"A well-told tale of Adventure with a capital 'A'."

—*Wooden Boat Magazine*

"Beautifully detailed! The impact grows with every page you read. You'll not put it down until Ladd is safely back home."

—*San Diego Log*

"Ladd's exploration of the human psyche will propel you through the pages. *Three Years* is a poetic saga that reads like a novel."

—*Northern Breezes Sailing Magazine*

"Stephen Ladd is authentic, and a good writer. If you want real adventure, try his book."

—*Bremerton Sun*

"If your dictionary doesn't define the word 'adventurous' as 'Stephen Ladd,' then wait for the revised version."

—*Ballard News-Tribune*

"For those of you with wanderlust nipping at your anchor line, *Three Years in a 12-Foot Boat* could be your guide to another world."

—*48° North*

"A fantastic adventure!"

—*The Adventurers' Club of Los Angeles*

"Wanderlust, voyaging, and earth awareness are woven together in *Three Years in a Twelve-Foot Boat.*"

—*Jefferson County Leader*

"One of the most fascinating, well-written voyage accounts we've ever read."

—*Latitude 38*

"Intelligent and delicious."

—*NewBuzz*

Three Years in a Twelve-Foot Boat

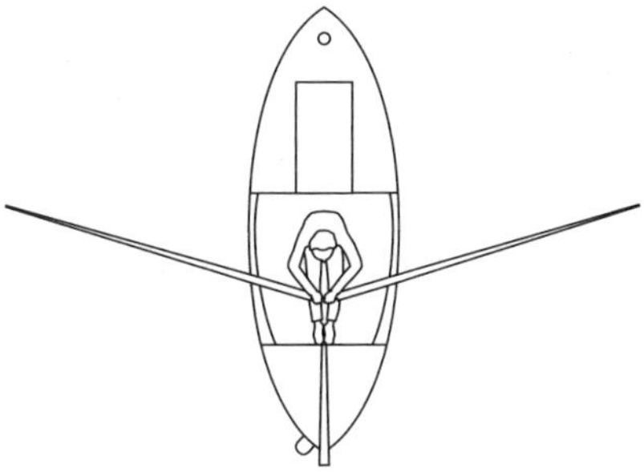

by Stephen G. Ladd

Adventure always!
Steve

Seekers Press

Cataloging-in-Publication Data
Ladd, Stephen G.
Three years in a twelve-foot boat / Stephen G. Ladd 2nd edition

ISBN 9780966933703 (paperback)
1. Voyages and travels--1990-. 2. Adventure and adventures.
Library of Congress Catalog Card Number: 99-93603
910.45 dc20

Cover by Richard Myers
Other design and artwork by Stephen Ladd

Published by:
Seekers Press
938 E. 31st Street
Bremerton, WA 98310
To order a copy transmit $25 (includes shipping and tax)

Manufactured in the United States of America

10 9 8 7 6 5 4 3 2 1

CONTENTS

DIAGRAMS of *SQUEAK*

MAPS

PHOTOGRAPHS

POEMS

FOREWORD

"You won't find reasonable men on the tops of tall mountains."
—*Hunter S. Thompson*

"The dangers of life are infinite, and among them is safety."
—*Goethe*

It's usually about the third or fourth night of a small-boat cruise when I start wishing I were home. Don't get me wrong, I love sailing and cruising little boats—I've made my living writing about the subject for almost 20 years—but after three or four days aboard a little boat the comforts of home begin to look really, really good.

I once spent five days and nights in an eight-foot plywood boat sailing down the hot and windy South Texas coast, spending as long as 13 hours at the helm one day. Within a few days I couldn't feel my backside—except for the nascent crop of sores—and my hands had swelled inexplicably. My boat was quite literally starting to come apart, and most of my "non-perishable" provisions were rapidly perishing in the sweltering heat. My nerves were seriously frayed. If I'd been anywhere near civilization on that third night I would have happily thrown in the towel.

Even short outings on a small boat inevitably involve bumped and bruised shins, cuts and scrapes, chafed hands, and assorted aches and pains. It's not unusual to wake up after a night on a camp-pad or thin foam cushion, stuffed into a small-boat berth, and feel as if you've been involved in a minor car crash.

What little movement is possible isn't accomplished by standing and walking as on terra-firma. Instead the sailor must slide, crawl, or shuffle awkwardly, often while compensating for the boat's heeling and bucking and trying to keep one hand always holding on. Frequently circumstances—shipping traffic, high winds, or weathering a point—require the sailor to sit, fixed in one strained position for most of a day. Alternatively, in a dead calm he might be forced to row until hands blister.

If the little boat has a cabin, standing below is out of the question, and even sitting headroom might be a coveted luxury. So the sailor sits hunched over or cross-legged trying not to bang his head on the nuts and bolts coming down through the deck, some of which already have strands of his hair hanging from them. Just slipping on his boots can require the contortions of a yogi.

Cooking aboard a little boat underway is a perilous adventure of its own, with open flames and boiling liquids, and even at anchor the smallest boats require cooking take place out in the cockpit, regardless of weather. And let's not bother to discuss considerations related to hygiene, buckets, and a little boat's lack of facilities.

I mention all of this only to help put Steve Ladd's remarkable voyage in perspective. While spending the better part of three years aboard a 12-foot boat will surely sound extraordinary, even to a non-sailor, I'm guessing most will still fail to comprehend the sheer audacity and severity of it all. Consider that it's common knowledge among cruising sailors that the smallest boat one should take to sea is something on the order of 34 feet and 10,000 pounds. Ladd's 12-foot *Squeak* weighed 250 pounds—which is, coincidentally, the approximate weight of a standard adult casket.

Of course if, like most of us, Ladd had limited his voyaging to the familiar waters of his home country—where the routes are well-worn and help never more than a VHF or cell phone call away—it would have been a less interesting tale. Instead, after sailing and rowing down the Mississippi River, Ladd and *Squeak* transited the Panama Canal and set sail south along the tangled, desolate, pirate-infested waters of Central and South America. What follows is an epic adventure—a dramatic voyage full of both predictable and unpredictable obstacles, and plenty of self-discovery.

When I first read it I couldn't help but imagine trying to be my best and most capable self—whether facing-off criminals or negotiating with crooked government officials, or landing my little boat in high surf—while I've been living day after day in a space smaller than most closets.

Like his writing, Ladd's voyage was honest and austere. He ventured totally exposed and vulnerable under an equatorial sun with swirling, turbulent foreign waters never more than few inches beneath him. Few people have the disposition for this kind of adventuring without a safety net. Fortunately for the rest of us, sometimes they make it home and write a book.

Joshua Colvin
Publisher
Small Craft Advisor magazine

PREFACE

Between 1990 and 1993 I rowed and sailed my twelve-foot boat 6,500 miles through some unusual places. *Squeak* and I traveled another 8,500 miles hitching rides from vehicles and ships. I knew from the start that I would write this book and that I would rely on words to tell the story rather than photos (the few herein were taken by others). The overall project consisted of boat design, construction, voyage, writing, and publication, all of which consumed ten years. But this is the story of just the voyage.

It's a true story, written as I went along and edited with reference to my detailed journals. To fit three years into a book I had to cut a lot, and synthesize much that remained. For instance, the dialogues are often composites of many conversations, and in one place I combined two minor characters into one. Consistent with the theme of self-reliance I created the boat graphics (following) and maps (at the beginning of each of the four parts) myself. Please use them to augment your mental picture as you follow along. Unfamiliar with boat terms? Read the call-outs in the boat diagrams. The poems help tell what I did, saw, and thought, so at least skim them for content. For the first edition (of which there were three printings totaling 8,100 copies) I created the cover too, but this time we have Richard Meyers of Port Townsend to thank. It, the foreword by Josh Colvin, and this preface chiefly differentiate this second edition. The text itself hasn't changed much. I've cut some of the more embarrassing excesses and clarified a few spots. It looks longer due to roomier typesetting, but is actually a bit shorter.

In my thirty-seventh through fortieth years I took chances and fended for myself. This book is about me, warts and all, and what I saw. If there's an 'ism' here it's individualism. We must all follow our own paths, for who else will pass that way? Perhaps no one, and we will have never found what only you can discover. But I wouldn't be an individual, or anything else, if not for my loving parents, one of whom I still live with here in my childhood home, along with my wife and children. So thank you! And thanks to the many that helped me along the way. You'll be learning about them in this book.

Stephen Ladd
Bremerton, Washington
February 2019

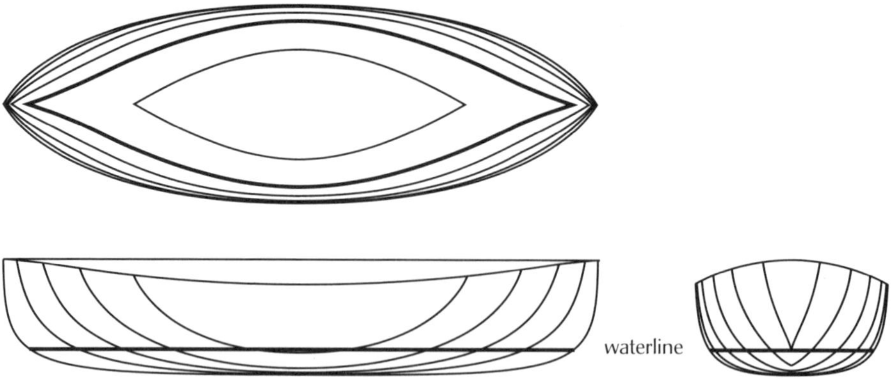

HULL SHAPE

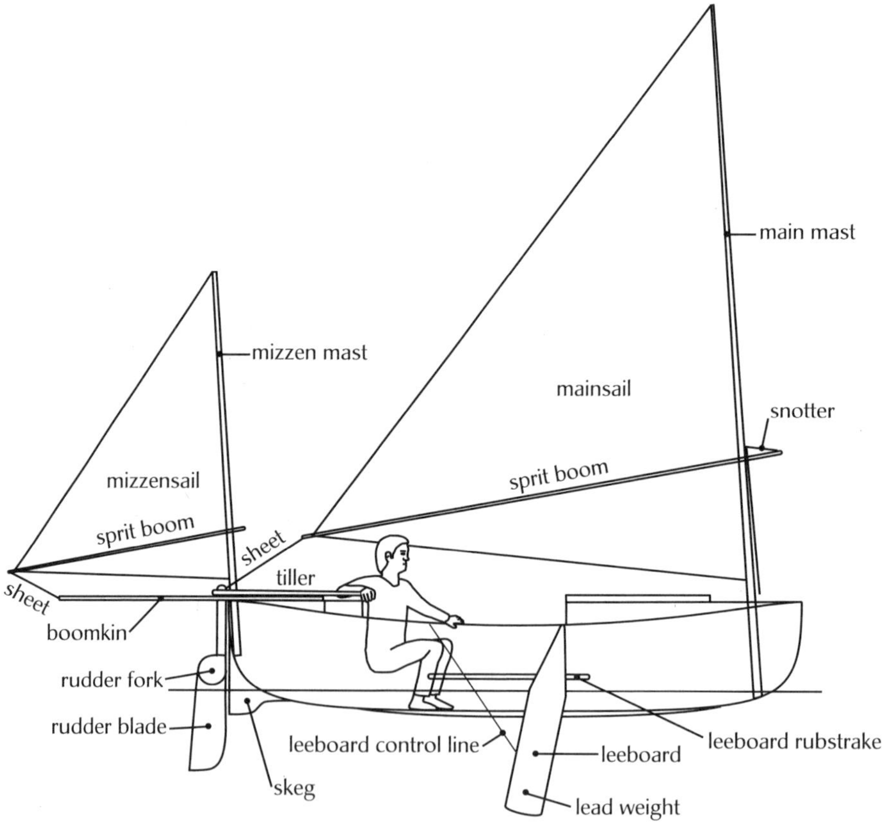

SAIL PLAN

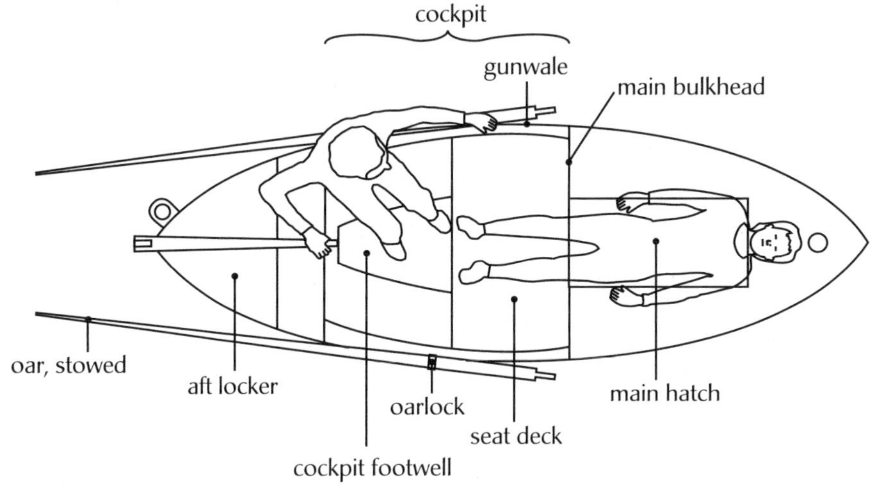

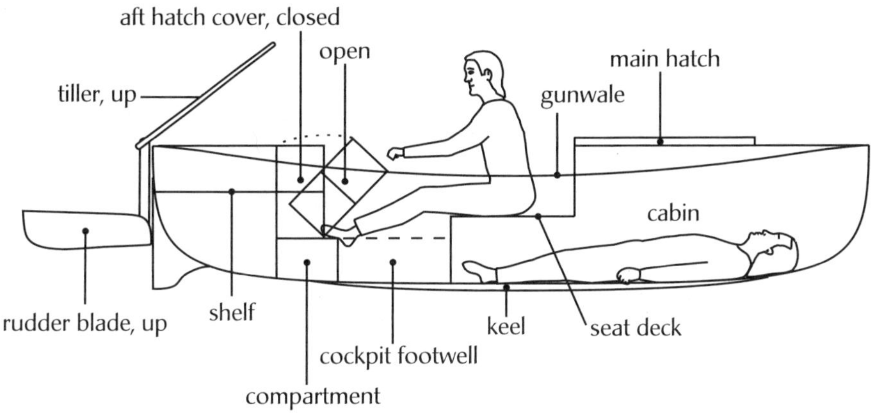

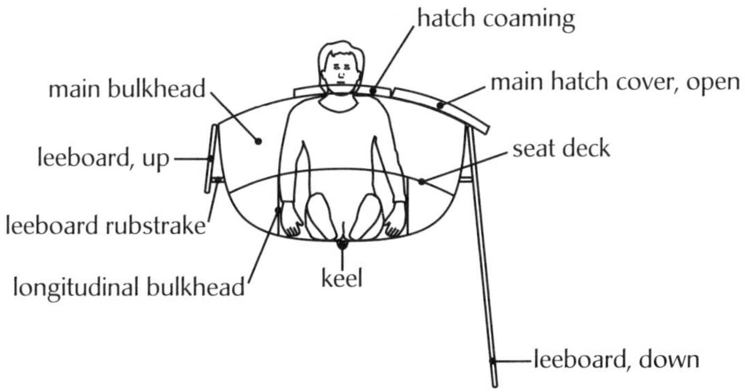

ACCOMMODATIONS

PART I
NORTH AMERICAN RIVERS

Rowing and Sailing

By Car or Truck

By Ship

0 100 200 300 miles
0 500 km
N
Lake Sakakawea
River
Bismarck
Pierre
Mississippi
River
Omaha
River
St. Joseph
Leavenworth
Kansas City
Boonville
Jefferson City
St. Louis
Washington
Ohio River
Cape Girardeau
Cairo
New Madrid
Arkansas River
Osceola
Memphis
Helena
Red
Greenville
Vicksburg
River
Natchez
Mobile
Panama City
Baton Rouge
Lake Pontchartrain
New Orleans
Gulf of Mexico

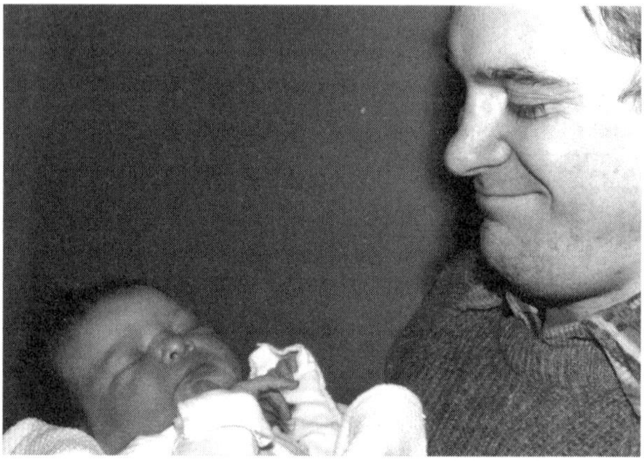

Brian and Steve, 8/9/90

CHAPTER 1

DEPARTURE

I gazed into my newborn nephew's face. His eyes were shut tight against the unaccustomed light. His dark brown hair was damp and tousled. His skin was almost translucent; underneath were veins like microscopic rivers of red and blue. My sister-in-law, who had gripped my hand so hard through the delivery, lay limp and sweaty on the bed, smiling like a wounded Sphinx. My brother Mike, more comfortable now that the fear had faded, took a picture of me holding his son. Brian's little fingers fidgeted weakly, but he didn't cry. He was moving into the unknown. Time for me to do the same. The date was August 9, 1990.

It had been half my life since I'd traveled limitlessly. The first time, in the year following my high school graduation, I had wandered alone through Europe, Asia, and Africa. Foreign cultures had swirled around me while I grappled desperately with my coming of age. Then I couldn't have explained myself. But over the years I realized I had gone where all was unfamiliar so that *I*, the only constant, might emerge.

I returned to my hometown of Bremerton, Washington, a pensive, rather hidden young man. I went on to college and became a city planner. Responsible jobs at courthouses and city halls in places like Coupeville and Sedro-Woolley helped me shed my shyness, but my introspection never really left. I had one worthy girlfriend after another, but never married. My continued wanderlust I assuaged by taking wilderness trips whenever possible. But the idea of a boat now plagued me.

There, I knew, lay freedom. I dreamed a thousand daydreams, spent untold evenings pondering the perfect vessel. I read every book in the Seattle Public Library on sailboats and naval architecture. For years I considered building a *Francis*-class double-ender, from plans by designer Chuck Paine. Then I discovered the shallow-draft genius of Commodore Munroe's *Presto*,

Philip Bolger's work with leeboards and sprit booms, and the advantages of cold-molded plywood and ultralight displacement.

No existing plans incorporated all these features, so during 1987 and 1988 I designed my own sailboat. It was thirty feet long, large enough to live aboard with Tammy, my girlfriend. But it would take years to build. Meanwhile, my relationship with Tammy was increasingly difficult. Should I commit to such a large project when I wasn't sure we'd stay together?

"Why don't you just shrink it down?" suggested my best friend, Jim Hogg. "Keep it the same, only a lot smaller." (There was never much love lost between him and Tammy.)

This threw me into a whirlwind of speculation. Could I make the boat light enough to drag up a beach by myself, yet big enough for an enclosed berth? I estimated the weight of a boat the same shape, unballasted, half as long. It exceeded the 250 pounds I set as an upper limit. I tried again, assuming a length of twelve feet. It worked! A cabin that would have been big enough for a game of ping-pong, in the original plan, became barely long enough to lie down in, and not quite tall enough to sit up straight. To enter the cabin at all I would first have to remove from it my camping gear, which would be the same as I used for cross-country skiing and backpacking. Two windsurfer masts, two sails, and two long, lithe oars would propel her.

It demanded to be, so I built a half-mold and started laminating thin veneers of Douglas fir. I molded the starboard half of the hull on the terrace of Tammy's and my apartment in downtown Seattle. The daily sight of a boat not intended to accommodate her naturally heightened Tammy's misgivings. My neighbors weren't thrilled either. "You gonna do that all night?" yelled a voice from another terrace one evening when I hammered a little too late.

I moved to my parents' house, quit my job, and labored another six months in their carport. To hold the veneers in place while the glue cured, I punched, and later pried out, approximately ten thousand staples. It was tedious, but I loved what I was building. I could never be perfect, but she could. Her sharpness and curvature delighted me. Her rose-brown wood glowed under the clear epoxy coat. I decided to name her *Squeak* after a dear, departed cat. There was no physical resemblance, but the other names I considered all seemed too serious for something so small.

Design choices were excruciating, like whether the main hatch should lift off or ride on hinges, but deciding what to do with her was easy. *Squeak* lent herself to river, coastal, and inter-island travel. I would exploit this potential in warm, foreign lands that could be reached without crossing an ocean. That meant Latin America, where I'd traveled for three months in 1973. To get there I wanted to drive as little as possible and take advantage of flowing water. That meant riding the Missouri and Mississippi rivers down to the

Gulf of Mexico. It would be nice if the North American and Latin American phases of the voyage could be symmetrical. That suggested sailing to the northwest coast of South America, then crossing that continent the same way I would cross North America: trucking her over mountains and descending rivers until I reached the Atlantic. How I would return home was too fuzzy to conjecture.

"How long do you think that will take?" Mom asked, trying to hide her concern. She and Dad had had thirty-seven years to get used to my adventures, but still worried.

"Oh, a year, maybe eighteen months. I'll give you a list of general delivery addresses, so we can write to each other. I'll call now and then. No problem." I hoped that if I treated it lightly, they would too.

I finished the boat and worked out the more obvious bugs. It was too late in the year to conduct lengthy sea trials; I needed to get through the Great Plains before winter. Jim Hogg needed a vacation from his job as a contractor, so he and his wife, Eileen, volunteered to drive me across the mountains. Meanwhile Cathi, my sister-in-law, expected to give birth any day. Might as well wait for that.

Jim is quite the amateur engineer. On August 4, 1990, I helped him dam a swale in his back yard, line it with plastic, and fill it with water from his garden hose. That evening some thirty friends and relatives came over, and at the appropriate moment we picked *Squeak* up, dropped her in the water, and spilled champagne over her bow. I had sent them the following invitation:

> To friends I've been scarce and will be scarcer
> but a boat is built so come help prepare her
> for the solemn quest that's our destiny
> 'cross prairies, plains, unto the sea
> to such wild shores and foreign lands
> as the goddess of that sea commands
> a fearful goddess, with rigid rites
> one such is the christening night
>
> To christen her *Squeak* for a cat I once knew
> is why I request this evening with you
> at set of sun on Saturn's Day
> August four, we toast champagne
> at Hogg abode, from whence she leaves
> inside their van to cross the peaks
> to softly slide down the further slope
> I pray thee come and give good hope

Our guests milled about the impromptu pond until midnight, feting *Squeak* and me equally. Unexpected faces from the past kept popping up. I wanted them to appreciate how light *Squeak* was. "Hey, Leah! You pick up the other end. Grab her by those handles. See? Just you and me can lift her." The attention both excited and fatigued me.

Five days later Brian was born. As I held him under the harsh hospital light and looked into his vulnerable face, another face came to mind. It was my own, captured in a grainy, black-and-white photograph in Kabul, Afghanistan in 1971. I had sometimes looked at the photo in the years since that first travel and marveled at how little the person in it resembled me, yet how much I wanted him to be me. The long-haired youth peered straight through me, unsmiling, unaware of the camera or of anything but—what? That snapshot captured not so much me as the crisis of my emergence, the unknowable force that compelled my earlier travel. I would seek *him* anew. I would return to the same crucible, that its heat might purge me. I was ready to change, to give my all. All this is true, yet it is simply an elaborate way of saying that I sought adventure.

Mom and Dad, Mike and Cathi's two girls, and my sister Susan and her kids had waited down the hall during the birth. Tammy was there too—though our relationship had failed, she had remained a friend of the family. Now they all crowded into the hospital room. While they passed Brian around, I confused the issue by hugging and kissing them all good-bye. Nobody cried. They were all too happy about the arrival of a new family member to make a scene over the departure of an older one. I walked outside.

The Hoggs were waiting for me in their long-bed van. *Squeak* lay in the back, on her side. Her stern pressed against the rear door, her bow came almost to the windshield.

I climbed in beside her.

CHAPTER 2

MILK RIVER

Jim, Eileen, and I drove across the Cascade Mountains, through Spokane, the Idaho panhandle, and Kalispell, Montana. Our goal was the nearest navigable point in the Mississippi river system: the headwaters of the Milk River, northernmost tributary of the Missouri. Three days later, on a dirt road just east of Glacier National Park, we found a trickle of water known as the North Fork Milk River. Not enough flow. Following it downstream, we came to where an aqueduct spills irrigation water diverted from the St. Mary River (which drains to Hudson Bay) into the Milk River (which drains to the Gulf of Mexico). We were half a mile south of the Canadian border, fifty miles east of the Continental Divide. The nearest town was Browning, fifty miles south. It was midafternoon, August 11, 1990.

After hugs, easy smiles, and a brief farewell, Jim and Eileen launched me into the swirling waters at the foot of the spillway. I flowed away from them while they stood watching from a bank strewn with yellow flowers, under slanting sun and cloud-puff skies. They were a picture of contentment. Already out of earshot, I wondered what they were saying to each other. My breast burst with joy for the water that ran so cool and fast, and the land, so rich in grass. With my oars I pointed *Squeak* downstream, and kept her off the banks as the stream turned. I floated northeast across the unmarked border. Four miles further, I pulled up to sleep under the infinite stars in my tiny sea berth with a see-through plastic hatch cover. A distant band of coyotes sang a mad, lonely chorus.

Dawn fired a low eastern cloud. I awoke from *Squeak's* belly as little Brian had seemed to wake from Cathi's belly: totally new. Sitting up, I saw high prairie: clean, quiet, undulating. Etched into the plain was a faint valley, where my little river meandered through green banks. Where it cut vertical walls in the valley sides, swallows made their wasplike condominium nests of mud. Ospreys and hawks soared and screamed. Cows cropped the yellow grass, one for every fifty or hundred acres. A lone fence line stalked off into the distance. I listened to the gentle day sounds:

water talking
breeze in ears and grass
short, sharp bird songs
a passing bee, a cricket

I rode the meanders endlessly back and forth, watching for rocks where the stream ran fast unto whiteness. The scenery flowed like a scrolled story. The day was hot until dusk, but I had only to dip and replace my hat, and cool water coursed down my neck.

The river was just right: big enough to clear my nine-foot oars, slow enough to manage, deep enough to keep *Squeak's* six-inch-deep belly clear of most rocks. There would be no road access for sixty-four miles, no civilization other than the lonely ranch houses I passed at the rate of one per day. Sometimes the river meandered through circuitous oxbows of cattail and pasture. Here I rowed with a pushing motion facing downstream. When necessary to reduce speed and minutely control lateral position, I turned the bow upstream and rowed with a pulling motion against the current. In violent rapids I stepped out into the thigh-deep water and anxiously lowered her through the boulders by hand. At first the Milk was clear, but gradually she owned up to her name. When her milkiness obscured the bottom, I learned to detect rocks from the ripple patterns. Then wind ripples obscured bottom ripples, masking once more the water's depth.

Each day I hiked up out of the valley and saw plains given to dry wheat. There were sways in the flatness, and distant heights. The breeze was steadier above, the sky bigger. The snowcapped Rockies had faded from view; the Sweet Grass Hills appeared to the southeast. Below, *Squeak* looked so sweet on that wavy ribbon of blue in a corridor of emerald river bottom.

A badger scuttled away with a gurgling growl; another hunkered down flat and glowered at me from its river bank den, showing his broad stripes. They dig out and devour the tall, erect gophers. The enlarged hole, often opening onto the cut bank, becomes the badger's new home. One morning I came upon a coyote drinking. He huffed off, seemingly incensed with himself at having been caught off-guard by his enemy, man.

I spooked blacktail deer, whitetail deer, ducks, Canada geese, great blue herons, and cormorants. Distraught waterfowl preceded me downriver with much honking and splashing of wing and web, as if warning the world of an advancing monster. Every disruption of a duck family was a drama. Would the scattered, peeping ducklings ever reunite with their mother? A mottled eagle landed on the flat inside a river bend, rather fluttery and mincing, as if hating to get his talons dusty, but there was nothing to perch on. A great horned owl huddled like a ball of gray fluff on the side of a tall bank. Marmots shifted from hole to hole. The second morning I almost stepped on a bottom fish that dumbly waited for me to get out my spear and skewer him. His flesh formed part of my supper that night. It was soft and bland.

From my point of embarkation it was ninety river miles to the town of Milk River, Alberta. I arrived on the third full day, pulled *Squeak* up into a riverside park, and walked into a town of nine hundred people.

Their dentist, without charge, prescribed an antibiotic for a wisdom tooth that had become infected. In his waiting room I met some Hutterites, members of a German-speaking religious colony that owned a large farm. A grandmotherly woman conversed politely with me while four young girls stole glances but did not speak. All wore long, handmade skirts, blouses, and bonnets of busy, clashing prints.

The next day I decided to hitchhike fifty miles northwest to Lethbridge to solve another problem. My clamp-on oarlocks had been preventing my oars from sliding in and out, putting my oartips at risk of breaking should they hit a rock on the backstroke. I needed the loose kind, so I stood in the heat outside Milk River until an old Ranchero pickup stopped. My host was an independent contractor, around forty, named George Truba. He was a good-looking man, average height, clear skin. While we drove I told him what I needed and why. My explanation sat well with him.

"I've had dreams too," he smiled. "Some have come true, like having a family of my own. Others never will now, I suppose, like restoring those old cars of mine." This and other grandiose hopes were now worn and dog-eared, but he nostalgically leafed through them with me, as if dusting off an old photo album.

George took me to a sporting goods store for oarlocks, then picked up some building materials. We drove back down to Milk River together, and kept on going to his eighty-acre farm near the border. He wanted me to meet his wife and kids.

Tony was a pretty woman in the late stages of pregnancy. Their six-year-old twins were named Torre and Guy. I fell for Torre, the daughter, because she engaged me sweetly and directly.

"You know why I like you? Because you let me sit on your lap, like Daddy." Guy, the boy, had a wiry, worried intelligence.

They put me up in a spare bedroom. George showed me his seventeen cars dating from the fifties and sixties. "None of them run, but I can't stand to get rid of them," he said. The next day I canned pickles with Tony, then

George and I customized the new oarlocks in his shop. Then it was the kids' birthday, and all their friends came to their party. I was comfortable with the Trubas—they were so happy together. Why did I seek my happiness alone?

After two days George brought me back to Milk River, where I bought enough food to last me to the next town, Havre, Montana. We launched *Squeak*, and at George's suggestion I took Torre and Guy along with me to our rendezvous, a picnic shelter eleven miles downstream. They were good and brave despite rough water and a big thunderstorm. We barely made it before dark. George and Tony met us, and we shared a dinner she had prepared. Then they left me, lonesome and worried about the two hundred miles to Havre. My only information was a rumor that the river ran underground a portion of the way! Unlikely as this sounded, it added to my disquiet as I unrolled my sleeping bag.

I dreamt about long-lost girlfriends, and that my belongings were scattered in all the different places I'd ever lived. I didn't remember how to find them, how to get back home. I woke up. The fire was out. It was raining, and the picnic shelter was dark and dismal. The Trubas' domestic bliss had piqued my loneliness. Perhaps it was a sign that I was getting ready to settle down, that the purpose of this great adventure was to get the wanderlust out of my system once and for all.

I had launched *Squeak* about four thousand feet above sea level. To reach the sea, the river had to drop four thousand feet in as many miles, but it wouldn't do so at an even foot per mile. A disproportionate share of the drop would occur on the Upper Milk. Accordingly, the river now wound through a sheer canyon with overhanging sandstone ledges, deep pools, and boulder fields. It undulated over hidden obstacles, and broke into whiteness as air mixed with water. It would have been challenging even in a canoe, but *Squeak* needs eighteen feet for her oars to clear. I couldn't afford to sustain damage, so I lifted the blades over tight boulders, and lowered *Squeak* by rope when necessary. It took all day to get through the canyon, some twelve miles. I pulled wearily into a small slough and cooked a stew on my Svea stove. The night being dewy, I retired into my bag fully clothed. The cabin was comfortable once I was situated. I adapted to the limited range of movement, and lit a candle lantern to read by before falling asleep.

It was August 19. As I set out, a golden retriever promptly followed me. Young and wiry, he stayed by me all day. At first he swam alongside with a possessed look on his face. Did he want me to pull him into the boat? I kept rowing. Then he ran along the bank, swimming only where rough terrain would otherwise have separated us. He swam through rapids I thought would kill him, and occasionally detoured to stampede cattle or deer. He was magnificent, but what was I to do if he persisted in adopting me? I called him Milky.

We passed through lush groves of cottonwood. "Hoodoos" appeared: sandstone columns with caps of harder, iron-bearing strata. In shape they mimicked mushrooms, wine glasses, sentinels, arches. They stood out, singly and in vast hordes, from the valley slopes.

Toward dusk a small "Archaeological Preserve" sign on the north bank told me I had reached Writing-On-Stone Provincial Park. I landed and climbed, with Milky, into the hoodoos. His vigor infected me. Soon we were scampering among the odd shapes, playing hide and seek. Then Milky smelled something and disappeared. I stepped onto an outcrop and saw, far below, a ballet of deer in flight. Only seconds had passed, yet Milky was close behind, hounding them across the river plain. The blacktails flowed and flexed like birds twisting in the wind, or a school of fish in breaking waves.

A rainstorm that had been threatening now fell. Unmindful, we continued into the uppermost hoodoos. They had only partly emerged from the eroding plain. Their sheer flanks were covered with prehistoric designs, carved or painted on blond sandstone. There were hundreds of them: mysterious stick figures, animals, and spirits, in different styles, from different periods. The most recent revealed the arrival of Spanish horses in the sixteenth century. To the Indians who created the petroglyphs this was sacred ground.

Washed-out daylight lingered long after it seemed night should have fallen. The valley was a wild gorge ringed by tall cliffs and contributing coulees. The south rim of the gorge rose directly into the Sweet Grass Hills, a wilderness of heaths and conifer. The rain had stopped, but the washes were now saturated. Waterfalls had sprung from the hanging gullies across the river. It could have been the beginning of the world.

In the morning Milky was gone, perhaps back home to await another river-runner. If so, his wait may have been long, because there appeared to be no other boats on the river. I was glad.

The hoodoos tapered off. Prairie and sky became too big to comprehend. On a distant slope, a coyote stalked a herd of unsuspecting antelope. Only I saw it. A tailwind blew up. The river became broad and slow. Countless shoals forced me to get out and push. I stopped in a plain of shallows and barely exposed sandbars, stripped naked, and played solo Frisbee against the stinging wind—

> bare feet leaping
> over rippled sand
> releasing sparks of water
> kernels of sun

The sun stimulated the parts of me that rarely see it. I was drunk with freedom.

I paused under a steel bridge. In a half hour two vehicles passed, each throwing up a slipstream of dust that drifted east with the wind. Fluffy clouds, some dark underneath, passed in endless armadas. I couldn't sail because there wasn't enough depth to put my rudder blade down, but I removed the main mast from its deck lashings and slid it into its hole in the bow. The bare mast alone blew me downstream, ahead of the current.

The sight of tended shade trees told me I was approaching a ranch. Pulling over at a cluster of buildings I met John Ross, a polite, third-generation cowboy. His face was fresh, his western clothes neat and clean. He owned twenty-five thousand acres outright and leased another forty thousand from the government—the biggest cattle ranch in Alberta. While we spoke his little boy played quietly on the front porch of the house. His wife came out and picked something from the garden. No one else was around for miles.

John answered my pent-up questions about ranching. He had about a thousand head. Thanks to his airplane, which he kept in a nearby field, he managed with only three hands. Except for aerial reconnaissance, they worked entirely on horseback: roping, branding, culling. Calves, heifers, cows, steers, and bulls all required separate management. They moved the cattle around to avoid exhausting the land. John gave me a name for the little black flies that bit my bare ankles at every opportunity. "They're called horn flies," he said, "because they suck blood from the new flesh at the base of the cattle's horns."

Now the river entered badlands: eroding strata of clay and rock. Each band was a different color: pewter, copper green, brick red. The hills were lifeless, but the streamside brush attracted deer. A white-and-black pelican flew by, en route to a new fishing hole. As I cruised along a bank with a trapped ledge a few inches above river level, I saw a rattlesnake, maybe four feet long and two inches thick. Was he stuck there? He stared uncomfortably at me as I hovered alongside. I tapped him with the tip of my oar and he rattled and reared, but didn't strike. He knew it was me, not the oar, that was alive.

I stopped at the last ranch before the Milk River crosses back into Montana and pulled up onto a low bank to pass the night. The Northern Lights illuminated the sky in fitful, dancing patches, like fluorescent light bulbs always warming up, never catching. A blonde, dimple-faced cowhand came down and crouched beside me on the bank. "How long you been on the river?" he asked. I couldn't remember. I looked at the dark, restless water and thought how it kept flowing while I slept. I wanted to be with it. During the day I rowed hard, but I would never catch up. The water molecules that cushioned *Squeak* when Jim and I first slipped her in would reach the Gulf of Mexico long before I would. I felt an urgency, as if life was passing me by. Yet I was living as fully as I knew how.

The river doubled back on itself with each bend, like the boundary between pieces in a jigsaw puzzle; I had to travel two miles for every mile a crow might have flown. The valley walls grew to five hundred feet high, a mile apart. I climbed to the top, to marvel at the windy vastness. According to my map, the valley side facing me was in the U.S., but the land itself had no inkling it was divided.

The river meandered east-southeast across the international boundary, but not all at once. That is, the boundary, running parallel to the equator, intersected three or four of the meander loops. The river carried me back and forth between the two countries before delivering me once and for all to Montana. The borderland was remote. There weren't any cattle, just deer, about fifty that day alone. They froze at my approach, then bounded off. Beaver jumped into the water from their dens in the banks. A flock of killdeers ran on spiky legs, cried their name, and swirled away. A dead fox lay washed up on a bank. The sunset was a huge interplay of gold, purple, and black.

My butt hurt from sitting all day. My legs craved relief from the cramped position that rowing face-forward required. It was now sixty degrees Fahrenheit by day, fifty by night. Gale-force winds blew constantly. A gust slammed me sideways onto a sandbar, levering my oar, cracking the gunwale. I could still row, but the damage would have to be repaired in Havre, the next town. The river level dropped, leaving a sloppy silt over everything. I quit early and camped in the middle of a vast marsh, hunched up in my cabin to escape the rain and howling wind.

Next day the valley became wide and shallow, broadening the stream to five hundred yards. Somewhere in this muddy sheet was a channel deep enough to float *Squeak,* but where? I groped with my oar tips, followed leads until I grounded, hauled, got constantly in and out of the boat. My skin pruned from the cold. My feet tracked water and sandy clay into the cockpit.

The river passed through an ancient lake bed dotted with willow groves. Was I the first man ever here? On the far side, the river entered a new valley, straight and fast. All around were new ecosystems:

stands of poplar
brush willow clumps
and the prickly, low cactus
each is a house that graciously accepts me
how could I be a stranger here?
each a tiny chapel
I am thankful for the earth, this gift

Now thick greenery lined the river, like a slipper over a lithe foot. Kersplash! Kersplash! Monstrously fat beavers crashed into the water from both banks. They looked like different animals in their different stances. Poised by their brush-covered holes in the banks, their backs hunched up, they looked like squirrels from the Dinosaur Age. Then they scrambled fleetly down into the water like sleek hogs. Swimming, they were hairy, brown logs with big, black noses and comical, curious eyes. Then they submerged with great splashes of tail. The streamside silt was now too soft to walk in. Green vines with magenta flowers extended over the shore. Something gave off a strange, chemical smell. Long worms, thin as fishing line, squirmed in the muck.

I saw the reservoir, that last major unknown before reaching Havre. I had known only that it existed and approximately where, because my only chart was a road map of Montana. Twenty miles long and one mile wide, it led southeast through a deep valley to Fresno Dam.

Judging from the vegetation, the lake appeared to be twenty feet below its normal level. The river ran fast to its end, then spilled through a channel in the lake's muddy drawdown zone. *Squeak* slid toboggan-like over corduroy waves, then grounded out. I got out to push; the bottom was sandy and firm. Suddenly my footing gave way, and there was nothing underneath. Quicksand! Luckily, I hadn't let go of the boat. I pulled myself up by her bow handles, then towed her into the lake with a crab-like shuffle.

It was August 25. Still water felt strange after so long on the river. The Sweet Grass Hills had disappeared behind me while the Bear Paw Hills had risen to the southeast. Supporting myself cautiously in the deep mud along the shore, I rigged *Squeak* for sailing. Then I flew down the lake on a beam reach while the sun burned down below the horizon and contrasts of dark and light deepened in the sky. A glorious sail! In no time I arrived at the dam.

I slept pulled up on a beach, and was woken in the night by young skinny-dippers. Their laughter and rowdy swearing carried over the water. It clashed with the quietude that had built up in me from being so long in nature, but appealed to my own fond memories of such play. One of the girls, undoubtedly very pretty without any clothes on (how I strained my eyes!), felt guilty. "Don't tell Jay! Don't tell Jay!" she begged her companions.

At the first hint of dawn I walked over to the dam. I had no idea what day of the week it was. The beauty of the land I had passed through glowed inside me. My step was light, almost intoxicated. I imagined I had become invisible to other people, and had lost my power of speech. I walked self-consciously up to a heavyset man in a red pickup parked on top of the dam. His face was ruddy, his whiskers white and stiff. A buxom sweetheart huddled beside him, an open whiskey bottle between them. He looked up, bleary-eyed, wary.

"Pardon me, good morning. Can you tell me where Havre is?"

"Twenty miles further down, back there," he pointed, with the quick control of a man who can hold his liquor.

"Any chance you could haul my rowboat around the dam? I can pay."

Dawn and I had caught them unprepared, like vampires not returned to their coffins in time. But the burly man came to life as the light grew, and my situation became apparent. He hauled me around and wouldn't accept payment. "Name's Henry Hickle," he said. "Look me up when you get to Havre."

Below the dam, the Milk was a different river. The silt had settled out in the reservoir, leaving the river clear, the bed firm. Crop-farming prevailed now. Coming around a bend I counted sixty-three rusty car bodies, side by side. They reposed at the steep angle of the bank, their grills in the water; someone had mixed auto wrecking with erosion control. A train chugged in the distance. The crickets sang sweetly. Cottonwoods stood in large, solemn groves. The sun came out. Succumbing to laziness, I dawdled for hours at a secluded bend, swimming in the bracing current, soaking up the sun. I looked up. So high it was barely visible, a vee of geese flew southeast. It crossed from horizon to horizon like a satellite.

The magic that is wilderness waned as man's influence increased. I portaged around the weir dam Havre gets its drinking water from, and started my forays into town. I was to stay there a week, repairing, provisioning, and drafting this chapter on a public computer at the library. Once I came back to the secluded bank I was camping on and found that someone had broken open *Squeak's* plexiglas hatch cover. Oddly, they hadn't taken much. I glued the pieces back together and hoped they would hold. Such was my return to civilization.

I ran into Henry Hickle, who insisted on bringing *Squeak* and me to his spread near the river, for security. He introduced me to his wife (different woman—bite my tongue!) and three boys. I watched TV with them in their mobile home, and listened to Henry talk. He was a ham-fisted railroad engineer, a gun nut, a blustery bullshitter. His massive face was always grinning, but the grin tapered uncomfortably if a silence ensued that he was unable to fill. He acted like a gun was being held to his head and if he failed to entertain the trigger would pull. His boys were perfect miniatures. There was no shortage of conversation at the Hickles'.

The local Bureau of Land Management office gave me some bad news about the Milk River's remaining three hundred miles. They said it became increasingly slow and mosquito-infested. Five more dams sucked water from it, virtually drying it up before its confluence with the Missouri. Fortunately, the Missouri River also flowed east, on a parallel path sixty miles south. It was only an hour away by Highway 87. Why not get a ride there, and hasten my switchover to the bigger river?

Henry agreed to drive me down to an old riverboat landing called Virgelle. Elk season was coming on, and it would give him and his eldest a chance for a little target practice.

I pedaled into Havre once more on a loaned bicycle, pausing on the bridge for a final look at the Milk River. She never looked better. I thanked her for what she'd done for me, and apologized for leaving so soon.

CHAPTER 3

UPPER MISSOURI

It was September 2, 1990. The predawn silence drew a rhapsody of distant coyote yelps. An owl hooted softly, monotonously. Day took root over the misty Missouri River as I joined Hickle and his boys for a breakfast of beef stew at the Virgelle landing. They had treated me kindly, but I was anxious to be free of their constant jabber, so at the earliest opportunity I pushed out into the stream and waved good-by.

I just drifted at first. The river was a quarter mile wide, smooth, deep, rather slow. Occasionally it divided, creating islands. The valley slopes were yellow of grass and green of shrub, with grays of increasing blackness higher up, where no soil covered the underlying shale. Cottonwoods grew inside the bends as the river meandered southeast. The sky was cloudless. A Sand Hill crane caught a fish with a spear-like thrust, and choked it down his long neck. Magpies winged past, black with long, white-tipped feathers, and giant pelicans with the opposite color scheme. Three cowboys worked a milling herd along a narrow riverbank. In the heat of the day I swam midstream, drifting with *Squeak*, splashing like a kid in the pale yellow water. The freshness seeped into me, releasing joy. Because *Squeak* and I drifted apace, it seemed we weren't moving.

The topography sharpened. The valley cut steeply through a sandstone mantle, forming buttes, hoodoos, running walls, spires, grotesque cathedrals. This country captivated Lewis and Clark too, as they struggled upstream in 1804, breaking a trail across the continent. Risk-taking settlers got off the pioneer steamboats and built homesteads along here, but the land was too rugged and dry. Now only a few abandoned log cabins remained.

At sunset I stopped by such a cabin and started split pea soup cooking. Catfish browsed in the reeds at the river's edge. A cottontail rabbit lurked among the splintered wood and rusty wire, so I worked my way within snub-nose revolver range and shot him. While a full moon slowly rose I dressed him, built up the fire, and roasted him over the hungry flames.

In the following days, the river seemed to penetrate a range of rugged hills. Pines, firs, and junipers thronged the forty-five degree slopes, while the canyon deepened. The third night I camped at a place called Cow Island Landing. An old gentleman I had passed earlier in the day pulled his kayak up alongside *Squeak*. His name was Jim Williams.

"What do you know about these hills," I asked after we had settled in.

"They're not hills," he said, in his sweet, southern accent. "We're in a gorge. This is a drainage pattern cut down into the plains, called the Missouri Breaks. I should know, I'm a retired geologist. I've also floated this stretch of the river every year for the last twenty-four years." Jim smiled modestly.

His frame was heavy, his lips full, his facial skin damaged from a lifetime of sun. He cooked us a gourmet meal and let me pull from his bourbon. I started on an after-dinner walk and promptly encountered a rattlesnake on the path. I laughed at how it circled up and cowered in the beam of my flashlight, but Jim didn't think it was funny. "I really wish you would wait until morning to go for a walk," he yelled from his bed. "*Please!*" Unable to resist his concern, I came back and crawled into *Squeak*.

The sun rose in the east while the moon set in the west, as if counter-balanced. Coyotes that had prowled the camp by night now slunk away. Jim and I pried our boats out of the riverside muck ("bensonite," Jim said) and set off.

A mule deer swam from an island to the mainland, only his head and rack above the brown-green water. Box elder and willow lined the river. Sudsy flecks swirled and sparkled in the sun. The river narrowed in the distance, like a highway. Crickets droned through subtle modulations of pitch. A pack of low-altitude bombers from a nearby Air Force base screamed overhead, following the river like nightmare birds of prey. High above, wispy mare's tails licked the sky's pale blue bowl.

By afternoon we reached the Robinson Bridge. It was the first road I'd seen in days, and the last I would see for many days more. We drank warm beers Jim had been saving in the bow of his kayak. Someone was coming to pick him up.

"My friends think I'm crazy to do this," he said. "But I need to shut myself off from society one week a year. Hard to say why." I felt his soul yearning toward mine, but we remained respectfully distant. Why can't men get close?

"I know what you mean. Since my first big travel, after high school, I've spent a week every winter cross-country skiing in the North Cascades. By myself."

Jim nodded gently. "Passing on the street we'd never've even noticed each other, but here it's obvious we have a whole lot in common. Only you've got it worse. Good luck to you, Steve."

We shook hands and parted, as if to get it over with, as if to exchange addresses would have been cowardice in the face of loneliness. I rowed away thinking how Jim's week was over. Soon he'd be with loved ones, and conveniences, and the pathos would fade. How long would it be before *I* returned home?

Below the bridge the canyon shrank, the air became muggy. Lightning lit the clouds on the north horizon. I pulled into the dry bed of a tributary creek. Its floor was cracked into large, irregular plates of mud, still quivery underneath, unable to support my weight. Every time I climbed back into the boat it took ten minutes to clean up my feet and the cockpit, because water didn't dissolve the greasy bensonite mud. Still, I liked my camp spot, because any confluence of streams is an important crossroads.

My back and hands were tired from rowing. I slept, and dreamt I was being carried from my parents' house in Bremerton down the long hill to the bay. Simultaneously, I was moving backwards in time. Homes that seemed old in my youth were just being built. By the time I reached the Coal Docks there were only the cabins of the first pioneers, but somewhere I heard the horrid screech of heavy equipment clearing out the woods. It was the sound of wilderness dying. I woke up. The moon was shining with the weight of eternity into my open cabin. "Least they haven't reached *here* yet," I muttered, and fell back asleep.

The sun rose. Yellow finches chirped softly as they worked through the brush. A few fleecy clouds moved slowly eastward. The smell of sage perked my nostrils. I found:

a downy white feather
as long as my hand

a clay-colored frog
that could sit on my thumbnail
but instead plops
across the broken mud
what if he falls in a crack?

the very tip of a cactus thorn
that could imbed itself
under my toenail, and does
these are the building blocks

I sailed that day. Meanders constantly changed my heading relative to the wind, forcing me to labor over the tiller, sheets, and leeboards. Near Fort Peck Lake the river straightened, in line with the robust wind. A hunter asked if I'd seen any elk and I said no. Five minutes later I passed a bull elk drinking from the river. "Hey, you best git!" I yelled. "Fella over there looking for you." He caught my drift and ambled off.

Fort Peck Lake was thirty feet low due to four years of drought. A swampy carpet of brush had sprouted in the exposed lake bed. The river flattened into a vast, meandering sheet flow. The water got shallower and shallower. I raised the rudder blade accordingly, losing steering control as I did so. The bottom was a light, organic muck that wouldn't support weight. When would I reach the lake? What if I got stuck?

Depth increased and current dropped off as the river bent around a steep peninsula to my left. To my right was a hundred square miles of cattail swamp. An orange moon rose. The sunset painted the hillside the same burnt orange. I had covered nearly fifty miles that day.

I landed and ate supper while mosquitoes ate me. To escape them I walked along the desolate shore. The wails of geese and ducks drifted over the lake. A browsing deer caught my scent, exhaled a sharp "huff!" and bounded off. Warty, fist-sized toads lassoed insects with their tongues. Eighteen-inch carp squirmed out of the water to feed in the mucky bank. What a strange land!

In the morning I hiked to the top of the peninsula and sat facing east. The sun peeked slowly, lightly over the horizon. I imagined him a face, and admired his gleaming forehead, until too much of his majesty showed, obliging me to humbly avert my gaze. I strolled through a prairie dog town on the flat above the hillside, and felt hostile eyes on me. They poised cautiously by their holes, and convulsed their bodies to emit sharp warnings. "Get out of town!" they whistled. I did so, via a long, serpentine trench that seemed neither naturally carved nor anything white man would make. It appeared to represent a gigantic snake, with a pit at one end, possibly representing a tail rattle. Had an ancient tribe dug the image as a message to the gods? The slopes leading back down to the lake were covered with cactus and a stalky, brittle shrub.

The lake was a fjord knifing through a mountainous desert. Sun and biting flies ruled out bare skin, so I wetted my clothes frequently to stay cool. Powerful tailwinds gave me good progress, but the waves grew to alarming size where the lake aligned with the direction of the wind. Still inexperienced, I concentrated on how best to sail my boat. After almost capsizing while struggling to reduce sail area, I changed the way the sail is lashed to the mast to make reefing easier.

The lake twisted and widened, beyond all sign of man. The wind blew ceaselessly, rippling the grass, ruffling the water. As the lake deepened it became clear. I camped away from the waves, in sandy coves, and listened to the coyotes as they sang their evening vespers. They howled with a passionate wisdom beyond my understanding.

On September 9 the wind faded. The sun was wilting hot. I rowed halfheartedly toward a distant, tree-covered island. The sun slowly burned down to the horizon on my right. I guided myself by reciprocal heading on the hills far astern, looking forward every fifty strokes for hazards and to correct my heading.

The island didn't show on the Montana road map, my only guide. I was far out in the middle of the lake, losing my race with the sun, which cast deepening violet across the heavens. Slowly, for it was further than I had thought, my isle grew and took shape. It became a very special place, my own discovery. The flatness of the water and my focus on reaching the island before dark put me in a trance. *Squeak* and I were one. We toiled smoothly, cleaving water apart and sewing it together behind. The sun set. Red, then orange, flared up from the place where it had disappeared. The evening star suddenly blazed through, like a pinprick hole in the iron wall of a furnace.

With the joy of a Christopher Columbus, I leapt onto the island's gravelly beach. Before white man it was simply a hill, but the reservoir had submerged it. The drought had then made it an island. Saplings grew up in nature's never-ending search for equilibrium. I ran to the highest point and was shocked to see, in the ultimate light, the dam only a couple miles away. It was detectable as a perfect flat on the northern horizon—an immense, earth-filled dam. The first of the great Missouri River reservoirs was almost behind me.

The next day I probed the irregular shoreline west of the dam until I found a narrow cove containing a boat ramp. A retired farmer named Jake Neufeld was there, checking lake conditions in preparation for a fishing trip. He offered to carry *Squeak* to his house, which was on the river below the dam, so we loaded her in the back of his pickup.

I took advantage of the occasion to refasten the steel runner on the bottom of the boat and gather provisions for the next stretch of river. Jake and his wife, Ida, were fundamentalists, and the only condition of their charity, most notably Ida's excellent cooking, was that I listen to their sermons without interruption.

"How do you suppose you've survived this adventure of yours so far? Don't you think the Lord is watching over you, and that you'd better take Him into your heart?" asked Ida over supper. She arched her eyebrows sharply as she delivered this final thrust.

"Maybe you're right," I returned, politely. But was it Ida's god I had been abstractly conversing with the preceding ten days, or gods more ancient, or no god at all, but simply Man's eternal yearning? I respected the Bible Jake and Ida handed me the next day, as I pushed *Squeak* back into the water. But it seemed mere printed paper compared to the river and sky that were my luminous house that fall of 1990.

The river whirled fitfully below the dam, like an innocent just escaped from prison, but its tension dissipated within a couple bends. According to the map, the Milk River was due to join the Missouri soon, on the left. In a sense, I had witnessed her birth at that spillway with Jim and Eileen. Now I would witness her end, her merger with a greater force. I was anxious, and, incongruously, thirsty for a beer.

As darkness fell I located a channel leading north. It was wide and without current. A white van sat on a grassy margin at the northeast corner of the confluence.

"Is this the Milk River?" I yelled.

"Yeah!" answered a tall man of rugged good looks. "Want a beer?"

I laughed. "As a matter of fact, yes!" I pulled up.

"Name's Chuck McCahon," he said. "This here's my treein' walker, Bandit."

"Korean Walker?"

"No, *treein'* walker. They chase the raccoon up a tree so you can shoot 'em."

Chuck had been raised on coons and carp in the hills of Missouri. He was at the mouth of the Milk to catch catfish, and before long we had skillets full of them. We drank beer, too, and talked of guns, rivers, critters, and women. As with Jim Williams, love of solitude united us. Chuck expressed it thus: "I like it when I hear the coyotes howl at night because then ain't nobody around to mess with me."

He confessed to being fifty, and shot me an appreciative glance when I said he didn't look it. He had led a rough-and-tumble life as an aerospace mechanic at air bases all over the Great Plains. He had been married three times, and kept showing me pictures of grown-up kids and ex-wives. He was a cowboy in dress and mannerisms. "I always meant to settle in the Rockies," he said, "but damned if I ain't still out here on the baldheaded prairie. Well, I ain't complaining."

I looked Chuck up when I reached the town of Wolf Point, two days later. He met me at the river and took me to the mobile home he shared with Babe, his "adopted mother." She looked maybe ten years older than him, and equally lively.

"Lookee here, Babe, here's that crazy river rat I was telling you about."

"Well I'll be, ain't you something. Come on in, come on in. I got a pot roast about done. He's staying for dinner, ain't he, Chuck?"

Their relationship approximated that of a younger brother and older sister who had chosen to live together in later life. Babe brought in the money from her job at the county courthouse, he did domestic chores. They showed me the little things that made up their life together: the pet salamander that ate liver, the pictures of the Old West trail ride they had organized. Chuck kept giving me things: a Buck knife, chokecherry syrup, homemade cookies, "sure-fire" fishing lures. It gave him such pleasure, I couldn't say no. It seemed he had a big heart confined to a small space. Chuck and Babe loved each other dearly, but he longed for the mountains, for a freedom that always eluded him. Or was his prison inside? Might freedom's air be too thin and sharp for a man bereft of wives and children?

It was cold that night back in the boat, and cold vapors shrouded the river at first light. The sun rose, burning the river clear. The sky became blue, ever deeper toward the zenith. The river braided through a broad floodplain, irrigation pumps sucking water at intervals. The main hazards were the fallen cottonwoods. Their massive roots snagged on the bottom, while their trunks and branches flagged in the current. Green water broke around them, white at the wound's jagged edge. Limbs thrashed back and forth, like metronomes wound by the timeless river.

The north bank belonged to the Fort Peck Indian Reservation. Following local advice, I camped on the south bank. Once a band of braves conducted a "sweat" just across the river from me. Drums beat long into the night, followed by the more conventional sounds of a rowdy drinking party. Other nights, muskrats, beavers, or carp woke me with curious scratchings and nudgings against *Squeak's* hull. Once I tied off on a root protruding from the bank. It turned out to be a convention center for Canada geese. Every time I stuck my head out of the hatch a hundred of them would honk and splash away. It embarrassed me to be the cause of such disruption.

I rose with the sun and strove all day for mileage. Rarely could I just float. Threading through the limbs of drowned cottonwoods, lifting my oars when the river snaked unexpectedly, I lost myself in the morning sun:

> big slow water
> foam fleck fires
> like skiing—the gleaming flakes
> like being forgotten
> and quickly remembered

I didn't mind the work, but winter threatened, and I hadn't even started to turn south yet. For two days headwinds held me back. Violent waves rolled upriver; I lost ground whenever I stopped rowing. The tall cottonwoods caused the wind to veer and gust.

The town of Culbertson lay two miles from the river, across open fields. I needed to make myself presentable before fetching food and drinking water, so I stripped and dove into the river. The cold shocked me. I stood waist-deep, feet braced. My body was taut, my skin tanned and goose-pimpled. I felt young and strong. I held no grudge against society. I loved my family. But only in nature could I feel this alive.

I looked again for the meaning of my voyage. I had feared that the actual event, so long in planning, might be anticlimactic. My post-high-school journey had been, at first. My best friend and I were enthusiastic when we agreed on the outline of the trip at the beginning of our senior year. But as graduation approached the joy of anticipation corrupted into existential dread. My future was too wide an abyss. An unformed identity stirred within me. Then we were traveling through Europe, and instead of the wild and crazy guys we should have been, we were still just Judd and Steve, trapped in an immature relationship. So I insisted we split up when we reached Istanbul.

The parting was traumatic. The journey didn't get easier, but this final break with the past allowed my identity to stir more forcefully. Wanderlust swept me to the Indus, where the 1971 Indo-Pakistani war entangled me, then back across Asia in the dead of winter, hitchhiking and sleeping on frozen ground. I picked up a motorcycle in Holland and struck out for Africa. But while preparing to cross the Sahara I got into two motorcycle accidents, the second of which landed me in a Moroccan prison.

My college years were still introspective, but mellower. Professional life drew me out, balanced me. But the wanderlust remained, that spiritual unrest inherent to life.

This voyage began with euphoria, not anticlimax. It was difficult, but not excessively painful or dangerous. Later I would know true fear, but now I was blossoming, unchecked. I had discovered a new way to travel. God's intimate details lay before me. My capacity for wonder had been reinvigorated, and the object of my wonder was as internal as external, for I was part of all I saw. Just as the photo of myself in Kabul in 1971 captures an enigma, so must I wonder at the thirty-seven-year-old man who felt himself such a young buck that autumn day outside Culbertson.

As for my itinerary, I still planned to sail out the mouth of the Mississippi, down Central America, through the Panama Canal, south along the Pacific coast, across South America by rivers, then back home. I was also ready to take on some environmental project in the Third World, or be diverted into whatever more thrilling adventure presented itself. In other words, the itinerary didn't matter.

Montana grew flatter as I approached its eastern edge. Ash trees mingled with the cottonwood on the banks, and red-throated turkeys lurked in the brush. I read the river almost unconsciously, identifying sandbars by slight signs. I rarely grounded anymore. I learned to embark and disembark without getting my shoes wet—it was too cold to go barefoot.

It was September 17. Oil rigs pumped like seesaws in a new range of hills to the east. The edge of a black high-pressure system swirled in the sky ahead. Wave after wave of darkness advanced while the forces of light rallied with flaming clouds and clashing sunbeams. The battle was vast and violent. The sun retreated steadily westward across the heavens, followed by angry black swaths of sky, until night imposed its inexorable truce. I had reached the mouth of the Yellowstone River. I was in North Dakota.

According to the map, Williston is on Lake Sakakawea, but as I approached town the next day I entered an exposed lake bed grown over with saplings and cattails. The river bent southeast without coming into contact with the town. Needing provisions, I attempted a reconnaissance, but the vegetation was too tall to see over, too thick to walk through, too weak to climb. The current was too strong to row back upstream. How would I get to town?

A half mile down, the river brushed against a cliff on the opposite bank. I climbed to the upper plain, five hundred feet above the river. No lake was visible. Williston was two miles away, across the floodplain. Vegetation and lagoons blocked a direct approach to town, but a dry channel entering the river from the northeast offered hope. It wasn't quite the right direction, but it would take me closer to town. So I returned to *Squeak,* crossed back to the other side, hid her in the mouth of the dry channel, and stuffed a few things into my day pack. I hoped to reach town and return in the three hours remaining before dark.

The drying slough had become a string of shallow ponds where carp wriggled fretfully. Herons and raccoons had hunted them, but they were safe from me, because the mud of the ponds' banks didn't support my weight. The slough continued straight for a mile without a clearing or vantage point, then opened onto a larger slough containing current. I followed this left, toward town, until a levee became visible on the far side. I stripped, crammed my clothes into my daypack, and attempted to ford. Halfway across I suddenly sank in to my crotch. A smell of clay and cellulose escaped from the muck. I squirmed back to the bank and soberly reconsidered. I found a stout sapling that a beaver had severed at its base, to hold me up if worse came to worse, and worked my way across via some sandy islands. I washed the mud off and put my clothes back on. A long walk through empty fields and rail yards brought me to a bar on the edge of town called the KK Korral.

It was too late to get anything done and still make it back to *Squeak* before dark, so I mingled and kept my eye out for a place to sleep. I told a fellow who claimed to know the sloughs how I had gotten to town. He didn't believe me. "Why ain't you muddy then?" he demanded, and afterward avoided me. I was either a damned fool or a damned liar, and he didn't want to know which.

The barmaid was friendlier. I told her my problem, and she called up a girlfriend of hers. "There's this guy here looking for a place to stay. He's not bad looking, either. How about your place?" It was a mischievous bit of matchmaking on her part. My needs thus assured, I enjoyed the bar scene, which grew livelier as the night progressed.

My hostess arrived. She was Mary, a chain-smoking, pool-shooting, big-breasted mother of two. She expected something for her effort, so I bought her drinks and gave her pocket money until I could have gotten a motel room for the same amount.

Several of us went to Mary's house and partied some more. Empty wine cooler bottles and junk food wrappers accumulated on the flimsy coffee table. When everybody else left, Mary popped in a pornographic video. She wasn't finished with me yet. The video had the desired effect. I paid this second round of obligations with some pleasure, and slept in her arms.

In the morning Mary yelled at her kids to get ready for school, while she prepared for a court appearance for DWI and driving with a suspended license. The dishes hadn't been washed. The house stank of cigarette smoke. She wanted to get together again later, but I escaped. Enough dissipation.

I procured candles, food, and secondhand warm clothes. A Corps of Engineers agent gave me maps of Lake Sakakawea, largest man-made lake in the U.S. He said that each year a few parties attempt to travel the length of the lake, but most either fail to negotiate the shallows at its entrance or are defeated by storms later on. Could I do it?

I slogged back to *Squeak* and rowed resolutely around a few semicircular bends, each a mile in diameter, to camp on a bank covered with tangled wood debris. The hills were sprinkled with a pink mineral. It had rained, and the bare clay slopes were gooey. With each step another inch of it stuck to the soles of my shoes, until I was walking on wobbly stilts of gumbo mud. The stilts constantly broke off and built back up as I hobbled up the slope to reconnoiter. Coming back down, the mud's greasiness made me glad of my ability to ski.

Morning brought heavy overcast and a tailwind so strong I dared not carry more sail area than the mizzen, which is about the size of a beach towel.

Squeak was surprisingly manageable in this odd set of sail, but the day was one long, grim battle. The river widened, slowed, twisted, became frantic with wave energy. In addition to the snags, rotten old trees, still erect, now rose up through the lake: ancient cottonwood forests, drowned when the dam was built. I sought a path, imagining how the river ran before the dam. I imagined wrong, and ran aground.

"Ran amuck" is more apt, because the thing I dreaded most had occurred. I was stuck in a bottomless muck the consistency of yogurt, far from land. Four inches of opaque water covered the muck, obscuring the channel, if one existed. The wind wailed furiously in my ears. My hands ached with cold and exertion. My eyes and nostrils rebelled against the groves of slimy, long-dead cottonwood.

There was no choice but to climb overboard, keeping careful grip on *Squeak's* handles. The mud was cold and creepy, too thin to walk, too thick to swim. But by getting out I reduced *Squeak's* displacement by a third. She was nearly afloat now. Experimenting, I discovered a "slurping" motion by which I could drag her, a sort of slow-motion sidestroke. Inching downwind, I saw that the river had circled more widely, and was brushing against the far side of the valley. I reached deep water, climbed back in, and let the wind fling me onto the far bank.

Solid land felt great! I put on warm clothes, cooked hot cakes, and climbed the slope for a reconnaissance. I had only to claw off that lee shore, proceed upwind through a deep bend, then round one more dead grove, and I would be home free in Lake Sakakawea.

Twice I launched, and twice the wind blew me back against the shore. The third time, rowing hard, I rounded the bend and cleared the grove. More groves followed, each a little easier to round because the lake was bending downwind. Some trees stood whole, others had broken off. Those that had broken off just below water level most concerned me. *Squeak* bumped over a hidden snag, and later side-slipped into a leaning trunk. No damage.

The lake deepened slowly, in measure with the pre-dam river gradient. Forest after rotting forest loomed up on the horizon; I weaved nervously through them. The prairie winds blew east down the lake, creating oceanic waves. I made mistakes, like snagging my mainsheet on the rudder while reefing. I refined techniques. Ashore, sand replaced the wretched mud. Sod now cloaked the rolling hills. Thickets of juniper and box elder clogged the draws.

On September 21, I camped below an abandoned house. It was open, clean, untouched. A 1949 Sears catalog lay on the bed. A trunk contained clean blankets. My air mattress had developed a leak, so I helped myself to two. Looking out the attic window, in the golden sunset I saw a skunk sniffing up my trail through the seared prairie grass.

I slept in *Squeak,* and in the cold morning returned to the house to calculate mileages on the kitchen table. The Missouri had started to veer south, but it was late in the year. Winter was advancing southward, freezing everything in its path. Could I outpace it?

I scaled charts, and multiplied by 1.5 to account for the extra miles added by meanders. I had averaged twenty-one miles per day, and had covered a quarter of the 3,600 miles to the Gulf. At that rate I would reach Kansas City in November, Memphis in December, and New Orleans in January. I'd have to buy cold-weather gear. At some point my drinking water would freeze, maybe even the river itself. Regretfully, I decided to rent a car when I got to Bismarck and drive *Squeak* south, just far enough to avoid the worst of it.

The following nights I camped in one or another of Lake Sakakawea's innumerable coves. One such evening I landed just after the sun had dropped behind the opposing hills. The line of shadow ascended my side of the valley, like a dark flood. I raced uphill, determined to feel the sun again before the cold, faint stars retook the sky. Foothold to handhold, I gained on the line of demarcation. Halfway up I reached it, but the sunshine wasn't complete; only the sun's forehead showed. Pressing on, I reached an eroding knob at prairie level in time to see the full orb. Winded and lung-cold, I sat down. This slight drop caused the sun's lower limb to set again, relative to my eyes, so I rose. It settled further. Soon, even my jumping couldn't further postpone the night.

Coyotes woke me in the chill dawn, their voices modulating as if to express trauma, or idiocy. That day I flew under full sail, then mizzen and reefed main, then mizzen alone as a gale slowly built. By afternoon the wind was so strong, and so nearly astern, that even under bare poles I achieved hull speed. I was petrified, but *Squeak* remained stable as long as I hugged the windward shores, where the waves were smaller. I was flying! Only when my course varied significantly from the wind did I ship a few gallons of water into the cockpit. It was a test of limits, happily concluded when I rowed to the head of a little fjord to camp. As usual, the wind died at sunset.

Dawn found a pair of owls cruising through my hollow. Three species of songbirds sang, each its own sweet melody. Honking geese flapped south in squadrons. They were happy, but not graceful like the kingfisher—

> kingfisher, kingfisher
> you are the best fisherman!
> so confident, purposeful
> of military bearing

your head is so big, body small
you must be smart
kingfisher, kingfisher
you are the best fisherman!

The leaves were turning yellow and red. I walked a tractor road to the top. A ruined house stood in a harvested wheat field. It had once been a log cabin, with mortised joints, adzed flat inside and out. It had been improved over time—stucco, wallboard, chimney—all long since gone to ruin. I returned to the lake. As always, the sight of *Squeak* waiting for me warmed my heart.

The dam was across the lake, ten miles away. The sail was pleasant except for whatever guilt I incurred in killing dozens of horn flies, all intent on a final meal before the cold put them to sleep. I had long since bought a fly swatter, and had become a crack shot.

The cove containing the boat ramp was hidden in a maze of inlets. I presented myself at the Lake Sakakawea State Park concessionaire store, where a park employee volunteered to haul me around the dam in his pickup. I had covered the lake's 180 miles in six days.

That night, camped partially afloat in the gravelly shallows below the dam, I was cruised by three raccoons. They rested their little hanni-paws against the gunwale and checked the boat out.

"What the hell's this, Charlie?"

"I dunno, Fred, but it smells like food in that sack!"

Before the third could speak I shone my flashlight in their eyes and they skedaddled, with plenty more terrain to cover in their nightly patrol.

I dreamt, and, instead of raccoons, three thinly clad warrior maidens visited me.

"We are the charming, beautiful people you encountered in your earlier travel, who touched you so in your impressionable years, and whom you travel to meet again," they intoned in sweet unison.

I loved them, and even in my dream knew such meetings would be fragile and transitory. Then I awoke, and a million stars, cold and bright as diamonds, filled me with an aching loneliness. Raccoons yes, but maidens? I was still deep in the winter gut of America, twisting slowly inside her. "I won't find them here," I sighed.

The land was no longer pristine. Factories and farm machinery emitted harsh sounds. A placard identified a cluster of mounds as an ancient Mandan Indian village, wiped out by European diseases two centuries before. A trim, Midwestern town named Washburn supplied me with candles and a hot lunch. Two days sufficed to complete this final stretch of the Upper Missouri.

Bismarck has four bridges. I camped between the third and fourth in a basin excavated from the bank. In better times it had been a marina, but now it was closed, up for sale, nearly dry in the low waters of late fall. Neglected boats and vehicles littered the weedy parking lot.

Scotty, the owner, let me stay there for free, and loaned me a bicycle. The bike took me to the library every day. There I tapped on their public computer, drawing from my diary. To get to the library I crossed the long, third bridge, trying not to look down through the transparent grating at the rippled sand far below. It was starting to freeze at night. The moon was coming full again.

I wrote and conducted repairs for a week, then called a car rental company. They had a car that needed to go to Omaha, Nebraska. It was mine for sixty dollars plus gas. I regretted the cold that dampened my curiosity and rushed me through my work.

CHAPTER 4

LOWER MISSOURI

On October 5, 1990, Scotty helped me lift *Squeak* onto the top of a new Oldsmobile Cutlass and tie her down. The car now appeared to wear a strange wooden hat, almost as big as itself. I drove out of Bismarck fretting at *Squeak's* unnatural perch, but she sailed effortlessly through the highway air.

What sudden, speedy mobility it was to drive a car! I relished each crossroad's choice. Where do they all go? I trended south alongside the river as it suffered through miles of drowned cottonwoods. I reached the bronzed, shrunken waters of Lake Oahe and followed it, still south, across a dozen counties. At dusk the air decided to come with me, and I sped south on the wings of a windstorm, crashing through tumbleweed stampedes. The headlights illuminated the fretful fleeing shrub ghosts. The air was too dusty to sleep by the side of the road, so I drove on to a parking lot in Pierre, South Dakota, and slept as best I could in the back seat with the wind rocking the car.

By morning the storm was spent. I killed time until the post office opened, then drove to Nebraska, reading my mail in two-second glances. Christian music played on the radio, tasteful and light, but ultimately commercial, formulaic. Garrison Keiller came on. He was better. Then I turned the radio off—better yet.

Pockets of bright grass shocked my prairie-seared eyes. Trucks lumbered past, mounded enormously with new-mown hay. Corn ripened. Streams flowed bountifully. The road crossed the Niobara River just below an ugly dam, from which chocolaty water gushed in shallow, chaotic waves. Vegetation thickened in the draws and crept up the shallow slopes. Somewhere in east Nebraska, prairie gave way to Midwest woodland. It got warmer. *Squeak* twisted and heaved in the crosswinds. I snacked as I drove.

At sunset I arrived at a riverside nightclub near the Omaha airport.

I eased *Squeak* into the new, improved Missouri River. She bobbed happily, restored to her intended medium. But I regretted the discontinuity in the journey, for we had bypassed about eight hundred river miles. The dent that *Squeak's* 250 pounds had left in the car's tinny roof also worried me. Fortunately, when I laid on the back seat and stamped upward with a stockinged heel, it came right out.

It was Saturday night. Floating household reestablished, I drove into Omaha's Old Market section, where I found the White Rabbit, a bar with sixties music and loose women. Several distracted me, but one stopped me cold. She had a Barbie Doll figure in a black miniskirt, mesh nylons, and a low-cut blouse. Her hair was long, black, straight. Her eyes pierced me through horn-rimmed glasses, but I walked up to her anyway. I started some little chat and hid my awe of her.

"Not many men have the balls to walk up to me like that," she said, begrudgingly. "My name's Barbara. It comes from the word 'barbarian.'" She offered me a cold hand, and stood close. The expanse of her breast under my nose made me giddy. It turned out we both appreciated Ayn Rand's philosophy of enlightened selfishness, so her opinion of me shot up even further. The Barbarian bragged for some time about her prowess as an attorney, and filled in her little self-portrait by noting that she lived in hope her severely retarded daughter would die. In short, any liaison with her would be fraught with both ecstasy and peril. Sounded good to me.

Two pitchers of beer later, we went to a late-night diner with another couple from the bar. The women sat on one side of the booth, I and a young black named Leon on the other. The ladies kept up a filthy banter we couldn't match. Any hint of arrogance or sadism on my part might have sustained the Barbarian's interest, but I was incapable. Her mood toward me soured. I was just another weakling, to be taunted and despised. Once again, good upbringing had thwarted my sincerely lustful intentions. They dropped Leon and me off back at the White Rabbit and drove off in search of more challenging prey, while I tried to remember where I had parked my rental car.

After an hour of politely walking around with me, Leon gave up and took a taxi home. I wandered the deserted streets several hours further, marveling at what a complete fool I was, and how someone can navigate a thousand miles of wild river and not find a parked car. At a very wee hour, when I had just about given it up for stolen, I found it, only three blocks from the White Rabbit, on a street I hadn't noticed before. A gust of lust had enfeebled my mind more than any of wind.

In the morning I drove the car to a lot at the airport, and jogged back to the brownish green river. It was no wider than in North Dakota, about two hundred yards, but it was faster and deeper because the Corps of Engineers had channelized it by projecting riprap revetments out into the riverbed. The four-m.p.h. current, plus the absence of sandbars and snags, meant I could go further in a day. I could also row facing backwards, a more powerful stroke. I had only to avoid the red and green buoys that thrashed back and forth in the current, marking the deep channel. Towboats passed pushing one to four barges each. Their wakes were uncomfortable, but not dangerous. Fishermen darted here and there in flat-bottomed, aluminum skiffs.

Cold, rainy tailwinds brought me 150 miles in three days. Iowa gave way to Missouri on the left bank, Nebraska to Kansas on the right. Boundaries were not apparent on the land, but river mile markers precisely metered my progress. Tall trees obscured the uplands. "A *sail*boat!" exclaimed a youngster on the bank, caught off guard by my quiet approach. Cheap cottages lined the banks within commuting range of Omaha. Further on the river corridor was wild. The Platte River entered, biggest tributary since the Yellowstone.

One day, after bathing distastefully in the cold, muddy water, I saw a buck enter the river downstream from me. Intent on swimming across, he hadn't seen me. I jumped in *Squeak* and followed. The creature heard me following him. Frightened, he swam incredibly fast. I had just caught up to him when we reached the far bank. He sprang shivering out of the river, stopped, and stared at me for a moment, terror and exhaustion in his eyes. Then he bounded off into the forest with a final reserve of strength.

On the night of October 9, I camped in a creek mouth. Strings hung from overhanging branches into the water. I pulled one up, and saw a hook weighted with nuts and washers.

Late in the night the sound of approaching machinery woke me. It got louder and louder: screeching metal, churning gears. Fear gripped me. Half-awake, I envisioned a monstrous barge tow bearing down, about to plaster me. The din climaxed. The monster was only feet away, just outside the cabin! Why hadn't it hit me? Then it dawned on me. I had camped beside a railroad, and a train was passing. My heart stopped thumping. I fell back asleep.

Sunrises and sunsets were the richest times because they are the boundaries of night and day, just as shorelines and forest edges are biologically rich because they separate ecosystems. I was active before dawn, not to miss a single second. It was luxurious to know I could lay abed and read in the dawning light, but instead I worked my way out the narrow creek and reentered the river, which jerked me around in its turbulent embrace, like dancing with a drunk. Frost lay thick on *Squeak's* decks. Swallows tucked and grooved through the swirling river fog as I rowed the last few miles to St. Joseph, Missouri. Above, icy mist diffused the sun. Below, the river was black and bubbly as a witch's cauldron.

Downtown St. Joseph, once the jumping-off point of the Pony Express, was now down-and-out, decayed brick and mortar. Someone told me about a mission serving free meals. While waiting in line there I met a roly-poly woman named Bonnie Brown and her eighteen-year-old daughter, Laura. Having heard on a TV newscast that I or someone like me was coming down the river, they invited me to their table.

Bonnie and Laura didn't have anything better to do, so they spent the day driving me around in their Oldsmobile. They cut capers all the while and made lively conversation. "The light ain't a-gonna get no greener," Laura teased whenever the stoplight turned green and her mother hadn't gunned it yet. Once I mentioned I was from Seattle, Washington, and the daughter asked, "Oh, did you ever saw the President?" And that was without knowing I had lived on Capitol Hill!

They took me to a laundromat, grocery store, gas station (to get a map of Missouri), and a secondhand store, where for ten dollars I purchased heavy boots, wool coat, and socks. We dropped Laura off at her boyfriend's, then I bought Bonnie dinner at a buffet restaurant out by the freeway. Her life had been hard, what with an alcoholic husband and physical disabilities, but she was zestful and gabby. To her I dedicate this poem, penned back in my bunk, at a lopsided dock on the waterfront:

The worst cities have the best secondhand stores
every ruined life an opportunity
and those four words
"I'm just passing through"
open such doors in the minds of those
who wish they were too
who know you know nothing of their past

The lowliest people are the easiest to talk to
joy and sorrow plain on their faces
their lives, a wilderness

In this wilderness, as in Nature's
I seek a vestige
of those who have gone before

Beneath the littered parking lot
crumbled brick ghosts of immigrants' tenements
below that a broken arrow
under all, slumbering earth

The wind shifted to the south, bringing sunshine and adverse winds. In Atchison, Kansas I toured the house where Amelia Erhardt was born. Newspaper clippings told her enigmatic story. Her brave spirit seemed to hover around me, in a lonely dimension peopled by disappeared heroes. But even she was not present when I clandestinely lodged that night in a creek mouth outside Leavenworth. After dark I followed railroad tracks in search of a tavern. I heard a snarl, and my flashlight beam found a possum beside the tracks. Slobber dripped from his sharp teeth; his eyes gleamed demonically. A night train passed: 111 cars, all groaning with ore and grain. Wayward corn kernels, escaping certain death at the margarine factory, had fallen between the ties. There they had sprouted new lives, regularly shorn by the thunderous steel bellies passing overhead.

Next morning, beside a garbage-can fire, an old cab driver smoked his millionth cigarette and told me what Leavenworth was like in 1945, when a dozen passenger trains came through every day. Literature told me that in 1850 it was a bustling riverport and jump-off for wagon trains. In 1827 it was a fort protecting fur traders and pioneers.

I passed a town per day, and in between it was just me, straining at the oars and squinting at the sun. I leafed through Lawrence Ferlinghetti's *A Coney Island of the Mind.* An endless reverie overtook me. I set my oars down and wrote,

Here, in the middle of nowhere
sleepy in the churning wind
where I have to think,
"Oh yeah, here I am"
this place least known
is the void round which my knowledge spins

If I dip two fingers in cream
and wipe it on the sky, squiggly,
scrape up the woody growth from leagues around
and spread it unevenly over these hills,
stream spider silk flags from my masts
and set a white house on a knoll by a cornfield
I will have recreated this noplace
alive with gusts and ripples
asleep with airplanes droning

I will have remembered to forget
I will have spaced out that certain way
step through a doorway, the room is moving
tie your shoe, your ears start ringing
like that deja vu at dusk
when I was nine crossing East 31st Street
I've never had it like that since

Exertion brought me here
but here I must not exert
because here, to try is to fail
to plan my words is to forget what I was going to say

Here, constants dominate
insect songs, cricket chants
and leaves, the billion, soon-dead flutterers
who talk of nonsense past
and what's for lunch
But passers-by punctuate:
dipping, river-sipping swallows
the lone sailor seeking secret fame

The cloud squiggles have squirmed down flat
the white house awaits another
is the corn ripe? (fool, long since harvested!)

It was a long, upwind grind to the mouth of the Kansas River, in the broken but mending heart of Kansas City. I tied up next to the Missouri River Queen, a tourist-toting pseudo-sternwheeler, then hoofed it over an abandoned bridge, across State Line Road, through deserted industrial yards, downtown. It looked better than in 1982, when I had attended a planning conference there. I considered revisiting the scene of my mugging to see if I could better remember what happened (I was hit on the head and woke up in a hospital with amnesia), but wasn't quite so foolish as to go there after dark again. Instead, I caroused at a wild bar featuring a band called the Night-crawlers, and drank their good microbrew with an absurd dude who, when he laughed, drunk and derisive, looked exactly like Teddy Roosevelt.

I was loaded myself as I wandered back through the industrial waste-lands, but so was the revolver in my pocket, and I feared naught. I re-crossed the roped-off bridge: a high, arching plain, sprinkled with rubble, and pigeon carcasses that rustled in the wind. It was a dark and stormy night. A shot rang out . . . from the barrel of my gun, down into the inky Kansas River. In my wantonness, I couldn't resist. The security guard admitted me back into the docking area, though he didn't know me from Adam, and I fell fast asleep in the belly of my little boat.

In the morning I sailed from Kansas City, elated to have escaped both harm and hangover. I now had to traverse the state of Missouri from west to east before I could resume my southward imperative. I passed under the city's great beltway bridges, admiring their architecture. Beyond, the river entered wooded hills. At the site of reconstructed Fort Osage, built by William Clark in 1808 upon his return from the Pacific Coast, I reflected on history's restless pace. By 1828 the frontier had shifted west and settlers had dismantled the obsolete fort to reuse its materials in building farms.

I was intent on reaching Lexington that day, but at the mouth of Fishing River a tall, lank man hailed me from the bank. Seeing the current was too swift for me to stop, he jumped into his boat, jerked his motor to life, and roared up alongside. With the offer of good company and certain creature comforts he lured me into accepting a tow back up to his camp on the narrow point formed by the confluence.

Dave was about forty, with long, graying hair and beard, and a bad knee. He spoke with such a strong Southern or Midwestern accent, I had difficulty understanding him. He had served as an electronics technician on the USS Ranger in the early seventies, helping bomb Vietnam "back into the stone age." He'd had good-paying jobs since then, but for the last three months had resided there in his tent, living off rabbit, deer, beaver, squirrel, catfish, carp, gar, and sturgeon. He ate a lot of snapping turtles, too. "This big around," he said, forming a circle with his arms. He taught me the names of the trees—mulberry, elm, locust. "Mulberry's best for the campfire."

While it was still light a friend of Dave's named Dan Pigg arrived with a big plate of food, which we shared. Dan was a handsome, blonde country boy. He kept repeating the twelfth step of Alcoholics Anonymous: "If I can't help a fellow human being I ain't worth nothing" (but Dave later told me to watch out for him when he's drunk). Dan gave me a can of beans and a can of spinach "for the road," and headed home.

Just as it was getting dark, and the campfire was starting to put out heat, Dan's brother Tom arrived with a bag of marijuana. Tom was less rustic in his speech than Dan, but equally fascinated with my journey.

"What are you seeking? Is it a quest?"

("He always talks mystical like that, but he never leaves Ray County," whispered Dave.)

Tom also was an alcoholic, dry just then. He talked about his family, the Piggs of Orrick, the nearby hamlet. He evoked a Ma-and-Pa-Kettle scene of broken windows, Saturday night fights, squandered money. They had always been considered the town fools, but now they were turning their dump into a big mansion with money that a third brother had made in Chicago. They were even building a swimming pool they never meant to swim in, just to spite their neighbors.

Tom left, and Dave continued his natural history lessons late into the night. Mice and frogs scurried about the messy camp, at the fringes of the fire's fading glow.

I slept a few hours, then rose at first light. As I pulled out into the current, Dave emerged from his tent and waved.

"Come again. I should be here."

He reminded me of the philosopher ferryman in one of Herman Hesse's novels, whom Sidhartha finds after a life of fruitless wandering among cults and temples. Dave had been around; now he had come back home to stay. No judgments passed his lips, but he was quick with a wry laugh, and with his motto: "The river gives me everything I need." He was self-reliant, yet quick to give and receive. Dan and Tom were his disciples. Of them Dave had said, in nearly these words:

> They are my reassurance
> for as long as Dan Pigg and Tom Pigg
> are Dan Pigg and Tom Pigg
> the sun will still rise

I rowed away in a pea soup fog with a robin's egg ceiling. The fog slowly burned off, until only a few mares' tails remained, high in the Missouri sky. Freight trains passed. Hardwood forests lined the banks. Hills were visible whenever the river meandered toward the edge of its broad floodplain. At Lexington I walked across soybean fields, up a hill, and across town for groceries. A cannonball from a Civil War battle was still lodged in a column of the old courthouse.

I passed the mouths of the Chariton and Gasconade Rivers. Indian summer had arrived, allowing me to bathe again. Leaves fluttered into the water like ticker tape from skyscrapers. Vines and creepers choked the woods. Herons squawked. A black water moccasin swam in the current. Snowy egrets preened behind the revetments. I stalked Peter Cottontail in the riverine brush, but he always escaped. Acting on a tip from Dave, I reached for a baby frog to use as live bait. He was too fast for my bare hands, so I clobbered him with a stick, intending only to stun him. He looked dead, and I was so glad when he finally revived that I let him go.

Three jet trails intersected at the sun. From the treetops came a strobing, electric sound of unidentified insects. Sometimes machines sounded: riverside grain elevators, farm machinery, chain saws. I realized that in rowing, as in bicycling or weight-lifting, the body has an optimum load range. *Squeak's* setup was fine except in headwinds, when a 'lower gear' (smaller blades or oarlocks further out) would have caused less wear and tear. My fingers were now chronically stiff and my shoulder joints were starting to pop with each motion.

The locals called the tugboats, together with the steel barges they push, "tows." One night, as I lay asleep behind a revetment, a tow passed close by, inching upstream against the current. The throb of its diesels and massive screws woke me. I rose to steady the boat. Blinding spotlights probed the shoreline from the tug's high bridge. When the tug drew abreast the cove opening, the water suddenly drained out. One minute *Squeak* was afloat in two feet of water, the next she lay aground. Little fish flopped madly in the mud. Then the water gushed back in, then out, then in, in lessening magnitudes, until calmness returned and the boat's lights disappeared upstream.

I savored the river towns: Glasgow, with its high hill, brick churches, and riverfront grain elevators where trucks delivered soybeans, corn, and hilo; Boonville, in a region where everything is Daniel Boone this or Daniel Boone that; and up-to-date Jefferson City, the state capitol, where I stopped for mail.

Thunderstorms struck. Rain fell so hard I couldn't see, but it was warm, exciting. I yelped with glee. Winds blew up, sometimes behind, sometimes ahead. One sunset it gusted so violently that trees broke with great cracking sounds, and I nearly capsized, though I'd already doused my sails.

Limestone cliffs now sprouted from the neighboring hills. The days grew shorter, and chilly again. I pulled on my woollies:

all bundled up
air clean and cold
trees aflame in red and orange
others, conservative green

sun remains in saucer blue
still he warms
and helps my worsted jacket
to hold off the robber wind

happy tools these mitts and socks
to take us where sun dips low at noon
as scuba takes us into the sea

ah! home among the trees
with others who breathe air like me
they in their fur, I in mine

autumn:
reflection, adjustment
and the swirling maple helicopters
of change

On October 19, approaching the town of Hermann, I saw bumper-to-bumper cars on a high bridge. Accordion music floated down from town. Oktoberfest! Hermann was a little German-American city, well-preserved. I walked the streets alongside a horse-drawn tourist carriage, eavesdropping on the driver's explanations of the town's architectural charms, then ducked into the Biergarten, where the accordion music was coming from. All they had was Miller Lite, but the gaiety was infectious.

I picked a yellow flower and gave it to a young woman grooving all alone to the music. She liked it, and asked for a purple one too. I got her that, and a beer, and another beer. I soon realized my southern belle was not demure. On the contrary, she swore like a fiend and staggered when she moved. But she was in high spirits and we got along famously until she needed to make a phone call. She tried to call collect, identifying herself as "his wife," but didn't get through. The operator told her how much it would cost to try again, paying in coins. She turned to me.

"Gimme a dollar and thirty cents."

"Pay for it yourself if you're calling your husband."

"Fuck you!" she countered, and threw the flowers in my face. The crowd soon trampled them into a yellow and purple pulp, and I was left laughing at the absurdity of our brief romance. I tried to party again, but the beer and polka music tasted stale after that. I retired to my residence on the river bank, where I was the object of considerable curiosity, until night extinguished all thoughts other than of sleep.

Back on the river, I tacked to windward, my leeboard control line humming in the water like a strummed gutbucket. I stopped for dinner at Washington, population 40,000. It was another Middle American town with German roots.

Seeing no place to eat, I was about to climb back aboard when a gray-haired, whiskery guy came up and started yammering at me in a broad, over-emphatic accent. At his insistence I tied *Squeak* to the barge he was renovating and rode with him in his old clunker up to Hardee's Restaurant. Nick Kagouris, retired army sergeant, was sixty-five years old but still husky, and appreciative of anything to "liven things up" in that boring town. He was a kind but moody man, shifting rapidly between ennui and foul-mouthed rage. Whenever he got a good dig in at somebody his eyes lit up and his mouth grinned into a V-shape, with big teeth showing at the bottom.

Next morning I was again about to slip away when Nick came to the waterfront to help me run errands. It could have waited until St. Louis, but my main halyard clamcleat was coming loose from the mast, so we looked for aluminum etch to glue it back on. The stores didn't carry it, so Nick took me to see "this weird Arab guy" who was a wizard at things like that, and also happened to be "filthy rich."

He took me to the fanciest house in town, a white, classical revival mansion overlooking the river. Its chandeliers had been given to King George of England by the Czar of Russia. The owner, Dibi Khanzada, was fifty-three, a Briton of Qatari extraction, veteran of the Suez Canal War, a brilliant engineer, restaurateur, and amateur taxidermist. He was small, brown-skinned, smoked a pipe, and spoke proper English. His wife, Zeena, was a plump Moor with a thick Arab accent. They had sold their restaurant near Buckingham Palace and moved to Missouri to retire and invest in real estate. Dibi loved America's wide-open spaces, and relished being called "Yank" whenever he visited his friends back in London.

Nick and Dibi's relationship was odd. Whenever they met they pulled out knives or hammers and pretended they were going to kill each other. They harried, insulted, and teased each other with passionate imagination. Their wives and I were all pawns in their telephone games.

"Tell him I'm on the john and to call back in ten minutes."

"Tell him he's a dirty son-of-a-bitch and I never want to speak to him again!"

Volatile Nick was the principal instigator, but Dibi loved the game too. Moreover, they united in their condemnation of "the Nazis" (mainstream locals), whom they resented for never fully accepting them into the community.

Just as Nick and I had quickly become friends, so did Dibi and I. He came up with an effective technique for reattaching my clamcleat, and adeptly repaired my Plexiglas hatch cover, which had rebroken. In turn, I helped him clean out his garage, which housed a Rolls Royce, a Cadillac, a Ford truck, several lesser vehicles, and tons of woodworking machinery he had recently bought at auction. Twice I went with Dibi and Zeena to their farm, an hour's drive away. Zeena cooked excellent Middle Eastern meals while Dibi and I hunted rabbits and cut wood. He seemed too delicate to handle a chain saw, but was actually quite good at it. He showed me his pet alligators and the little brass cannons he made, yet another hobby. We talked endlessly of life and what should be sought from it. He admitted to having become tied down with material possessions. Real estate investments had gone bad. Like Nick, he and Zeena had come to hate Washington, Missouri. They longed to move somewhere else in the States, travel, and lead a simpler life.

When not with Dibi and Zeena I was with Nick, eating his wife's Greek cooking, watching the news on TV, or playing the piano at a local lounge. One day we passed a Greek-American friend of his. Nick gave chase. He drove wildly, honking his horn and shouting out the window, "You *milakka* (jerk-off)!" We caught up with him and they bantered jovially for awhile. Driving on, Nick heatedly informed me of the guy's shortcomings: his incredible stinginess, and how the local preacher had caught him in the act of banging one of his waitresses in the cooler of his restaurant.

Nick was a little down when it was time for me to go. Wife Jean needed hospitalization for a pain in her leg. Financial difficulties weighed on them. "I'm sure glad you showed up, Steve. This week would have been real boring if you hadn't."

This was the bittersweet crux of traveling. On the brink of leaving, loneliness held me back, binding me to newfound friends, yet it pushed me away too, in search of a fuller love. The balance had now tipped in favor of leaving. Indian summer was over. The mornings were frosty again.

By evening I was in St. Charles, founded by the French in 1780, jumping-off point for the Lewis and Clark Expedition, the beginning of the Santa Fe Trail. Its charming historic district evoked powdered wigs and flintlocks, coopers and stonemasons.

The following day I rowed the remaining twenty-eight miles to the Mississippi River. On the bank, the white-on-blue river-mile signs passed at seven-minute intervals, like a slow-motion countdown: "10—9—8—7—6—5—4—3—2—1."

CHAPTER 5

MISSISSIPPI RIVER

At 3:45 P.M., October 26, flush with excitement, I pulled up at the confluence of rivers. The intersection was T-shaped, the Mississippi draining south, the Missouri joining from the west. Not a soul was in sight. Out-of-service barges lined the banks. The upland was a forested floodplain, littered with flotsam. A hundred yards inland a levee protected a vast field, tilled bare. The Mississippi upstream of the confluence was wider than the Missouri, but not as fast. The volume of the combined rivers would be two to three times that of the one I had followed for two months.

With deep satisfaction at completing a phase of the voyage, and plenty of daylight remaining, I left for St. Louis, twenty miles south. Across from the Missouri's mouth was the entrance to a canal paralleling the river. Its sign read, "ALL BOATS," but I chose the more circuitous main channel to avoid barge traffic. My course now being less opposed to the wind, I hoisted sail.

I passed under a bridge and saw the city in the distance, but a noise of rushing water disturbed me. What was it? It grew louder. It came from ahead, but the river looked normal—no, a faint mist. I stood up. Fifty yards ahead, the river disappeared. Waterfall! I was in the middle, a half mile from either side. The wind dictated that I steer for the left bank. I angled sharply upstream, devoting most of my speed to keeping a constant distance from the drop-off. Blow wind, blow! I inched over to the Illinois side, my heart pounding. Safely ashore, I climbed an abutment and beheld a low dam over which the river flowed with even, crushing power.

"That's the Chain of Rocks. It raises the water so's to be able to operate the lock," said a fellow fishing from the abutment. He showed me a string of saugers he had caught.

At Kimmswick, Missouri, 10/29/90

The sun was just setting. The abutment precluded portaging here, so I rowed upstream a quarter mile, then across to the Missouri side. Here, rather than dropping in a single fall, the water did so in a series of rapids through tiers of riprap (jagged boulders) in which logs had accumulated. Determined to sleep with the trial behind me, I stripped, donned sneakers, and slipped out onto the sharp boulders, feeling carefully for footholds. I tied a long bow line, nudged *Squeak* just so, and reined her in when she had drifted beyond the white water of the first chute. Then I waded down and repeated the process on the second chute, and the third. It was now dark but for a bright half-moon. On the last chute I nudged wrong—the current caught her broadside, obliging me to let go the rope lest she capsize. Scampering and wading faster than I would have thought possible, I caught her before she sustained any serious knocks. Exhausted, I drifted clear of the disturbing sound of falling water and slept in the lee of a wrecked barge.

In the morning I tacked into town and landed front and center before the stainless steel Gateway Arch. Tourists who had bent backward to photograph the arch leaned forward and snapped *Squeak* and me instead. I spent all day begging permission to tie to one of the docks serving the many tourist stern-wheelers, to no avail. "Sorry, our insurance doesn't allow it," said the manager of a floating restaurant. After dark I found a security guard willing to look the other way for just one night.

The nearest marina was in Kimmswick, twenty miles downstream. There I met a young couple from New Mexico who were descending the Mississippi from its headwaters in Minnesota in a canoe of their own design. The girl, Diane, was delicate and pretty. She rarely spoke, but urged the conversation on with attentive smiles. Paul, lanky and animated, raved over my undertaking and begged for details.

"Well what are the locks like on the Missouri?"

"There aren't any."

"You're kidding! God, how many have we gone through, Di? Twenty?"

We had dinner together, then I pulled out a phone number my mom had given me. It was for her Cousin Bernice, whom I knew only faintly.

"Oh, Stephen, of course! No, I want you to come stay here. Can't you leave your little boat there at the marina? Of course you can. I'll just come pick you up first thing in the morning."

I stayed at Bernice's home in suburban St. Louis six days while working on Chapter 4 on a computer at the library. It was like living with a daintier, Midwestern version of my own mother. Bernice lavished me with kindness, yet sensed my need for privacy. I took the bus downtown each morning and stayed at the library until closing. St. Louis was thriving but colorless compared to the smaller river towns. When I hitched through in 1973, on my way to Miami, a slum landlord had paid me five dollars to clean up a vacant lot. I saw no vacant lots this time. Halloween arrived, and I haunted the downtown hot spots, sadly costume-less, admiring from afar the Sisters from Hell, the Human Fly, the Pumpkin Lady. Once again, romance eluded me.

On November 4 Bernice drove me back down to Kimmswick. My distant relative no longer seemed distant. But it was the nature of my voyage to approach briefly, then draw away. Bernice later sent me prints of the photos she had taken of me, including a series that captured the loneliness of my departures. In the series I am sailing away. In each frame, river and sky are a uniform blue-gray. Across this expanse, *Squeak* and I shrink, and shrink, until her sail is but a tiny speck.

A north wind now sped me past cliffs and forests. I camped in snug coves while rain pummeled the hatch cover eighteen inches above my face. I woke in the night with moonlight seeping through clouds, and ghosted through eerie morning fogs, giving wide berth to the tows. Alternating green and red buoys marked the river channel. The massive deciduous trees that populated the low hills had lost half their leaves. Those still clinging were dying and burning with color.

At Cape Girardeau I answered the hail of a trio of white college boys who offered me beer and a fire to sit beside. I contributed gin, potatoes, and carrots. They debated, two in favor and one opposed, whether "niggers" deserved to be discriminated against.

"*You* guys sound like niggers, the way you talk," I said, meaning they seemed to have adopted the slang of the race whose worth they were deciding. They blushed and changed the subject.

It was a joy to sail downriver and downwind at the same time, to go doubly with the flow. The countryside melted away at ten miles per hour, half from current, half from wind. But the north wind also froze me, while humidity dampened clothing, bedding, and matches. Through long hours at the tiller I shivered and tensed to keep warm. To make light of myself, and work my vocal chords, I concocted a shanty:

Well I guess this song has now begun
but will we still be friends when it's done?
I leave that up to you to say
I'm off to the Caribbean

Where the fish can fly and the birds can swim
and the water's so warm that you want to jump in
That's reason enough right there to go
off to the Caribbean

Well I left my home in Seattle town
liked it just fine but I gotta move around
Kissed my Ma and promised not to drown
then off to the Caribbean

Where the fish can fly and the birds can swim, etc.

Well to drive would cost too much in gas
so I went in a rowboat like a stupid ass
down the Missouri and the Mississippi
then off to the Caribbean

Where the fish can fly and the birds can swim, etc.

Well my boat ain't big but at least she's slow
and every day we do a do-si-do
I row her and she sails me
off to the Caribbean

Where the fish can fly and the birds can swim, etc.

When I get down to New Orleans
I plan to find me a Cajun Queen
Make her take a bath if she ain't clean
then off to the Caribbean

Where the fish can fly and the birds can swim, etc.

Well I left my home a little too late
Didn't realize how long it would take
Winter in North Dakota ain't
my idea of the Caribbean

Where the fish can fly and the birds can swim, etc.

Well in case you didn't already know
the moral of this story I've told
is I don't really care for the mist and snow
I care—to—be—in
  the Ca—ri—bbe—an!

The tows became more numerous, and larger: four barges wide by six long, then five by six, six by six, seven by seven. They were floating football fields, moving islands. Sometimes their skippers razzed me over their loud-speakers:

"Say, you in the little boat, kindly move aside so I can pass," or

"Living proof that damn fools never say die," or

"Hey man, ya havin' fun? Tell ya what, I almost ran over you!"

A work crew suspended beneath a railroad bridge stopped its clattering and clanging to laugh at me. Workmen in the grain terminals, power plants, and shipyards stared, waved, shouted. They were small as ants against the backdrop of their man-made marvels. I rarely was close enough to see their expressions. Our connection was weak and passing, like eye contact between a passenger on a speeding train and someone standing by the track. Soon the train will have passed, and, for the person left standing in the blank silence, there will be no sign of what has occurred but a faint reverberation. My journey was like that, except that I was both the one in motion and the one left alone in nature after the contact. Drifting, I saw the world while remaining still. I had the active sight of the mover and the passive sight of the motionless. I existed in the same dimension as the workers on the bridge, and in another, quieter one as well.

On November 6 I rowed through wild meanders overhung by weathered snags, and on into the night, eager to reach the confluence of the Ohio River. A fish jumped, a bank sloughed. Rowing tentatively, straining my eyes, I turned left at the junction and ascended the Ohio to the town of Cairo, Illinois. Barges lay double- and triple-parked all along the bank. Tiny tugs busily reshuffled them into new tows. I pulled up onto a flat in the revetment and explored the town. Once the goal of runaway slaves, exemplified by Huckleberry Finn's Jim, Cairo was now derelict. Many of its red brick buildings were abandoned, their cast-iron facades rusty and loose. A mark on the floodwall recorded the height of the 1937 flood, which covered the entire town with six feet of water.

Cairo still stands at the greatest confluence of rivers in North America. The Ohio is as wide as the Mississippi, but slower. Both are the color of lightly creamed coffee. Joined, they constitute the Lower Mississippi. Downstream of Cairo, on a straight stretch, the river ran so wide and far, it met the sky at the horizon, as if I were looking out to sea. Out in the middle I nearly forgot the water was flowing, so smooth and even was the current.

On the left bank, Illinois gave way to Kentucky, then Tennessee. The land was wild because the river had washed away the pioneer towns. Islands were numerous, and would increase in number as the river rose to winter stage, filling the chutes (side channels). Somewhere beyond the scrub willows and cottonwoods was always a tall, grassy levee. Beyond that lay flat farmland. This is the longest continuous line of levees in the world, protecting a floodplain that gets ever wider until it reaches the sea. Heights of land are visible only where the river meanders near the floodplain's edge. So far, the river has endured the widely set levees, but it chafes at even these strictures. Someday it will wipe them out, too.

I imagined the Mississippi during the Civil War, when the Union ironclads pressed inexorably southward under Admiral Porter and General Grant. Major battles occurred at Island 10, Memphis, and Vicksburg. Another Union fleet captured New Orleans and worked its way north. The fall of Vicksburg split the Confederacy in two, but rebels continued to fire on federal shipping, and Union commanders continued to burn towns in retaliation. Thus, few antebellum structures remain.

Until the migrant river erased it, Island 10 was near New Madrid, Missouri. I stopped at this town, so named because it was founded under Spanish dominion. As I ate lunch in Tom's Grill, a TV news crew pumped the old-timers at the table beside me for their attitudes toward a psychic's prediction that on December 3 the New Madrid fault would experience an earthquake like that of 1811, when a region 150 miles long and 40 miles wide suddenly sank and was filled by river water. They responded with a mixture of Southern nonchalance and black humor, at once irritated and delighted at being the center of attention.

"Wife said she was thinking 'bout going to Pennsylvania to stay at her sister's and I told her, 'You go on, Ruth, I'll just stay here and ride it out.'"

"Yeah, earth might swaller the whole town up, but at least we'll be through with this nonsense."

I wished I could be there on the big day, but snow was also predicted, and that worried me more than any earthquake.

Each day I sailed on the cold north wind, and each sunset I sought a chute away from the wash of the towboats. There I nudged *Squeak* onto the sand and dropped her leeboards to anchor her. I cooked and ate. If any daylight remained I walked the spits and fired a few rounds at the plastic containers, bottles, and light bulbs that littered the sand and clogged the brush. One dreary dusk a cloud of birds advanced over the sky, and a noise like angry waves;

> blackbirds swarming, blackbirds swarming!
> they twist and turn and merge and churn
> like smoke under a glass

with all the shapes that clouds have been
one fast upon the other
and all the patterns of leaves long fallen
and caw! voiced all together

was this the sound that Van Gogh heard
before he killed himself?
a being made of a million beings
a river of feathers
a rope of birds

I sailed a whole day in ceaseless downpour. The wetness slowly found the gaps in my raingear. The north wind picked up, so I reefed, clinging stubbornly to the tiller, bailing the cockpit. I had to find a laundromat to dry my clothes, or remain miserable. My road map indicated towns that never revealed themselves. I now pinned my hopes on Osceola, Arkansas.

The Lower Mississippi's few harbors are old river bends that have been bisected by the river having taken a shorter course. Man blocks off the old bend's upstream connection to the main channel, leaving an arc of still water. Harbor depth fluctuates with the river, through an annual range of forty feet. At dusk I rowed up such a chute, through a gauntlet of moored barges. The river having not yet risen, the banks were tall and muddy. I tied to a barge being loaded with grain, to avail myself of the precarious plank by which the crew climbed ashore. A bargeman in a stocking cap paused to grin at me. "Come all the way down in that little thing, huh? Bring any *weed* with ya?" His voice was twangy.

"Sorry. But hey, which way's town?"

It was a mile and a half away. I traipsed down a country road through muddy cotton fields. It had stopped raining, but the sky was dark and gloomy. I was wearing all my clothing, my winter boots, my thick wool coat. All of it was wet. "Laundromat, laundromat!" I gasped, as a man dying of thirst might gasp for water.

The laundromat was full of poor black mothers and squirmy kids. I stripped down except for T-shirt and cutoffs and dried my clothes. The hot, dry clothes felt marvelous. Now for something to eat. All I saw was a McDonald's down the road. Traffic was heavy. The shoulder was narrow and full of puddles. I entered the McDonald's and got a tray full of food. An adolescent supervisor yelled orders at a pimply employee.

"Mop the floor!"

"I already did!"

A little boy ran around yelping and his father kept warning he would whip him, but he never did.

I finished my meal, then considered whether to attempt a sponge bath in the men's room. I hadn't bathed in a week, but I was afraid of being caught. Business seemed to be dying down. I went in the bathroom and hung out awhile. Nobody came in. Go for it.

I stripped off my sweater and T-shirt and put them inside the sink cabinet to stay dry. I had just worked my head up into a lather when they started coming in. A convoy of beer-drinking teenagers had arrived and were now lining up to use the john. They crowded all around me. Nobody said anything. I hurriedly scraped off most of my beard. I couldn't seem to keep the water from flowing all over the floor. Then I reached inside the sink cabinet for my clothes. They were sopping wet! The drain had been leaking on them the whole time! I wanted to cry. I gritted my teeth and pulled the soggy mass over my head. Just then Pimple Face and his boss came in with mops.

"Seems to have been a leak," I mumbled before they could speak, and fled into the darkness. I dried my clothes all over again, bought some groceries at the Piggly Wiggly, and trekked back to the harbor. Such was my night on the town in Osceola, Arkansas.

Next morning the sun rose through the orange haze like a hot-air balloon. Birds sang the local songs, unfamiliar to me. The north wind had died. The land was flat, the treeline scraggly. The newly accreted lands inside the bends were thick with the bright dwarf willows that survive submersion. At the outsides of the bends the Corps of Engineers had laid vast sheets of riprap or concrete matting to stop the meanders. Near towns these revetments were often supplemented by wrecked barges, car bodies, and obsolete concrete castings. Dikes (riprap jetties projecting into the river to concentrate flow) became fewer. Velocity dropped off.

An old fisherman approached me in an aluminum skiff. He was a fleshy man with soft, waterlogged skin. Beaming with contentment, he showed me the catfish he had netted: spoonbill cats, yellow cats, blue cats, buffalo carp. He gave me two small channel cats to eat. He drank his whiskey, I my gin. We drifted awhile together. "I always pays my respects to you kooks runnin' the river," he said, politely. "Can tell you a mile off."

Memphis, Tennessee is named for the ancient Egyptian city, and its self-image is one of classical splendor. The first inkling was a bridge with a double arch in the shape of "M," for Memphis. The second was a basketball stadium in the form of a pyramid. I moored at the fanciest marina on the whole Mississippi. It was Saturday night, so I showered and walked to Beale Street, home of the blues and once a center of Southern black culture. Out-of-town tourists thronged the nightspots and perused the plaques memorializing great stars of the past.

I settled into a club with a rock band and got drunk, secretly refilling my cocktail glass from the pint in my pocket. I chatted but didn't connect. I saw young lovers, and their kisses gave me a bittersweet pleasure—bitter because I didn't want to feel old, sweet because sentimentalism is one of middle age's few rewards. But must life's phases be sequential? Can one person combine the innocence of a child, the lust of an adult, and the wisdom of an elder? If yes, what is the price of such complexity?

Perhaps my philosophy was therapeutic, because my hangover the following morning was mild. I dried blankets and sewed buttons, enjoying the sun, sitting on the dock beside *Squeak*. People came by asking questions. One donated charts, another a history of the Mississippi River. A lovely young sculptor named Susan gave me a glimpse of Memphis's art community by taking me that evening to the unveiling of a major painting. It was a storm of yellow and dark masses titled *Solar Wind*. The artist was dark, possibly gypsy, full of a gentle, nervous energy. The guests—photographers, musicians, painters—clowned and danced for hours. Then Susan took me to her apartment, where we fried okra and talked of individual expression, the struggle between commercial and artistic success, and her belief in the occult until four in the morning.

Her companionship, though platonic, still warmed me when I rowed out of the harbor the following noon. I was glad no one saw me leave; what good are farewells? Besides, I had just picked up a packet of mail. I situated myself midstream, set the oars down, and eagerly read letters from Jim and Eileen, Tammy, Mom and Dad.

The price of warm weather was light, contrary winds. The stiffness in my fingers returned. My calluses built up. I ate breakfasts of whole wheat bread and fruit, and suppers of potatoes, carrots, and onions. My upper body was hard as a rock, but my legs had atrophied. The birds were all south by now except for the odd flock wintering locally. I camped in calm lagoons and walked sandy shores carpeted with raccoon and heron tracks. Slim, bare branches protruded from the silt. The State of Mississippi took Tennessee's place on the left bank. I was getting close to the Gulf.

On November 15, 1990, I reached Helena, Arkansas. It was to be a memorable stop, not for the fast food I treated myself to, but for the young woman in a checkered flannel shirt, jeans, and tennis shoes who stood behind me in the checkout line at the supermarket.

"Not from around here, are you?" the cashier asked me. "I can tell by your accent."

"Hey, you people talk funny, not me," I kidded, and told her how I had arrived.

"Finally, I'm not the only stranger in town anymore!" the woman behind me chimed in, then blushed and lowered her head. "Just a bag of dog food," she said while I bagged my groceries.

We walked out of the store sufficiently close in time for me to hold the door open for her. "I've got a shower you can use if..." she volunteered, at the same instant that I blurted an invitation to come see my boat. "Okay, boat first," she laughed.

We walked along country roads leading toward the river and talked while Traci's nervous German shepherd, Poco, darted about and waded in the stagnant ditches. The sun set as we crossed the wide, green floodplain.

She was twenty-three, my height, slim. The touch of acne on her face didn't diminish her beauty in my eyes. Her body moved gracefully yet with a hint of awkwardness, as if she were in metamorphosis, or distracted by an internal dialogue. Traci never knew her biological mother, and her stepmother died when she was young. Her relationship with her father, a college professor in Lubbock, Texas, caused her an anguish she didn't fully understand, that had something to do with her innermost challenge. Always precocious, she left home early and went to Austin, where she waitressed and attended the university for years without getting a degree. She had bought a little pickup truck with an installment from an inheritance her father held for her, and now was traveling around the country taking pictures. Things were coming together. She prided herself in her progress as a photographer and looked toward to a career. She had been in Helena two months, shooting the black faces there. She called it her "Delta project."

Traci fell in love with *Squeak*, and I with Traci. I taught her how to row on the dark river, behind her with my arms around her, all four hands gripping the oars. I tied *Squeak* to a piling and swam back to shore, naked, to keep my clothes dry, and because I wanted her to see me.

I spent five days in her apartment in an old house overlooking town. We busied ourselves with putting a new alternator in her pickup; with beer, music, gin rummy, boat rides, and sunsets on top of the hill. She was fun-loving, thoughtful, almost compliant, yet her pattern over the past few years was that of a misfit, a rebel. How could that be? In the quiet times she castigated herself for neglecting her work. She showed them to me: stark, black-and-white photographs that revealed hidden qualities, like an old woman's endurance, or the brittle hostility of a girl forced to grow up fast.

Helena is in the heart of the Delta, the poorest corner of the United States. The cotton industry had been mechanized, leaving the blacks unemployed. The buildings were dilapidated. Restless youths jived on the street corners, old folks sat on porches. We ate catfish and grits at a soul-food restaurant, and went to a funky pool hall she knew. It was a small, bare room in an ancient brick building. We horsed around with "the brothers." I was still unaccustomed to being around blacks, but Traci played a tune on the juke box and danced the "electric slide" with them. I marveled at her, and she at me.

"Steve," she said, across a table from me, our hands touching, "what you're doing with *Squeak* is so—perfect. I want to stay close to you, but it wouldn't be right to distract you from your journey."

"You're journeying too. It's all what we make of it. *Squeak's* too small for us to go together, but how about if we meet up periodically? I'll sail down to the Gulf coast and find us someplace uninhabited. We can build a camp and hang out for a few weeks."

"A paradise for two! With my truck and your *Squeak* we'll be amphibious! We even have Poco to—I don't know, a neurotic shepherd must be good for something."

I looked at her, and ached with desire. Our possibilities were so staggering; why did I doubt? What was I afraid of?

I had lived with Tammy for four years prior to the journey. I loved her, but she was unhappy, difficult. I became remote. She took refuge in another man, I in my boatbuilding. We started drifting apart a year before my departure, but I still hadn't come to terms with losing her. The rivers filled with beauty all of me except the void she used to fill. When I thought of her it hurt. I told myself it wasn't too late, that we could get together after the voyage.

Now I knew it would never happen, and accepted it. Traci had healed that wound, filled that void. My love for her was that of a man still grieving, who falls in love too fast. My lust for her was dizzy, unstable. We agreed to meet in Greenville, Mississippi, three days downriver. I watched her until she faded from view, and thought of her constantly.

The river was big and monotonous. Water, sand, willow thickets, forest—they all blurred together. Chutes and lagoons became less frequent, but I always found a place to camp. To avoid barge traffic I often sailed in the shallow water near the edges. Their wakes annoyed me, but I benefited from those of the upriver-bound towboats by cutting in behind them as they passed and getting a push from their wash. It was like riding a roller coaster, because their immense propellers produced a jet of ten-foot-high swells that shot me downriver several knots faster than the normal current.

Winds arose, and died again. Clouds gathered and dispersed. I saw a wood tick wriggling in the water's surface tension, and scooped him up. Other times it was a honeybee, or spiders. A green grasshopper with red eyes, minus a rear leg, kept me company for hours. Yes,

Hitchhiking insects are desperate fellows
when saved from their watery graves
They'd hijack your boat if given a chance
for they are all scoundrels and knaves

But they haven't a chance—you're too big for them
besides which they don't even know
that but for your kindly indulgence, they
to Davy Jones's locker would go

So give them a ride and don't be afraid
they'll charm you with quaint insect tricks
like crawling and buzzing and rubbing their legs
and jumping with one-legged kicks

Besides, it'll all soon be over
they'll fly and you'll see them no more
and all night long you'll worry, in doubt
'bout whether they made it ashore

I passed the mouths of the White and Arkansas rivers—wild-looking places, perhaps not much changed since 1541, when De Soto's crew was here, except the tall, straight cypresses have long since been logged off, never to return. De Soto himself, that brave but cruel man, lies somewhere nearby, for he died of fever at their winter camp on the Arkansas. His lieutenants wrapped him with weighted shrouds and sank him into the river so the Indians wouldn't know the man they feared was dead.

I arrived at Greenville just as canoeists Diane and Paul were leaving. We had crossed paths in Memphis and Helena, too, one of us always leapfrogging ahead of the other. I went farther in a day, but my stopovers were longer. I moored *Squeak* at the marina and walked around town until I found a ruined factory with water running from a broken pipe. No one was around, so I bathed. I found a laundromat in the black quarter and did my clothes, jogging back to the marina between cycles. Each time I ran a gauntlet of scruffy youths who wanted to sell me pot, or panhandle, or know what I was doing there. I rarely understood their words, but I knew enough to walk quickly by and not look afraid.

I worried that Traci wouldn't show up. Just before dark her truck rolled onto the dirt levee. Relief flooded over me. She was a dream: so tall, so sweetly shaped. She got out and faced me, her shoulder-length, brown hair swaying across her face. She brushed it behind an ear, and smiled. "Hey, sailor!"

Our five days in Greenville together passed quickly. We had Thanksgiving dinner at a friendly cafe. I replaced oarlock sockets again. She gave me a jitterbug lesson on the lawn at the base of the levee, but it was quite beyond me. We sailed, read poetry at the library, caroused with new friends, exchanged puns. I struggled to keep up with her wit.

"I planned on wintering in New Orleans anyway," she said one evening at the marina lounge. "Why not get an apartment there together?"

"Sounds good. But how about after that?"

"Where do you plan to go?"

"The idea was to keep going south, but I don't know how. Maybe sail west along the coast of Texas, to Mexico, or maybe east, to Florida. What do you plan to do?"

"I still want to loop through the States over the next year or so and build up a folio, but right now I want to be with you. Whichever way you go, we'll find a way to meet up."

We slept in the back of her truck with Poco tied outside. We touched and talked until we ran out of things to say. I felt nervous with her again, like we had just met.

Something weighed on her. On her car stereo she often played a tape by a female vocalist, a fellow Texan whose name I don't recall. The songs were about wayward womanhood, about heroines who refused to be imprisoned in small towns, or possessed by men. Traci still behaved civilly, but I sensed volatility. Whatever it was, she denied it, fought it. She didn't understand herself, and admitted it, joked about it.

"I'm not comfortable with my sexuality," she dropped, with a little smile that quickly vanished. She wasn't implying homosexuality; it was something else. "I can't tell my dad about you. I have to pretend I'm chastely working on my pictures, when really I'm shacking up with a sailor and haven't concentrated on my work for weeks. Maybe Poco is my punishment for violating the Protestant work ethic." The dog was physically healthy, but she whined constantly, and freaked out if Traci left her alone.

On the morning of my departure we made love with unusual intensity. I rubbed my torso on her, kneaded her breasts through her flannel shirt. She murmured, squirmed, smeared her mouth on me, then resisted, though not with her full strength. My blood leaped. She thrashed her head from side to side while I pressed her hands down by her shoulders. I reached down to lift her shirt, and with the freed hand she pulled my mouth down onto hers. I entered her, and her eyes shot open, then clenched again. We tussled, exploded, sank mutely into aftermath.

Suddenly Traci pulled away and sat up. "Get out of my truck!" she screamed.

I gasped. "What?"

"Get away from me, you're bad for me, let me go." She started to cry, then leveled out. "I'm not kidding. I never want to see you again. Get out."

I could no more reason with her than with a wild animal. A spell had come over her, or perhaps our intimacy had been a spell, and now it had broken. Another Traci faced me, and this one was not civil. She brushed her tears away as if they disgusted her. She tensed, rocked forward and backward, fixed hateful eyes on me.

"What's wrong? Talk to me. Please, don't do this." But begging did no good. She was fleeing me, just as she had fled her father, college, Austin.

I gathered my things. Traci got Poco into the cab and started the truck. The back wheels dug into the loose gravel of the levee.

"Please, meet me in Natchez," I said through the glass, but she only looked away, slammed her hand onto the dash, spun the wheels again. I got behind and pushed. The wheels caught. She sped away. I had no telephone number, no address. She would move out of her apartment before I could ever get there. I would never see her again.

There was nothing to do but get in *Squeak* and resume my voyage. I was listless, almost nauseous from the shock. Losing her so suddenly was a nightmare that wouldn't go away. Was this the end of my reborn youth? Had I bungled my last chance for a young, vital woman? I pondered and agonized for days, but I didn't blame Traci. Perhaps it was her better judgment that had surfaced. It had been warning her not to get entangled, not to jeopardize her emerging identity. The wild card in her had surfaced, and it was the card of solitude. I too had chosen to travel alone. My mind whirled as I sped away on a new north wind.

Slowly, the river mended me. I was in its almighty embrace. It flowed, I with it. Its power and pace reached down into me. The pain was similar to that of my drawn-out separation from Tammy, but because I hadn't known Traci as long, it tapered sooner. In the final analysis, I couldn't fault the way I had handled my affair with Traci. "You took the big chance and you tasted the candy," I said. I said it quietly, but it sounded loud. "You're still intact."

In Vicksburg I visited the battlefields and toured a reconstructed Civil War ironclad. Vicksburg was the Gibraltar of the South, and when it fell, so did their cause. I sent four books back to the St. Louis Public Library, and got four more from the Vicksburg library. That night, while I looked for a place to eat, a huge black man asked me for money, and when I refused he chased me down the street yelling things I couldn't understand. I kept ahead of him until a cop car happened by. The policeman got out and cuffed him to a halt.

"He stole my money!" the giant bellowed.

"You haven't *got* any money," said the cop, his voice dripping with scorn.

I found a hamburger joint, and told the waitress what had happened. "Things like that aren't supposed to happen in downtown Vicksburg," she said, troubled.

But always cushioning my prickly city experiences was the softness of the river. Wispy tufts of cotton floated by on an imperceptible breeze. ("Spoor of cottonwood," someone said.) I dipped my fluted oars gently into and out of the still water, not to make a splash. In the cool, damp morning gulls flew silhouetted against trees made gray by distance and mist. Four hundred and five pelicans, symbols of the state of Louisiana, flew directly overhead like a squadron of World War II bombers. As it warmed, chinks in the cloud cover admitted sunbeams at angles that seemed to lack a common vertex. The river upswelled in gushes and puckered into whirlpools, causing *Squeak* to yaw and veer. I wondered, which was the more logical being for the ancients to worship, the sun or the river?

The days were short and sleepy—winter solstice was near. My average dropped to thirty-five miles a day. I welcomed darkness because it meant rest, but the nights were too long. My candle lantern worked overtime to light my reading book. Its faint glow emanating from my hatch cover must have presented a mysterious picture. I woke to a heavy fog, and all day hugged the bank, listening for towboat motors. Sights and sounds were muffled. It grew warm and bright despite the heavy vapor. It felt strange to drift through a fog bank wearing T-shirt and sunglasses.

I convinced myself I didn't really love Traci, that love only comes with time. But what a riddle she was, and how hard that my curiosity must go unsatisfied. In her wake my voyage looked different. I felt good with *Squeak*, and with the river journey I would soon complete, but I had no further ambition. Should I continue into the Gulf though my gusto had gone? I hoped my spirit would rekindle, that some daring exploit would reveal itself, impel me. And I longed for the new people I hoped to meet in New Orleans. Perhaps I could still find my Cajun Queen.

Diane and Paul were in Natchez, Mississippi when I arrived. As usual, they were busy being shown around town and reported on in the local news. Paul was the social dynamo, but Diane yearned to please, too. They were still in their twenties, but had already racked up some fine travels together in the Far East and Latin America.

Like St. Charles, Natchez was originally French. Its fabulously rich cotton planters were ruined by the Union blockade in the Civil War, but the town escaped physical damage. French colonialism still shone through succeeding layers of American architecture. In the Catholic cathedral a choir practiced Christmas songs. Old-time artifacts and nude paintings festooned the Under the Hill Saloon on the waterfront, where a local dance band attracted a sizable crowd for Sunday night in a small town.

Traci was supposed to have met me here the following day. Should I wait around? No, no point. I left early, and camped that night at the mouth of Washout Bayou. It was aptly named, because a storm the night before had made it a raging torrent. Yet louder than the rushing water was a regular, mechanical screaming that came from the woods. The trees were bare, the forest open and easy to walk through. I followed the ear-splitting racket to an unmanned oil well. An unmuffled propane engine powered the pump. I stood by the well, and the huge lever head worked up and down above me, like a tyrannosaurus devouring its prey. Beyond the well, soggy fields stretched for miles. My bailing towel froze stiff that night. Spanish moss dangled from the trees like solemn beards, flagging in the bitter wind.

On December 6, I approached Baton Rouge, head of navigation for ocean-going vessels. I hadn't planned to stop, but halfway through town I saw a multistory docking structure of painted steel girders rising from the river on the opposite bank. Curious, I crossed over. A boy wearing a shirt and tie helped me moor.

"Where you going?" the boy asked, shyly.

"Oh, just down the river. How 'bout you? From around here?"

"No. I'm here for a—well, sort of a convention for kids that are supposed to be gifted." He explained it to me as we ascended together the spiral ramp that led, counterclockwise, to the top of the structure. After the first full revolution, where the ramp neared the steep bank again, I noticed a tall, young woman with a German shepherd watching me, fifty feet below and to my right.

A buoyancy seemed to lift me. Momentum carried me around and up, but my eyes wouldn't let go. My neck twisted more and more, down and to the right, until I had to stop. I couldn't believe it.

I turned to the boy. He had stopped talking and was staring at me, startled. "I know her," I said, blankly. "Excuse me." I looked at Traci again, then let the buoyancy carry me up the ramp, over an elevated promenade to the top of the levee, and down to where she stood, waiting.

I took her hand. I felt joyous, cautious, calm. "Hi."

"Hi."

Silence.

"Shall we walk down the bank?"

"Okay."

After a few minutes Traci stopped and faced me, eyes lowered. "Steve," she said, "usually when I have an impulse it's right, but the one in Greenville was wrong. I had to see you again, if only to apologize." She looked up, searched my eyes. "I've been looking for you this whole past week, in Natchez,

St. Francisville, wherever there's a road to the river. I waited for you to sail by, but I was always ahead of you or behind you. Then a half hour ago someone said they saw a little rowboat, and I looked through his binoculars, and it was you. I was afraid I'd never find you. Steve, can you forgive me?"

I took a breath. "Traci, everything about you is so—sudden. Thank you for finding me. I don't know if I can open up again. Let's just see how it goes."

She took me to a park where I could shower, then to a laundromat. We picked up a bottle of dry sherry and parked in front of the laundromat, sharing the wine, waiting for the clothes. My reserve started to lift. Exuberance leaked out. In front of the laundromat a black man was doing upside-down push-ups for the benefit of two buddies. I went over and said, "In high school I used to be able to do sixteen of those. Let's see what I can do now." I put my porter-style Swiss army knife down on the pavement so it wouldn't fall out of my pocket, placed my hands nine inches from the wall, and did a handstand, heels resting against the wall. I lowered myself until my head touched. To my chagrin, I couldn't go back up. I struggled, then dropped my feet down. The three blacks roared, doubled over and shaking.

"Well at least I made you laugh." I dusted my hands and looked for my knife. It wasn't there.

"Hey, who took my knife?"

"Man, don't look at me."

"I wouldn't take nothing of yours!"

"Didn't none of us see no knife!"

"Come on, it's a kind that's very hard to find." They continued to profess innocence. The upside-down-pushup expert did so the loudest, so I targeted him. "Please, give me a break." I wasn't getting anywhere. "Okay, I'll give you five bucks for it."

"Now you're talking," said my suspect. He produced it from a crevice in a nearby picnic bench.

"So, you're not only an acrobat and a thief, you're a magician too, huh?" I grumbled. I passed him the fiver as he passed me the knife, both of us wary.

I decided to be a good loser. "Well, I guess I had that one coming. Hang on a sec."

I walked back to the truck. Traci had watched the whole thing.

"You mind if we share the sherry with them?"

"Of course not."

"Thanks." "Hey! We got a bottle here. Come on over." They cordially clustered around the cab, and we passed the sherry. The magician now entertained us with *one-handed* push-ups. His name was Dare, and he had just been released from nine years in Angola State Prison. He and one of the other guys were supposedly going straight, but the third was openly dealing drugs.

"I guess I'm pretty stupid to get myself into a situation like that, huh?" I said to Traci.

"You goofball, I loved every second of it," she said, and kissed me.

The old feeling was coming back. I stayed in the truck with her that night, touching, not ready for sex, unable to sleep for the shock, the gladness, the caution. In the morning we went to a restaurant and had an all-you-can-eat breakfast. I had taken it into my head to learn sea shanties, so Traci took me to a music store, where I bought a tin whistle, then to the university library, where I checked out a book on shanties.

"Meet you in New Orleans in four days, right?" I said. "You know the spot, I marked it on the map."

"Don't worry, sailor, I'll be there." She released my line.

I held her eyes with mine as I rowed away, singing "What Do You Do With A Drunken Sailor," arms and voice in rhythm.

The end of phase one was in sight. The river trended southeast, then east. Human presence was heavier now, but natural beauty did not suffer greatly. Snowy egrets still hunched like hoodlums in the silent dawn. They faced the new sun, which cast a violet over their plumage. The kingfisher still stood on his overhanging branch, looking like a naval officer with a punk hairdo. Swallows flitted over the river at sunset just as they had back in Alberta. The sand looked like brown sugar. Rains had loaded the river with debris. The winter rise had started.

Levees now pressed tightly on the river, eliminating islands and bayous. Like an ant on a basketball court, I picked my way through work boats, tows of all sizes, and ocean freighters. The freighters went faster, but at least they parted the water instead of steamrolling over it, like the tows. They were tall and shapely after the squat barges. Their names, painted on bow and stern, evoked all the seven seas: *Pacifico Mexicano*, *Singa Sailor*, *Golden Crown*, *Sunny Clipper*, *Capetan Lefteris*. They hailed from Manila, Singapore, Panama, Limassol, Oslo, and from ports unintelligible because written in Greek or Russian. Most were high in the water, bulbous bows half awash. Those heading out to sea floated deeper, their holds full of oil and grain.

I remembered my first "DO NOT ANCHOR OR DREDGE" sign, in eastern Montana. There it stuck out like a sore thumb; now I passed many such signs. Office towers and fuel farms sprouted on either shore. Jumbo jets arced gracefully over a nearby airport.

On December 10, I passed under the soaring bridge just west of Kenner. There would be no place to moor now until I got to Lake Pontchartrain, so I rowed continuously, southeast four miles, then northeast four miles, then counterclockwise around the great, semicircular bend that forms New

Orleans's southern edge. I rowed past Downtown and the old French Quarter, a compact cluster at the semicircle's east edge. The waterfront was alive with ferries and fake sternwheelers. Then I entered the man-made canal that connects the river with Lake Pontchartrain.

Just inside was a lock. I arranged to go through with a towboat bound for Florida pushing six barges of Ohio coal, then killed three hours exploring the neighborhood. It was inner-city, black, heavy with rush-hour traffic. The night was warm. The moment came. The towboat churned its mighty engines. The tow slowly started to move. We squeezed in, the lock's doors closed behind us, we dropped two feet. The north doors opened. The tow turned east, toward the Intracoastal Waterway, while I rowed to the lake, three miles away. Factories and fishing vessels thronged the shore, but all was quiet. I blew my whistle and a second drawbridge opened. Then a third bridge opened, and a tidal gush projected me out into a horizon-less lake, illuminated in the foreground by the glow of New Orleans, fading into a darkness relieved by only a few twinkling lights. Suddenly the lake flashed white as acres of small, closely packed fish jumped all at once. Just as suddenly it was calm again.

My river voyage was over. I tied to a piling, turned in, and added it up. In four months I had rowed, sailed, and drifted nearly three thousand miles. The emotional weight of so many joys, travails, and friendships overwhelmed me. But mostly I felt the North American continent. It ached in my callused palms, and in the muscles of my shoulders and back. The world's longest river system streamed through my consciousness as I sank into sleep.

CHAPTER 6

NEW ORLEANS

The sun rose peacefully on December 11, 1990. Marbled sand showed through the clear, slightly salty water. I sailed west along stair-stepped sea walls to the marina, where a snappy little man called Pee Wee invited me to moor in a shallow corner of the U. S. Power Squadron facility.

I was a furloughed sailor in a new port, glad to be done with rivers for a while. Traci showed me the apartment she had placed a deposit on, then returned to Helena to conclude her affairs there. I met a Tulane University engineering student who got me into her computer lab so I could word-process the preceding chapter. The marina and university being on opposite ends of town, I took a lot of streetcars. I played my tin whistle on the bus and the driver almost kicked me off. Was I that bad?

Reading was allowed, so I pored over my sea shanty book and photocopied the best pages. When again faced with endless rowing I would sing songs proven to lighten the load: "Rio!" "Maid of Amsterdam," "Rollin' the Woodpile Down." They oozed camaraderie, adventure, tragedy, sexual humor, joy. Shanties summarized life in the days of working sail. They evolved over decades and spun off countless versions as befitted the various shipping trades and the art of the individual shantymen. Only the most popular survived to be documented by researchers around the turn of the century.

I lived aboard *Squeak*. Ducks and geese paddled among the yachts of the marina. They deserved cleanliness, so I picked the floating garbage out of the water. The temperature was in the sixties, the sky overcast. The air was so humid even waterproof matches wouldn't light. Mosquitoes forced me to shut the hatch and screen the vent. Late at night the city hushed until only fog chimes and the cries of birds were heard.

I attended a Power Squadron function wherein jolly gents and shipshape little wives conducted long ceremonies, with plenty of giggly cocktails before and after. Their accent was more east coast than southern, New Orleans's roots being different from those of the rural south. The French Quarter was mainly white too, both its residents and more numerous tourists. The latter ate hot dogs and drank 'hurricanes' while gawking at the girls who bumped and ground in their glass cages facing Bourbon Street. Live music blared from every open door: blues, dixieland, rock, cajun, latin. A drum and bugle corps clashed in the main square, while a sidewalk chess player took on all comers.

Elsewhere I saw blacks. They rode the dreary ferry across the river to Gretna, performed public service jobs, and hung out in their neighborhoods, which dominated the inner city. French 'gingerbread' still adorned their tired houses. I struggled to understand their dialect. Supermarket clerks hadn't been trained to smile or exchange greetings. The cultural barrier was high, but penetrable. Once, while I waited for a bus next to the Superdome, thousands of black children suddenly streamed from the dome's many exits, each clutching a Christmas present of cheap plastic. Like steam released from a pressure cooker, they dispersed over the vast circumferential parking lots, shouting joyously, then faded into the city, the smaller ones hand-in-hand with their mothers, the bigger boys running in bands of three or four.

As my bus neared the marina somebody grabbed my shoulder from behind and shouted, "Hey stranger!"

"Paul! Diane! All right! You made it too, huh?"

"Yep," said Paul, "just pulled in yesterday. New Orleans! *Nawlins*, I mean. Gotta get that straight. Hey, good to see ya!"

We found a bench where we could sit together.

"Isn't it a great city?" continued Paul. "Oh, the dazzling prize that awaits the diligent river rat! We got us a nice little hotel close to the lake. Only problem is, Di's Uncle Jack's meeting us tomorrow to haul us back to New Mexico."

"Couldn't you have given yourselves a little more time?"

"It's a shame," said Diane, "but the trip took so much longer than we planned."

"Yeah, Di's overdue at her lab tech job, and I gotta get back there and pound nails. Gotta start saving up again. While paddling our little arms off the past couple months we've done nothing but dream about our next trip. Pretty silly, huh?"

"At least you know what you're doing next. I sure as hell don't."

Their stop was coming up. We noted each other's addresses and exchanged hugs.

"Dammit, Steve, keep in touch. Otherwise we'll go nuts wondering whatever happened to you." Then they were gone.

On December 17 I finished my writing. Traci returned from Helena, and we moved into the place she'd rented, 2633 Carondelet, Apt. C. It was small, with white paint and tall ceilings, in an old two-story just one block off St. Charles Street. In one day I switched from boat bum to respectable land-lubber, complete with apartment, girlfriend, and neurotic German shepherd. We arranged and rearranged our diddly furniture. We got the mattress from the back of her truck and threw it on the floor. I tumbled her down onto it. She fell willingly.

"You still my girl?" I asked, my eyes an inch above hers.

"Yes," she gasped, and dropped her eyelids, like the original Squeak used to dim her eyes at me to express her love when I returned home from work. Traci was a rebel, yet her passion could be unlocked only through surrender, because surrender terrified her, and was therefore sweet.

In my heart I knew the sweetness wouldn't last. *Squeak's* voyage wasn't finished. Neither was Traci's. She was easy-going, but I sensed that other persona lurking inside her.

That evening the side of her I called Beta made her little appearance. Traci had worked for hours setting up her developing equipment, then brooded, too tense to move. She sat on the bed, in the corner, arms clasped around her knees. When she looked up it was with fear and hostility.

The nauseous dread returned. "Traci, what's going on?"

"Who are you, anyway?" she cried. "You're not like me. I'm an artist, I'm fucked up. You're a machine, so orderly and disciplined. I've got work to do and I can't do it when I'm around you. When are you gonna leave?"

"Who am *I*? Who are *you*? The mad genius locked up inside Traci Harding?"

She fixed me a stare like she had me pinned to the ground and was about to ram a spear up my nose. "I'm who I am, and don't fucking analyze me, and don't plan on staying too long, because I'm not gonna let you move in on me or mooch off me or…"

"I'm not trying to do those things. Traci, I'll pay a share of the rent. I'll give you lots of space. I *want* you to work." Under the nausea I admired Beta's perception, her cold magnificence. But she couldn't be reasoned with, only placated, tolerated.

In the morning I woke to sweet, indolent "Alpha." I told her what I had seen. We talked about it.

"Beta's gonna be back, isn't she?" I said.

"Yes, if that's how you want to put it. I'm sorry. I love being with you. I want it to work out. But we have to be realistic."

"Traci, you've got to finish your Delta project."

But it was difficult for her. She kept agonizing over details, putting it off. Better to simply enjoy our time together, to build memories—

of bed
of long-lingering breakfasts
grits, toast, fruit, coffee
frisbee in the park
flowers on the table

of gin rummy and beer
how do you keep beating me like that,
brainy woman?

of nights on the town
tavern characters
stumble-dancing
(I stumble, you dance)
you out-punning me
I marvel at you
and at me, with you

We adopted a nearby bar, the C-Note, where the bartender played the piano while the regulars gathered around and sang. Some of them lived in cheap apartments above the tavern. Traci befriended a weak-chinned fellow named Patrick who spoke with whimsy of his life. Had he wasted it? Odd things interested him, like cloning and yo-yos. I preferred Jose, a short, barrel-chested Mexican. He was a party animal, with a macho gleam in his eye and a street-smart charm. He showed us an old bullet wound under his ribs and described what it was like to get shot. "It didn't hurt. I just felt sleepy and had to lie down. That's all."

Poco, Traci's dog, whined from some basic unhappiness, except when we took her for a run on the levee. I did more than my share of the housework. Traci appreciated it, lavished me with love. When Christmas approached we decorated a wreath with tiny, multicolored lights and endlessly admired the effect. We visited the art museum, cooked crayfish and oysters, played gin rummy, war, king's corner, tic-tac-toe. She won at everything. On Christmas Day we partook of a free dinner at the C-Note—an annual showing of thanks to their customers. On New Year's Eve we soaked in the tub, drank champagne, and listened to a radio broadcast: "It's New Year's Eve, live, from Tippy Tina's in New Orleans!"

I bought an old Schwinn five-speed, because a bike's great for covering a lot of city without getting mugged. I biked to the marina to work on *Squeak*. When Traci drove to Tuscaloosa to visit relatives, I people-watched and drank dollar-a-cup beer in the French Quarter. Suave talkers and flashy dancers cajoled passers-by into their establishments. One night a pair of whiskery roustabouts howled and jeered at a woman, or a man dressed as a woman, baring her breasts from a second-story terrace. "They're fake!" they yelled. I checked out the gay bar. It was packed with short-haired, neatly dressed guys all drinking and watching pretty-boy videos. I had feared somebody would try to seduce me, and was almost disappointed when nobody did.

Beta returned periodically, until I almost got used to her. I worked through the pain, accepted the fragility of our relationship, and promised to leave by January 10. Meanwhile, Alpha and I tentatively agreed I would sail east along the coast, and that she would meet me occasionally. Once I got to the Florida Keys I would either follow the Antilles south and east, or follow the Cuban coast west and cut across to the Yucatan. We talked of possible adventures together in Haiti or the Amazon. I also looked for passage on a ship crossing the Gulf of Mexico. My bones were still cold from my river trip, and a ship would be my fast track to "where the water's so warm that you wanna jump in." I doubted a ship would take me.

My first encounter with a shipping agent confirmed my doubts. "Freighters stopped carrying passengers twenty years ago," he said. But the second agent simply listened to my story then said, "I might be able to help you." He was a tall Scandinavian-American named Torberg Ulltang. Perhaps I stirred his Viking blood.

I called Torberg constantly over the next few days from a pay phone down the street from our apartment. One ship refused me for liability reasons. Then the owner of a freighter bound for Panama gave permission. "You'll be working for your passage, no money exchanged. We still need the captain's approval."

Beta, convinced I would soon leave, remained in remission the last few days, or perhaps Traci balanced her components better. Perhaps Traci was like a congress whose minority faction, Beta, refrained from filibustering so long as the majority respected its rights. That is, Traci was pleasant and conciliatory, but more up front, to me and herself, about her need to eventually slay every dragon, even if some were imaginary. Then again, when Traci smoked marijuana she became aggressively witty and less caring, in a manner consistent with neither Alpha nor Beta. Anyway, it was all amateur psychology on my part. All I know for sure is that *someone* maddeningly beautiful drove me all over town in her Nissan pickup, helping me locate supplies, get a visa for Panama, and generally prepare for whatever I was getting myself into.

On January 9 Torberg said, "No, I still haven't connected with the captain, but why don't you go ahead to Mobile anyway. That's where the *Tramarco Trader* is. She'll be sailing on Saturday the twelfth. I don't foresee any problem at this point."

"Torberg, if this works I owe you a big debt."

"No problem whatsoever. I hope you accomplish your mission."

We loaded *Squeak* into Traci's pickup and drove the hundred and fifty miles to Mobile. Guards permitted us into the Alabama State Docks, where we drove until we found Pier B North. There she was: a 430-foot bulk carrier, black with white superstructure, five holds, four cranes, Norwegian flag.

Traci waited while I climbed the gangplank. It was my first time aboard a freighter. A Filipino officer said, "Yes, we were expecting you. I'll show you to your *cabina,* number 118." It was a small room for one above the engine room, third deck down from the main deck. The communal head down the hall reeked of urine, but that didn't matter, I was so excited.

I went back to the truck. "It's all set! I can move in right now!" Traci helped carry my gear aboard, except for *Squeak,* whom we set down on the pier to await loading. Then there wasn't anything else to do but wait.

"Want to walk to the end of the pier?" I asked.

"Okay."

A breeze was blowing from off the Gulf. I smelled salt air, change, destiny. Lucking onto this ship was the spark I had hoped for. My passion for the voyage was back. The Amazon had always been my favored goal. A shortcut to Panama would put it within reach. My leaving would take the pressure off Traci, allow her to focus on her work, build up her self-worth. But I didn't want to lose her.

"Let's keep it alive between us. Will you write?"

"Of course."

"Will you fly down at some point and visit me in Panama or Colombia? You've got the money. We can travel together awhile, or hang out in a village."

"I'll come down at least once, but I can't say exactly when. I'm going to be real busy for a while, finishing the Delta project and making a folio."

The docks were deserted. Mobile Bay was a vast, gray haze. The *Tramarco Trader* was still being loaded.

"Traci, there's no hurry, but maybe there's no sense dragging it out either."

"I know."

"I love you." I'd never said it so out loud before.

"I love you too," she murmured, with less conviction. "I'll miss you incredibly. But I support your journey. You and *Squeak* are going to do something great together. I just know it. The easy thing would be for you to stay here with me. But you don't do the easy thing."

"Neither do you." We kissed again, then she got in her truck and drove away. Whatever should happen, I was proud to have possessed her, and been possessed by her. The world was at my command. What could I not do?

PART II
PACIFIC COAST of PANAMA & COLOMBIA

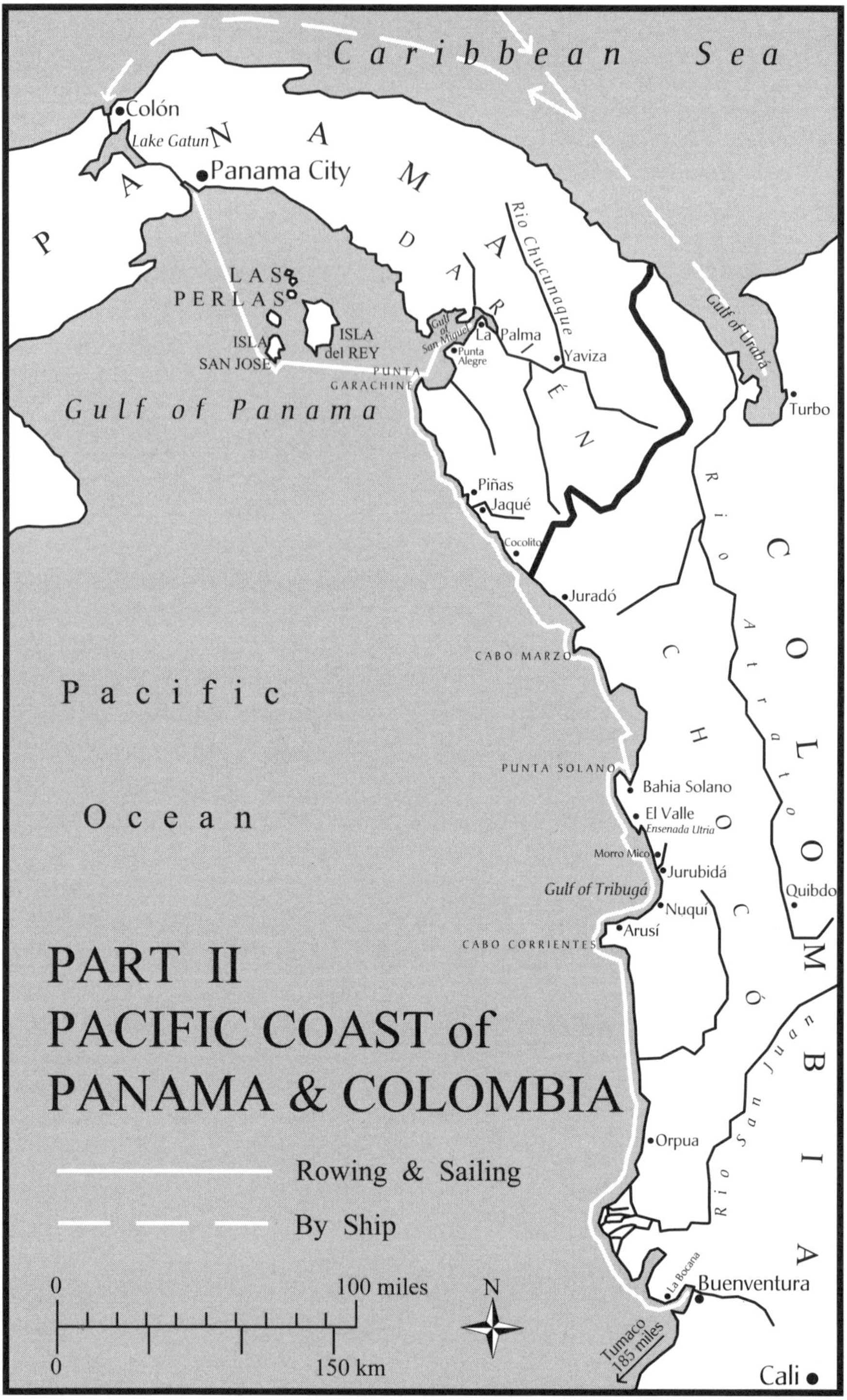

CHAPTER 7

TRAMARCO TRADER

While I settled into my *cabina,* door ajar, someone tapped.

"Come in."

A hand held the door by its edge and opened it further. A torso leaned in. His skin was brown with a honeyed, orange glow. He was a shapely young man, but his smile was shy, guarded.

"Dinner ready—you want come up?" His English had a Caribbean lilt.

"Sure. My name's Steve, what's yours?"

"Hernando Wright."

He led me to the men's mess, a white room with two formica tables fixed to the floor. Benches flanked each table. A door and window opened onto the aft deck.

Following Hernando, I dished myself up at a serving table and sat with him and four other Latin Americans. They spoke Spanish, of which I had learned a smattering on a jaunt through Colombia seventeen years before. Seven or eight Filipino men and officers sat at the other table speaking Tagalog. They switched to English to welcome me.

"First time American man work this ship."

"Yes, and he bring little ship with him! Littlest ship I ever see!"

"Very brave or very crazy."

After dinner I roamed, alone and spellbound, through all five floors of the superstructure, down into the engine room, and forward, past the holds, to the forepeak compartments. I had never seen so much machinery, so many dark, steel enclosures. Not until midnight did I retire to my tidy *cabina.*

I spent the following day in town acquiring documents. *Squeak* was too big to classify as a personal belonging, so a shipping agent prepared a bill of lading. U.S. Customs signed an export declaration, allowing me to import her back into the States without paying duty. I got a yellow fever shot, bought malaria and dysentery pills, and had a plastics fabricator reinforce my hatch cover, which had never fully recovered from the treatment it received in Havre. I ran wherever I went, despite rainstorms. When I returned to the pier, the rain had filled *Squeak's* cockpit like a bathtub.

While I bailed it out, Captain Abrahamson found me. He was a portly Swede, of moderate height. His black and white uniform was newly pressed. His hair and beard were red, turning white. His round, ruddy face expressed brisk competence.

"Mr. Ladd, you will not be signed aboard unless you obtain personal travel insurance. Sorry, I haven't time to explain. You will speak to Sparky, the radio officer."

I found him, a bookish Filipino. "But I thought everything was approved!"

"Sorry. Captain says, I do. You better hurry, go look around."

I raced to a telephone booth, looked up "insurance" in the Mobile Yellow Pages, and called ten companies. None had even heard of travel insurance. I ran back to the ship and found the captain.

"I'm sorry, once we have loaded if you do not have travel insurance you will be put off the ship. No, I don't know where you get it. It's just called travel insurance." This gave me an idea. I ran to the local American Express office. Eureka! They gave me an application form, which I filled out and mailed, together with a money order for eighty dollars.

I brought the stub to Sparky. "See, says here I'm covered as soon as it's in the mail."

He didn't examine it closely. "Congratulations Mr. Ladd! I add you to the crew list now." He typed a new list. The last entry read, "Stephen Ladd…Deck Boy."

"So I'm a thirty-seven-year-old, Harvard-grad deck boy. Wouldn't have it any other way. Thanks, Sparky!"

I exercised my new title by lugging tarpaulins from deck to forepeak and cases of beer from dock to galley. The stevedores manning the ship's cranes loaded huge rolls of brown paper. When they left, my supervisor, Boatswain Leopoldo, Pol for short, took charge of loading *Squeak*.

I had been trying hard not to think about her being lifted so high in the sky. "You'll be careful, won't you, Pol? Does the lifting harness look okay?"

He waved his hand palm-down to quiet me, looked at the harness, clipped the lead to it. He lifted a palm, and another mate hoisted her straight up forty feet, over, and down onto a hatch cover just forward of the superstructure. I patted their shoulders. "Good job! Thanks, guys." They smiled and carried on, under pressure to ready the ship for sea.

At eleven P.M., January 12, a throaty rumble permeated the *Tramarco Trader*. Deckhands retrieved the docking lines while the officers in the bridge conned her into the channel. She left Mobile Bay, and began to roll.

I woke dreaming of Traci, of the dancer's legs which I lifted and spread, my palms under her knees, until her thighs were beyond vertical, until.... I quenched myself with my hand, and lay still while the charging sweetness settled in my veins. I opened my diary and pined for her. When daylight sifted through the porthole I swung my feet to the linoleum floor and pulled on a pair of old jogging pants.

The day was cold and clear. To complete our lading we sailed for Panama City, Florida, holding a couple miles offshore. It was Sunday, so only a skeleton crew was working. I went forward and watched the prow slice through the azure water. The ship seemed to be stationary—wasn't it the eager sea which advanced upon the blade and broke into a snowy wound that proceeded apace to the horizon behind our stern? Landward, the blueness paled where its bed of ivory sand became visible through the shallows, succeeded by the sun's blinding reflection on the beach, and a verdant shoreline strung with condominiums of white, beige, and tan.

At Panama City, Florida, port employees on the quay below twirled light ropes weighted with monkey's fists. They released—the lines traced parabolic curves up to our men, who tied them to the ship's thick warps. The port hands then hauled in our warps and tied them off on bollards. Squared-off pine logs were loaded through the afternoon and evening. After supper, as I drifted to sleep in my bunk, the mechanical sounds of the ship's lading were just audible. As the hold was filled, my soul filled with electric anticipation.

When motion and the drone of engines woke me, around midnight, I dressed and climbed the five flights of stairs to the bridge. I cracked the door open. Inside was dark and silent.

"May I come in?"

"Yes, but go quietly," answered Captain Abrahamson.

I glided to the continuous band of windows, stopping near two shadowy figures. They were the pilot and the captain, conversing in low tones. Two Filipino officers stood by. An A.B. (able-bodied seaman) was steering.

"Eighty-four degrees," said the pilot, his voice hushed, commanding, richly Southern.

"Eighty-four degrees," acknowledged the helmsman, turning the wheel. "Now on eighty-four degrees," he repeated when the ship was on heading.

It seemed I was looking down from a skyscraper, so tall was the bridge. We were winding through a narrow channel marked by parallel lines of lighted buoys, green to starboard, red to port. The sky was starry. Waves that would have bobbed *Squeak* uncomfortably, here were minute, glittery brushstrokes.

My eyes now adjusted to the darkness, I made out the pilot. He was dressed like a neatly attired bass fisherman. He specified several more compass headings, then a rudder angle where the channel bent sharply. I saw it through the windows, and on the chart in the adjoining chartroom. Finally we passed through a man-made gap in the barrier island and proceeded past two anchored ships waiting to come in.

When deck hands had lowered a rope ladder over the side, the pilot spoke into a hand-held radio. "Pick-up boat, this is pilot. Ladder ready, port amidships." A boat drew alongside, kept pace. "See you the next time through, Captain," said the pilot. He shook his hand and left the bridge. The captain walked onto the port wing deck and trained a spotlight on the ladder. Minutes later the pilot descended the ladder and dropped onto the leaping boat. Facing the spotlight, he waved his arm in a slow arc. The captain switched off the light and came back inside.

"All ahead full, hundred and eighty degrees." The Yucatan Passage was five hundred miles away, due south.

In the morning I helped Hernando dump galley scraps over the aft rail. North America had disappeared. Already it was warmer.

"Thanks for helping me practice Spanish yesterday, Hernando. And for coming to wake me up this morning."

"I don't want you miss your breakfast." He giggled, then became serious again. "Thank you for playing cards in my *cabina*, being my friend. You sleep too late, I'll always wake you." He smiled shyly at me. His body was tall and muscular, but his moods were those of a dreamy child.

"Hernando, where'd you learn English?"

"My parents come from Jamaica to Costa Rica. So I am black man. Only black man on the ship."

"That shouldn't matter," I said, but obviously it did. He mixed little, and spoke to officers only to acknowledge orders. He faded from view when others were around, but cautiously revealed himself to me.

"Last man hired, too. I fraid they lay me off."

I valued Hernando, but I couldn't be a fellow outcast. When that chore was done he withdrew below deck while I followed Boatswain Pol in hopes of another assignment. The little man's bowed legs paced incessantly. His trousers were baggy, his butt small and flat as a scrap of armor plate. He roved with ant-like haste. When he found a problem his eyes darted about, judging distances and forces. His wind-etched face, under its black bangs, was a mute canvas for those eyes, until he realized he must speak. Then he smiled at me for an instant, agreeably, self-consciously.

"We pull ladder more up," he said, and had me crank a handle up and down, pawl disengaged, while he tugged and relashed the heavy boarding ladder. He used his strength well. His hands plied ropes and machinery with joyful precision.

When seaworthiness was complete, Pol settled me into scraping and painting. I scraped incipient rust spots on the superstructure's exterior walls and ceilings, then painted them with orange primer, then a white or brown finish coat. It was tedious, but I was outdoors and unsupervised. Now and then I stole a moment to marvel at the sea's complete emptiness.

I marveled at that emptiness at night, too, when I went to the bridge and set my face down on the goggle-like opening in the radar screen's cone-shaped hood. The sweep-line revolved without a blip in its ghostly orange bowl. That screen contained a secret world, exactly thirty miles in diameter. The *Tramarco Trader* was always at its exact center. The ship carried that world around with her like an inner eye. It was always nighttime inside the radar scope.

Shipboard rhythm was precise: breakfast at 7:30, work from eight to five, hour for lunch, two coffee breaks. Permanent crewmembers worked an additional eighty-five hours per month in late-night shifts, but not me. I gained weight on the food: rice three times a day, augmented by breakfast items in the morning, and by vegetables and meat or fish at lunch and dinner.

We communicated through a strange complex of languages. The placards explaining the ship's equipment were in Norwegian, but no one was Norwegian. The captain and chief engineer spoke Swedish to each other, English to everyone else. The Filipinos spoke Tagalog among themselves, English to the Swedes and myself, and a blend of English and Spanish to the Latinos. The Latinos had no common language with the Swedish officers.

I ate with the Latinos because they were the only people who spoke among themselves in a language I remotely understood, and for their joviality. They were seamen and technicians. Claudio, the Chilean, was the electrician. The Chief Repairman was a Salvadoran named Chavez. He was assisted by a fellow countryman, Miguel. Costa Ricans Hernando and Alejandro were the lowest ranking men in the deck and engine crews respectively.

I spent time with the Filipinos, too. Rudy, the steward, welcomed me to his commodious cabin one floor below the bridge, and to his beer-filled refrigerator. He was excessively polite, westernized, hung up on cultural superiority. He slicked his hair back, and wore a silk scarf in the open collar of his white shirt. "Every day I struggle to keep my head above the barbarism around me," he said. "Work, eat, sleep, fuck, that's all the seaman knows. No good! Duty to God, to country, to family and employer, this must be our watchword." When the Persian Gulf War broke out we listened to the Voice of America on his shortwave radio. "Thank God for America!" he enthused. "The world needs a strong hand to guide it, to squash these dirty little Arab tyrants." The Filipinos of lower rank were also pro-American, also married and piously Christian, but less moralistic. Their gay, Tagalog conversations usually concerned pleasures of the flesh they had experienced in ports-of-call.

One evening I sat with the Filipinos in the Crew's Dayroom and watched *Romancing the Stone,* about a wild adventure in Colombia. That's where *I* was going! Yet the movie was pretend—my adventure was real! After hero and heroine had lived happily ever after, the Filipinos filed off to bed, but my imagination was too fired for sleep. So I exited to the side deck, then lurched forward across the flat, massive covers that kept the sea from the holds. The covers were as wide as the ship, and comparably long. Because the *Trader* was plunging at eleven knots, they pitched like basketball courts in an earthquake, basketball courts that dropped off into dark sea. I walked across the first hatch cover, jumped down three feet, jumped up again onto the second, and so on across the third, fourth, fifth. The bow was smashing with a shudder through each curling swell, flinging tons of phosphorescent foam into the air. A euphoria swept over me like I had experienced only once before, one morning in 1972, when I woke up in the mountains outside Barcelona. I had slept on the ground next to my motorcycle, and upon waking stood, stretched, and beheld the wild hillsides below. Then, as now, I tingled with inexpressible joy. The world seemed so precious a gift.

For three days the ship sailed due south. The engine maintained a steady rumble, felt as much as heard. The prow sliced inexorably—flying fish fled from it in long, lizard-like skims. The seas came from the port beam, rolling the ship. Could I survive in *Squeak* in such conditions? I worked shirt-less until my shoulders burned, then covered up. As I scraped peeling paint near the galley's greasy exhaust vent, I became queasy.

"I don't feel very good," I said to Pol.

He looked at my pallor and smiled. "It's okay. Go take a siesta." A nap cured me of my seasickness, but my mates ribbed me at dinner.

"So, your belly stood on its head today, Estevan?"

"His appetite returns quickly!"

"Ah well, it happens to all of us sooner or later."

That night we entered the Yucatan Passage, ten miles from Cuba. It was too dark to see, but in the hot morning a jet fighter swooped low over us. Its only markings were the letters AG on its tail. "Cuban plane," said Hernando.

Two days later we sailed through the banks off Honduras and Nicaragua. We saw no other vessels, but fishing boats sometimes manifested in the radar scope at night. I once noted the bearing of a blip on the five-mile-radius circle, picked up the binoculars, checked the compass, and peered in that direction. Blackness, blackness, blackness. Ship heaving, horizon indiscernible. Check the compass again. There! A speck of light swirled with distance in the lens of the binoculars, like a firefly in a jar.

It was eight P.M. An A.B. was steering 149°, same heading we'd been on for two days. The third officer, a slender Filipino, was in the chartroom with a low light, plotting the hourly position on the chart: another X in an evenly spaced line of Xs marching toward the southwest corner of the Caribbean Sea. On the counter beside him were the Loran and Sat Nav digital readouts where he got our latitude and longitude. In a corner, the gyroscope that ran the main compass whirled mysteriously in its metal box.

Someone entered the bridge and walked to the windows. I joined him. It was the chief engineer, a pensive, athletic Swede in his thirties. To the crew he was an iceberg, but I had conversed with him in his cabin about motorcycles, computers, environmental degradation, my voyage.

"Peter."

"Ladd. About the Pacific coast. I'm thinking you'd better have a sextant and tables. Stay offshore as much as possible. All the dangers are close to shore: reefs, surf."

"*Squeak's* too small to carry much stores. No, I'm gonna have to stick to the coast. Why, do you think I'll have trouble finding places to land?" We talked through the dangers and strategies, working our imaginations where we lacked information.

"I think your mission is possible, but you will have to take precautions against illness."

"Such as?"

Captain Abrahamson came in, conferred with the third officer, scanned the sea. He stood nearby, but didn't enter the conversation. Suddenly he broke in. His voice was controlled.

"Mr. Ladd, I'd say you have a ninety percent chance of being robbed before completing this voyage of yours, and a fifty percent chance of being killed. There, I've said my mind. I needn't repeat myself. After all, it's your concern. Good night." He and Peter exchanged some words in Swedish, then the captain retired.

Peter chuckled. "The old man may be right, but I don't expect that will stop you from trying."

I heard the wind whistling outside, and sensed clouds flying overhead, obscuring the stars. I was uncomfortable being the object of concern. "I'll just see how it goes. One day at a time."

Now my Spanish-English dictionary went everywhere with me. I also practiced each day from a self-instruction book. Starting January 13, I wrote my diary in Spanish. Much of my practice was with Alejandro, from Limon, Costa Rica. At lunch he would come up from the engine room, grimy from head to toe, and push the hair from his sweaty face with the back of one hand. "Aiieee, what an ugly heat I suffer down there today. Pray to God I don't go mad." Then he washed his hands, sat down, and massaged the depression from his temples, eyes, cheeks. "Friends, what amusing events have we to discuss today? Estevan, 'Mario Brothers' in my *cabina* tonight again?"

After dinner I knocked on his door, and a different man answered. Cleaned up, elegantly dressed, his ebony hair slicked back, Alejandro was suave.

"Estevan! Beer!" he said, and handed me one. "Music!" He put a cassette of Caribbean music into his tape player and turned up the volume. "Mario Brothers!" He turned on his TV screen, and gave me first crack at the controls.

"I'm not as bad at this as I was a few days ago," I said, "but I'll never catch up with you." The little action man too often fell off the cliff or was brained by flying objects.

Hernando and Claudio dropped in. Beer gave way to vodka. Alejandro turned off "Mario Brothers" and plugged a porn movie into his VCR. By the time it was over and the others had left, he was quite drunk.

"Look, Estevan, my daughters. Beautiful, no?" He picked up a framed picture of two solemn, richly attired girls undergoing some religious ceremony. He fingered the photo lovingly, then sank onto his bed, hand over his eyes. *"Hijo de puta, hijo de puta!* (Son of a bitch, son of a bitch!)"

"Yes, they're beautiful, Alejandro. What is it?"

He passed it off, got up, wavered to his closet. "Look, the sneakers I bought for them in Mobile." He pulled out L.A. Gear shoe boxes. "Eighty dollars a pair. They'll have the finest shoes in Limon. And this television back here. For the home. All my money goes to a house I rarely see."

"Do they pay you well?"

"Almost a thousand dollars a month. And what can I earn in Costa Rica? Nothing. So I have no choice. I can be with them, or I can provide for them. I cannot do both. See, Estevan? For you, working on the *Tramarco Trader* is a lark. For us it is a hard life. We love the sea, yes, but only because it is empty and turbulent, like our hearts."

He sat wearily back down. "And still I haven't told you the worst part."

"Your wife?"

He looked at me, his anguished eyes eager for understanding. "Yes. Unfaithful to me. *Hijo de puta!* I know about the man. In Limon nothing is secret. But how can I satisfy her needs when I am not home? I could never beat her, and if I could it wouldn't do any good. Oh my God, you condemn me to a bitter life." He sobbed, one hand over his eyes, the other crumpling the knee of his pants. I put my hand over his. He sank, then abruptly straightened, swayed. "We drink," he said, and lifted his glass to his lips, motioning me do to the same, but I'd had enough. Then he lay down, closed his eyes, and curled up on his side.

"Sorry, *mi amigo.* Sleep well," I said, and went to my *cabina.*

On January 18 the captain called a crew meeting. "We're nearing Turbo, Colombia," he announced. "As they have no port facilities, we will discharge our cargo of paper at anchor in the Gulf of Urabá, onto barges. The people in Turbo are the world's most vicious thieves, with the possible exception of Colón, Panama, which is the next place we will stop. We must take extraordinary precautions. Before we get there we will secure *all* deck gear below, even mooring cables and the barrels of lube oil on the side decks. No stevedores are to be allowed below deck *under any circumstances.* Someone must be on watch whenever they are present to make sure of this. Are there any questions?"

"Can we go ashore?" I asked.

"*No*, Mr. Ladd. This is *not* a tourist boat!" Alejandro giggled beside me, but not loudly.

We had been a week without sight of land, and our arrival at a new continent filled me with suspense. That night Panama's San Blas islands showed up on the radar screen. I went to bed, and returned to the bridge before dawn. Shore lights were visible. The captain and several officers carefully maneuvered us into the shallow gulf. The day dawned on cloudy skies, muddy water, and rafts of seaweed studded with stems and sickly flowers. The air was humid, the coast low and jungly on one side, mountainous on the other. The chart showed converging river mouths and mangrove swamps. Strange beetles and moths alighted on the decks and bulwarks.

We joined several ships at anchor. They were loading boxes of bananas from lighters. We were there to unload the paper that would be used to make those banana boxes, but today was Sunday. The Filipinos spent it fishing off the aft deck. They caught catfish, which in the evening they barbecued and consumed with vodka. They shared generously. "It is for times like this that we work so hard," said Max, the mechanic's mate.

After so much paranoia about thievery, the arrival of the Colombians made me uneasy. First came two customs officials, one of them armed with a club, and a machete that fit into a scabbard concealed under his shirt at his back. He pulled it out for us by reaching behind his neck and withdrawing it upward, then brandished it with mock ferocity. He turned out to be more fawning than threatening, however. He tried to bum a dollar off me. "For college," he said, but I didn't bite. His superior was expensively dressed, polite, inscrutable.

The stevedores were black, barefoot scarecrows, thrice as many as necessary. They lounged on the long, narrow side decks while cranemen lifted the paper rolls and set them onto barges. Dreary little wooden tugboats maneuvered the barges and towed them up the Atrato River. Everyone bantered and gesticulated, as if competing for control. One was a woman. She wore an American flag sewed to her jean jacket.

"Americano?" she asked when my business took me near her. She said it almost reverently.

"Sí," I replied and walked on, shy of her, worried about when I wouldn't have the structure of the ship to insulate me from these people.

In the evening a boatload of brown and black prostitutes motored up, a young black man at the helm. The motorman stopped near the foot of the gang plank and yelled words I didn't understand, yanking his arm back and forth in the air. Crewmembers clustered at the top of the gang plank, eager for a look.

"Sorry, the captain has forbidden them aboard," said the first officer in Spanish, smiling familiarly. "He's afraid their fingers will be sticky." Even the girls laughed at this.

Their clothing was drab. They were plain in my eyes, but others gleefully pointed out their favorites.

"That one's not bad, in the brown dress, near the stern."

"No, I'll take the black one any day. *Hijo de puta,* those tits!"

The helmsman circled twice, allowing us time to change our minds. A girl and a crewmember exchanged comments that caused merriment all around, but I missed their words. Then they sped off to another ship and we reluctantly dispersed, pleased to have at least seen the forbidden fruit.

The unloading took two days. When the stevedores left we checked for stowaways and freed the anchor, Pol and I coiling the thick anchor line as it came aboard. The anchor had dug itself into the clay bottom, and took a half hour to free. Then we sailed for Colón.

It was January 22. In twenty-four hours I would be ejected from my safe cocoon into a town infamous for thievery. I faced many uncertainties: would *Squeak* be unloaded onto the dock or into the water? What paperwork would be required? Would I find a safe haven? Could I go through the canal under my own power? Beyond that the uncertainties only intensified, because nobody knew anything about the coast from Panama City to Tumaco, Colombia, where I hoped to arrange transportation across the Andes. I photocopied the ship's chart of Colón Harbor and nervously packed my gear.

CHAPTER 8

CANAL ZONE

Just as inbound and outbound bees become noticeable as one nears a hive, shipping increased as we approached Colón, at the Atlantic entrance to the Panama Canal. A dozen vessels lay at anchor near the opening, but the *Trader* wasn't going through the Canal, so we sidestepped them and docked in the harbor.

The warehouses and administrative buildings reflected what the Washington of Woodrow Wilson's day thought an American empire should look like: bigger, whiter, and stodgier than anything Madrid or London had produced in places like Lima or Calcutta. The lack of maintenance ever since, and the majestic palms, added a touch of Tikal or Angkor Wat. Soon docking was complete, the gangplank was lowered, and I got my first close-up of the Third World since 1973.

"Careful, Estevan!" warned Alejandro. He was freshly bathed and neatly dressed. He and a half dozen other guys were walking in a group to shop at the Duty Free Zone.

"Don't worry, I'll run all the way to the yacht club." And run I did, out the port gates, through streets thronged with fruit stands and gaudy buses, through agitated crowds of blacks, mestizos (people of mixed white and Indian blood), Chinese tradesmen, and Cuna Indians in native finery. The sun was scorching hot. A boy trailed me on his bicycle, begging, but nobody else even got a good look at me. An iguana scurried away as I cut across a vacant lot.

An armed guard admitted me to the yacht club. Whoever might have preyed upon me outside could never get in here. Panamanian businessmen drank beer at the air-conditioned bar. European and North American yachtsmen were doing laundry and checking for mail.

I showed a picture of *Squeak* to the lady at the office.

"I don't see why you shouldn't be able to keep it at the dinghy dock," she said.

"How much will that cost?"

"Twenty-five cents a day."

"Yeah, I can swing that. Thanks."

My next stop was the office of the Canal Port Captain, an elderly American. "Sorry. I can't let you go through without a motor," he said. "Currents are too strong on the uphill stretch. You'll have to find a ride, either by truck or ship. Shouldn't be too hard. Probably cheaper, too." That eliminated one option for crossing the isthmus. My chief concern, however, was to settle into *Squeak* as soon as possible, in control of my own situation.

Back aboard the *Tramarco Trader* I waited for Captain Hudson, the local shipping agent. He arrived late and unapologetic, a tall man with white, crew-cut hair in a tan uniform.

"I'd prefer to be unloaded into the water and row over to the yacht club," I said.

"Okay, that's what we'll do. Customs can check you there." He was Panamanian, but his English was good.

Pol and I had *Squeak* all ready to go on the aft deck. Ten stevedores rushed up and demanded the job be turned over to them, but Pol was already cranking the crane's control levers. *Squeak* was soon in the water, on the side away from the dock. I followed her on a rope ladder, a drop of thirty feet.

I had just climbed aboard when a commotion brewed up at the top of the ladder. A woman in a navy blue uniform, clipboard in hand, seemed to be the cause of it. Captain Hudson called down to me.

"Customs lady's here. Says your boat's gotta go onto the dock, clear customs."

"What? Can't they just…"

"Don't argue. We'll get your boat out first thing in the morning."

Another sling was lowered. I secured it and climbed back up the ladder. *Squeak* went up, over, and down onto a palate on the dock. I had just enough time to grab a few essentials before a forklift trundled her into a security compound inside the warehouse.

"The ship's leaving at midnight! Where am I supposed to sleep?" I asked Captain Hudson.

"Just stay close, we'll fix you up."

Cranes unloaded the pine beams and arranged them in huge stacks on the dock. Crewmen drifted back from town and prepared to sail.

"Okay, let's go," said Captain Hudson.

I found Hernando. "Hang in there, buddy."

"I never see you again," he said. His eyes were doleful, almost reproachful.

"Adios," I said to Alejandro, and squeezed his hand, then followed Hudson down the gangplank. At the bottom I wished I'd hugged him. Too late.

Captain Hudson's jeep had a pair of crossed fire hose nozzles painted on its door. "I'm the municipal fire chief, too," he said. It must have been an important post, because he frequently stopped his vehicle to confer with men on the street.

"How'd Colón make out in the invasion?" I asked. The U.S. had invaded Panama to arrest Noriega the year before.

"See for yourself." He swung by the remains of a multi-story concrete building. "Used to be the prison. When the helicopters came the guards gave the prisoners rifles and told them to go up on the roof and shoot. Not much left of those prisoners anymore, or the roof, as you can see. I made out okay, though." He chuckled.

"Yeah?"

"Yeah, the GIs distributed M16s to forces they thought would help them mop up. I ended up selling a bunch of them to some Colombians for seven hundred bucks each. Not a bad day's work, huh?"

The man disgusted me. "How about just dropping me off at the yacht club? I'll find a place to stay there."

"All right. Pick you up here at nine o'clock tomorrow morning."

"Right. Thanks for the ride."

I called Traci from a pay phone, told her I was all right, begged her to meet me in Panama City. She said she couldn't break away just then, and promised to visit me later, in Colombia. Somebody let me crash in the cuddy of their day-sailer. I spent my first night in Panama curled up on sailbags, miserable with heat and mosquitoes. Would Traci ever deliver on her promise? When would I get *Squeak* and my stuff back?

Captain Hudson was two hours late picking me up. I needed him too much to tell him off, so I just tagged along as we visited various offices. I didn't catch what was going on but it looked tenuous. Minor obstacles were erected and overcome, but the fact that *Squeak* was not a registered vessel really bothered the bureaucrats.

"But little boats without motors don't *have* to be registered where I'm from, in Washington State. Do they here?"

"That's beside the point," said Hudson. "They just want something official. I know, the American consul. Come on."

The consul notarized an affidavit to the effect that boats such as *Squeak* don't require registration in the U.S., but the customs officials still weren't satisfied. They insisted that a Washington State attorney prepare a document for me, get it notarized by the Panamanian consul in Seattle, and forward it to them.

"That could take days! Weeks!" I said. "In the meantime all I have are the clothes on my back, my Spanish dictionary, and a ratty blanket. I also have hardly any money, because none of the banks here will take my traveler's checks."

Hudson looked at his watch. "Sorry, gotta go now. Good luck," he said, and marched away. Now I didn't even have an interpreter. I sat numbly in the consul's waiting room for an hour, imagining my things locked up like the treasures of King Tut, until cloth turned to dust and leather to glue. I was too confused and depressed to move.

Suddenly, "Excuse me."

I looked up at a balding Panamanian in a striped shirt and tie.

"I'm a clerk in the shipping agency next door, and I couldn't help overhearing your problem. I've spoken with my manager, and he says we might be able to cash a couple of traveler's checks for you. Also, I've written a name and a referral note on this card. He may be able to help you."

Never had I received a kindness so unexpected or helpful. Cash in hand and a spring in my step, I ran to the Duty Free Zone and found the referred-to person, a sweaty, heavyset man. He was busy with a subordinate, but interrupted their conversation to hear me out. Forced to fend for myself in Spanish, I found I could manage. He seemed to suggest that the prohibition against entry of a non-registered vessel could be circumvented by declaring *Squeak* to be a vessel "in transit."

He sent me to another office, which sent me to another, then another, then back to the first, and on and on. The offices were unfurnished, dismal. Finding them was difficult—many lacked even a sign outside. I understood little of what was happening except that I was swept up in a foul current and if I could stay afloat long enough I might get *Squeak* back. Whenever I reached a dead end I twisted and turned until I was back in the flow. New officials raised new reasons why *Squeak* shouldn't be released. They savored their self-importance, but eventually grew tired of my face, at which point I started gathering stamps and signatures. My folder of papers was expanding. Then the offices closed. Exhausted, I guzzled two beers at the yacht club bar and spent another sleepless night on the sailbags.

The next day was Friday. The offices would be closed over the weekend, so I was motivated. First I ate breakfast in a cheap, working-class restaurant. A Rastafarian man walked in. Upon seeing me he swiveled on his heel and left saying, "I'm not eating in any restaurant that serves gringos!"

A more serious hostility came after I had finished my meal and was hurrying toward a hotel to get a map of Panama. Along the way, the sidewalk passed through a sort of canyon formed by the building on my left and a parked van on my right. It was a major street. The people in the "canyon" appeared to be deliverymen and shopkeepers. But a mulatto youth suddenly stepped into my path, yelling in another direction by way of distraction, and held a small knife to my navel, while someone unseen hugged me from behind. I thought, "Well, at least the blade's not very long." It took them five seconds to search my pockets, check for money belt, and run off. "Not my passport," I yelled, and started after them. Dropping it, they disappeared around the corner of the building. I grabbed the passport. At that moment someone stepped from a shop into the "canyon" with a revolver at ready. "Assholes!" he muttered, but they were gone. He and the deliverymen, who hadn't moved, laughed off their brief tension. "Careful here," he said. "It's dangerous."

I had hidden my larger bills in my sock and left other valuables in the day-sailer. The thieves got my wallet containing three dollars and the Swiss Army knife I had lost and regained in Baton Rouge. This time it was gone for good. On the surface I reacted calmly, but the emotional shock showed up later. I took to running again so robbers wouldn't have time to set up on me. If the sidewalk looked doubtful I ran down the center of the street.

No more paperwork could be done until I had a way to transport *Squeak* to the Pacific side, so I hustled around looking for a ride. In the yacht club parking lot I noticed an elderly Panamanian whistling and poking around under the dashboard of a Dodge Dart. He was a pudgy little man in white shorts and long-sleeved shirt.

"Excuse me, sir. Speak English?"

He straightened up and nodded.

"Good. I'm in a bit of a jam. Customs won't give me my boat back until…" I presented my case in the simplest, most optimistic light.

"Hmm," he grunted, and glanced regretfully at the dangling stereo wires he was working on. Kindness, not my offer to pay, induced him to help. "I am Ochoa. I don't have time to go to Balboa today, but I can move your boat here, to the yacht club. Will that help?"

I didn't know if the "in transit" scheme would succeed if *Squeak* was only going to the yacht club, but it was better than nothing. "Sir, I can't begin to thank you. Yeah, I think that'll work. Let's go!" I secretly prayed he would stick with me.

Sure enough, I still lacked certain forms and clearances. We went back to the same old offices and collected a raft of new stamps and signatures. Officials who had missed out on sabotaging me the day before presented fresh reasons why I shouldn't get my boat back, but they were flimsy arguments, halfheartedly presented. A slight black man named Feliz, apparently an unemployed porter, joined the campaign on my behalf. Momentum was building.

Feliz's social status didn't allow him to argue forcefully, but he was shrewd, diligent, and knew the actors. Ochoa wasn't the kind of guy to throw his weight around either, but he was guileless and fondly regarded in the community, therefore a valuable advocate. I was a quixotic *norteamericano* of limited funds, whose darling little boat (I showed her picture to everybody) had been cruelly impounded. Together we were unbeatable. My friends considered the matter from all angles and decided the time had come to approach Señor Castilla, the customs chief.

He received us doubtfully. "After all," he murmured, "the vessel *is* unregistered."

"Oh come on, it's just a tiny little thing!" said Ochoa, shoulders shrugging, palms lifted and waving.

Castilla tapped his desk.

"Please, sir!" I begged.

He sighed. "Well? Shall we go take a look at it?"

Our faces burst into grins. Ochoa slapped his thighs and stood up. "Yeah, let's go see what's been causing all this ruckus!"

By the time we had all piled into Sr. Ochoa's clunker, even Sr. Castilla was appreciating the humor of the situation.

We drove to Dock Six and walked into the warehouse containing the meshed enclosure. There she was, *Squeak,* in all her innocence.

"Let her out!" I pleaded.

Sr. Ochoa opened the gate and walked inside. A man with a clipboard rushed up. "Hey, you can't go in there!" Ochoa didn't even turn around. Then we were all inside, checking her out. Hope overwhelmed me. I picked up one end to show them how light she was.

"See? No problem putting her up on the car!"

Castilla talked to the man with the clipboard while Ochoa drove his car up. I laid my air mattress on the roof as a cushion. A couple more forms were signed, then some stevedores lifted her up on top. We drove back out to the main gate, where Sr. Castilla said *adios.* I paid Customs $12.25 to have one of their employees ride with us to the yacht club and verify that *Squeak* got there. The "in transit" clause was now satisfied, not that it made any sense. Soon *Squeak* was happily afloat at the dinghy pier. I thanked everyone profusely, especially Sr. Ochoa. Nobody asked for a dime. I was ecstatic, but also a nervous wreck.

Over the weekend I fell into a depression. I had pulled through, but was left with a heaviness of spirit and a fear of walking outside the yacht club. The other yachtsmen were getting robbed too; one guy stepped out of a bank and was promptly relieved of a thousand dollars. Knifings were witnessed. One couple was set up and blackmailed by plainclothes police. Panamanians were always accosting me, begging, performing unrequested services, scamming. I was oppressed by heat and not sleeping well. To top it all off I slipped and banged my knee, which left me limping for a week. I needed friends.

Fortunately, nearly everyone who sails around the world funnels through the Canal. Several such circumnavigators introduced themselves as I moved back into *Squeak* after six weeks of sleeping in other beds. They were waiting for Tuesday, when the accumulated yachts would be taken through the Canal all together. Buford and Jeri Beach, owners of a sixty-foot trimaran called *Beachouse*, asked if I would serve as a line-handler for them. *Squeak* could ride on deck. I agreed.

Also transiting on Tuesday were Ralph and Don on the trimaran *Wind Chime*. They invited me over for much-needed drinks. The boat was spartan, meticulous. They had charter-skippered in St. Croix the past fifteen years and were now shaking out cobwebs with a technically difficult cruise to the Tuamotus, Tahiti, and Hawaii.

Ralph had a sincere, worldly strength. He was fair and rugged, with a tanned, hairy chest. His speech was a charming blend of New England and the Caribbean. Don had an Iowa accent, and had lived harder. "If I'd known I was going to live so long I'd have taken better care of myself," he said. As examples he related Vietnam combat experiences, a four-month motorcycle trip through Mexico, and an interlude in a Guatemalan jail. Don had long ago baked off his natural endowment of skin and had to keep covered up. He shared many of Ralph's good qualities, but when the topic switched to the Persian Gulf War he became vicious, and apocalyptic. "We should have nuked Saddam," he seethed, "but our politicians are too chicken-shit, and now we're in for a world war. Fucking planet's gonna blow, and I wanna be as far from civilization as possible when that happens."

The yacht club's most mysterious denizen was Peter Francis, a gaunt, beanpole figure who walked with a fast limp, never stopping, eyes darting here and there. His hair and beard were gray, closely cropped. He always wore the same worn-out sandals, olive shorts, and white, unbuttoned shirt.

Sunday he approached me. "So the pricks have robbed you as well, have they?" His voice was working-class British, his eyes gray and penetrating. A deep scar ran the length of his thigh, others showed on his chest. His lips had a disdainful or pained curl. "Here's how I intend to handle the bastards next time." He pulled a box-opener from his shorts pocket and thumbed the blade open.

"You might as well see mine." I showed him the Buck knife Chuck had given me in Wolf Point. I had strapped it to my belt.

"Very nice," he said. "So you're thinking of going down the Pacific coast to Colombia, are you? Sailed to Buenaventura myself five years ago with a partner. First yacht to enter the harbor in fifteen years. Engine broken down most the time, too. We tried to start a logging business with the harbor master, but he ended up double-crossing us."

"What other ports did you stop in?"

"Don't recall exactly. They're all shitholes." His eyes shifted uncomfortably under questioning. "Least I still had a boat then. Cock-suckers."

"Who?"

"Rammed me and sank me without warning, they did, couple years ago. One of Noriega's fucking patrol boats. Charged me with gunrunning and locked me up for fourteen months. If you Yanks hadn't invaded I'd still be in there. Lousy food screwed me up. I'm still pulling my shit together." He looked away. "That's alright. I've still got the map."

"What map?"

He eyed me. "You're not cut out for the yacht club scene, are you? Little cushy here, aye? Sheltered? Stand me a beer and I'll tell you about it."

We sat in a corner of the yacht club bar. He looked around, leaned forward.

"I met an old guy one time in a bar in Panama City. He gave me the map to the *Playa de Muerto* treasure. It's all a matter of historic record. In 1837 the Catholic church took all their gold out of Peru and put it on a ship sailing north out of Lima. But Cavendish, the pirate, he knew about it. The Spaniards saw him chasing them, and they stopped at a beach and buried the gold, tons of it. But Cavendish caught them before they could get away. He tortured them into showing him where the gold was, then he massacred every one of them. Ever since they've called the place *Playa de Muerto.*"

"Beach of Death? Where's that?"

"About a hundred miles south of Panama City. Then Cavendish reburied most of the gold, made a map, and took a little gold back to England with him. He never got around to coming back for the lion's share. Lots of people have looked for it, but they didn't have the map. Me and my partner looked five years ago and didn't find it, but I think I could now. Hell, the whole time in prison I didn't think of anything else. All I need's about five hundred bucks and a boat." He leaned back. "You're going that way. Maybe we can work together."

It was tempting, not so much for the gold—that sounded too good to be true—but because he was bold and knew the coast. "Tell you what, I'll go with you and help you look. My boat's a little small for two people, though. Can't you find a little dugout or something and come along with me?"

He looked doubtful. "Let's talk about it again tonight. I'll meet you here at seven."

He never showed up. I saw him the next day. He said the boat he'd been staying on was being sold and he didn't know where he would go. We set another rendezvous, which he also missed.

I was due to leave the next morning. Was he purposely avoiding me? Should I give up my ride through the Canal in hopes of connecting with him? I decided to move on, at great cost to my curiosity. Oh well, perhaps I'd run into him again.

I had climbed out of my depression and was getting things done. I rigged a sun awning over the boom and got some letters off. Ralph loaned me charts, which I photocopied, taped together, and shaded with colored pencils. On Monday evening, January 28, 1991, I rowed out to the *Beachouse*. We lifted *Squeak* aboard with the halyard winch and stowed her on the broad deck. Jeri Beach settled me into the port pontoon of their trimaran: four skinny compartments all in a line. She had decked it out with linens and toiletries like a hotel suite.

Buford and Jeri had designed the boat and overseen its construction in Houston. They were strong-willed people, in their sixties. Another couple moved into the starboard pontoon, giving us the required four line-handlers, one for each corner of the vessel. White-maned Buford drilled us on locking procedure. "I've been through the Canal before," he said. "I took my vessel through without damage that time, and I intend to do the same this time. Understand?" We did.

When our Panamanian pilot came aboard we motored in convoy to the first Gatun lock. It had more than enough room for the seven yachts. The pilot explained that the Panama Canal consists of three locks on the Gatun side and three locks on the Pacific side. Each lock is actually two locks side-by-side, for two-way traffic.

Upon entering each lock, Canal employees twirled to each line-handler a monkey's fist, which we attached to our docking lines. The Canal employees pulled up the docking lines and secured them to bollards. The gates shut. We line-handlers took up slack as the lock filled with water. We then proceeded to the second lock, and the third, for a total lift of 110 feet. Buford snapped like a mean dog whenever someone didn't follow a command to his satisfaction, but Jeri's pleasantness made up for him.

On top was man-made Lake Gatun, the waters of which gravity-feed the canal system. We motored through its jungly islands to a cozy anchorage, where we all swam in the cool, fresh water. A big moon rose out of the jungle while Jeri mixed gin-and-tonics. The air cooled nicely. Jeri and the other couple went to bed early, but Buford and I stayed up to watch President

Bush give his State of the Union address on their television in the main salon. Bush bored me, but Buford's snide criticisms of him tired me even more. "Well, guess I'll turn in," I said, halfway through.

The next day we motored through the Gaillard Cut, then down through the Miraflores and Pedro Miguel Locks. Everything went smoothly, but as soon as the pilot left, Buford groused, "He didn't know his ass from a hole in the ground. Why the hell'd Carter give the Canal to the damned Panamanians, anyway? The whole things going to pot." I might have agreed with him if he wasn't such a redneck.

The channel flowed swiftly. The height of the exposed mud indicated a tidal fall of up to twenty feet. On the left bank, near the Pacific entrance, was Balboa, an American-made suburb of Panama City. The Beaches dropped me off there. The date was January 30.

I had a lot to do before continuing my journey. As a center of operations, the Balboa Yacht Club (BYC) had advantages. The manager, Larry Liberty, didn't want to charge me moorage, but I insisted on paying a dollar a day. Only boats with expensive equipment were getting broken into. As in Colón, plenty of interesting sailors were passing through. Unfortunately, the only moorage was a hundred or so buoys, all fully exposed to the wakes of ships transiting the Canal. To get from buoy to pier we yachtsmen had to make noise and wait up to a half hour for a ramshackle launch to pick us up. The club was several miles from the city proper. I didn't care to spend money on taxis, so I walked a lot.

The Canal Zone was still U.S. territory. A naval installation enclosed the BYC on three sides. Forts and air bases surrounded the city. GIs were all over, and for every one there were three or four slender, seductively dressed Panamanian girls. In the words of one soldier, "If you can't find a girlfriend here, you can't find one anywhere." Our armed services were trying hard to keep a low profile, but the invasion's scars were still fresh. Shot-up buildings hadn't been repaired. Anti-U.S. slogans were spray-painted all over the slums. But the Panamanians also loved America. They used U.S. currency, ate hamburgers, and paid extra for the "Made in USA" label. Those who owed their jobs to the military presence were vocally pro-American.

The BYC bar was a meeting ground for people of all stripes. Graham was a painfully shy Englishman with glasses and long brown hair. On rare occasion he skippered a charter boat. Otherwise he sat at the bar, wasting a fine intelligence. I once asked him how he ate. He gave me an apathetic, faintly humorous look. "Frankly, Steve, I don't eat unless somebody feeds me." The one time I saw him with any money, two dollars, he insisted on buying me a drink.

Avis I met one evening while she was alone at the bar, downing her fourth rum-and-coke. "I've had a hell of a day," she groaned, "battling those Panamanian *señoras* I work with. I swear they don't like me just because I'm American. Or maybe it's because I'm blonde." I drove her home. Her husband, Boatswain's Mate Mike Pine, was a pint-sized, nasal-voiced Portuguese-American from New Haven, Connecticut. Mike found a gallon of Coleman fuel for me, and hollow-point bullets for my revolver. Either he picked up the tab or Uncle Sam did.

I could have sworn I saw Willie Nelson in the bar one day, but it turned out to be John, a single-handed sailor from California. He laughed more and louder than anyone I'd ever met. A couple weeks before, John had fallen off his boat, at sea, at night. "So there's my boat sailing away," he said. "It looked real pretty just then, with its lights shining and everything. I watched it a long time. Well, it was a nice night and there wasn't anything else to do, so I figured, what the hell, might as well swim. Swam for three and a half hours, and would you believe it? This boat comes by, right past me. I says, 'Hey,' and they stop and pick me up. Ho-ho! I always been lucky!"

Completing our little circle was Papillon, a retired American serviceman and guru on how to get things done in Panama. "Always be friendly, even if they're not," he advised, in his deep, Texan voice. "And remember. This here's Mañana Land."

It was indeed challenging to get things done. I found a map of the city, but each new dictator had renamed the streets, and my map was about two dictators behind. The Embassy of Brazil, located in one of the city's affluent neighborhoods, issued me a visa. Not a single bank in Panama would cash my Bank of America traveler's checks, not even the Bank of America itself, but the BYC gladly did so without charge. I bought white cotton pants and long-sleeve shirt for sixteen dollars on the bustling Avenida Central, where the clothing stores congregated, and paid a dentist ten dollars to extract the wisdom tooth that had bothered me on the Milk River. The empty socket became infected and I spent three days in my wake-tossed berth, too feverish to get up.

My errands often took me along the palm-lined sea wall that runs from San Felipe, the ancient quarter containing the Presidential Palace and Plaza de la Independencia, to the skyscrapered financial district. The sea wall and its adjoining boulevard looked out over the limitless Pacific. What would befall me in that awesome void, and in the dark lands bordering it? On a beach at the San Felipe end of the wall, fishermen mended nets while shipwrights repaired brightly painted boats, each a hollowed log with additional planks for freeboard. Fishing vessels and small freighters tugged relentlessly at their anchors in the exposed harbor. A rusty wreck protruded from the shallows. At one point, a square-sectioned sewer ran out into the bay, its top perforated with one-foot-diameter holes, a hole every ten feet. The sewer carried a pungent brown effluent. At the last hole before the sewer disappeared underwater a bronze-skinned, nearly naked man fished with a line and hook, as if through a hole in ice. He baited his hook with entrails, dropped it in the hole, jigged two or three times, and pulled out a foot-long catfish. He repeated this again and again, filling a bucket in the short time I watched. Mm, yummy. Shitfish!

I spent hours on rattly, crowded buses. Outside they were gaudily painted, inside they were plastered with a bewildering array of decals: Jesus Christ, skulls, German shepherds, the playboy symbol, WD-40, a voluptuous mouth, Cupid, maudlin sayings of love and nationalism. My fellow riders were dour-faced and insular, as are bus-riders everywhere. The drivers showed us as much consideration as they would a load of cattle, and ground their transmissions as though crushing blocks of ice.

One day while I checked for mail in the yacht club office, a footnote was added to the Peter Francis affair. Among the dozens of letters for so-and-so aboard the such-and-such, all unattended in a series of bins, was one addressed to him. It had just arrived from England. It was wrong to open it, but I did.

The letter was from a woman with a different last name, perhaps an aunt. It began:

> Dear Peter, another year has gone without hearing from you. Today you are forty-three; how time does fly. I myself am now seventy-five. It is three years since you disappeared, and I worry constantly about you . . .

The letter was long, full of tender detail about how family members were doing, and about the new little ones. She begged Peter to write soon, or she would report him as a missing person. Moved, I promptly wrote the woman a note telling her when and where I had last seen Peter, how he seemed, and that I didn't know how to reach him. Without identifying myself, I mailed my letter, then guiltily taped up Peter's and put it back in its slot.

There was a package for me, too. Brother David had registered *Squeak* and sent me the papers so I wouldn't have a repeat of my Colón experience. He also enclosed the map of Colombia I had used in 1973. With his own preparations to climb Mount McKinley in the spring, he had plenty to do without helping me.

Anxious to clear my mind of my voyage to date, I located a word processor at the Fort Clayton library. Larry Liberty connected me with a lieutenant colonel who arranged to get me on-base, and I spent a week writing. The facilities were excellent, like being back in the States, but I was a ponytailed, aging hippie in a sea of combat fatigues. Everybody acted like they didn't see me.

In the evenings I rode the bus back to Balboa, picked up a snack if anything was open, and walked the mile from the highway to the BYC. Then I walked down the long pier and got one of the Panamanian launch operators to take me back to *Squeak*. They all thought I was nuts—the other boats were cruise ships compared to mine. But I was dependent on them, so I employed Papillon's advice and stayed on their good side.

Life at a mooring was a drag. I discovered why they call them "wakes": every time a ship goes by it wakes you up. The waves were so big I was afraid I might roll over, which would be a real eye-opener with my gear loose and the hatch open. Also, a strong north wind blew day and night, which acted on the windage of my mainmast to cause *Squeak* to tack back and forth. It was like trying to sleep while water-skiing. Early each morning, lest I oversleep, a construction crew on the other side of the channel set off underwater explosions, which kicked up some interesting mini-tidal waves. Then there were the popping sounds I always heard through *Squeak's* hull. Sometimes they roared as loud as a bonfire of pitch pine. "Ha! That's tiny shrimps making that noise," said "Willie Nelson" John. "They're feeding off the algae what's growing on the bottom of your boat!" My only neighbors were the little gulls that shit all over the adjoining boats, and the pelicans that plopped into the water after fish. At least it didn't rain.

Besides Peter Francis, from whom I never got any details, I met only one person with experience of the Pacific coast of Colombia, a Colombian who had driven a boat up from Buenaventura. "*Es sano* (It's safe)," he said, but he wouldn't discuss it further. Maybe he'd smuggled drugs up. Everybody else warned me against going until I was sick of listening to them. Horror stories of piracy and cocaine-smuggling were coming out of the area. "They're not leaving any witnesses," said Mike Pine. "Yachts and fishing boats have disappeared without a trace," said Graham. Nobody navigated the Colombian coast, nor remembered a time when anybody did. I wondered, if nobody goes there, how do the pirates support themselves in the meantime? Perhaps by fishing or smuggling. But would they want a boat as little as *Squeak*, with no motor? Nobody knew.

Nor was piracy the only mysterious hazard. The chart showed a geography totally foreign to me. Could I land through the surf on the exposed beaches? What's it like to sail along a hundred miles of mangrove swamp with a tidal range of up to twenty feet? Could I obtain food and water? My experiences thus far in Panama had shaken me, yet I had barely opened a door onto a long, twilit corridor through which I must pass.

Then Traci wrote that she had come to feel distant from me, and would not meet me in Colombia. She seemed amiable but guilt-ridden, like she had taken another lover, like she respected but did not love me. I was crushed. Lottery tickets fluttered forlornly in their sidewalk clipboards in the dirty wind. An old woman's gray hair, pulled into a tough, bobby-pinned bun, symbolized the knotty self-discipline I held within. Fearful and lonely, suffering from the heat and dust, I dreamed of a cool, clean, soft place, a nirvana of my own making. I was scared, but I was going anyway. Tumaco was six hundred miles away, not so far really. From there I shouldn't have any trouble getting a ride to Puerto Asis on the Putumayo, if the dry season still held. Then the Amazon. One careful day at a time, and all mysteries would be revealed.

I longed to move on, but still had some tasks requiring a metropolis. My last few days in the city yielded tide tables, mosquito netting, soap, a new tooth filling, vaccinations against hepatitis, tetanus, and poliomyelitis—and two trays of gin-and-tonics, shared over happy hour with newfound friends in the BYC bar. The syncopated beats of the Panamanian folk music swayed us back and forth. I left our little party feeling rather sleepy, and couldn't resist stretching out, just for a second, on a delightful pile of leaves near the telephone office. I woke at dawn, surprised to find my wallet still on me.

One of my new friends was Christian, a young Swiss traveler seeking passage to Ecuador. He had a crisp, pleasant style. Our tasks being related, we knocked around together for a few days, practicing our Spanish on each other. One evening Christian telephoned me at the bar.

"Please, come join me for a double date. I'm with two Panamanian women, and they want to meet you."

"Are they pretty?"

"Mm, more or less"

I met them at a good restaurant. The ladies were airline office employees: intelligent, financially independent, unattractive. Their figures were lumpy, their conversation moralistic and predictable. I excused myself at the earliest opportunity and returned to the bar, populated as it was with more typical Panamanian women: dirt poor but alluring. Yet this too was a frustration, for they spotted me for a cheapskate and avoided my advances. Their culture demanded that their sex appeal determine their standard of living, and they couldn't afford to let anything but money affect their mating behavior. Prostitution was a matter of degree, ranging from the simple bordello girl, to the woman supporting herself through a stable of boyfriends, to the cash-conscious husband-seeker. Dates were bargaining sessions, the man maneuvering for sex, the woman for food, drinks, presents. The prices were reasonable, but I was too proud to pay.

Also seeking passage south were Alistair Price and Coco Schneider, young lovers who had met in Mexico some months before. Lank, blond Alistair was a Devonshire lad with a fertile imagination. His enthusiastic statements often ended with the word "really" or "actually," quaintly inflected. His eyes hid behind thick-lensed glasses, and his jaw dropped slightly inward when he spoke. I fell into a sort of love with Coco, the cosmopolitan Berliner. She had dark hair swept from left to right over her head, deep eyes, sharp nose, and the shiny smile of a tease. She was older than Alistair, and an intelligent warmth radiated from her soft body.

Alistair and Coco soon joined forces with an eccentric Frenchman named Michel, who would drop them off in Salinas, Ecuador, then continue alone to the Marquesas. Sun-bronzed, quiet, scrawny little Michel had spent his life in Reunion, Madagascar, and Morocco. He had been a mathematician, a teacher, a jeweler. He moved in an entirely different plane from the other yachters. His stubbly Sindbad face lacked a front tooth but contained the mysteries of the seven seas. He communicated with nature through an inner sense, not electronics.

"At night, when I am at sea, I listen to the water through the hull: '*Swish swish, swish swash…*'" While whispering the syllables he swayed his hand tenderly back and forth. "Sometimes I understand the water's words. Someday I learn speak back to the sea."

Michel's boat, *Alefa*, was a low-tech plywood tub. Of its cockroaches he said, "Sometimes I say, 'Kill, kill!' Sometimes I say, '*ça va*.'" But the *Alefa* was homey and safe. When Alistair and Coco moved aboard I joined them for an evening of rice and vegetables, gin, fresh-squeezed orange juice, sea shanties, Eric Clapton and Jimi Hendrix. I broke out my tin whistle while Michel produced a recorder, a conch, and a ceramic bead with intricate air passages. We were all of different nationalities, yet we sang from a common pool of favorite songs.

We slept, and began the new day with readings from the Rubaiyat of Omar Khayyam in French. Michel, great lover of his native language, soon resurrected what little remained in me of that beautiful tongue from my early travel days. He showed me, with evident pride and grief, pictures of a previous, much larger *Alefa* he had spent three years building, only to lose it off the coast of Brazil through a crewman's negligence. Never has man crafted anything more graceful than the wooden sailboat in that photograph. With him in the photos were a lovely woman and a young son, now living in Reunion. I didn't need to ask. His sense of loss extended to them too.

As the crew of the *Alefa* readied for departure, so did I. I secured my exit permit and hurried back to the yacht club, relieved to see *Alefa* still there. It had become important to me that they not leave me behind—alone I might not have the courage. At Michel's suggestion, I tied *Squeak* to the aft rail with a long line. At nine in the evening, February 19, 1991, we left for *las Perlas,* the Pearl Islands.

CHAPTER 9

ISLA SAN JOSE

Breeze and tide nudged us out the Canal's Pacific entrance, past a dozen anchored ships, and on into open sea. Panama City glittered astern. *Alefa's* foresail billowed and swayed, drawing us like a team of horses through the starry night. Sixty miles ahead lay Isla San Jose, southwesternmost of the Pearl Islands. Someone had described it to Michel as a paradise. It lay on Michel's and my way out through the Gulf of Panama. Alistair drew watch by virtue of not being able to sleep. Michel catnapped beside him on deck.

When Michel woke me at first light, no land was visible. The sea was mild. *Alefa* rocked and pitched before the slack wind. *Squeak* followed willingly a hundred meters astern.

Alistair now slept while Michel and I steered a course of 150° through the long, hot morning. Michel moved slowly, curiously, like a bird. He wore only a short, black, pajama bottom. He trailed a lure, and caught a bonito, a beautiful creature with sharp lines and metallic skin. He stroked and spoke gently to it in French until it died. I filleted the firm, bloody meat, which Coco sliced into sushi.

Toward noon we saw land. The wind died, and we motored with islands on our left, ultimately rounding Isla San Jose to enter a southeast-facing roadstead. It received a degree of protection from a partly submerged reef a half mile offshore. From the reef's clefts rose a huge pillar of stone, a statue-like monolith that seemed to guard the harbor. Other satellite islets stood somewhat further away. The shore was rocky and irregular. Two German-flagged yachts lay to anchor opposite a big rock near shore. One we knew from Balboa: the Haering family. We anchored by them.

With a couple hours left before dark, Coco and I rigged *Squeak* and sailed to a large beach a half mile to the north, where the shoreline curved east. I landed through mild surf onto pink-gray sand. A giant lizard scurried away. Crabs darted in and out of holes in the sand. Behind the beach was a stream-fed lagoon. To the right, steps led up through a stone retaining wall to a road that disappeared into thick forest.

We swam in the lagoon—its water was cool in the upper six feet, hot below—then lazed on the sizzling sand. Her closeness soothed me.

"I'm hurting, Coco. Traci's cutting out on me. It comes at a hard time."

She frowned. "Alistair and I have problems too. I want to return to Germany now, for family and work. I stay with him until Ecuador, then I go back. Neither of us are ready for this separation."

"Funny," I said. "Alistair never talks about you, just about his trip through the Amazon after he gets to Ecuador. I think he's more in love than you are. Concentrating on the journey is his way of dealing with the situation. He's brave."

"Alistair's younger than me. He needs this hard travel to build his strength and to find himself. I don't need that now. He's covering ground I've already covered."

"I feel for him. In a way he's where I was in 1971, when I split up with my best friend and started traveling alone. In another way he's where I am right now. I'd hate to have to break up with you."

Coco smiled, then sat up. "Steve, this place makes me uneasy."

I also felt it, something brooding and timeless. "Me too. Let's go."

As we reached the anchorage a man approached us in a dinghy. He held up a dead iguana and cried out sharply in German.

"He wants to know if we want it," said Coco.

"Yes!" I answered, but in maneuvering alongside him I underestimated my turning radius under sail, causing *Squeak* to catch on a pole protruding from one of the anchored yachts. While I struggled to disentangle us, the German rowed up and threw a four-foot-long iguana onto Coco's lap. She screamed and slid it off. I brought *Squeak* under control, trampling the gross reptile underfoot, and sailed away from that impulsive man.

In the morning, after breaking fast on eggs we had found in the iguana's belly, Coco, Alistair, and I went ashore and formally met the German. Coco translated: "For eight years Dieter and his mate, Gerda, have been making a farm here." Dieter had a lean frame, fierce eyes, and strong teeth that showed through a square, silvery beard. He hurriedly shook our hands, then swept his German-speaking guests—Coco and the Haerings—off on a tour. Meanwhile, plain, survival-oriented Gerda showed Alistair and I how to start a fire using dry banana leaves. We gutted the iguana and roasted it over the fire, both of us eager to become jungle-wise. Wood smoke mingled with the smell of singeing flesh.

Coco later took Alistair and me where she had been taken. The farm consisted of a small beach camp, a dozen white chickens, shacks, bee hives, and a few acres of fruit trees and pineapple plants. The soil was red and barren. They took water from a stream. For protein they shot iguanas and doves, trapped tailless rats, and netted fish. Never having had time or materials to build a house ashore, they lived aboard their rusty ketch, the *Seepferdchen (Sea Horse).*

We continued along an old jeep track with sea views on both sides. West lay the blue, uninterrupted Pacific. East lay the anchorage with its three large and one tiny sailboats, and the guardian rock, a hundred feet tall. It had the form of a human bust, with an oversized head. Eyes, nose, and mouth were formed by patches of brown grass, lighter than the black rock. The figure faced the high point of the island, directly above the farm. "Its Spanish name is *Mono Ahumado,* Smoked Monkey," said Coco, "but Dieter and Gerda call her Mona. They believe the Indians worshipped her, and now *they* worship her and ask her for help. They believe a high priest and perhaps a treasure lie buried on that rocky hill there, which the Mona faces. While clearing the jungle they found pieces of Pre-Columbian pottery, and ancient bottles, perhaps brought by early pirates."

Sawgrass cut our bare legs. The equatorial sun beat down on our heads. The track ascended the island's spine, traversed dark woods, and crossed a cool clear stream that ran copiously through a bed of gnarly basalt. Vines hung down into its shady pools. Little lizards ran on hind legs across the water, without sinking. We followed the stream into the lagoon Coco and I had discovered the day before.

In disrobing for a swim we found ticks. They had buried their heads into our skin and were sucking blood. We plucked them gently, not to leave the heads inside. We returned to the farm by scrambling along the shore, which was of the same basalt we'd seen in the streambed. It was broken into massive chunks, and studded with sharp protrusions.

Michel had kept to himself since our arrival at the island. He remained aloof while Alistair, Coco, and I talked late into the evening. The subject of spirits came up.

"I've had experience with them," said Coco. She seemed reluctant.

"Come on then, tell us," urged Alistair.

"Well, when I was young my family owned a farm in the country. The family that kept this farm for us was rustic, but intelligent. Once they gave us a very unusual stool. One of its three legs was hollow, and inside this hollow they told us to put a pen. The stool was placed on a large sheet of paper, and the people present sat around, each with a finger on the stool. The stool moved and the pen wrote out messages. They were from the spirits of dead people, always a different person from a different time and place, each writing in his own hand. Some wrote in ancient script. Some gave information about themselves which we verified from historical records.

"The stool became the rage of Berlin, but it went too far. My sister developed emotional problems, and a friend of the family was haunted by spirits when he tried to stop communicating with them. You see, the spirits don't tell you anything valuable. They only sap energy from the living because they're bored, or in limbo, or trying to work out wrongs they committed when they were alive."

"Can we do it here?" I asked.

"Yes, let's have a go!" said Alistair.

Coco gave in. "If you must, I'll try a shorthand, Ouija version." We wrote letters on scraps of paper and spread them in a circle on the cabin's bare plywood floor. A low-wattage bulb cast a dim pool of light on us as we each placed a finger on an upside-down glass in the center of the circle.

"Come forth," whispered Coco.

It was a dark tropical night, between cool and warm. The north wind murmured in *Alefa's* rigging and raised short, uneven waves that bobbed her slowly up and down. A two-inch roach ventured from his hidey-hole, scurried softly, then disappeared.

I chose to concentrate on *Alefa's* wooden mast, once a tree in Madagascar. I imagined watching the masthead from above as it swayed with the boat, describing ellipses of infinitely varied shape all around the zenith. I sighted down the mast, down the imaginary line projecting from its base. It probed the dark center of the earth, had always probed, would always restlessly sway and probe, seeking the center, where is it? I remembered floating, submerged, fetus-like, in a hot spring near Glacier Peak, in midwinter, and feeling the hot bubbles stream over my naked body as they emerged from deep within the planet. An image of orange-red fire sizzled inside my eyelids.

"No spirits," said Coco, waking me from my trance. The glass hadn't moved. "Maybe the motion of the boat kept them away, or maybe you two are too skeptical. Spirits are choosy about who they communicate with."

We relaxed on the soft cushions. "Let's make up a story," I suggested.

"I'm no good at that, but Alistair certainly is," said Coco.

"Righto. Sounds fun, actually. Shall I go first?"

"By all means," I said.

Alistair settled into his pillow. "Captain Silas Greenback," he declared, "was already a man with a rather shady past when he was marooned by fellow pirates on a desert island somewhere in the Gulf of Panama in the seventeenth century. Inexperienced at scavenging, he wasted away and recorded time by carving notches on an old whale bone. Unaccustomed to such loneliness, old Silas resolved to escape the island or die trying.

"With nothing more than the dirk he kept in his boot, Silas split a balsa tree into planks and laced them together in the overlapping style of his native Dorset. Within a month he had a leaky boat and a pair of oars fashioned from ironwood saplings. He packed water away in hollow gourds and rowed out through the surf. Soon he was far out to sea, adrift, hoping for a favorable outcome." Alistair waved the show to me.

"Meanwhile," I said, "on an island just beyond the horizon, lived a young Indian by the name of Cuan Tru. He belonged to a band of hunters and gatherers. They were a happy people, but Cuan Tru was restless. At the age of fifteen he had a vision that told him to seek a spirit that resided somewhere beyond their island. So Cuan Tru wandered until he saw a tree leaning out over a rocky stream. The trunk had the shape of a banana, and in it he saw the canoe that would help him fulfill his vision.

"Moving to the site, he took the tree's life. Then, with tools of chipped basalt, he hollowed the giant trunk. He built a fire and baked stones, the heat of which he used to steam the log's gunwales outward. Cuan Tru heaved his dugout out the stream's narrow gorge and into the sea. He paddled for two days, then his water gave out. With the sun burning directly overhead, Cuan Tru soon became delirious.

"He'd have died, but a jolt aroused him. Lifting his head, he saw a man with white skin and a long, red beard. It was Silas Greenback, but to Cuan Tru it was the white spirit of his vision. Take it, Alistair."

"Okay. The two men instinctively trusted each other. Silas shared his water, and they worked up a crude language of sounds and gestures. Together they paddled until they reached the Darién coast, where they set up camp in a cove. The coast wasn't as remote as the islands, really. Buccaneers roved about, and the descendants of *conquistadores* still wandered the jungle in search of gold. Silas and Cuan Tru assembled a band of desperadoes hailing from the four corners of the world. There was Jombo, the giant black harpooner, Jan the treacherous Dutchman, Diego the deserter from the Spanish outpost at Nombre de Dios, even an Orinoco cannibal. So motley was the crew, in fact, that nobody spoke the same language as anybody else, so the co-captains taught them the language they'd developed. Silas's cat-o'-nine-tails provided discipline, and Cuan Tru's quiet strength inspired them.

"They designed a vessel capable of taking easy prey. The crew salvaged cannon from a wrecked galleon, and manufactured powder from the guano that coated the nearby rookeries. Finally, launch day arrived. The moon was full, the tide was high. The crew cheered as the little ship slid into the water.

Then they sailed in the direction of a rumored island, whose beaches were littered with emeralds and pearls.

"After four days they came to a tall, jungly island, and anchored at sunset in a bay surrounded by oozy mangrove flats. Before daylight, a noticeable tilt showed they had underestimated the tide and had gone aground. They were stuck until the next high tide. This was unfortunate, because as it grew light they beheld hundreds of native canoes approaching from a village at the head of the bay. The warriors carried blow guns and spears. Silas and Cuan Tru, considering their limited gunpowder, decided to try diplomacy. They loaded their longboat with cheap trade goods and met the leading canoe.

"Far from expressing gratitude, the savages seized Silas and Cuan Tru and stormed the ship. Everyone was bound and taken to the village, which went into a frenzy. The chief, seated on a golden throne, gestured instructions, and braided vines were laid out from shore to the ship, which was now high and dry. Fifty natives pulled on each of the twenty braids, dragging their ship toward the village, leaving a deep trough that filled with water.

"By evening the ship lay at the edge of the village. The natives lit fires. Some of them danced while others rolled cauldrons into place then forced the crew, kicking and screaming, into the cauldrons."

"Allow me to rescue our heroes," I said. "You see, Cuan Tru had a trick up his sleeve. Before leaving in the longboat he had instructed his chief gunner, who was a dwarf, to squirm down into the powder keg to avoid detection, then blow up the ship at his command. When the water grew uncomfortably warm, Cuan Tru pulled a small, perforated shell from a string around his neck and blew a long, piercing note.

"The drummers paused, the dancers stopped. Even the flickering flames seemed to hesitate. Then the sky was rent with a deafening blast as the ship exploded. The concussion knocked the chief on his ass and upset all the cauldrons. Debris showered the village. The pirates quickly dispersed into the forest. Once the natives had pulled their wits together they ran howling after them. Cuan Tru ran until he reached the top of a cliff. Darts and spears whizzing all around him, he dove into the water far below."

Alistair picked up the thread. "Meanwhile, Silas had jumped off the other side of the island. At daybreak he was picked up by a ship flying the Jolly Roger. The captain, a one-eyed, one-legged bully, first proposed to keelhaul him just for the fun of it. But old Silas, always quick on his feet, said he knew about a buried treasure. If he died, the knowledge of it would die with him. If, on the other hand, the good captain should give him his own cabin and decent food and drink, he'd take him to the gold, and they would all be wealthy men.

"Old One-Eye didn't entirely swallow this, but he granted Silas a fortnight to find the gold or be drawn and quartered. Meanwhile, he'd have to earn his keep by washing dishes in the galley. Silas gave sailing instructions toward the make-believe cache, and pondered how to get out of this scrape. In the meantime, he befriended Chan, the Chinese cook, and took to engaging in late-night drinking bouts with him.

"Seeing Chan was easily gotten drunk, Silas concocted a scheme to poison One-Eye and take over the ship. He left an iguana carcass in the bilge until it grew a yellow mold with purple shoots growing out of it. When the maggots all died he reckoned it was ready.

"That evening, Silas and Chan played mah-jongg while the soup simmered. They broke out a bottle of rum, and Chan was soon passed out in his chair. Silas crept down into the bilge. He scraped a thimbleful of mold off the carcass and slunk back into the galley. He had no sooner ladled out a bowl of soup and mixed in the fungus when One-Eye, whose cabin was directly overhead, banged on the ceiling with his wooden leg. 'Chan, my supper!' he bellowed. Old Chan jumped up and staggered to the door, taking the bowl Silas handed him. He went to the captain's cabin, returned, and passed out again.

"Silas waited. From above there came a long silence, then a moan that grew into a pitiful wail. 'Greenback!' he screamed, and pounded his wooden leg once. By the time Silas got there, One-Eye was convulsing on the floor.

"Guess I've done for you now, you old shitbag,' said Silas, and pulled a pistol from the corpse's belt. Swiveling on his heel to face the crew, which had gathered at the doorway, he cried, 'I be now the captain of this ship, and what man of you dares deny it?' None did, and old Silas was once again master of a fighting vessel." Alistair waved the floor to me.

"Cuan Tru's luck started out pretty slow, too," I said. "He swam away from the island until night fell. He lost consciousness, and came to the following morning lying face down on a deserted beach, his mouth full of sand. Slowly his senses came back. The wildlife being similar to that of his home island, he soon nursed himself back to health. The trees were heavy with fruit, the hives were full of honey, and the lagoons teemed with fish. It seemed he was alone in that tropical paradise.

"So he thought until he came upon a basalt ridge. He scaled it and peered over the other side. Below he saw a village inhabited solely by girls and women. Garlands and bright cloths adorned their honey-colored skin. The huts and landscaping were neat and efficient. Fowl and domesticated deer were carefully tended. One particularly lovely woman, seated on a low platform, was apparently their queen.

"A row of huts aroused his curiosity. Sneaking down to it, he saw a sight that made his blood run cold. Under each thatched shelter lay a man, or what could have been a man. For they were apparently nothing but vegetables whom the women fed and cleaned, but had never allowed to move. Their senses and muscles hadn't developed. While he watched, an old woman entered one of the huts and, massaging the creature's penis, extracted a palmful of sperm. She then walked to a nearby couch where a young woman lay waiting. The old lady took sperm and a reed into her mouth, and blew the sperm into the young woman's vagina.

"Cuan Tru went back to his side of the island, no longer at peace. He feared the woman village, but he feared loneliness as well. Finally he decided to surrender, so he returned to the ridge and descended into the woman village. He walked slowly up to the platform and knelt before the queen. The women froze still and gazed at the first real man they had ever seen. They glanced anxiously at each other while the queen stared at the kneeling man. Her hazel eyes revealed worry, wonder, and dawning purpose. Finally she went to Cuan Tru, lifted him gently by the chin, and sat him down beside her.

"Cuan Tru submitted to the women as they fashioned rich apparel for him and laid out a larger pavilion. He came to love his queen, and appreciate ever more fully her beauty and wisdom. From then on, mothers raised their sons humanely.

"Life was good, but Cuan Tru, searching for a purpose in all that had befallen him, dreamed of a ship that would transport the colony to a new land, the location of which God would reveal. Cuan Tru shared this vision with his queen, who agreed it was true. So he meditated on shapes and dimensions, which the women translated into a frame of aromatic wood. The dreamship rose and changed fluidly, like sculpted clay. Its lines were long and flowing. They fastened a skin of pure, straight grain, and wove rainbow-hued sails. The ship took to the water like a living creature. All came aboard, and away they sailed.

"On the third day, a cruiser flying the Jolly Roger bore down on them. In the rigging was Silas Greenback, who laughed at seeing his old partner so well ensconced. Cuan Tru beckoned. "Come Silas, for we go to create a new world!" Silas hesitated a long, wistful moment, then grabbed a rope and swung down on deck. They embraced as the dreamship disappeared into the twilight, never to be seen again. But somewhere in the vast Pacific there may still exist the Garden of Eden founded in the seventeenth century by Silas Greenback, Cuan Tru, and the women of Paradise Island."

It was past midnight. Coco lay yawning on a cushion. Michel had curled up on deck hours before. Soon we were all asleep, and the tropical night was sowing dreams in our fertile minds.

The following day, Alistair, Coco, and I went in *Squeak* to play on the big beach. It was a calm day, yet there was a swell. Upon reaching a threshold ten yards from shore, the swell rose into a breaking wave perhaps three feet tall. I stopped in the surf zone, bow shoreward, and held *Squeak* while the others got out. A wave caught the raised rudder blade and slammed it over, splitting the rudder stock vertically. Worried about how to fix it, and what would happen when I encountered worse surf, I no longer enjoyed the outing.

On our return Michel said, "I go now. Ecuador." He'd been withdrawn since coming to the island. Perhaps he felt crowded with four aboard, or worried about dwindling provisions, or feared that the north wind wouldn't hold. He didn't say. I wasn't prepared to part so suddenly with Alistair and Coco, nor they with me. But we had no right to question Michel's wish. They had no alternative but to leave with him. I had none but to stay behind.

Alistair bravely shook my hand. "Well, old man, see you at Puerto Asis, on the Putumayo?" he asked.

"I'll look for you, but you'll probably have already passed through."

I held Coco for a long time. My sunglasses hid my tears as I got into *Squeak* and untied our boats. Michel leaned toward me, sensing my distress. "You go by the coast. You be all right, Steve." They weighed anchor and sailed away, Coco gazing at me from the stern with an enigmatic expression on her dear face. I was wretched, because in them I had hidden from my grief at losing Traci, and from my fear.

I saw now that it was a mistake to have taken the ship to Panama. I had zero experience with ocean sailing or survival in the tropics. Had I worked my way from New Orleans along the Gulf coast, I'd have acclimatized slowly, within easy reach of materials, services, and information. Also, I'd have been better able to fight for a continued place in Traci's heart. Instead I poised, alone, before a void.

The green and white speck that was *Alefa* vanished on the bright horizon. Following Dieter's suggestion, I tied to a buoy and killed the rest of the day bobbing uncomfortably in the short waves and hot sun. I thought of October, 1971, when I separated with my best friend in Istanbul, he on his way to Egypt, I on mine to Afghanistan. Then, as now, I suffered a separation compounded with the shock of an alien environment. Perhaps I hadn't changed much since that day twenty years before, in the crisis of my youth. I was still lost, still close to that pathos, that faraway-ness, that compound of all emotions that is my spiritual core. I kept seeing more that needed to be done before it would be remotely sane to continue the voyage, but all I could do was cry. I cried for myself, for my fear, for loved ones who might never know my fate. I cried for Earth's cruel beauty, and the slenderness of Man's hopes. I cried for myself, but the ache in my heart seemed peopled by long-ago lives, from all the civilizations of which we have record, and by beings of whom we know nothing but who cry, as I was crying, before the lonely mystery of life.

Finally I started to move. I cleaned up epoxy resin that had leaked from the shampoo bottle I kept it in—the cap had come loose. I made places for new equipment acquired in the city. As night took hold I ate whole wheat bread, margarine, oranges, and raw carrots. My supply of these things wouldn't last long. I resolved again to proceed slowly and patiently, to accept the delays and the horrible bogged-down feeling. According to Dieter, the iguana-killer, I had two months before the north wind would stop and the rains and south winds would begin. Maybe before then I could still make it to Tumaco, 540 miles due south.

I kept to the sidelines the next two days as Dieter and Gerda visited with fellow Germans Eddi and Ute Haering, their teen daughters Katje and Iris, and son Marco. Like Michel, the Haerings had heard about Dieter and Gerda's farm, and used it as a final stop-off. Their next run, to the Marquesas, would be the longest of a circumnavigation that had already consumed twelve years. The kids knew no other life. Fixing roots in the sea itself, and in New Guinea and South Africa, where Eddi had found temporary jobs as an aeronautical engineer, they'd sprung up hale and wise beyond their years. Ute, a teacher, educated them herself. Their sailboat was neat as a pin. When it came time for the Haerings to leave I wrote in their guest book:

round the world in many ways
by seas and dreams and turns of phrase
expand our minds and fashion days
of learning in the sun

making friends where terra ends
before the haul around the ball
Pacific gleaming blue

our boats are set, good friends well met
good voyage to us both
my dear Swiss Family Robinson
adieu! adieu! adieu!

It was February 26. Gerda rang their great triangle, Dieter blew the conch. We waved until they were out of sight. "It's hard when friends leave," said Dieter. "All sailors are a family."

His sentimentality didn't last long. He gripped my arm and drilled me with his wild eyes. "You must understand this island," he said. "It is Paradise! Paradise! But it is hard! We discover it eight years ago while sailing around the world, and never leave. But there is no time to lose! The jungle fights us. The insects and animals kill our young trees. The blacks come and steal. Sun! Ants! Sawgrass! Ticks! Sandflies! You can stay here with us. We help each other. But you must understand."

I did. Now it was my world too. I immersed myself in it.

It was summer in the tropics—the leaves and soil were dry. The forest had never been logged. It was thick, but penetrable. Some trees were slim and gnarly. Others were covered with thorns. Birds were everywhere: brown pelicans, terns, green parrots, doves, songbirds. Iridescent hummingbirds hovered about my head. There were dwarf deer, feral pigs, and herbivorous rats. Lizards came in several sizes, from the dragon-like iguana to tiny geckos. There were thin, brown snakes which Dieter killed at every opportunity. None of the crabs were large, but each species possessed a unique skill: translucent red crabs that darted quickly, black crabs that leaped and scaled rocks in the crashing surf. The beach and forest floor crawled with hermit crabs. Each boasted a shell a little different from the others, many quite elegant. Coral grew on the rocks of the bay's floor. I once broke a hollow stick on the upper beach, and black bees the size of my thumb flew out. I jumped into the sea to escape them.

The island lent itself to objective analysis, but the feeling it gave me did not. It was a sensation of time flowing rapidly and evenly—endless sun and wind, interlocking cycles of mystery so deep we don't know how to frame the questions. I didn't believe Mona was a god, but in some sense I must have believed it. Her presence colored my experience. The human resemblance was too uncanny. Her eyes never closed. She had captivated Dieter and Gerda and induced them to settle under her direct gaze. Now I was there too.

I moved *Squeak* to the beach to escape the harsh sea motion, and started hunting. I had limited success spearfishing because fish large enough to be worth cleaning rarely let me get close, and the water was too cold to stay in for long. Better to collect snails and giant limpets at low tide, then scoop their meat and grind it in Gerda's grinder. I hunted iguanas with Dieter, but never caught any. Once a six-foot monster ran past, too suddenly for us to react. "I kill the females when they come out of their holes where they lay their eggs," he said, "or shoot them after Zulu trees them." Zulu was his black South African dog.

Gerda generally stayed aboard the *Seepferdchen*. She was tall, quiet, in her mid-fifties, with short brown hair and limited English. She was strong, but no longer happy there. "I want return Deutschland," she said. "See grandchildren."

Dieter maintained a rough, chauvinistic affection for Gerda. Once, as we returned from an outing, he paused to cut flowers for her from a shrub with his ever-present machete. "Thirteen years today since I meet Gerda," he said. But whatever Gerda did, he planned to remain there until his health failed. There was no sign of that happening yet, though he was sixty-three. On the contrary, I had difficulty keeping up with him.

I accompanied Dieter on any pretext. He showed me how to dig in the sand next to a lagoon and collect the water that comes up, filtered of pathogens. He showed me how to spot wild pig sign, and heal a cut by rubbing it with the flesh of the aloe vera plant. Dieter loved to talk, smile, and laugh, but he rarely had time.

"I vas in Hitler Youth when the war started," he said in his rough English as we marched to harvest a papaya from the upper orchard. "When I am only fifteen I operate an antiaircraft gun every night in Berlin. Very funny! In 1945 I fight on the Russian front and the western front too. I loved the war because no more I had to go to school! One time, while I hide behind a tree, I shoot an American tank with a bazooka. But the American army vas smart! They had concrete around the top. It bounced right off! The Russians capture me, the British capture me, the Americans capture me. Always I escape."

"You must have known you were losing the war."

"No! We were young, we were strong. We thought we would win!"

After the war, he and a fiancée built a boat and sailed out the mouth of the Rhône River, only to be shipwrecked in the Mediterranean. He'd been a shrimp fisherman in Spain, a marine salvager in Morocco. His ultimate exploit, a circumnavigation, he forgot when he saw Isla San Jose.

When I wasn't roaming with Dieter I worked in the tiny beach camp. It was the focus of the farm, though its only improvements were some plank furniture and sheet-metal wind screens. It was at the edge of the forest, separated from the beach by a screen of vegetation, near the outlet of a small, mangrove-choked lagoon. The lagoon, fed by the same stream from which they got their water, was handy for washing clothes and for rinsing off after swimming in the sea. Most of the streamflow sank into the sand, but a rivulet always snaked down the beach. When the moon was full, and the tide high, waves washed into the lagoon. The beach was framed by basalt outcroppings. In its center, forming a separate islet at high tide, was a rocky spire which lined up with the *Seepferdchen* and Mona. Usually my only company were Zulu, the white chickens, a carpet of clicking hermit crabs, and the wind in the leaves, which were large and round, or thin and palmy, or oblong and bright. Here I repaired the Plexiglas hatch cover again, made a mosquito net to fit the hatchway, and mended clothes.

An hour before sunset, Dieter would return to the camp, strip naked, swim vigorously a few minutes, then row out to the *Seepferdchen*. He always left his cap hanging on a dead branch that protruded from the sand of the upper beach. This cap epitomized him. It was an adjustable baseball cap in a military camouflage pattern. Around its bottom Dieter had sewn a fringe of cloth to keep sun and sandflies off his neck. I had seen such caps before, perhaps in WWII photos of jungle or desert combat. The cap hung there as the evening faded against the backdrop of spire, bay, Mona, and distant Isla del Rey. I played "Danny Boy" or "Tennessee Waltz" on my tin whistle, Zulu howling plaintively by my side. I slept, and in the morning the cap was there still. Then Dieter rowed ashore, and the cap took its place on that grinning, warrior head that looked so naked without it.

The summer winds abated, and a cloud of sandflies ("no-see-ums") enveloped me day and night. Their bites weren't as bad as those of the mosquito, but they were much more difficult to avoid. The insect's minuteness allowed it to pass through mosquito netting or a buttoned shirt front. Insect repellent kept ninety-nine percent of them away, but one percent of infinity is still infinity. The first fifty or hundred stings hurt individually. After that my entire skin would burn and itch like a single, inflamed organ. The only solution, though uncomfortably hot, was to thickly clothe my entire body, including gloves, three pair of socks, and a hood drawn closely around my nose and eyes.

I reconciled myself to a trip back to Panama City before proceeding south. Nowhere else could I get the fiberglass I needed to repair the rudder, and the only thing left in my food sack was white rice. But distance and the north wind precluded rowing there. Dieter said that, besides him and Gerda, only a dozen or so Panamanian laborers lived on the island, near a dirt airstrip twelve kilometers away. Dieter discouraged me from approaching them, so I kept my eyes open for a passing yacht or fishing boat that might give me a ride.

On March 1 a jeep stopped at the larger beach, flashed its headlights, and left, leaving someone behind. Dieter and I fetched her in his dinghy. She was a middle-aged woman with curly red hair, plump but capable.

"You are Dieter?" she asked.

"*Ja.*"

"I am Annie Marie, from Belgium. Sorry to bother you. My boyfriend's yacht has come aground at Playa Grande, six kilometers away. A worker on this island brought me here thinking you might help us." She was quite chipper for having just been shipwrecked.

She and Dieter walked to the wreck while I rowed there. The *Melissa* sat stern-to-sea on the upper beach. She was a thirty-nine-foot, cold-molded sloop of superb craftsmanship. Her owner, Jacques, was thin and withdrawn. His brown hair was tousled, his face puffy from sandfly bites. His round glasses kept sliding down his nose.

"I anchor yesterday here. I don't look the tide, so stupid! It drops in nighttime. We pound, pound. I try motor but it gets hot, stops. The waves push us onto a rock, bend the rudder, break a hole. Water comes in. Annie and I get ashore okay, but the invisible flies sting us all night. No sleep." His eyes were bloodshot, his shoulders stooped. "Six years I build her. All my money. No insurance. She cannot be saved, I am certain."

"But you *can* save her! You *must*!" cried Dieter, tense all over.

Jacques shrugged weakly.

Dieter appraised him. "Okay, we save her for you. Come, Steve. The tide soon fills her again with water. We first keep her from moving sideways or more up the beach."

While Annie Marie held *Squeak* steady in the surf, Dieter and I gingerly hoisted aboard the *Melissa's* fisherman's anchor. It took up the entire cockpit, making it impossible to row, so I swam *Squeak* seaward. Three hundred yards out we dropped it overboard. We then ran its line to the *Melissa's* stern and tensioned it with a winch. Waves were beginning to break over her. We next removed outboard motors, wooden interior components that had floated loose, and assorted equipment and stores. I worked inside, handing things out through the forward hatch. The water got deeper and deeper. The waves lifted and dropped the stern, causing the water inside to gush back and forth the length of the boat. Everything was coming loose and breaking. Everything that floated became a battering ram.

"*Ach,* the sea, it is terrible!" Dieter lamented, as if cursing an evil god. But he also enjoyed himself immensely. "More beer, more beer!" he cried. I scooped dozens of floating cans into bags and passed them out. We guzzled, ate cookies, and blew the boat's horn, but kept our pace until the tide made it unwise to stay inside any longer. Then we gave the Belgians a few last words of encouragement and rowed home. We took with us a soaked Honda generator so Dieter could get it into fresh water.

Next day Dieter worked on the generator while I returned to the wreck. Waterlogged clothes, cushions, and ropes covered the surrounding beach. They'd had six months of food and supplies aboard. Most of it was now worthless, including their hoard of Venezuelan cigarettes, which floated about inside the *Melissa.* With insect repellent and a tent made from a spinnaker, Annie Marie and Jacques had managed to get a little sleep.

They had met three months before in the Caribbean. She was an educator and translator, he a newly retired industrial programmer. Jacques despaired of salvaging even the most valuable equipment, such as the Aries self-steering vane or the Avon life raft. He wanted to pick up what they could carry and return to Belgium, where they could get work. Annie Marie was inclined to fight for their dream, but being a latecomer to it she had less say. "We've decided to stay together," she said. "We can be philosophical. We can make new dreams."

"I hate to think of your boat breaking up and being stripped by fishermen," I said. "The hull's basically sound. The rigging's good. Perhaps Dieter and I should buy the salvage rights from you." The Belgians were amenable, but Dieter decided we lacked the necessary tools and materials.

Dieter and Gerda had helped the Belgians out of compassion, and to be first in line for whatever gear they might abandon. I helped them from compassion, and because they and I now shared a need for transportation to Panama City. The third morning after the wreck, Dieter, Gerda, and I motored there aboard *Seepferdchen* to see what more could be done. When we arrived, with the Belgians was a small man about Dieter's age in a pilot's jumpsuit. "It is Otto Probst!" Dieter said as we rowed his dinghy ashore. "Owner of the island. He is born in Panama, but German parents."

Otto had hosted Jacques and Annie Marie in his trailer near the airstrip, and agreed to purchase the salvage rights for three thousand dollars. He already had several mestizo laborers there. We all worked, lightening the wreck and salvaging gear. English, Spanish, German, and Flemish were spoken equally. Rum and beer flowed freely. When I made my need known, Otto said he would send a Jeep to pick me up the following morning and put me on a plane to Panama City. Jacques thanked me for my help by giving me his slightly damaged sextant and other items. Dieter and Gerda were ecstatic over the coffee and other trivia they came away with. By the end of the day, Dieter was so tipsy he rolled us over while rowing through the surf toward the *Seepferdchen.*

It took most of the following day to travel from beach camp to airstrip. A plane was expected, but nobody knew when. There wasn't any radio or telephone—I just had to wait. The sandflies precluded rest, so I paced the airstrip under the baking sun. A small boy sat in front of a nearby hut, constantly rubbing the sandflies from his bare arms and legs.

"Can you get me a drink of water?" I asked.

He fetched me one.

"Thank you. Say, what are the little flies called?"

"*Chitras.*"

The airplane never came. Otto took me into his trailer, as he had the Belgians. It was a comfortable single-wide. "Help yourself to the food in the kitchen," he said. "I'll be busy with the wreck most of the time."

Like Dieter, Otto had fought with Germany in the war. Military discipline showed in the thin coat of grease he kept on the metal parts of his constant companion, a Beretta semiautomatic rifle. But whereas Dieter never learned Spanish and hated blacks, Otto was proud to be Panamanian. "Panama is my birthright, not a wilderness to be conquered," he said. His employees revered him. He'd built businesses dealing in lumber, shrimp, heavy equipment imports, and lighthouse repair, and was now an advisor to Panama's post-Noriega government. He told me much about the Darién coast, having logged there for years.

For two days I waited with Annie Marie in the trailer, listening for the sound of the airplane. Otto and Jacques updated us on the salvage process. They had patched the holes in the hull and removed the sand and water. The tides were swinging back toward neap—the *Melissa* was no longer jolted by waves at high tide. They wouldn't know until the next spring tides if she could be pulled off. Jacques and Annie Marie were still working out their trauma, and laying plans for the future.

A six-seat plane arrived on the afternoon of my third day at the trailer. I climbed in beside an elderly campesino. The rest of the passenger area was filled with live chickens, dead iguanas, and sacks of *marañones*, the fruit from which cashews are extracted. A half hour later we landed at Panama City's downtown airport. It was March 6, 1991, and I was back in the city that had failed to arouse much affection in me the first time around.

I took a room for eight dollars a day at the Hotel Caracas, on the Plaza Santa Ana, at the southern terminus of the Avenida Central. At almost any hour the plaza was full of workaday Panamanians, passing time. This part of the city was old and poor, but how wonderful to have restaurants and fruit vendors close at hand! I bought fiberglass cloth, sight reduction tables for the sextant, machete, batteries, pens, sunblock, insect repellent, socks, shoes, cap, flight suit (copying Otto), lighters, locks, hammer, screwdriver, acrylic solvent, and a pocket knife. I repaired the sextant, had plywood parts fabricated for a new mizzen mast step to replace the one on the rudder post, studied my Spanish, and wrote another chapter at the Fort Clayton library.

One day, while scrounging information at the Balboa Yacht Club, I met an Englishman named Jim who claimed to have sailed to Buenaventura five years before.

"That's odd," I remarked. "I met another Englishman, named Peter Francis, who sailed to Buenaventura five years ago."

"We sailed together."

They'd been partners, but Jim had given up on Peter. "The man's a sad case, a pathological liar," he said. "Noriega's gunboats didn't sink Peter's boat; his own negligence saw to that. Maybe he was in prison, I don't know. Or maybe it was for something he really did. As for the *Playa de Muerto* treasure, that legend's been floating around here for eons."

The mystery had not been solved, only transformed. Peter Francis was just another bit of human flotsam, accumulated where Man had dug a ditch cutting America into North and South. Others, less extraordinary, were the destitutes who came into restaurants to beg from me while I ate. Their slums defied gravity in not having fallen down yet. They packed the sidewalks with makeshift stalls, forcing foot traffic into the snarled street. They crowded buses, honked horns, preached the Gospel through loudspeakers, clapped and shouted to get you into their stores lining the Avenida Central. They breathed filthy air and maneuvered around mounds of rotting garbage. Their colds and sore throats became my cold, my sore throat. Half the city was unsafe to walk in the daytime, all of it at night. I peered constantly over my shoulder, and ran where it looked iffy. I saw two policemen beat a cowering man with nightsticks, and laugh with pleasure. The newspapers had photos of bullet-riddled bodies on the front page.

It was a city of darkness, but it was a city of life. Its terraces, workshops, and bars teemed with vendors, tradesmen, revelers. Its ancient streets formed a tight, organic whole. Its noise was a grand tapestry of voices and blaring rhythms. Its filth was a by-product of life. And what Panama City now was, so it had been since before English-speaking America was conceived. From here, in 1524, Francisco Pizarro sailed to conquer Peru. I would be retracing his route. The ruins of Panama Viejo and the fallen cathedrals of San Felipe were markers of a more glorious past.

A fan spun on the ceiling of my white cubicle in the Hotel Caracas, drying my sweat as I lay on my cot looking up. Roars of unmuffled trucks filtered through a small, barred window seven feet up the wall. My normal 150 pounds had melted to 130 from the heat and my privations on the island. *Steve,* I said, *you're pushing yourself. That's good, but rest is necessary for work. Let the bogged-down feeling sweep over you, then move on.*

I laced my fingers under my head, palms up, and stared at the fan until the images of my recent experiences—people, places, nature—shifted in fragments, like looking through a kaleidoscope. As in my earlier travel, I had immersed myself in the foreign until only *I* remained constant. I had left my supports, and now the universe outside me was a collage, churning in the metal blades of a ceiling fan. Through a different lens could those shards become a lovely, logical whole? Could any belief system piece it all together? Perhaps, but piecing it together wasn't my concern just then. My concern was to be more intensely myself. In that, I was succeeding.

On March 18, 1991, someone at Otto's office said a plane would leave for the island that afternoon. I settled my affairs, caught a taxi, and was soon skimming high over the Pacific Ocean, its mighty swells reduced to brush strokes on a blue canvas. As we approached the Isla San Jose airstrip, I saw the *Melissa* anchored in the bay. Otto had saved her! The Belgians were gone.

The gentle rhythms of the island again enveloped me. Mona the rock sentinel kept her vigil. Gerda and I collaborated on small tasks, and fell back on each other as someone to care for. The daily struggle to retain even the most modest of comforts absorbed all her energy, and Dieter was too Superman to be tender. I suffered two days of listlessness, then, over the coming fortnight, built a secret compartment for documents and cash, repaired the rudder, installed the new mizzen mast step, and learned how to use the sextant. According to Dieter, the rainy season would begin, as always, at exactly 2:00 P.M. on May 1. Would I reach Tumaco by then?

It was good to live with so little footprint on the land. I came to know the bluish lizard who lived by the shady camp in which *Squeak* and I resided. I recognized individual hermit crabs by their shells. A little red crab snuck into and out of his burrow at my feet, no more nervous than usual. At night larger, blue crabs clicked and scratched under my boat, and Mr. and Mrs. Parrot still flew past the hilltop each day. I fought a long battle of wits against a colony of midget ants determined to ransack my food supply. The individual ant was insignificant, but the colony was a wily, implacable foe. The sandflies worsened in measure with the waxing moon.

New yachts came. Now an old hand, I led shore parties to the sand filter where water could be fetched, and showed them through the farm, to the top of the hill. "That's Mona," I said. "Believe what you will, but Dieter and Gerda pray to her." They turned to the harbor monolith and smiled uncertainly, like tourists disoriented by the gloom within a cathedral.

For a while we had three Finnish and three Swedish sailboats all at the same time, a sort of Scandinavia Week. Others flags were German, French, English, Greek. All were poised for the Milk Run, the trade-wind cruise to the Marquesas. Every time one departed, the anchorage resounded with horns, whistles, bells.

"Good Luck!"

"Bon Voyage!"

"See you in Tahiti!"

I shared my evenings with Zulu, the impetuous South African dog. She added her mournful voice as I sat under the moon on a bench made from a whale bone and piped my favorite tunes. I was lonely, and envious of the laughter that drifted to me from the yachts, but the beauty of the tropical moon over the rock-shattered coast soothed me.

By April 3 the Milk Run season had nearly passed. Only a few stragglers remained to see *me* off. For my work was done. My turn had come.

I hugged Dieter. He helped me launch, and I passed by the *Seepferdchen* to say good-bye to Gerda. I choked back my tears. She had already given me three papayas and a bag of sour oranges. It was hard to let go of my friends, yet I couldn't think of anything to say. I rowed out to the sound of trumpets, until Mona dwindled small, and recorded my good-bye to the island:

Once more I sit on the old whalebone
and look out over the black rock
palm-screened shore
You fill me as well as this poor vessel can hold

Once more the horns of parting sound
this time for me
as I shrink before my friends into the Pacific
as so many others have for me

A jumping off with no return, an emptying

But live in me, shady greens,
scuttle, crabs, and know you no time
grind in my veins, tide-pulsed surf

Hold me in your deep sleep, Mona
if there be such
below your undying gaze

CHAPTER 10

TO BAHIA PIÑAS

Sunblock saved the backs of my hands and tops of my feet from actually burning. Still, the sun hurt wherever it touched my skin, so intense were its rays, while a north wind took me past the southern tip of Isla del Rey, then another ten miles to tiny Isla Galera. It was uninhabited, wild, maybe two hundred acres of forest skirted by rocky precipice, and a clean, sandy beach on its west end. The Las Perlas were visible to the northwest. Otherwise the horizon was empty.

I wanted to sleep on land, not adrift. The beach was exposed, and dropped steeply underwater, so the massive waves didn't break until just before they hit shore. There would be time to land between waves, but once I hit the beach I needed to stick, not get sucked back down as the wave receded. If that happened, the next wave would grind me up. The anchor! I tied it to the bow with twenty feet of line, landed, and at the same instant hurled my anchor up-beach. As *Squeak* slipped backward it dug in, and caught her. Success!

I unloaded and dismantled as necessary to haul *Squeak* to the high tide mark. An hour of daylight remained. I palmed my revolver (Dieter had warned that wild dogs might attack me here) and explored.

Machete-breached coconut husks lay about the palm grove behind the beach—the island was visited, but not occupied. Higher up were bigger trees, with buttress roots that radiated from the trunk, like ten-foot-tall rocket fins. In their crests roosted hundreds of large seabirds with crimson balloons of featherless skin on their breasts. The balloons inflated and deflated in slow cycles. A dragon-like iguana spooked and ran heavily across the dry forest debris. No trails. Portions of the forest floor were burning—a slow, creeping blaze of narrow tentacles, each recorded by a path of scorched earth.

Come morning, I studied the surf. The waves arrived at thirteen-second intervals. One wave reached its highest surge just as the following began to break. Good and bad waves alternated in series, but there was no pattern to the number of waves in a series. Accordingly, I decided to drag *Squeak* down to where the waves barely reached, anchor her, and load her. Then I would stow the anchor, close the hatches, pull her lower on the beach, and launch just as the first of a series of good waves passed the break zone.

I miscalculated by loading her too low on the beach. An unusually large wave rolled her, sucking away my pot, spoon, cap, and notebook containing two weeks' worth of diary, sea shanties, pens and pencils. Replacing these things wouldn't be easy.

Apprehensively, I finished loading and pulled *Squeak* down a little further. I struggled to control her in the smaller waves while waiting for a big one, but the fourth surge sucked her away. I ran to keep up, then jumped aboard as if onto a galloping horse. Her momentum propelled her through the break zone just before the next wave arrived. I grabbed the oars, but the critical point had already passed. I was safely at sea.

Having landed and launched through heavy surf, I had confronted the first of the four things I most feared. The remaining three were to cross a water too wide to see the other side, to land at a native village, and to spend a night adrift.

The second fear now faced me, for the mainland was twenty-five miles away. I sailed into that apparent nothingness with a sinking feeling. How beautiful was the sea, and how terribly empty! *Trust the map, not your eyes*, I said. *Hurry, wind, blow!*

Two hours later the mountainous spine of the Garachine Peninsula began to show. The peninsula didn't creep up from the horizon. It had been there all along, but only with proximity did its blueness differ from that of the sky. The wind slackened and I rowed, wondering how currents were affecting my course. A huge shark followed me lazily, his black fin wagging above the water like the tail of a friendly dog. Whatever his interest, I feared him no more than the dolphins that played around me, or the giant manta ray that passed below, a darkness in the water like the shadow of a passing airplane. The open sea now seemed a benevolent place, but I was anxious to reach land before nightfall. Then a pretty breeze sprang up and got me around Punta Garachine just at twilight. I landed on a gravel beach in the protected water inside. It was high tide, so I didn't have to pull up very far.

Something soft ran across my feet, waking me. What could have gotten inside the cabin? I emptied everything into the cockpit until only I and a nimble brown mouse remained. With nowhere left to hide, he cowered in a corner, eyes reflecting in the beam of my flashlight. He could have been an appropriate mascot for a boat named *Squeak*, but I caught him and put him outside as the day dawned foggy and temperature-less. The new high tide offered easy access back into the water.

Before proceeding southeast along the coast, I had decided to enter the Gulf of San Miguel. That way I could provision at the town of La Palma, test my seamanship before tackling the harborless coast, and explore what on the map seemed a fascinating piece of geography.

First I rowed eight miles northeast across the entrance to Ensenada Garachine, a southern appendage of the gulf. Big shrimpers worked the calm shallows. Outboard-motor canoes passed. The water teemed with jellyfish, like tepid soup. The sky brightened but remained overcast. The air was muggy.

As I proceeded east along the south shore the gulf narrowed, until the north shore became visible. The village of Punta Alegre appeared on my right. Otto Probst had recommended it to me. It was time to do the third feared thing: enter a native village.

The Canal Zone was urban, accustomed to foreigners. Isla San Jose was private, without native population. But here, in the Panamanian hinterland, a white man in a strange boat was unheard of. I dreaded entering the village out of shyness as much as fear of violence.

A crowd was already gathering. I landed among the dugouts that lined the beach, and a sea of dark faces engulfed me. They were male and female, old and young, mostly Negro, some Indian, in ragged, factory-made clothes, no shoes. Some wore shorts, others trousers. Some wore shirts, others didn't. They touched the boat, marveled, laughed, asked rapid questions. Where was I from? Was I all alone?

Feigning nonchalance, I gave each child a pencil from a stash I had bought for that purpose. Some accepted shyly, others wanted more. Now my Spanish was vital. *"Es seguro dejar aqui mi bote?* (Is it safe to leave my boat here?)" I asked.

"Nadie toca nada (Nobody will touch anything)," they assured.

They conducted me to a shady yard of packed dirt. A girl poured water from a pitcher while I rinsed my hands. A woman sat me on a block of wood and fed me a dish of steamed shrimp and rice, deliciously seasoned. After I'd thanked my hosts, a troop of boys guided me through the village: dirt streets, planked shacks, school, health clinic, manual water pumps, seemingly happy, carefree people.

Enough exposure for now. I returned to the beach, where an excited crowd continued to examine *Squeak*. True to their word, nothing had been touched. I launched, relieved to be free of their stares and questions. They stood watching me a long time.

I rowed toward the head of the gulf, through craggy islands and foothills. There was no sign of man in the matted forest that covered the land, nor in the bizarre plants that draped themselves over the streaky granite cliffs. As evening approached, cliffs gave way to mud flats and mangrove, a spindly, weblike tree that grows in saltwater.

I passed the night as dictated by the tides. The tidal range along the Pacific coast of Panama and Colombia is about six feet during the neap tides and sixteen feet during the spring tides. Every twenty-five hours the tides go high, then low, then high, then low. Thus, the cycle lags an hour further each day. During each lunar month the tides go spring, then neap, then spring, then neap. Since it was laborious to haul *Squeak* by myself, beaching for the night was only practical when the highs more or less coincided with sunset and sunrise, especially in spring tides. Also, beaching required a protected shore. This evening the water was calm, but mangrove swamp lined the shore. With my lead line (a string with a weight on the end) I found a spot near shore deep enough not to go dry at low tide and dropped anchor. My net kept out the mosquitoes, but not the *chitras.*

In the morning I approached La Palma, agonizing over how to keep my revolver handy should thieves attack by boat, yet hidden from officials. Would anyone notice that my visa had expired? I rowed with the incoming tide around a sharp bend into La Palma, on the gulf's upper extremity. According to my map, this was the capital of The Darién, one of Panama's ten departments. It had two thousand residents, an airstrip, no road access.

I pulled *Squeak* through thigh-deep mud to the foot of a low sea wall. Opposite were the town hall, soccer field, and military post. People met me, but not many. It felt safe. I washed the mud off my legs and walked the paved street along the waterfront. The people lived on the steep hillside above, in small houses accessible only by foot. The town was clean except for the waterfront, which served as dump.

I made purchases and performed small chores until April 7, when I went to a *cantina* to drink beer and listen to folk songs sung to the guitar. Seated with the musicians was a tall, white Panamanian, about thirty-five years old. His forehead was broad, his eyes steady, his words reserved and thoughtful. *"Mucho gusto,"* he said. "I am Tomas, owner of *El Corredo."* Our conversation was in Spanish, as all would be in the coming months. *El Corredo* was a small wooden freighter, docked there for the night.

"Come with me upriver, to Yaviza," he said, after I had told him my story. "I want you to see it. It's at the end of the line, a real frontier town."

"What about my boat?"

He shrugged. "We'll tow it. Please, I want to share with you the wild beauty of this region which I have made my second home."

I accepted.

Sky and water were dark. I tied *Squeak* to *El Corredo's* stern. She was a chunky, fifty-foot cargo-carrier, tall in the water. She faced into the current, so *Squeak* streamed aft, behind her. I fell asleep.

Shouts woke me. It was still dark. "Untie!" they called. The freighter's engine was running.

"No, I'm going with you. Ask Tomas!" They tried to explain something, then suddenly the freighter's gearbox slammed into reverse. She started backing. *El Corredo's* stern, tall and broad as a barn door, bumped into *Squeak* and started pushing her sideways. I was going to capsize! Frantically I untied and slid out of the way, my heart thumping. Now I understood: to finish loading they were re-mooring, opposite side to the dock. It was an inauspicious beginning, but at their invitation I retied and climbed aboard. Minutes later we were steaming upriver in the misty dawn.

The saltwater gulf slowly became a freshwater estuary, narrowing and winding through jungly floodplain. Of the twenty or so rivers that join to create this estuary, the largest is the Tuira. This river we ascended with the rising tide, past the mouths of tributaries. The Colombian border lay to the south, beyond a line of peaks. We stopped at a haphazard pier of poles and planks to discharge cargo, then continued, now up the Chucunaque River, to Yaviza.

Head of navigation for vessels carrying goods from Panama City, Yaviza was also at the end of the unfinished Pan-American Highway. Even this link was passable only four months out of the year. Yaviza was the trading center of the wild borderlands. Though within the tidal influence of the Pacific Ocean, it was actually closer to the Atlantic, only twenty-five miles northeast across a cordillera. "The Yavizans are mostly blacks from Colombia," Tomas explained. "Such thieves they are! They'll steal an outboard motor, take it apart, and carry it in pieces across the mountains to Colombia. But the small rivers that radiate from Yaviza belong to the Indians. Some are Cunas, a highly organized tribe. Others are Chocó."

The narrow, brown river was the village water source, bathroom, dish sink, washtub, and garbage dump. There was no dock, just a muddy bank. *El Corredo* nudged up to it and bottomed out as the tide dropped. The crew unloaded boxes of flour, cooking oil, soap, and canned goods, then started loading logs and thick, chain-sawn timbers.

We loaded wood for three days. Some of it was hard and blood red. The rest was a heavy yellow wood called *pino.* Father-and-son teams floated the wood down with motor-driven dugouts. Grunting and splashing in the muddy water, they lifted the timbers to the gunwale. Our bare-chested seamen pulled them on deck and passed them down through a roomy hatch to two other men, who stowed them in the hold. There was no machinery, but the men were strong. No one wore shoes or gloves, yet no one was hurt.

Meanwhile, Indians arrived in dugouts laden with plantains. Black idlers thronged the town's dirt streets, shouting and laughing.

One night I went to a bar with Tomas and Gregorio, *El Corredo's* captain. The bartender knew my friends. He sat us at a quiet table and clunked down a bottle of *Ginebra Caballito* (Little Horse Gin) and three glasses. On the wall behind us was a larger-than-life mural of a voluptuous woman in a pose that revealed a pantied crotch, and the words "*Solamente Para Ti* (Only For You)."

I focused on understanding my friends' words, but couldn't help noticing when three mestizas sat at the table beside us. One of them, a pretty woman in her twenties, caught my eye, smiled, extended her arm, and ran her finger down the line of the painted figure's vulva, all in a fluid motion. I turned quickly back to the conversation, but Tomas was watching.

"Try her, Steve," he said, a smile playing on his lips.

"Naw."

"Why not?"

I shrugged.

"How much can you pay?"

"I've only got eight dollars."

Tomas tipped his head for her to come. She stood before him.

"Ocho (Eight)," he said.

"Bien (Fine)."

Five minutes later I was copulating with her on a cot in a lantern-lit back room. *"Rapido, rapido* (Hurry up! Hurry up!)" she urged. "I need to get home to my kids." Her eyes, so alluring before she'd taken my money, were now lifeless. Her hands tugged my back woodenly. "Please, my life is hard." I finished up. I'd have added some little tenderness, but she threw her clothes on and ran out the back door into a heavy downpour, the first of the rainy season. It rained every day after that.

I ate and slept with the crew: wise old Captain Gregorio, Cepallo the purser, Panchi the good-natured cook, three young seamen with beautiful, black bodies, and ten-year-old Jimmy, the ship's boy. They laughed a lot, especially at Jimmy's pranks. The boy loved to boast, and dance to the radio—a sly, suave shuffle. He once bested a town boy in a fight of flailing fists and feet, and returned to the boat panting, strutting, wide-eyed. The men howled and slapped Jimmy's back in an accolade that lasted forever, and that rekindled whenever they were ready to throw back their heads and laugh again. They talked of sex, violence, and money with boyish innocence. "Hey you!" they called. "Gringo! You like Yaviza woman?!" They addressed me thus not out of disrespect, but because they knew no other formula. I was the honored guest of their *patrón.*

Tomas was soft-spoken and erect. After schooling at the University of Bologna, Italy, he had returned to Panama with a passion for leftist politics that almost got him killed, when he and a fellow demonstrator were beaten by a death squad in El Salvador. He became a professor of statistics at the University of Panama, married, started a family. Courage and love of nature balanced his intellectuality. The Darién drew him, and taught him its rough ways. He had purchased *El Corredo* a year or two before, and was trying to make a go of it financially while retaining his teaching post. For hours Tomas shared with me his encyclopedic knowledge of the Darién: its people, politics, economy, plants and animals.

On April 10, I passed the siesta outside the post office, waiting for it to reopen at one o'clock in accordance with a note attached to the door. At two o'clock it was still deserted. While I walked back toward the waterfront a woman waved and shouted, "There you are! *El Corredo* has left!" I ran the rest of the way. *El Corredo,* and *Squeak*, were indeed gone. Happily, two men in a dugout loaded with wood were waiting to pick me up. We caught up with *El Corredo* at the juncture of the Tuira and Chucunaque Rivers, where they were taking on a final boom of logs.

"The tide was falling," said Tomas, laughing. "Gregorio waits for no one when the tide falls, not even me."

"Tide waits for no man," boomed the captain from the door of the pilot house.

The lumbermen had nothing solid to stand on. They sloshed and heaved well into the night while seamen stowed, Gregorio and Tomas directed, and Jimmy danced with some local kids to Latin pop tunes on deck, aft of the cargo hatch. A storm of moths battered about the only light, a twelve-volt lamp affixed to the cabin top. Then the cassette-player was turned off, most went to bed, and strange animal calls floated over the water.

We got underway at two in the morning. I stood at the stern all night, fighting sleep, shivering, ready to cut the towrope with my knife. *El Corredo* was exceeding *Squeak's* hull speed—I feared she would be swamped or damaged.

When we reached La Palma, at dawn, Tomas urged me to stay. "Come on! There's an Indian village I want you to see. It's so beautiful, the people so happy."

"Thanks Tomas. It's tempting, but I've got to go." I pressed his hand, then spread *Squeak's* sails.

A breeze blew us around the bend and out a few miles into the open gulf, where an uninhabited island offered protection. From its treetops and angular clefts emanated insect sounds like a thousand tiny chain saws. The sun warmed my skin. I anchored, swam ashore through cool water, and walked a pebbly beach, naked as Adam. It could have been the first land to lift up through the primordial sea, so new did the world seem, and full of mystery.

The next day I tacked into a stubborn headwind, first of the southwesterlies that would plague me for months to come. At Punta Garachine, where the stowaway mouse had woken me, low tides at dusk and dawn precluded dragging *Squeak* up-beach. I anchored offshore and lay down in the cabin, but the wind changed. Sharp waves jarred me. Currents swung *Squeak* one way, then the other. Rains wetted me. Mosquitoes flew out to bite me. A skin infection was spreading across my face. No sleep.

Morning. Time to tackle the harbor-less, mountainous, nearly uninhabited coast. When could I sleep again? Where would I shelter if a storm came up? Was this really the Land of Pirates the Panamanians made it out to be? I feared for my life, but I wouldn't stop the voyage. And there was only one way: by the harsh ocean rim.

I left the gulf and sailed southeast. I skirted offshore rocks, where the constant southwest swell rose and broke in combers like hills of avalanching water. It got hot—I removed my dark green pilot suit. A sea turtle lolled on the surface, and fixed me with a glassy eye. The sun burned—I donned my whites, and poured water over myself.

As evening approached I lucked onto a beach protected by a cluster of rocks. According to the chart this whole stretch was the *Playa de Muerto*, Peter Francis's Beach of Death. I landed without difficulty and pulled *Squeak* over a short, steep beach to a cool lagoon the size of a swimming pool. Leaf-filtered sunlight dappled its crystal water, and played on its sandy bottom. The pool was fed by a mountain stream that dropped down through a bed of boulders and water-carved rock. An otter passed by on his way to the sea, swimming underwater and emerging at boulders to eye me. Kingfishers of various colors flashed about. Trees of many kinds crowded around, some very large. Fragrant red orchids hung from their branches. The forest floor was shady and pleasant to walk on. I cooked rice and vegetables and slept afloat in the lagoon. It was absolutely calm except at high tide, when the sea gently surged into it, mixing saltwater with fresh.

I remained there another day. Each high tide reconfigured the chute through which the lagoon drained into the sea, and smoothed the sand. Like a snowfield in early winter, the beach was always new. While I rested and performed chores, a species of shore crab caught my attention. They were six inches across their dark purple backs, with violet pincers and orange-and-white legs. When seized by a pincer, they simply detached it and scurried away. Presumably, it was no great bother to grow a new one. I thus acquired a potful of pincers and steamed them for lunch. Evening came again, and large bats flitted about in the gathering darkness. The Beach of Death was full of life; only human life was absent. What would it be like to stay here, as Dieter and Gerda had stayed on Isla San Jose? What natives would eventually find me, and what would they do? Were a treasure chest and a pile of skeletons buried somewhere under my feet?

Underway the next day, sizzling sun alternated with thunderous showers. I constantly changed clothes. The wind was against me. The current was against me, especially further out. I hugged the rocky coast, though the waves, reflecting like sound off a wall, made the water rougher there. I bobbed and sweated only a few yards from the cliff faces which rose straight from great depths; from submerged pinnacles over which the ocean swells heaved and broke; from steep, mossy forests echoing with bird and insect sounds. In a long, backbreaking day I made good only eight miles.

At nightfall I came to a bay called Caracoles (Snails), at the foot of a mountain valley. Its waters boiled with schools of a small, black-and-silver tuna. I pulled *Squeak* up into a stream sheltered from swells. It issued from a swampy forest, at the edge of which I saw canoes and a clapboard shack. A family of Indians stared at me from its doorway and windows. They didn't respond to my greeting. Fear was on their faces.

The next day I arrived in Bahia Piñas (Pineapple Bay). In a corner of the bay I found the Tropic Star, a fishing resort known as the final speck of civilization before crossing the border into Colombia. It was neither large nor luxurious, but its eight Bertram launches were well-maintained and well-skippered. A handful of Europeans were there, paying a thousand dollars a week for some of the best marlin fishing in the world. My goal, however, was to seek a ride back to Panama City. The lesions on my face were now large and numerous. A different kind of sore had spread over my buttocks. In the city I could get medical attention, and purchase materials for various projects to protect my health: a sun awning, a rain fly, seat cushioning.

I tied to the dock and introduced myself to the manager, a middle-aged American woman. She was strangely aloof. "Sorry, you can't stay around here—members only. I can get you to Jaqué, though. That's the village a few miles south of here. You can catch a flight there. If you give our policeman a few dollars your boat should be safe until you return."

I threw a kit together. A launch picked me up. Half an hour later we were crossing the bar at the mouth of the Rio Jaqué, running at twelve knots, keeping pace between bone-crushing breakers forward and astern of us. I could never have entered in motor-less *Squeak*.

No one was able to serve me food in Jaqué, so I bought a pineapple and a package of crackers. I devoured them under a metal shelter at the airstrip, where a short, chubby idiot pestered the waiting passengers with pranks and gibberish. I didn't want to go back to the city.

It was Wednesday, April 17, 1991. A light plane carried me back over the now-familiar coast, covering every five minutes what had taken a day in *Squeak*. I got a room at the Hotel Caracas, made purchases, and went to a public health center. My skin infections responded promptly to antibiotics.

Unable to make the Friday flight back, I resigned myself to a final weekend in Panama City. Still skinny, I gorged on meat and vegetable dishes, juices, and ice cream. The restaurants were open to the street, and vendors traipsed through selling lottery tickets, gum, cockroach poison. Some were run by Chinese who had gotten into Panama by buying visas from corrupt immigration officials during Noriega's time. "We paid $10,000 apiece, everything we had," moaned a woman of twenty-five, slumping onto the seat opposite me, a washrag in her hand. "Now the new government is threatening to deport us." She and her fellow countrymen were bored, dispirited, so unlike other Chinese I'd ever met.

I took long walks through the San Felipe neighborhood, on a peninsula west of the city harbor. Its quiet plazas, ruined cathedrals, and ramparted sea wall felt Mediterranean, timeless. I thought of Traci, and how my sex with her was always desperate, as if I knew it wouldn't last. I was always lonelier in the cities. On Monday I flew back to Jaqué and caught a ride to the Tropic Star.

Before proceeding into Colombia I needed to construct the rain fly and other projects I had bought supplies for in Panama City, so I rowed to the village of Piñas, across the bay from the resort. Three black youths in one-man canoes accompanied me. They were employees at the club, returning home for the evening. We raced, I in my heavier, wider boat with long oars, they with their pointy paddles. It was a draw.

At Piñas the lads showed me how to enter the mouth of a little river, and helped me haul *Squeak* up into the calm water behind the beach gradient. The river was shallow, with a bed of gravel and sand. We landed where the villagers came to fetch water, bathe, and wash clothes. From there a trail led inland a hundred yards, then across a shaky footbridge spanning a muddy slough. The first houses of the village were on the far side of this slough, to either side of the trail. The trail continued another third of a mile to the center of the village, which fronted the bay.

"I need to stay in Piñas awhile," I explained to my three friends. "Is there a place where I can sleep in my boat, but sheltered from the sun and rain?" They ran off, made inquiries, and returned.

"Under the empty house!" they cried. Soon people were packing my equipment, then *Squeak* herself, into the village. We slipped her under a vacant hut on the bank of the slough, by the trail to the river. Being elevated five feet off the ground, it didn't afford standing headroom, but would protect me from the elements. It was to be my home for the next two weeks.

The three nearest houses were Indian, and similarly elevated. These households were headed, respectively, by Cabeza, who was somber and honorable; Adolpho, lighthearted and wistful; and Pedro, the pensive one. These men and their boys became my friends. The wives and daughters were too shy to approach, and tended to speak in their native tongue, Chocoeí, rather than Spanish.

Piñas had no restaurant, but a woman named Andalucia gladly cooked for me. The $1.50 I paid per meal was a rare windfall for her. In her home, a single room with a kerosene lamp, she fed me rice and fish, or lentils and meatballs, or soup. Andalucia was a pragmatist, a reader of cheap novels, a voluptuous woman no longer in the bloom of youth. Her son Ignacio lived with her, one of the three boys who had raced me on my way into the village. He was shamelessly lazy, but Andalucia adored him. Once, in the middle of my supper, the *corregidor* (village official) paused in the doorway, as if to see who was inside. He was a tall, powerful man—I had met him, but never discerned his responsibilities. Before he could turn away, Ignacio sprang to his feet, his face alight, and grabbed his forearm. "This is my father!" he exclaimed, turning to me. The *corregidor* shot us both an annoyed look, as if caught to disadvantage, and stalked away. He hadn't denied Ignacio's claim, but by his expression he wished he could have.

Food availability was my principal reason for choosing Piñas as a site to get some things done. Working in or around the vacant hut, I built a reel on which to wrap my lead line, covered my portable cockpit seat with foam rubber and vinyl, made a plastic rain fly to drape over the boom, and painted a map of the Western Hemisphere on my aft hatch cover, with my route in red, and the words, "*El Viaje de Squeak*" (The Voyage of Squeak). The map would facilitate my innumerable self-explanations. To explain the meaning of *Squeak,* which they could not pronounce, I learned to say, *"Significa el chillido que hace un raton* (It means the shriek a mouse makes)."

Piñas had perhaps a hundred and fifty houses interspersed with groves of coconut palm, mango, and bamboo. Chickens, frogs, and crabs roamed the sandy streets, which flooded during downpours, then quickly drained. Insects much like fruit flies kept trying to fly up my nose. I saw how their larvae infested the open sores on the village dogs, and learned to wave them away.

The population was about half black and half Indian. They didn't noticeably conflict, but they lived differently. The blacks were more gregarious and acquisitive. The only people in town with money were the black store owners and Tropic Star employees. Yet they tended to be idle. Most males did little more than chop firewood, fetch water, and catch fish for the supper table, leaving most of their day free. The blacks' homes were gloomy, wood-frame structures with cement floors, lockable doors, and corrugated metal roofs.

The Indians worked harder but were poorer. Their homes were of sticks and thatch with unenclosable doors and windows. I asked why they were elevated. Cabeza said, "Our ancestors still wander this ground, but they are sort of groggy, they don't see well. We build our houses up, so they won't bump into them." The heart of the home was a chimney-less fire pit in which they burnt green mangrove. Every morning the males marched upriver, their machetes over their shoulders, like rifles. *"Al monte!* (To the hill!)" They usually returned with a bunch of plantains over a shoulder, or suspended from a pole carried by two boys. They wore the same cheap, factory-made clothing as the blacks. They showed no pride of tribe, or knowledge of native handicrafts, yet they considered themselves outsiders to western culture. They never bragged or begged, but addressed me with a shy smile. The high esteem in which they held me almost bordered on adulation. I tried to deserve it.

The Indians grew the local produce, and built the boats. The *panga* was an outboard-motor dugout with strakes added for extra freeboard. The *lancha* was a large, paddled dugout with sharp ends. The *chalupa* was the river dugout, with flat projections at bow and stern on which to stand while poling or paddling. Finally there was the *piragua,* the one-man canoe. Boats were important because they had no wheeled vehicles. Nor was there a water system; everyone fetched from the river and boiled it before drinking. Corn was ground by hand. The only machines were a dozen or so outboard motors and three small generators, one for each store, to power their lightbulbs and refrigerators. There was no post office or telephone.

I was the nearest thing to television. With little else to do, the villagers marveled over me. Everyone lingered to gawk and chat on their way back from the river, their grab-bag assortment of plastic containers balanced on their heads. Kids especially crowded all around and watched, sometimes for hours, while I worked, ate, or read. When would they ever get another chance to see a real live gringo up close? They raved over my possessions. Sometimes they displayed a few English words: "Hello!" "How are you?" Usually they just watched, blankly, as if hypnotized. They blocked my light. To stretch an arm or swing a tool I had to move them first. But it seemed unfriendly to complain. I forced myself to ignore them, to carry on with my work. If after a while I should look up and return eye contact, they would snap out of their trance, explode with embarrassment, white teeth flashing, their voices flying off into laughter. I never quite got used to it.

"Are there Indians in the United States, Estevan?" asked Pedro, the pensive one. It was nearly dark. I was sitting on a log stool, shaping a piece of wood into a handle for my lead line reel. Pedro kneeled in front of me. His arms and legs were bare, his skin dark brown. He brushed back the ebony bangs that dangled over his smiling face.

"Yes, we have Indians. Different tribes."

"How do they live?"

"Oh, not much different from anybody else."

"No?!" For once Pedro's smile faltered. "You have Indians, and they live like Americans?"

"Sure. Well, they're not as well off as the average American. But they own cars, or pickup trucks, houses, the usual stuff. What's the matter, Pedro? Are you feeling sad?"

Usually the sight of my flashlight, better built than any of theirs, or my sturdy food buckets, or stove simply dazzled my Indian friends. This time, Pedro slipped into self-pity.

"I am so poor," he said.

"You're as happy as we are. Maybe more."

"Are we happy, Estevan?"

"Yes."

He smiled again. "Thank you, my friend."

Because I had enough money to buy a bottle of gin, I was highly prized as a drinking partner. I played dominos with Ignacio and other boys in the billiards hall above the store, and learned to slap my domino down with a loud whap! like they did. I learned to avoid certain tedious fellows who, when drunk, thought they could speak English, and pestered me with grandiose, repetitive expressions of brotherhood. It was often necessary to deny people the pleasure of wasting my time along with theirs. The kids, however, were always sweet. I taught them how to play frisbee, and commissioned them to perform small tasks, like guarding my boat while I went out at night. Once I chastised two of them for leaving my frisbee on the beach, and they soon returned with a gift of four mangos as a sign of atonement.

My friends comforted me, but I wasn't one of them. They had each other; Piñas was their home. Whereas everything I saw and heard, being strange, washed through me, cleared my thoughts, removed all but the essential mysteries, like the dualities of love and loneliness, freedom and fear. I felt sad, but rich. I had no one, yet my capacity to love was heightened. I loved my loneliness for its intensity. Just as a positive wire craves to pass its electrons to a negative wire, so did my loneliness burn for love. This burning potential was of value in itself. It found expression in my love of nature, always nearby. No lover held me, but nature held me.

Nature's hold can be whimsical. One evening, while I sat in *Squeak's* cabin with the hatch open, flying ants swarmed. They landed on me, dropped their wings as casually as one might a pair of slippers, then crawled inside my clothing. At first I laughed; their tickles were almost sensuous. Ultimately I was forced to crouch inside, close the hatch, disrobe, and pick the squishy bugs from my clothes.

Curious how man and nature interacted outside the village, I followed Pedro to his *monte*, that is, the patch of forest he cultivated. It was an hour's hike away, on the side of a steep hill. He had cleared by machete and fire, sewn seeds in a seemingly random fashion, and never weeded, but simply harvested things as they ripened. That day Pedro dug up some yucca, all but lost on the brushy slope, and climbed trees to harvest avocado, papaya, guava, and a foot-long, woody pod containing sugary sweet "beans." On the way back we encountered a large, green serpent in the trail. It raised his head, and shook a small tail rattle. Pedro threw a branch—it crawled away. "Very poisonous," he said. "Death comes quickly."

But the mosquitoes and the microorganisms in the river posed a greater health risk than snakes. My mosquito net kept the large, iridescent blue mosquitoes from stinging me at night, and I still ate two malaria pills a week. I managed to avoid drinking unboiled river water until Andalucia negligently served me a tainted Kool-Aid. The next day I came down with a diarrhea which I identified, by the rotten-egg smell in my mouth, as amoebic dysentery. I'd had the same thing in Colombia in 1973, when I traveled that country for six weeks with my brother Mike.

"Go see the doctor," advised Andalucia.

"What doctor?"

"El señor medico. He's down on the beach today."

He was a roving homeopathic researcher, a kindly, middle-aged Colombian. "Everything I know, I taught myself," he said. "I travel around gathering traditional cures. When I can help the people, I do. They call me 'doctor'," he laughed. "I'm not one, of course. But you can't blame them for coming to me when there is no one else." He prescribed massive amounts of lemon juice mixed with Alka-Seltzer. In the following four days I consumed forty-five lemons, and was cured.

By May 7, I was ready to continue southeast across the international boundary. Many had warned that the Colombians would kill me. I made light of it. "No, *I'm* going to kill *them!"* I would say, and gnash my teeth. But their predictions filled me with gloom. Aside from hiding my cash and passport in the compartment I had built on Isla San Jose, and keeping my pistol handy, what could I do? I had racked my brain for defensive strategies, and always came up with the same answer: a man with a motor-less boat and a snub-nosed revolver is at the mercy of men with faster boats or longer-range weapons. Courage and luck would decide it. Or karma?

I purchased rations, hauled everything to the river, and loaded. At high tide I exited the river mouth, waving good-bye to my friends. They stood a long time, watching me go.

CHAPTER 11

TO BAHIA SOLANO

I needed to mail letters at Jaqué, but surf blocked the river mouth and pounded heavily on the beach beyond. Ultimately, the beach bent around like a fish-hook, the tip of which was a rocky promontory. In the cove thus formed I landed and pulled *Squeak* past the high tide line as darkness fell.

To my knowledge, no one had witnessed my approach. Hoping that night would hide her, I left *Squeak* unguarded and walked toward town, about two miles away. The beach was wide and sandy. The sky was overcast and dark, as always during the rainy season.

Halfway to Jaqué, a flashlight shone toward me from up ahead. I reciprocated with a flash from my own light, and kept walking until I made out a small black man with sharp features. He was watching the waves, probably as a preliminary to going fishing.

"Buenas noches," I said. "I need to find the postmaster. I met him in Piñas once, his name is Jaime. But I don't care to enter the town alone at night. Will you guide me there for two dollars?"

"It's not worth it to me," he answered. "And you shouldn't walk this beach alone at night. Two years ago a gringo was killed and buried on almost this exact spot by someone assuming he had money."

That convinced me the letters weren't so important. "Never mind then," I said, and started walking back toward *Squeak*, ready to run once I was out of sight.

"Wait!" he said. "Okay, I'll do it. My name is Oscar. You can trust me."

Hoping I could, and that the story of the buried gringo had been merely an attempt to raise the fee, I followed him up a trail. It led to the airstrip, to one side of which was his house. It was an old U.S. Army ammunition bunker, window-less, with thick cement walls. Oscar's surprisingly attractive wife and small children entertained me with light conversation just outside, while he changed into long pants and a clean shirt. I began to feel better about him.

It was Friday night. Electric lamps lit the main streets. Under one lamp we found several tables, and people of all ages milling about. The mood was festive—lottery tickets were being sold. One of the vendors was the post-master, a gentle, rather effeminate man.

"Hola, Jaime," I said. "Remember me?"

"Estevan! Que tal? (What's going on?)"

"Finally leaving for Colombia. Here, could you post these letters for me?"

"Of course. Where's your little boat."

"Not far," I whispered, anxious that not even he should know.

Oscar and I had a couple beers, then returned to his house. He changed back into his shorts and sweatshirt while his wife served me starchy, orange-red fruits the size of golf balls, with hard pits inside.

"I can find my way back alone," I said.

"No, I must come with you."

Oscar accompanied me to the dark beach, and down it toward *Squeak*. He was business-like, reserved. Crabs scattered as we advanced across the firm, damp sand. The tide had risen, forcing us to wade at one point, where jagged bedrock protruded into the surf.

I was relieved to find *Squeak* unmolested, but uneasy that anyone should know my whereabouts. "You won't tell anyone where I am, will you?"

"Don't worry. I've come to fish. I'll be close by." Sure enough, he pulled a *piragua* out of the brush, launched, and lit an oil lamp. He fished long into the night, floating just offshore, while I slept as well as the *chitras* and my overwhelming sense of caution would permit.

When the sun rose I hauled *Squeak* into the water, rounded the promontory, and continued along the coast. After my trek through the shadowy night, the sea seemed bright and stark. Studying its undulations, I noted two types: ocean swells and local waves. The former were constant, of long interval. They advanced from southwest, the direction of prevailing wind, in long, straight rows. Hardly noticeable in deep water, they rose like monsters upon entering shallows, steepened until they broke, and carried on as rolling breakers.

Superimposed over the swells were the locally generated waves. More chaotic and variable, they responded rapidly to changes in direction and intensity of wind. Since the winds near the equator are light, these waves posed no great hazard, but they required me to continually counterbalance and brace, which tired me. The chop and *Squeak's* tippyness precluded standing up, so my legs weakened and my buttocks became sore. Also, *Squeak* lost much of her momentum plowing into these short, steep, waves.

Anxious to reach a haven before nightfall, I developed techniques for dealing with the headwinds. In light breezes I lowered the mainsail and rowed. With a little more wind it was faster to tack to windward and row at the same time, rudder blade and lee board down. For this maneuver I lashed the tiller at such angle as provided neutral helm, sat off-center to balance the boat, and looked over my shoulder to check my course. When the wind exceeded about six knots I unlashed the tiller and sailed, grateful for a respite from rowing. The wind varied, forcing me from one technique to another. The constant rearranging of gear irritated me.

The currents were also unfavorable, and more difficult to gauge. The best indicator was to come close to an exposed rock, stop, and see how I moved relative to the rock. In shallow bays there wasn't much current, but off points of land and in deep water there was. My Pilot Chart warned, "Northwest currents of up to 1.5 knots." It seemed greater than that—rowing *Squeak* at three knots I sometimes made no noticeable progress. To minimize the problem I hugged the shore, and followed the curve of bays rather than cut from point to point. I often rowed within twenty feet of the swell-washed rocks.

The cliffs were typically a hundred feet tall, backed by jungly ridges and mountains. Streams fell from high places in slim, white lines. The water didn't free-fall, but rather adhered and curved with the rock. At sea level the waves had eroded caves and arches. Beaches had formed in the larger bays. Here coconut palms grew: thin, gently curving stems capped by massive, radiating fronds and clusters of green or yellow nuts. Sometimes a deserted Indian hut nestled in these groves.

As night fell the coast became very irregular, in a small, tight pattern. Someone had told me about an Indian hamlet called Cocolito, the only place in that stretch where a boat can land, but where was it? I hugged the cliffs, skirted the foaming rocks, and peered into each concavity. A rainstorm hit. Lightning lit the jagged coast, brightly but briefly. Otherwise, only the patches of white foam penetrated the gloom, each warning me of a rock that could stave in *Squeak's* soft belly.

Just as it seemed hopeless, a fire appeared onshore, above a cove. I approached until I felt the waves rising up—too much surf to land in the dark. I anchored in the center of the cove. It was barely big enough for the swing of my anchor line. Relieved to have again avoided spending the night adrift, I draped the rain fly over my boom and slept.

Daylight revealed a semicircular beach, topped by two handsome, almost wall-less huts. The land behind the beach was low. Anchorage and lowland were sheltered from the sea by a hill of bedrock. A devil's garden of rocky crags lay partly submerged to the northwest, where I'd come from.

Upland was the American continent at the very point where the Isthmus of Panama joins South America: a tall, narrow, forest cordillera.

A bare-chested youth ran down from a hut and paddled out to me in his *piragua.* "Come ashore with me," he said. "My father wants to meet you."

"Bueno," I said. His canoe was tippy and had almost no freeboard, but he effortlessly brought us in.

His father, Leonide, was an Indian of about forty in neat, western dress. "So you're sailing to Colombia?" he said. "Very dangerous—bad men there. You can stop in Punta Ardita, it's several hours from here by *piragua.* The people are harmless. But don't stop in Juradó, the next village. They're evil there. And whatever you do, circle wide around Cabo Marzo (March Cape). I mean far, far out to sea, to avoid pirates. They will be looking, and they're merciless. Then don't go ashore until you reach Bahia Solano (Sunny Bay)."

I looked at my chart, which I'd brought ashore with me. "But Bahia Solano is sixty miles away!"

"Yes, very far."

Meanwhile, elsewhere in the hut, two women and a girl cooked, several children played, and a young couple kept to themselves behind a screen. The women fed me fried fish and plantain. I gave out pencils.

"Come on," said my young canoeist friend after I'd eaten. "I'll show you my grandparents." Together with two male cousins, we walked to another hut. Inside, an old woman tended a cook fire while a man sat on a stool, whittling a stick. "He is one hundred years old," said the boy. The old folks smiled serenely, but spoke no Spanish. His tan skullcap and her gray dress were hemmed with straps of colored embroidery.

We continued across a gravelly stream to the extensive coconut grove for which the hamlet was named. They had more than they could ever eat, or drink, since they valued the water more than the flesh. One of the cousins climbed a tree, his knees pointing straight out to either side, bare feet under his buttocks, gripping the trunk. With each upward advance he paused to stick his machete into the trunk a little further above his head. He cut several nuts loose—they dropped heavily. My friend chopped off a portion of a husk, revealing the hollow core. "Drink one now," he said. The water was milky, almost sweet. "Here, take two more with you."

Back at the main hut, I asked Leonide how far to the Colombian border.

"It's just here," he said, waving his arm, finger outstretched. "Before Punta Ardita."

"Are there trails there?"

"We go only by *piragua.*"

"Do many boats pass here?"

"No. We hope you will stay for a while."

"I'd like to," I said, "but it's ten o'clock. I'd better leave now if I'm to reach Punta Ardita before nightfall. Thanks for everything."

"Que le vaya con Dios (May you go with God)."

I left Cocolito, and Cabo Marzo immediately came into view, twenty-five miles south, a mountainous peninsula projecting mightily into the sea. Adverse wind and current made it impossible to cover more than a mile per hour, so I had plenty of time to study each rock, each shattered islet. The shore was a lofty wilderness. There was no marker where I estimated the Colombian border to be. The sun slowly arced, overheating me. A marlin leaped, a glassy-eyed beauty in white, silver, green, and black.

Evening approached. I rowed harder. The sea became rough from the sustained south wind, and from the swells that reflected off the cliffs, superimposing a second layer of waves. My hands hurt, my butt hurt. Darkness fell. Still no campfire, no Punta Ardita. The coast was a maze of sea stacks and booming foam. I poked among them, hoping for a cove large and shallow enough to anchor, but the swells threatened to dash me on the cliffs. My chart wasn't detailed enough to navigate in the dark. This time I had no choice but to distance myself from the coast, to not be blown onto rocks while I slept. This was the fourth of my four fears: to spend a night adrift.

I rowed directly offshore for two hours. Then I tied lines to my bailing bucket and water bags and threw them overboard to act as sea anchors, that is, to hold *Squeak* in place relative to the water. I secured everything, lay down, and repacked my gear around my body to hold me in place despite the motion. I felt precarious—a capsize with the hatch unsecured and my gear loose would be disastrous. But I slept well.

In the morning it appeared *Squeak* hadn't drifted very far. There no longer seemed to be any point in going to Punta Ardita, so I steered for Cabo Marzo. I hoped to round this cape four or five miles offshore per Leonide's advice, then proceed to Bahia Solano, the next safe place. I worked my sails and oars all the hot, quiet day. No other boats. The sky was blue, gray, pink, white. All day I toiled, but my headings to land features never changed, which meant I hadn't moved. I rowed harder. It didn't help. The current was too strong out here, while to go closer was to risk being seen by pirates. I despaired. I began to doubt my capacity to complete the voyage. Night came, and with it a shore breeze. I sailed for hours toward the Cabo Marzo light, even catnapping with the tiller lashed. My wristwatch had died in Piñas, so I don't know what time it was when I finally dropped sail and went to sleep.

At dawn I woke to a strong south wind, a bad sea, and thick overcast. My location was about the same as it had been the previous morning. The chart showed 1,500 fathoms. I couldn't fight the Humboldt Current in this deep water. To go forward I had to go closer to shore. That would put me close to the village of Juradó, the supposed den of cutthroats. Whatever pirates awaited me at Cabo Marzo would have an easy time of it, because the only way to round that cape was to stay within a stone's throw of it.

The wind blew up until I had to reef, then a rain fell, killing visibility and chilling me into shivers. I lowered sail and clambered back inside. Not bothering to rearrange the cabin, I lay contortedly on top of my gear, barely able to move, and ate moldy bread, peanut butter, and a tin of prepared chicken.

Rain and wind stopped. I pried myself out. A muggy fog hid the land. The water was silver-gray, calm, undulating. Only a quarter-mile radius of ocean was visible—I was at its center. Nothing else floated there, nor flew overhead. I had the eery urge to get out and walk, so metallic was the water. I rowed by compass, and the fog burned away, starting from the zenith and working down to the horizon, until only the muggy heat remained, now stoked by the glinting sun.

Moving again! I reached the base of the cape and worked my way seaward along its lofty flank, until it disintegrated in a vast confusion of cliff-sided islets. The peninsula's tip had crumbled into a labyrinth of land and sea, projecting seaward another four miles before tapering to nothing. But I didn't have to go that far. Through the channel between the mainland and the first islet I saw, like a new world, the next major cape: Punta Solano, thirty-eight miles further south. I entered the crevice-like channel. The swells surged through, raising and dropping me relative to the glistening walls on either side. Further in the surge dissipated, leaving the water calm. Seaward, waves broke on the far side of a low screen of rock. Patches of sand drifted over bedrock and boulders. Here the channel was about seventy yards wide, fifteen feet deep. The bottom was a flat, pebbly plain.

Thankful for this unexpected haven, I anchored and dove. The water was warmer than in Panama. Uh-oh, the protective stainless steel strip running down the centerline of *Squeak's* bottom was coming off. I would have to resolve that in Bahia Solano. I pried a scallop off the bottom, and speared a brown triggerfish. I cooked them with potatoes, ate, and still had an hour of sunlight left to dry my gear. After three days and two nights of bumping around, the calm water soothed every cell in my body.

The drone of a motor—a powerboat, entering the channel! I jerked up, grabbed my revolver, and held it low, out of sight. But the boat was full of what appeared to be recreational divers, not pirates. We stared at each other as they passed.

I calmed down again, and did some figuring. Since leaving Piñas I had averaged eleven miles per day, a third of what I used to cover on the North American rivers. I had spent $3,600 of my $6,200 in traveler's checks, $13 per day on average. I had been in Panama three months, triple my original estimate. How long would I be in Colombia?

Cabo Marzo! I felt as if I'd climbed Mt. Everest and found the Garden of Eden on top. As I drowsed in bed under slanting sun, the images of the past few days jostled in my subconscious. Sea-beings, watching me from below! I shook myself awake, picked up my notebook, and struggled to capture the sensation of…

Rowing, rowing on the roof
of a world that's made of water—
who are they below who raise
their heads as at the sky?

They who ask me of the land
"Does a falling tree where no ear hears
still make the crashing sound?"

I answer:
"Without me do searocks still bare like teeth?
the ocean suck and seethe?
oh! and under do your talons
still yearn to stave and scratch?"

They say:
"We hear of handsome Indian boys
like Captain Cook's Hawaiians
thick of chest, strong of arm
open-faced and new
born of sea, born of me
tell me, is it true?"

And I:
"It's true that giants walk
the land with giant steps
and fire burns that never can
deep down within your depths

but tell me now where sleeps the serpent
of black and yellow stripes
who swims your sea along with me
and when I call him, dives?"

But they unknown can only ask
so on I row and wonder
at seacaves crashing black inside
and pelicans in diagonal
in my sky above theirs

I sailed from Cabo Marzo under a brilliant morning sky. The coast still provided no shelter, only precipices, stranded fragments of green-capped rock, and the booming of swells in crevices. But the current no longer gripped me, and a breeze came up with just enough westerliness in it to sail, close-hauled, toward the entrance to Bahia Solano, the place Oscar had recommended. I now made out that bay as a pocket opened toward me, sheltered from the sea by Punta Solano, a peninsula projecting north like a barb from the generally west-facing coast. Another bay opened to my left. I cut straight across, eight miles from shore. The land was all mountainous jungle—no clearings or roads. I was making good time! Where two days before I was desperate, now I looked forward to my first port of call on the Pacific coast of Colombia. What would it be like?

At dusk, still short of the bay, I pointed *Squeak* at one point of land, then another, and noted the bearing of each from the compass affixed to my hatch cover. I then drew on my chart the reciprocals of those bearings as lines emanating from the respective points. Theoretically, I was where the lines intersected.

In the morning I fixed my position again. I had drifted three miles north and three miles west. Still, Bahia Solano was only ten miles away! I felt as if I had passed a test, and was now truly a sailor. With that realization came an intoxicating sense of freedom: the ability to go, with *Squeak,* anywhere in the watery world, unhindered, self-reliant.

Freedom from man, but never from nature. The breeze died—I dropped sail. It returned—I hoisted again. It died—I rowed. If I reacted promptly to each change of wind, I spent too much time sail-handling. Squadrons of brown pelicans flew close overhead; the sound of the air in their wings approximated that of a distant train heard by an ear pressed to the track. Marlins or sailfish jumped happily from the sea. And I saw more speedboats.

For four days the fear of pirates had followed me like a cloud. An official at the U.S. Consulate in Panama City had said the Colombians would "kill me for my shoes." Mike Pine, my Navy buddy, warned that crews were being murdered on the high seas, their boats used to smuggle drugs. Yachtsmen sailing from the Panama Canal to Ecuador stayed a hundred miles off the coast, and ran with their lights out at night. I had kept going on a hunch that most of the fear was paranoia.

But the human mind is impressionable, and each approaching speedboat brought surreal dread. The boat came near, and I imagined scenarios: what they would do, what I would do. It was a daydream, and I was the director of the dream, so I never died. When a fatal bullet was fired I stopped the action, considered alternatives. I stopped the bullet but I couldn't stop the dread, because the approaching boat was real, would reach me in a few seconds, and then I wouldn't be the director of the dream.

I didn't particularly fear accidental death because I had years before accepted the outdoorsman's responsibility to understand natural laws, and his motivation for exposing himself to them. I knew my motive: intensity of experience. The intensity was worth the risk. That calculation came automatically, but the danger posed by people seemed different. Nature is unintelligent and orderly, therefore predictable. Killers are intelligent, therefore malicious, unpredictable. I hypothesized that it was preferable to die by my own incompetence or bad luck than to be murdered. But with passing time I realized one danger was simply more familiar than the other. My responsibility was the same: weigh the odds, and minimize risks.

I'd been keeping my sails down as much as possible, since a small sailboat in the distance might be mistaken for a yacht, and I kept my stainless steel .38 Special at hand whenever a speedboat approached. Some passed near, but none attacked, nor looked like pirates, nor looked like they themselves were worried about pirates. Still, I kept my gun on the seat beside me, and often touched it. It felt good in my hand.

In the entrance to the bay, a cluster of spires protruded from the sea, like a fern whose fronds were fifty-foot needles of rock. I passed them and saw, at the head of the bay, the town of the same name: Bahia Solano. Along the shore to my right, modern vacation homes intermingled with indigenous dwellings such as I'd seen in Panama. Two motor yachts lay at anchor. White people snorkeled in the bay—they stopped on the surface to stare as I passed.

These signs of affluence astounded me. On the Panamanian coast, the few people I had seen lived primitively. Now I felt as if I had passed a forbidden frontier to discover a land of surprising wealth, just as Francisco Pizarro, following the same path almost five centuries before, had discovered the Inca Empire. After so long in the Third World, this outpost of First World sophistication appealed to me as a haven in which to prepare for the remainder of the voyage to Buenaventura, the first place with a road leading to the interior of the continent, or Tumaco, the second place. Of late I was increasingly inclined to use Buenaventura as my jumping-off point for truck transport across the Andes, to the headwaters of the Amazon.

Besides the usual provisioning and letter-writing, I hoped to add a shallow keel to *Squeak* in Bahia Solano. Due to the absence of bulkheads in the cabin, she was alarmingly flexible in her belly, the spot most likely to hit a rock. I hadn't added the keel originally because I wanted to minimize draft, but now strength seemed more important. The loose stainless steel strip decided the matter, because to secure it I needed something to screw into. To build the keel I needed a workplace, tools, and wood.

The two yachts, a coastal freighter, and several smaller boats lay clustered around a fuel dock on the right side of the bay, near town. I rowed up to a speedboat in which sat three young men. *"Hola!"* I said, in my best Spanish. "I'm a *norteamericano,* on my way south, and I need to stay here awhile to work on my boat. Do you know anyplace where I can haul out?"

They wore bright shorts and sport shirts. After so long with blacks and Indians, their skin seemed nearly white. They gaped a moment, asked a flurry of questions, then the one at the wheel, a baby-faced mestizo in his mid-twenties, turned toward town. He stabbed a blunt finger toward a large house. "Go there, we'll pull you out."

It felt safe. "Okay, meet you there!"

We each landed on the beach, then the four of us carried *Squeak* up a concrete boat ramp to a paved, cyclone-fenced compound behind the house. The compound contained a sportfishing boat on a trailer, two jet-skis, piles of lumber, and a generator shed. The house was two-story, not quite finished, with sophisticated cement work, covered verandahs, and woodwork left unpainted.

"My name is Juan Carlos," said Baby Face. "And this," he waved proudly at the house, "is La Cherna, so named for the local game fish. I'm getting it ready to open as a fishing resort. We plan to accommodate two couples at a time—lodging, excellent food, and the best fishing in Colombia!"

Juan Carlos was short and patricianly handsome under a layer of fat. "Allow me to introduce my associates," he said. "This is Casañas." A black laborer with a long, patient face reached forward to shake my hand. "Zuly, my jewel. What would we do without her excellent cooking and cleaning?" A beautiful young black woman smiled at me self-confidently. "You already know Nelson, my fellow *Paisa.*" One of the three that had helped me carry *Squeak* up the ramp, a tall, slim youth with a sharp face, grabbed my hand and shook it, then threw his head back and laughed at my quizzical expression.

"What, my friend? You don't know what a *Paisa* is?"

"No."

"*Paisas* are people from the department of Antioquia, the capital of which is Medellin. They say we possess *malicia indigena.*"

"What? You're malicious?"

"More like sly, sly like an Indian," said Juan Carlos, smiling. "We're famed for our business talents, creativity, and aggressiveness. *Paisas* control all of Colombia's industries, including narcotics. You've heard of the Medellin cartel?"

"Of course. So you're a narco-trafficker, Juan Carlos?" I asked.

"No no!" he tutted, wagging his finger. "Now come here, I want to show you my kitty."

Juan Carlos led me to a small cage under a ramp of concrete steps. Inside, an ocelot paced frenetically. It was half again the size of a house cat, with a yellow coat and black spots. Juan Carlos poked a finger through the wire mesh. The cat lunged and stood, paws resting on the mesh, claws wiggling through the openings. Juan Carlos tapped the claws' sharp tips—the cat pressed its muzzle against the mesh, fangs gnawing the wire, tongue licking. "Pss! pss! *Gatica! Gatica!*" He laughed and cooed. "My pet! Isn't she a beauty!"

His gaiety faded to a polite smile. He turned to me, eyes slightly narrowed. "Now, you say you designed and built your boat yourself?"

"Yes."

"Then you have skills. You're obviously an intelligent gringo, or you wouldn't have made it this far. This is my proposition. You pay for the groceries during your stay here. Don't worry, only you, Zuly, and I will usually eat in the house. Also, do a little work for me. I need a larger ocelot cage. I want you to design it. Also, I need you to advise me on how to repair the launch. The fiberglass is damaged and the foam flotation has soaked up water. Nobody here knows how to do such things. In exchange I'll give you a spare room, access to my table saw, plane, and other tools, and whatever wood you need to repair your boat. So, Estevan, is it a deal?"

"You bet it is."

"Good! Come then, I'll show you around."

He settled me into a small bedroom with its own bath, then brought me into the spacious front room. Zuly, the maid, served fish soup. The tall ceiling, supported by exposed beams, continued forward to shelter a porch deck. The wall between room and deck was only waist-high, allowing ample air, and an expansive view of the bay.

"The soup's fantastic, Zuly," I said. "I'm a lucky man to be placed in your care."

She glanced up from the kitchen countertop, where her strong, shapely hands patted corn flour into griddlecakes. She flashed me a half-smile, half-grimace. "Oh go on," she said.

Night having fallen, Juan Carlos took me for a walk through town. The streets were muddy and unlit, but some of the buildings were substantial, with crisply stuccoed walls and factory-made doors and windows. He showed me the telephone office—finally I could call home—and a new, three-story hotel of whitewashed masonry.

"The owner is Pablo Escobar, head of the Medellin cartel," said Juan Carlos. "He never comes here, though." Soft light emanated from the doorways and windows of its street-level bar. The bartender was one of the skin divers I had seen in the bay: a suave, pensive fellow with gentle eyes and wavy, brown hair.

"Have an *aguardiente,* it's on the house," he said, and poured a shot of a clear liquid that smelled of licorice. I remembered it from 1973: an anise-flavored brandy.

"Thanks," I said, and sipped. "Mm, this is good."

Juan Carlos and I were the only customers. We sat at a table by the window. "And thank you for taking me in, Juan Carlos. Bahia Solano seems so quiet and safe. I still can't get over it."

"May your time here be profitable," he said.

In the morning I walked to the office of the Port Captain, a black man in a tan shirt and tie. "No," he said, "We have no customs or immigration procedures here. Just give me your boat papers to hold during your stay." I gave him the registration my brother had sent me, then continued through town. The locals were black, some with added Indian blood, producing skin the color of dark honey. Culturally they resembled Panamanians. The more important businesses, however, particularly those catering to the developing tourism industry, were run by whites and mestizos from Colombia's interior.

"Some of us *Paisas* and *Bogotanos* (residents of Bogotá, the capital) come to build vacation homes or make money. But my friends and I came for the relaxed atmosphere, the pristine environment." The speaker was Camilche, the tall, happy-go-lucky owner of a homemade, open-air bar called *Los Helechos* (The Ferns). Camilche served drinks, cooked food, and played British and American rock on his stereo for the clique of alternative-lifestyle types that made up his clientele. There was André, the notary public, who looked like a Latin version of Michael Jackson, and whose true vocations were dance, Tarot, and African mysticism. White-haired Gustavo, a Chilean dramatist who had fled to Colombia when President Allende was overthrown, treated us to homemade marañon wine. Fernando, the hard-drinking comic, once donned a huge Afro wig and wandered around town, his arms up in a V, fingers waving the peace sign. When sober he read novels. Adriana, the town beautician, had brown eyes and a childlike beauty that filled me with longing. Long after the rest of the village had gone to sleep, she loved to talk and laugh and share tender thoughts with her friends. After my grim passage through the border lands, such sharing was tonic to me.

One afternoon while I drank a Poker Beer with them, for they rarely seemed to work, a slender young man with curly hair rode up to Los Helechos on a bicycle. The exterior wall being only a waist-high partition of sticks nailed vertically, he stopped just outside from where I sat and excitedly asked, in English, "Are you the person who sailed down from Panama?"

"Yes."

"Incredible! What, from Panama City? With no motor? How do you navigate?" His voice was gentle, yet electric. His face reminded me of Christ's in a small portrait I'd seen in the Sistine Chapel when I was nineteen. Half-mesmerized by his hazel eyes, I answered questions. Then Juan Uribe, for that was his name, told me he had a degree in marine studies from Rhode Island and was developing new techniques for catching the local fish. He later gave me valuable information about the coast ahead, and some extra anchor line.

My work at La Cherna went smoothly. I propped *Squeak* upside-down on a sawdust floor under a shed, then glued in place a 1"x1.5"x7' keel from a hard red wood called *abarco,* shaped it, fiberglassed it, and screwed the stainless steel strip in place. This took ten days. I then designed a new ocelot cage and helped with some land-levelling. Meanwhile the meals were tasty and the house stayed neat. Every few days I asked Zuly to be my girlfriend, and she good-naturedly declined. I resumed the stretching-and-breathing exercises I did whenever ashore. To condition my lower body I ran each morning to the ice plant and back, a mile each way, past men and boys carting dripping blocks of ice by wheelbarrow, bicycle, and horse.

One day Juan Carlos and I played frisbee on the sand flat that each low tide exposed in front of La Cherna. He soon became too winded to go on, so I continued alone down the beach, throwing the frisbee up into the wind and catching it, boomerang-style, past a soccer game, to the mouth of a small river emptying into the bay on the far side of town. Inside the mouth, boats lay pulled up around a wooden building with a sign that read "*Gasolina*" in childish, hand-painted letters. A woman sold fried dough and meats from a mobile stall. I crossed the river on a shaky footbridge from which black children fished, and toured a recently built slum. The people lived in shacks on the margin of a mangrove swamp that once encompassed the river mouth, but was being cleared and filled. Tiny sloughs snaked here and there. They dried out with each low tide, and served as driveways and parking lots for dugout canoes.

That night, back in my room, I unfolded my map of Colombia onto the floor. The yellow-shaded area along the Pacific coast was labeled "El Chocó." Like the neighboring department of Darién, in Panama, the yellow area was covered with the squiggly brown lines that meant mountains. Thunder crackled. Rain pounded outside the open window. I looked at the short, steep rivers the map showed entering the ocean every few miles along the coast, and visualized them rising under this rain, shedding the torrents that fall on these mountains throughout the rainy season. Like ambassadors of the rain forest that pressed in around Bahia Solano, thumbnail-sized crabs snuck under the door into my room. Finger-sized geckos crawled the walls. I opened the door, and pondered again the fist-sized toads that sat under the electric lights illuminating the verandah. They were slow of body, and so numerous it required care not to step on them. But their tongues were a blur. Now and then a toad would convulse, and a moth that had been nine inches away would find itself clamped inside a cavernous mouth.

The keel was done. My obligations to Juan Carlos were fulfilled. On my last night in town I drank Poker Beer and *aguardiente* at Los Helechos with Adriana, Camilche, and Fernando. We listened to Tracy Chapman, the black American singer, and I tried to translate for them her sorrowful lyrics. The lights in the houses went out, but we carried on for hours. The sky cleared. Moonlight filtered through broad leaves, half-illuminating the village. The still air smelled faintly of flowers. A young soldier on night patrol strolled by on the far side of the street. "Hey, lonely man, come have a drink with us!" said Camilche. The soldier hesitated, then came over and leaned his rifle against the wall. For ten minutes he added his polite laughter to that of my friends. His uniform was olive green, baggy. He continued his rounds, and the quiet grew ever deeper. From across the darkened street came a wailing animal sound—it rose in quick desperation, then tapered slowly, slowly, like the final chords of a Chopin dirge. "A weasel killing a hen," said Adriana, sadly.

In the morning Adriana helped me buy provisions. She was sweet as a child, yet voluptuous. I hugged her. "Thanks for caring for me," I said. Casañas helped me launch *Squeak*. I anchored near the Port Captain's Office and swam in for my *zarpe* (permission to weigh anchor).

"I've received reports of piracy around Buenaventura," he said. "I suggest you put *Squeak* on a coastal freighter rather than proceed alone."

I sighed. *"Gracias, señor,* but I'm determined to complete the voyage under my own power."

He frowned. "You'll have to sign something then." He prepared a note to the effect that he had warned me and whatever happened was not his responsibility. I signed it, then swam back to the boat, holding my *zarpe,* boat papers, and clothes up out of the water with one hand. People gathered on shore to see me leave, but none were my close acquaintances. Then I saw Casañas watching me from the high porch of La Cherna, with the passivity of a Sioux warrior watching a wagon train roll across the prairie in a Remington painting.

Earlier that day Juan Uribe, the U.S.-schooled fisherman, had returned from a trip to Medellin and invited me to spend my last night in Bahia Solano at his house. I found it, at dusk, in a cove on the bay's northwest shore. Some black children helped me pull *Squeak* up among the palm trees, beyond reach of waves. "No, no danger of theft," they said. "Juan's house is up here." They led me up a steep knoll.

"Good evening, Stephen," beamed Juan Uribe. "What an honor! And especially fortunate, because my father is visiting. He's anxious to meet you. Oh, here!" He handed me a new Casio wristwatch. "I bought it in Medellin. 'A watch for the watch,' as they say. Whoever is on duty must know the time."

The house was spartan, airy, of unpainted wood, curiously dimensioned and joined. Juan led me to a dark patio overlooking the bay. Through wispy palms I glimpsed the moon, and its reflection on the far waters. Beyond, the coastal range stood like a black wall.

"*Papa,* this is Stephen." A white-haired gentleman rose to shake my hand, then sat me comfortably beside him.

"I'm fascinated by your travels," he said, in slow, easy-to-understand Spanish. "Please, tell me how it is you come here." He was a retired executive for the Coca-Cola Company of Colombia, still robust and patriarchal.

The youngsters had sat on the floor inside, drawing pictures and chatting. Now and then one would bring his or her creation to Juan. The child, without speaking, would hold it up for him to see. He would praise it, and tenderly stroke the child's nape. "They are the neighbors' children, but they stay with me whenever I'm home." Love shone in Juan's eyes, and fatigue. "My, but I'm tired. Too many nets, and motors that won't start."

"Yes, *mi amor*. We'll eat something, then it's to bed with you."

We ate a meal of boiled fish and rice, then turned in, they in rooms below, I on cushions in the loft. In a corner was a stack of religious pamphlets. I picked one up. It was the official newsletter of the Rosicrucian Church, in Spanish. I remembered a Rosicrucian girlfriend I'd once had, and attending with her a service full of mysticism and ritual. Who was this Juan Uribe? I would never know, because my anxiety to complete the voyage necessitated that I leave in the morning.

CHAPTER 12

CAPSIZE

When I woke, at 6:30, May 31, 1991, Juan had already left to set a net. *Squeak* was in better shape than ever. I saw the remaining miles to Buenaventura as something to get over with, perhaps ten days of concentrated effort.

A breeze took me to Punta Solano, then deserted me amongst the reefs at its tip. Some of the rocks showed, others were evidenced only by the breaking of swells. I cut the corner, passing inside some of the rocks. Now a stark coastline loomed ahead: the mountainous peninsula that separates Bahia Solano from the sea.

The day was long and hot. I broke for lunch near an offshore rock which bared in the troughs and buried in the swells. By my drift relative to the rock I saw the current was flowing north at a mile per hour. Every few minutes I set my sandwich down and rowed back to the rock, as if it were traveling south and I were catching up with it.

An hour before sunset I reached the village of El Valle. The bar at the entrance to its harbor was impassable, so I continued toward Ensenada Utria, eleven miles away. The breeze swung to the northwest, but the current remained contrary. I paralleled a long beach, then the ridge-like peninsula that encloses Ensenada Utria. The map showed the *ensenada,* or bay, as a long, narrow inlet. The surrounding land was a "national conservation park." My friends in Bahia Solano had said the park was very beautiful, and administered by gentle scientists.

Darkness came before I had reached the screen of islands that extends seaward from the tip of the peninsula. First the shape of the waves was obscured. Then the physical relief of the peninsula went, then the shoreline, then the seaward horizon, until all I could distinguish was the intersection of black land and charcoal sky: a downward taper from left to straight ahead, representing the tapering peninsula. I pushed on for another two hours, consulting my compass, straining all my senses for the rocks I would have to pass through before I could anchor in the *ensenada.* Then even the skyline disappeared in the inky darkness. Impossible. At 8:15 P.M. I turned and sailed away from the coast.

I no longer feared sleeping while adrift, having successfully done so three times. I sailed southwest on the breeze, now fully swung to north, until 9:15, then dropped the main. I was glad to see the breeze continue into the night because it would counterbalance the current, and prevent me from losing ground. On previous occasions I had dropped both sails. This time I left the mizzen up and sheeted it tight, causing *Squeak* to face into the wind. To encourage wind drift, I did not set a sea anchor. I put the two five-gallon water bags in the cockpit footwell and packed the rest of my gear tightly around me. It began to rain. I closed the hatch, laid back, and fell fast asleep.

I don't remember what I was dreaming, only that it was very pleasant. My actual situation, however, was deteriorating. While I slept, an intense downpour filled the cockpit with rainwater. The rainwater's center of mass was higher than *Squeak's* center of buoyancy. The wind increased, the waves built up. Inevitably, *Squeak* started tipping.

I woke to the sensation of *Squeak* rolling over. Still on my back, I opened the hatch and sat up, intending to stabilize her. But the roll continued, and my quick reflex only cleared the way for the sea to pour into the cabin. I ejected myself into the dark water, turned around, and watched incredulously as *Squeak* slowly rolled through 360 degrees and returned upright, now full of water and unstable. I was treading water, aware of the gravity of my situation, astonished at the severity of the storm, and at how calm I felt. Tepid rain stung my face, like a shower massage turned up high. The waves were four feet tall, sharp and agitated. Suddenly there existed before me a pillar of light, bright as the sun, seemingly fifty feet in diameter, reaching up into the sky like Jack's beanstalk, blinding and deafening me. A fraction of a second later it no longer existed, but other lightning bolts struck here and there, and the sky was blinding, then black, then blinding, then black. Thunder shook the air. I looked at my watch. Eleven P.M.

The mizzensail, still intact, flapped furiously. I let loose its sheet and began securing floating objects. I put my mapcase and water containers inside the cabin and clamped the hatch. I inserted the clips into my oarlock pins so my beloved oars wouldn't come out of their sockets, but the clips promptly deformed from the force of the waves on the oar blades, pulling the pins up through the sockets. I secured the oars with the ends of my leeboard control lines and prayed not to lose them or be struck by lightning in the long night ahead.

There was no hope of bailing *Squeak*, or even of sitting in the cockpit. Every time I climbed aboard she rolled over. A dozen times I righted her with my body weight, but she wouldn't stay up with me on top; I couldn't balance her. The water sloshing inside the cabin caused the hatch to break off—my gear was vulnerable to loss again. I was starting to shiver, so I got my life vest and rainsuit from the aft locker and put them on, with the life vest inside. Opening the locker caused that compartment to flood too, but I had no choice. I took the belt off my khaki shorts and secured it tightly around my waist to maximize the wetsuit effect of the raingear.

I had done everything I could to minimize loss and breakage of equipment. I was shivering again, and needed to get out of the water. It was about 75° F—cold enough, with the wind, to sap my body heat. *Squeak* was more stable upside-down, so I climbed up onto her bottom, my head aft. The bow was underwater but the stern floated high due to the foam flotation inside the cockpit seats. I held onto the skeg, laid my cheek on the backs of my hands, and spread my legs to embrace the hull. My bare feet dangled in the water which now, with the wind chill, felt warmer than the air. I had no hat, so I sunk my head down inside the rainsuit and shivered.

The rain continued, but the wind and waves slowly let up. *Squeak* still wasn't stable, so I shifted my weight as necessary to keep her masts pointing down toward the bottom of the sea, perhaps a hundred fathoms away. As the night progressed and the sea calmed I rested better, entering at times a state of near-sleep. Once I saw the lights of a fishing boat, but my flares were in the cabin, inaccessible. Some of my hard-to-replace equipment had probably already fallen through the open hatch. Would my oars and sails still be there in the morning? If no boat found me, how long before I would die of exposure, thirst, or sharks? I supposed I should regret having taken such chances. I wished I could yell, "Help, Mr. Wizard!" and be magically transported home, like the adventurous turtle in a cartoon series during my childhood. I thought about my family, and how hard it would be on them should I disappear.

What to do, what to do? At first I assumed all would depend on whether a boat should find me in the next few days. But as I pictured techniques whereby *Squeak* could be saved with the assistance of another vessel, I realized I might be able to do it by myself. If only I could stabilize her in an upright position and cause the cabin hatch to float above the waves, I could bail the water out. Stability might be induced by removing the masts and leeboards. Buoyancy might be increased by stuffing makeshift air bags inside the cabin. I pieced together the details and waited anxiously for dawn.

It came almost suddenly at six A.M. All that remained of the night's storm was a residue of waves, like the surface of a swimming pool after being emptied of swimmers. The sky was gray and windless. The shore was perhaps five miles away. No boats. I felt all right. Activity would warm me up. With a prayer of hope, I slipped into the water and went to work.

Swimming around the boat, I removed the oars, rudder, leeboards, masts, sprit booms, boomkin, and damaged Plexiglas hatch cover, tying each to one of *Squeak's* handles or to each other by odd bits of rigging. The mainmast I removed by turning *Squeak* on her side and pulling on the mast while pushing the boat away with my feet. Fortunately, most of *Squeak's* components floated. As I rotated the hull, equipment previously trapped inside floated loose. I swam here and there retrieving whatever warranted the effort: first aid kit, sextant, food containers. Boat parts came untied and I retrieved them, glad there was no wind to scatter us.

When she was fully stripped I was able to stand up in the cockpit. She had survived the night without major damage. The oars were there. The masts and sails had held up despite seven hours of rocking upside down in the waves.

Now to remove the water. I emptied one of my collapsible five-gallon water bags, blew it up like a balloon, stuffed it into the cabin, and secured it as far forward as it would go. It was enough: the hatch coaming was now an inch above water.

Waterlogged gear clogged the hatch opening. I was especially relieved to see my pack since it contained the bulk of my tools and supplies. To clear the way for bailing, I slopped my pack and sleeping bag into the cockpit, then released my three-gallon bailer from its shock-cord retainer. Within three minutes I had removed the lion's share of the water. She was a boat again! Euphoric, I bailed out the cockpit, then bailed the cabin some more. I opened the aft locker and water gushed into the cockpit—I bailed that too. Then I pulled the boat parts out of the water and reassembled them. The hatch cover had come loose and sank, taking my compass with it. My Danforth anchor had slipped from its retaining straps, but its line had snagged on something. It was still there, dangling in the water far below. My clothes bag was missing, along with both flashlights, main halyard, main snotter, nautical chart, half my food, and my lead line and reel. But that was nothing; I was alive, and could continue the journey! It was now seven A.M.

The wind had kindly held off during my self-rescue, but as soon as I gripped my oars a strong wind blew up from shore: one final challenge. Unable to sail, I had to row into it, or spend another night at sea.

Four hours later my hands were blistered, but I had nearly reached a small island. I couldn't remember having seen it on the chart. About twelve miles north I made out what could only be the entrance to Ensenada Utria. The storm had pushed me that far south! Twelve miles further south was the village of Nuquí. Which way to go? The park personnel at Utria would undoubtedly help me, and security shouldn't be a problem. Nuquí, on the other hand, would more likely have the tools and materials I needed to get my boat and gear back into shape. Furthermore, I had a contact there, a woman I'd met briefly in Bahia Solano, who worked for some sort of rural development agency. I chose Nuquí.

It was Saturday, June 1, 1991. I felt renewed joy in the ability of my hands to grip the oars, of my eyes to scan the horizon. I wouldn't take those joys for granted again soon.

After the capsize, Nuquí, Colombia, 6/1/91

CHAPTER 13

NUQUÍ

The wind died, the air turned muggy. I rowed through a group of rocky islets, then along the broad arc of beach that defines the Gulf of Tribugá. After several miles the surf lessened, and the beach became strewn with plastic and rotting garbage. Inland, beyond a no-man's land of sand and shrubs, I saw buildings—the village of Nuquí. Four young black males in cut-off trousers stood waiting for me. I landed, and they bombarded me with helpful hands and suggestions.

"Pull it up higher, higher!"

"Turn it, other end!"

"Come with me, I'll show you a hotel. Don't worry, nobody steals nothing."

"Hold it!" I said, anxious to keep control. "I need to find Claudia, from Cali. She works for something called CODECHOCÓ."

"Sure, I'll take you, come on."

"Wait. Which of you can I trust to watch my boat while I'm gone?"

"Choose Eleimo, he's very serious," said one, indicating a quiet teenager.

"Okay?" I asked. The boy nodded. "Alright, let's go."

The other three led me across the beach to a street of compacted sand. It led into the village, with small houses to either side.

"This is where Claudia lives," someone said, indicating the first house on the right, a brown bungalow. I knocked—no answer. A crowd quickly gathered, people of all ages in light, colorful cotton garments.

"Who's this?" they asked. "What's going on?"

I decided to move everything to a patch of crabgrass beside Claudia's house. The distance was about five hundred yards. The faster I got it done, the sooner I could guard my belongings. My guides agreed to help, and several smaller boys as well.

By the time we'd set my gear and *Squeak* down on the grass, the crowd had grown to a hundred people. They pressed so close I could barely move. Their voices combined to create a din of laughter, questions, and suggestions. The sight of all my strange, waterlogged possessions excited them greatly. A woman picked up my soggy diary and started reading. Children leaned on the gunwales and peered into the cabin—were they stealing? A reporter for a Buenaventura-based newspaper interviewed me. A policeman advised me to go to the police station. How could I ever sort and dry my things without them getting stolen?

"The woman in the house across the street says you can stay with her," said one of my helpers, gesturing wildly. "She has dinner all ready, and an extra bed. You can keep your boat in her lean-to. So, you'll go, right? Yes or no?" Others also urged me to move. I hesitated—people grabbed things and started carrying them across the street. Allowing myself to be swept away, I carried my pack into the cement-block house. A woman of about forty with brown skin and full figure showed me to a small, dark room. For another hour I sorted and carried stealable items into my room, frazzled and hungry. Finally, I ate the offered meal at the table in her front room, and relaxed.

After nightfall I went out to get my gun. I had tried to remove it before landing on the beach, but the wooden dowel which the barrel slid onto, thereby holding the revolver in place in its hiding spot, had swollen, gripping the barrel and preventing removal. I now reached inside to where the gun should have been, and found only the splintered end of the broken dowel. Someone had stolen it.

My high on having saved myself evaporated. Now I was easy prey, while the bad guys were better armed. I cursed myself for not guarding the boat better, and the thief for taking advantage. I didn't have a Colombian gun permit, so I couldn't report it to the police.

I returned to my room. Strangers appeared at my doorway and stared into the gloom, trying to make me out. The room had no door closure, no light, no window. A drinking bout ensued between the lady of the house, whose name was Eulalia, and several friends. I tried to socialize, and an old drunk pulled me onto a stool. "Drink!" he said, shoving a glass of clear liquor into my hand. "We're friends, right? Brothers, forever! Yes or no?" He slammed a sentimental fist over his heart, fell over from the blow, straightened again. He pawed my knees and forearms with damp hands. "My friend!" he pleaded. I scootched my stool backward. He shifted forward. I retreated to my room.

All night long music blared from a cassette player. A second night without sleep. I had done so many things right, I should have been proud, but instead I was depressed, insecure, uncomfortable.

The party culminated at dawn with shouts, and a booming of drums. I came out. A seven-piece drum band stood in the front room, beating drums of three sizes, in a breakneck rhythm.

"What's all this?" I yelled into Eulalia's ear, willing myself to be gay.

"*Dia de Campesinos* (Day of the Peasants)!" she exclaimed from her stool. Her eyelids drooped from drink and lack of sleep; her hands and torso swayed chaotically to the music.

Claudia appeared at the door, a beautiful mestiza in her mid-twenties, slightly overweight, with liquid brown eyes and tan skin. "Estevan!" she said. "Come outside, it's less noisy here."

We stood in the street, already half-filled with people. "Sorry I wasn't here when you arrived," she said. "I've been at a conference in Quibdo, the departmental capital. My work is giving me troubles."

"What do you do, anyway?"

"Oh, CODECHOCÓ is a government agency. We're supposed to provide technical assistance to rural communities. But we have no money! What can we do without a filing cabinet or photocopier? I don't want to talk about it. How are you? Is everything okay?"

I explained the capsize.

"How horrible!" she said. "I *am* busy, but for you I have time. Come on, let's go to the beach. This commotion drives me crazy." We walked for hours over the warm sand, far from the holiday clamor. Claudia told me about work and health problems, and listened to my woes. Her concern was sisterly, not that of a potential lover. Still, it soothed me.

The next day, Claudia gave me space in her house and back yard to salvage my gear. Everything was clean, wet, and salty from having sloshed back and forth inside *Squeak* for seven hours, as if in a washing machine. I began drying my maps, passport, traveler's checks, and books. My last two weeks' worth of diary had dissolved into an alphabet soup. I rinsed and dried my remaining clothes, sleeping bag, awnings, lines, repair materials, and spare parts. I cleaned and oiled my tools. With my little remaining cash I bought new rope, towel, flashlight, medical supplies, and a pair of pants. Claudia introduced me to her boyfriend, Alejo, who ran the Yamaha outboard motor shop. I copied Alejo's tide table by hand. Then I taped notepad paper together into a 5"x35" sheet and traced that portion of his nautical chart covering the coastline from Nuquí due south to Buenaventura. To improve my ribbonlike map's legibility I colored the land green, the water blue, and the coral reefs red. This miscellaneous recuperation consumed a week.

The books never completely dried. It was cloudy most of the time, and so humid it was unnecessary to wet my face before shaving. Mold grew on my clothes. Mushrooms sprouted in the corner of my bedroom. The temperature was always seventy to seventy-five degrees Fahrenheit. Some nights it rained so hard, so long, so monotonously, it seemed the roof would break. Any vessel left outside would be full in the morning. I read in a book at CODECHOCÓ that the Chocó gets 472 inches of rain per year. Seattle, notorious for its rain, gets only thirty-five. Thirteen and a half times as much rain as Seattle!

In my weariness following the capsize, I had moved in with Eulalia without inquiring as to cost—bad policy. Finally I asked how much she expected me to pay for the fried fish, plantains, and white rice she cooked for me. The price seemed reasonable.

"But I don't have any money now," I said. "You understand, don't you?"

"That's okay. I don't have any either, but the stores sell to me on credit. I'll pay them back whenever you pay me."

"Thanks for trusting me, Eulalia."

My hostess moved about the house wearily. She was single, uneducated. Dark fatigue rings surrounded her eyes, which were large, and showed a lot of white. Fortunately, Eulalia rarely drank as much as on that first night. We got along well, but I cooled toward her when, after I'd been there ten days, she announced that she also expected 1,500 Pesos a day ($3 U.S.) for the room.

I paid, though Claudia advised that it was too much. The house was just a concrete slab, walls, and an asbestos roof supported by a framework of poles. Partition walls separated the rooms, but didn't extend to the ceiling. A central hall, with one bedroom on either side, connected the front room to the kitchen, in back. The only light came from two small windows facing the street. Day or night, I needed a flashlight to see inside my 6'x8' room. The only plumbing fixtures were a faucet at ankle level near the back door, and a toilet in the kitchen, screened by a ragged scrap of plastic sheet. At night Eulalia's three chickens slept beside the toilet. The chickens created dung, cockroaches ate the dung, and rats ate the cockroaches. The rats scurried in and out through a hole in the floor, and scaled the rafters. Furniture consisted of a table, two chairs, and two stools, all crudely hewn and nailed together.

The house's only adornments were three posters of Christ. They hung in the front room, each on a different wall. In the first he flows with blood, nailed to a splendid golden cross. In the second he floats in the air before a red sky, right hand upheld in benediction, a blue heart visible inside his chest. In the third he wears a rich blue cape and a pink shirt embroidered in gold. His bosom reveals a crimson heart. This heart is being tortured rather remarkably: burning on top, bleeding on the bottom, and encrusted throughout with thorns. Yet his face is tranquil, his eyes are blue and dreamy.

Eulalia's house shared a common wall with Daniel and Purita's restaurant/tavern/convenience store. They had seats for twenty people, and a cassette player which usually played *vallenato,* a folk music originating on the Atlantic coast, featuring strings, accordion, and male voices. The rhythm was allegro, tightly subdivided, syncopated. It was happy, yet full of pathos for the common man. Like most of Nuquí's businesses, Daniel and Purita's place combined diversity with poor selection. Nuquí's numerous cubbyhole stores all featured the same dry foodstuffs and cheap manufactured goods.

Nuquí sat in a mangrove swamp where three small rivers joined, a half mile upstream of their common mouth on the Gulf of Tribugá. Activity centered on the riverfront, where boats could moor, not on the beach. Tentacles of tideflat invaded the town, from the riverfront inward. Parked *piraguas* lined these drainage ways. Shacks of warped, rotten planks stood on stilts over muck sprinkled with trash and mangrove saplings. The sandy streets crossed these drainage ways via small, concrete bridges. The air smelled of sewage, mud, and salt.

A water system supplied the houses but it came straight from the river, certain to make you sick unless boiled. Garbage was dumped on the beach. As in Bahia Solano there was a power plant but it didn't work. The only vehicle was a truck with which they hauled sand from the beach to build up the streets. Malaria was endemic, cholera was spreading up from Peru, and the hordes of children suggested contraception was not practiced. Skinny dogs roamed the streets, their bodies covered with sores, misery in their eyes.

The population was mostly black. They were talkative, gesticulative, curious, covetous, opportunistic. Children shuffled over the reddish dirt, bellybuttons protruding. Young men in faded caps and striped T-shirts played dominoes under a thatched roof. They were satisfied with life as they knew it, yet quick to volunteer if I needed manpower, and eager to impress. When I walked the street, kids chanted "Estevan! Estevan!" Adults cried "Meester!" or "Gringo!" I answered if the tone was friendly. "When are you leaving?" they asked, not to imply that I should leave, but simply because it was one of the few formulas they knew for initiating conversation. The blacks loved to sound authoritative, and to pronounce grave warnings.

"Beware the pirates in the approaches to Buenaventura!" said one.

"Yes, two years ago they killed a cousin of mine," said another.

The sound of English, the language of technology and T-shirt slogans, awed them. "You speaking English?" the kids would ask, having learned this phrase in school. *"Hable, hable un poquito* (Speak, speak a little)."

I gave a few English lessons to Marco Milton, the obese notary public, in exchange for meals at his house. Marco was slow and smug, but he was ambitious, and that set him apart. He made a show of being the all-powerful male to his wife and the sentimental patriarch to his kids.

Once, after dinner, I told him how my gun had been stolen. "I wish I could get it back," I whispered. "It kind of bothers me."

"Tsk, tsk, too bad. What kind was it?"

"A .38 Special."

"No kidding? Wait a second." He got up and returned with a revolver.

"Let's see." I verified it wasn't loaded. "Yep, just like mine, except it isn't stainless."

While we discussed the chances of getting my gun back, Marco's year-old boy waddled up to his thigh. He whisked him onto his lap. Soon the infant was toying with the revolver in front of him. "Oh, look," said Marcos, grinning. His massive arms encircled the infant. His thumbs and forefingers formed protective loops around his wrists, which were no thicker than Marco's thumbs. Marco giggled as the infant jerked and stroked the pistol. "Guns and babies!" he squealed. "How cute."

While Marco pursued his dream of learning English, I coped with the black coastal dialect of Spanish. *"Die peso,"* I learned, meant *"diez pesos* (ten pesos)," because they always clipped the final *"s."* I was jolly with the blacks, but couldn't sustain a conversation because the narrow range of subjects we were mutually able to discuss bored me. Intellectually, the relatively few *Paisas* and *Caleños* (natives of Cali) stimulated me more. They included the town doctor, the pharmacist, the tourists at the guest lodge, and a handful of white settlers that had hacked homes out of the jungle ringing the gulf. Rowdy survivalists canoed into Nuquí periodically to buy provisions and chase women, like cowboys in a frontier town. They bought me drinks and gloried in posing with the a*venturero norteamericano* while someone snapped our picture. Nearly naked Indians came into town too, their canoes full of foodstuffs. The women had long black hair and big bellies; their men were small, with Dutch Boy hairdos and sharp faces.

Once I'd organized my gear, I designed the new hatch cover. It would be temporary, and would serve as mold for the permanent cover, which I hoped to laminate in Cali, the city just inland from Buenaventura. Alejo, Claudia's boyfriend, donated shop space and some red cedar planks. Surrounded by boats and outboard motors, using manual tools, I built an arched frame and covered it with 1"x1" wood strips. Then I added brackets for the clamps to grab onto, handles, and elastic strap attachments. My hand-held compass would have to suffice for direction-finding.

The shop was hectic during the day. In the evening, when it had settled down, Alejo often turned up the *vallenato* and sent a kid down to the store for beers. Then Alejo, a sidekick of his named Juan, and I would sit in plastic chairs around Alejo's desk and talk for hours about women, adventures, and American cooking. Rain would drum on the tile roof, and thunder would rumble for hours. They both spoke English, having lived in the States, and appreciated me as a reminder of their time there. "Everything's so *funky* here!" I exclaimed one evening, as we rode bicycles among the rotting shacks.

"This is Colombia!" Alejo beamed, with a pride at once mock and real.

Alejo wasn't quite handsome, but he was strong. His skin was light, his hair medium brown, his hands and face rugged. He knew how to grab things and bend them to his will. He had built a business hiring and catering to the local blacks: "The hardest thing I've ever done," he said. He had a knack for joking sexually with the local girls, for nonchalantly fondling a bottom and getting away with it. They enjoyed the opportunity to laugh, be embarrassed, and refuse his advances. But actually, Alejo had his hands full with Claudia, his moody lover.

Juan came from the same small town in Antioquia as Alejo, and performed odd mechanical jobs for him. In contrast to Alejo, Juan hated the blacks, and they him. "Steve, do you have anything I can put on this?" he would ask, and show me a sore oozing with white pus, the result of a recent fight. "Cocksuckers. Please to God I get out of here before they kill me." Juan was skinny and sly, with huge eyes that showed a lot of white, and lashes that made him look like he wore mascara. His gestures were intense, especially those expressing apprehension or alarm. With his friends, however, he was intimate, conspiratorial. He once showed me his most cherished possessions: his pictures of the United States. "Here I am with my Camaro," he said. "Man, what a hot car! And this is the house I used to live in in New York, before they deported me. Someday I'm going back to the States, where things are *nice*. Not this shit," he added, waving his hand disdainfully over Nuquí's mudflats and sandy streets.

When I'd spent my last peso Claudia said, "You should go see Luis Eduardo Gonzalez. He's the richest guy in town, even has his own plane. Owns a factory in Cali. He could probably cash your traveler's checks for you."

I walked east along the beach to a modern vacation home with a tall concrete porch, and knocked on a door made of hard, red wood. A maid answered.

"I'll get him," she said. Then a dark, handsome man of about fifty appeared in shorts and sandals. Bands of needlework ran vertically to either side of the buttoned opening of his white cotton shirt.

"Hi, my name's Estevan…"

"*Mucho gusto,* Estevan!" he exclaimed, pumping my hand. "Yes, I heard about you. Please come in."

After drinking his cold beer and recounting my voyage, I asked Luis Eduardo if he could cash two hundred dollars' worth of traveler's checks. He promptly arranged it.

"If you want, I'll also take you and your boat to Buenaventura aboard my yacht."

I wasn't sure how to respond. "Thanks. I must admit it's tempting. But I'll probably continue under my own power."

Luis Eduardo smiled. "I was hoping you would say that. I admire bravery. Actually, it was Marco Milton, the notary public, who persuaded me to offer you a ride. He's worried about you."

I chuckled. "Good old Marco. Are the things he says about killers exaggerated then?" I asked.

He shrugged. "The people here are like children. Don't take anything they say too seriously. But when you get to Buenaventura, go immediately to where I keep my boat. No place else is safe." He gave me directions to a boat landing. "And after Buenaventura where will you go?" he asked.

"Originally I planned to sail to Tumaco, but now I think I'll go from Buenaventura overland to Cali, and build my permanent hatch cover there. Then I'll arrange transport either to the Putumayo River, which feeds into the Amazon, or the Meta, one of the tributaries of the Orinoco."

"Cali is a wise choice. Will you stay at my house while you're there?"

Again, his generosity stunned me. "That's very kind. I'll definitely call you."

"Good. It's decided then."

I passed Luis Eduardo's place each morning while jogging. The beach stretched in a vast semicircle of breakers and palms, from the mouth of the river to the sharp islets I had passed through in coming to Nuquí. Little red crabs dodged into their holes as I passed, then returned to their work of shoveling bits of sand into their mouths with their pincers, right pincer then left, hurriedly, while darting back and forth on spiky legs. At high tide the waves rolled right up to the driftwood line, and I continued apace, stepping carefully among the shifting logs and debris. The water was the same temperature as the air. Out on the gulf, skinny black fishermen stood in skinny black canoes, forming upside-down Ts. Their dugouts were thinly carved and warped by time and moisture. Because the canoes were nearly semicircular in cross-section, it amazed me the men could keep their balance while paddling standing up. Each trolled a single hooked line, wrapping and unwrapping from a spool-shaped piece of wood or foam. When done for the day they would paddle to the beach, drag their canoes up, arrange the sword-like bills of four or five long, skinny fish so as to grip them all in one hand, and drag them into town.

On June 11, my thirty-eighth birthday, I sat for an hour and a half in the telephone office. All the international lines were busy. I knew Mom and Dad would be thinking of me, and worrying. Hoping to at least celebrate with a good supper I walked back to Eulalia's, only to find her sick in bed with a coterie of dour old housewives caring for her. "It must have been the ice I used to cool that sweet oat drink a couple nights ago," she said.

"They don't boil the water before they freeze it, do they?"

"I don't think so."

I had taken a glass of it, too, but had realized the danger and put it down after only a sip. Hoping that wasn't enough to give me dysentery, I left to satisfy my hunger at a thatched rain shelter where a woman fried fish and dough pancakes over an open fire. While I sat on a stool eating an oily pastry we had an *aguacero,* as they called the frequent downpours. Puddles soon formed in the streets. A girl of five chose the stool next to me to wait out the storm. Her shoes were both plastic, but one was pink, the other brown. Paying me not the slightest attention, she stood on her stool and bounced and swiveled to her own beat, singing over and over a tune frequently heard on the village's transistor radios.

I liked this little girl very much, and all the dreamy coastal gaiety she represented. I didn't feel particularly gay myself just then, however, because a nausea was spoiling my enjoyment of the pastry. I remembered my sip from the tainted oat drink, and realized I had the amoebas again. Soon I would be as sick as Eulalia.

Even before, I had grown tired of fish, of the bland starches, and the taste of cooking oil in everything. My body craved nutrients that were unavailable. With the amoebic dysentery back, this craving intensified. There were no lemons to be had, so I was unable to fully cure myself. Nonetheless, by mid-June I had finished the temporary hatch cover and expected to leave soon.

The night before my departure the bar next door rocked with *vallenato.* Diners were still dining, and drinkers had began drinking. Moneyed townspeople like Marco Milton and *Paisa* tourists from the hotel crowded the bar and overflowed onto the street. On the outskirts of the crowd, barely illuminated by the tavern's harsh lights, a bare-breasted Indian woman stood, hand-in-hand with a young daughter. Both were perfectly still, absorbed in the scene.

I went to bed. Around midnight the bar shut down, but still I couldn't sleep. Mosquitoes kept coming in through the holes in my net, obliging me to hunt them down with my flashlight. I got out my notebook, and wrote:

> One can only write poetry
> of one's own country
> of the wild that's yours

How then to describe the sullen frog
I found crashed in my room?
or thin mud?
black girls in pink dresses?
or a massive greenness outside
that broods, and presses in?

Two A.M., and cocks crow all across the village
children and parents sleep under mosquito nets
rain drips from gray shanty eaves
insects sound like birds

At the heart of this strangeness:
temperature that never varies
bare-toothed laughter
a scrap of jungle scraped clean
and soiled as only people can soil

Yet the black and green butterfly
does not disdain to land here
the blue-tailed lizard scrambles over concrete stubble
as readily as over muddy sand

I, tiny satellite, rove these parts
conscious of germs
fighting the tendency of things stirred to become one

Here I am more fully myself
because here I don't belong
here I thrive only through insistence

My poem is the song of a satellite
that passes, insistently
and changes nothing

On June 18, 1991, Alejo opened the shop's double doors and helped me carry *Squeak* down the ramp to the edge of the greenish brown river. Boats and crude docks lined the waterfront, but the far side of the river was virgin mangrove swamp. Alejo passed me gear while I stowed.

"Steve," he said, "before you leave for Buenaventura you should spend some time in Morro Mico."

"Morro Mico—that means Monkey Hill. You mentioned that place before. What is it?"

Alejo paused. "Paradise. That's all." He swung a water bag up to the gunwale; I strapped it inside, behind the mainmast. "I know, I helped build it. My big brother, Javier, lives there. And La Negra, his wife, and Melissa, their daughter."

"Where is it?"

"After your capsize, you said you rowed to an island that isn't on the map. Well, that island is Morro Mico, and the property on the mainland behind it is also called Morro Mico. It's on a bay facing southwest."

"I remember the bay."

"Good. So go spend the weekend there."

"Maybe I will."

By now a dozen men and boys had knotted tightly around us. "Hey, give me some room," I said, switching to Spanish. "I've got to swing this oar!" They moved just far enough, then crowded in again.

A murmur passed through the crowd. "Look, it's Luciano!" Alejo turned.

"Luciano!" he said. "What the hell?"

A tall, erect man of about thirty walked slowly down the ramp, set his duffel bag down, and received Alejo's bear-hug. His skin was pale, his short hair slightly reddish. "Just got off the plane." He shifted his gaze dreamily from person to person. "I'm on my way to Morro Mico."

"Well, you're just in time for a ride, if Steve doesn't mind. Steve, this is Luciano. He's from the same town as Juan and the rest of us."

"Ciao, Luciano. Want a ride?"

"Please."

I stowed Luciano's bag, sat him in the cabin facing forward, then pushed *Squeak* off. The crowd, which had grown considerably, shouted and pranced as I gripped the oars.

I rowed out the mouth of the river, protected from swells by a rocky island. Then I moved Luciano to the seat deck, closed the hatch, and set sail. He kept his weight low, and handled those parts of the boat I couldn't reach with him in the way. When not adjusting a halyard or leeboard for me, he sat still, attentive. We cruised north on a southwest wind, through the spiky rocks, toward where I'd capsized.

"Eighteen days I was in Nuquí," I said. "It's great to have a change of scenery, even if this first twelve miles is a backtrack for me."

"Have you been sailing long?"

"Almost a year. See the map painted there? That's my route."

Luciano studied it. "What an adventure."

"True. But there've been so many delays. I try not to think about it anymore—just go with the flow. I've been through a lot. Alejo's right, I need a rest."

"Morro Mico will be perfect for that," he said. "I lived there with Alejo, Javier, and La Negra for a few years, fishing. Bought some property of my own, too. We'll be going right by it. Then I went back to Medellin to study agriculture. This is my first time back in three years." His Spanish was deliberate, thoughtful, musical.

"I bet you're anxious to see your friends again."

"Yes, and my property. Look, we're beginning to see it now. That point there, that's all mine. To the right of it's the mouth of the Jurubidá River."

When we reached the island near which I had capsized, we turned right into a bay. It was semicircular, about a half mile across. Two rocky points framed its entrance. The land around the bay was steep. A semicircular ridge started at one point, climbed up and around, and descended to the other. The distance from beach to ridgetop was about a half mile. Five streams drained the bowl, each with its own mouth on the bay. Thick jungle covered the land except for one clearing, on a gentle slope at the head of the bay. There a house stood.

"They own everything to the top of the ridge, all the way around," said Luciano. "As long as you're in Morro Mico, you'll neither see nor hear anything of the outside world, except the ocean." I turned around. The bay faced west-southwest, straight into the prevailing wind and swells, like a porthole at the bow of a ship.

The surf looked questionable. "Wait, let me out," said Luciano. He got into the water and held onto *Squeak's* rudder. "Okay, row." His body acted like a drogue, holding *Squeak's* stern to the waves as I came in. Then we pulled her up, and ascended a path to a campus of pebbled courts, landscaped with indigenous plants. A pair of brilliant clown parrots chattered in a papaya tree beside the three-story house.

Luciano paused. "Look at it. We got all the wood from trees here on the property, sawed it up with chain saws, planed it smooth, and left the boards clear. Now, inside."

There were no doors or glass panes. Only railings or low partitions separated the rooms from the outdoors. The bottom floor, a flush slab, housed the kitchen and living area. The second floor, which was split into two levels, contained hammocks, a woodshop, and small bedrooms. The partial third floor was the master bedroom. The leafy, floral smell of rain forest flowed throughout. "Eleven years it took to build this," said Luciano.

Behind the kitchen, a man with shoulder-length brown hair was fitting a piece of wood for a new partition wall.

"Javier! Don't you ever stop working?" asked Luciano.

Javier spun and froze, mouth agape, a tape measure hanging limply from his hand. He was better-looking and of slighter build than Alejo. He embraced Luciano and kissed both his cheeks. *"Hombre,* don't tell anybody you found me at a loss for words, what will they think? Why didn't you write to us you were coming? Never mind, I like surprises. And who's this handsome devil?" he asked.

"Estevan, from America."

Javier held up his hands, palms outward, as if to resist arrest. "My God, a gringo! Are you with the CIA?" Then he smiled and took my hand in both of his. "Just kidding! Alejo told me about you, the American Viking, invading Colombia. Welcome to Morro Mico!"

"Luciano!" A little girl ran through the rear door and hugged Luciano's waist. He loosed her grip, knelt, and hugged her chest-to-chest. "Can this be my Melissa?" he asked. "Impossible, you're far too tall!"

A woman of thirty with long black hair and high cheekbones entered, set a basket of lemons on the kitchen counter, and embraced him. She was tall and stately as an Inca queen. Her skin was the color of caramel, her body exquisitely sexy in a light cotton robe. They called her La Negra.

After joyous greetings she said, "Go on you two, take a bath, and bring me your dirty clothes back. I'll make up some beds."

"Yes, Mom!" said Luciano, smiling. "You'll love this, Estevan."

He led me out the back door and seventy-five yards up a gravel path, to a stream which formed a natural pool the size of a hot tub. The crystalline water felt cool and fresh on our salt-laden skin. "For a massage, do this," said Luciano, positioning himself under the three-foot waterfall that fed the pool.

While La Negra cooked yucca and grilled snapper, Luciano produced fruits and vegetables from his duffel bag and squeezed a pitcherful of dark, pulpy juice. Afterward, I sat back from the table and exclaimed, "Have I died and gone to heaven? This is everything I craved in Nuquí: nutritious food, cleanliness, peace and quiet."

"It's good to get a fresh perspective," said La Negra. "It reminds us how fortunate we are."

"Fortunate, hell!" roared Javier. "Stubborn, that's all! You must be stubborn too, Estevan, to have come so far in that nutshell of a boat. So please, stay as long as you like."

The following day was Melissa's seventh birthday. She was fair-skinned, austerely beautiful, quiet, used to being around grown-ups. At her invitation, a boatload of little black friends arrived from a village at the mouth of the Jurubidá. Alejo and Juan came too, to attend the party and relax for a couple days.

The high point was an outing to the furthest stream. Seven of us, kids and adults, walked north over the damp beach sand. The tide was out, and Alejo, Javier, and I played frisbee along the way: long bombs, rapid-fire, passing while running, break right, break left. Then we reached the stream and waded up through its calm, knee-deep water. We stooped to clear hanging branches and vines. Rotting bits of driftwood crowded the banks. Fifty yards up we climbed the first fall, an ascent of ten feet. Above, another cascade fed a pool. It was of sculpted bedrock, goblet-shaped, just big enough for all of us.

"Watch," said Alejo. He swam under the fall and surfaced in an air pocket behind, half visible, then swam back. "Your turn," he said.

I took a breath. Eyes open, I frog-kicked down and through the foam. Inside, I stood half out of water, back pressed to the wall behind. The water fell a few inches before my face, thick and clear. I watched the others as if through a kaleidoscope—they seemed to be joking and playing, absorbed in each other. Water encompassed me, yet I could breathe. The crash of water filled my ears. The laughter of my companions, only a few feet away, barely reached me, as if from a different world.

Leaving the others, I scaled the slick rock to the head of the fall. The gorge's flanks shimmered strangely. I looked close, and made out thousands of minute, transparent crabs, wiggling in the surface tension of the wet rock. Above, the stream filtered through boulders. Here and there, eddies had scoured spherical cavities in the bedrock. The streambed curved and gently climbed. Broadleaf forest lay close and dark to either side. Branches met overhead, but sunbeams penetrated, illuminating leaves, and firing the water. I fell into a near-trance.

That night I tried to capture the feeling:

> Above the falls, beyond the laughter
> sweetwater pools sleep in cavities
> embroidered with miniature palm
> anchored in living stone
>
> In a pool is my face
> in my face, a snail
> in the snail, an indelible secretion of life
>
> Above the rock-scour slide
> quiet now the shower
> the brook falls calm in green-capped boulders
> arm-breadth of clear earth blood

Float now, out of body
through green-shadowed space
forest giants, high-held orchids
into the great crowns: chlorophyll, cellulose
Pierce now the sky, the sun
silver fire irradiant
pure energy
melt

to reincorporate in the upper vale
where none live
and few come to find the peace
eternally offered

I ask: why so quiet? alone?
why so faint the pathway to heaven?

Luciano was usually quiet, absorbed in a new form of exercise he was developing. It entailed a series of difficult positions accompanied by meditative effort. One position stood out. He stood on the beach, closed his eyes, balanced on his right foot, bent forward, held his body and left leg horizontal, outstretched his arms, and craned his neck and fingers upward. He didn't hold this position statically, but rather quivered and shifted, striving for spiritual balance. He looked like an airplane flying through turbulence.

My diarrhea tapered off. La Negra's cooking put the weight back on me, and every day we swam in the surf. The bay floor was a vast expanse of sand. The slope was gradual, so the swells started rising far out, near the entrance of the bay. At six to ten feet they broke, then carried on to the beach, slowly weakening. We dove under them. I found a bamboo log and hung on to one end while Melissa held onto the other. The waves crashed and twisted us around underwater, but we held onto our respective ends of the log, and soon saw each other again on the surface, ready for another wave.

I donned my mask and explored the surf zone, sensing the wave energy at different depths. I lay on my back on the sandy floor in ten feet of water, where the rolling waves didn't reach, and watched them pass overhead. I went where the water was shallower, and saw the waves sweep across the bottom, sending the fluffier deposits violently landward then back again—the shock wave reminded me of film footage I'd once seen of the effect of an atomic explosion. I gauged the depth of water where the swells rose up, and where they broke, in anticipation of navigational challenges on the way to Buenaventura.

One day Luciano and I hiked around the bay's rim. First we waded up the northernmost stream, crossing logs and scaling waterfalls. Shrubs choked the stream corridor. Leaves blocked the sun. When the ravine became too narrow and steep, we climbed a flanking hillside. Thin organic soil scraped away under our tennis shoes, revealing red clay and slick roots.

We reached the sharp ridge, and followed it south. The trail was faint. Black frogs with red spots crawled over decaying leaves. "The Indians extract poison from the red spots," said Luciano. Emerald hummingbirds browsed among budding shrubs, blue berries, and orange flowers. Some of the trees were very large, others small. Species intermingled.

Forest blocked our view inland, but as we negotiated the ridge, the trail suddenly opened onto the ocean. It was as if we saw it from an airplane, so high were we, so completely did it fill our vision: silver-blue, ruffled, empty. How many tens of miles to seaward did my gaze penetrate? I saw the curvature of the earth, and wondered where an imaginary straight line would end. Would it bump into one of the thousands of islands that make up the mid-Pacific archipelagos, or slip through, to reach the Philippines, or Australia, a third of the world's circumference away?

We followed the southernmost stream down to the house, completing the loop. Because we had circled the entire realm of Morro Mico, it had seemed a great odyssey, but the actual distance was not great. "Two hours, Luciano!" I said. "We were only gone two hours!"

The next day Luciano and I rowed, without the sailing rig, to his property. We cut across amphitheater bays, and rounded points. The sea was deep and restless. To our left, black cliffs shot up through explosions of foam. My oars felt precise and powerful, like surgical instruments.

I dropped Luciano off at his property and continued through the river bar, centering myself in the deep channel, which was clear of breakers. Inside, the river curved right, around the village of Jurubidá. It was smaller and neater than Nuquí—many of the cottages were painted. I saw a malaria control center, a school, and a woodshop in which an old man was carving a waist-high pestle for crushing grain.

I rode the rising tide upriver. It was a hundred feet wide, clear but brown-tinted. It meandered first through mangrove swamp, then lowland jungle. An unfamiliar bird broke the silence with strange calls, and flew from tree to tree in a scalloped trajectory, the way power lines look from a speeding car. I tasted the water—it grew less and less salty. The trees were tall where the land was high, short where it could flood. Only tall grass carpeted the low peninsula inside each bend. Narrow sloughs branched off. The river shoaled, clarified. A vista opened. I traced the valley ten miles, to the river's birthplace in a wall of mountains.

By noon, which coincided with high tide, I had ascended about two miles, to the upper limit of tidal influence. The current became neutral, then contrary. I rowed until it became too swift, then got out and towed. The bottom was gravel and cobble. Snags and islands clogged the channel. Time to return.

I coasted back down, checking into sloughs along the way. One looked like it might be a meander cutoff. At first it was wide enough to row, but soon I was lifting my oartips over obstacles, then pushing against the rank vegetation to propel myself. The slough wound through marshy forest, narrowed. The sun being directly overhead, I lost my bearings. I wormed deeper and deeper, until *Squeak* was tightly wedged. Water grass and lilies closed in behind us, reeds and branches blocked the sky. In every direction plants limited my field of vision to a few feet. I sat still.

This is what I came for
to be intimate unto claustrophobia
where water, land, and life intersect

where shadows have gravity
where I would never be found
in the center

I gave rein to the silence, until the hum of an insect mattered, until the plants had personalities. I imagined myself truly stuck there.

A black insect, seemingly between a bee and a fly, entered my space. It stopped in midair, wavered slightly, and studied me with multiplex eyes. He shifted position a few times, processing data like a tiny machine, then he was gone. What had he concluded?

I rowed the ebb tide back to Luciano's property. He was clearing a hillside with his machete. He showed me a hut, ruined by rain and rot. "I lived here for a year, and planted a lot of pineapples and yucca. Now I need to weed out what's grown up around them." I helped with my machete, striving to keep my balance on the steep slope, and to slash the weeds without harming the pineapple plants inside.

We weren't as careful in our second landing at Morro Mico as we had been the first time. "Go!" said Luciano, judging that a gap had opened. I didn't even close the hatch. The beach was perhaps 150 yards away. Before we had covered a third of the distance, swells rose up behind us, as if from nowhere. I rowed harder, but the first one overtook us. It was three feet tall, not yet breaking. I corrected my way out of a broach as the wave passed beneath us. The next wave was taller, steeper. It surfed us toward the beach, lifting my stern to starboard. I contained it with desperate pulls at the port oar, then lost control. *Squeak* rolled. I floundered underwater for a moment, unable to tell up from down, then found land under my feet.

The water was only waist-deep. *Squeak* was on her side, the cabin half-full. My oars were floating away, along with the bread and oranges I had bought in Jurubidá. Luciano and I righted her, rescued the important things, and bailed. I would have to dry my gear again. The consequences weren't severe this time, but the incident heightened my fear of the long, shoal coast I would have to navigate after leaving the Gulf of Tribugá.

The following day I practiced boat-handling in the surf. I equipped *Squeak* for rowing only, strapped fifteen gallons of water inside to simulate normal weight, battened down the hatches, and launched. The waves were too big in the center, but by moving toward the south end of the bay I could select whatever size I wanted. To practice launching I positioned myself as far seaward as possible without the waves pulling *Squeak* from my grasp, then rowed out fast when I detected a lull. Launching was safer than landing, because with boat and wave moving in opposite directions there was less chance of being carried away in a surfing motion.

Next I tried surfing small waves. Due to *Squeak's* buoyancy I was able to surf her on waves less than a foot tall. She always wanted to broach—turn her beam to the waves—but I straightened her again by backing with one oar while pulling with the other. Soon I was surfing with good control, and riding waves high up onto the beach. Finally, I landed through the center of the bay. I waited outside till the waves seemed smaller, then rowed. I had about ten seconds of rowing time between waves. When a wave approached I slowed down to avoid being surfed, even backed up if necessary. They were six feet tall. Halfway through, one caught me. I applied torque and shifted my weight to the uphill side, controlling the broach, until I was high and dry on the beach.

By June 28 Juan and Alejo were back in Nuquí, and Luciano had moved to his property. My weekend with Javier and La Negra had stretched into ten days. Now I was packed and ready to launch.

"Well," I said, "if the purpose of Morro Mico is to make people feel like new, you've done your job well."

"We were just getting used to having you around," said La Negra, her hands on my shoulders. "Won't you stay another day?" Melissa stood shyly by my side. The waves lapped at our ankles.

"Oh, but he's a Viking," said Javier. "We've got to let him go so he can plunder new lands. But first, Señor Viking, you must see Ensenada Utria. It's only twelve miles north."

"The national conservation park? I meant to go there the night I capsized. Yes, maybe it deserves a quick look before I proceed south. Thanks, guys. I'll write." With that I climbed aboard and rowed through the surf. By nightfall I had passed into the shelter of the islets that protect the approach to Ensenada Utria, and anchored in glassy water in the bay's bottleneck opening.

In the morning I saw an inlet three miles long by a half mile wide, surrounded by forested hills. The only sign of man was a cluster of wooden buildings on the east shore of the opening. I swam there, just in time to help a handful of men and women in their twenties and thirties move a pile of whale bones from the upper beach to a shelter for sorting and preservation. Afterward they invited me to share breakfast with them under a roofed platform set in the woods, above a steep gravel beach. The tide was high, and the sight of gray gravel under clear water reminded me of the Puget Sound.

"Because the park's so remote, we rely on each other for everything," explained Fabio, a roly-poly marine biologist with a black goatee. "The emphasis is on conservation research. There are usually about a dozen of us here: park employees, scientists, and graduate students."

"Where are you all from?"

"Bogotá, mostly. Except the motorboat operator—he's from around here. We seldom receive visitors, so I hope you'll stay awhile."

He excused himself to wash the dishes. We would have plenty of time to talk, however, because for the next three days I would eat with them, gather wood for their fire, and go with them on outings. Meanwhile, I'd try to postpone my worries about the road ahead.

First, the boatman took Fabio and me to one of the islands at the tip of the peninsula. Fabio dove in with an oxygen tank and tallied fish by species, on a greaseboard. I snorkeled alongside him. The reef was of sculpted bedrock, drifted over with sand. Where the sand was shallow and flat tan coral grew, one to two feet tall. Noting my interest in the wispy coral, Fabio caught my attention and wrote, "Fragile!" on his greaseboard. I nodded, and avoided touching them. Inch-long, neon-blue fish lurked inside the coral clusters. An olive puffer lay on the bottom, deflated—he watched me through huge eyes. It was raining, and droplets bounced over the sea's surface, like popcorn on a frying pan.

When Fabio had finished he showed me to a camp in the middle of the island. A large rain tarp had been slung under the trees. Under it a cauldron of fish soup was boiling. We stood around it, along with several other people, strangers to me. We were all in wet swimsuits, but the air was warm. A bowl of soup was passed to me. Fabio pointed to the black man with the ladle. His body was small and sinewy, his kinky hair grizzled with middle age.

"This is his camp," he whispered. "He was a great pirate once. Very bold, very feared. He's quite a man." I didn't understand how a thieving murderer, if that's what pirates are, could be such a swell guy, but I shook his hand. He seemed innocuous. When Fabio told him how I'd arrived he eyed me curiously, and seemed to check an impulse to speak.

The next day I went with a mestiza biologist named Marta for a hike west across the peninsula. She was tall and lean, unmarried, about forty, quieter than the others. The trail was a jumble of rocks and roots. Marta walked in front. She moved casually, observing every detail. In the way she performed the thousand-odd motions required by the trail, I saw that she had walked a lot of trails, that she mused over signs, and asked herself questions. I sensed that she was used to being alone without feeling alone. The wild was her home, her family, her love. It wasn't a new love, but it was the one that would last. The science she practiced was very applied: an accumulation of small, good deeds.

"The little holes in the clay banks are made by armadillos," she said.

"That rustling and snapping of twigs in the treetop there is a troop of monkeys."

"The Indians use the buttress roots radiating from these trees to make platters with which to toss and blow the chaff from grain."

We crossed a divide, descended a shallow creekbed, and emerged onto a sun-dappled beach, where pink-gray sand drifted around pockmarked protrusions of black rock. Marta pulled a shovel with a broken handle from behind a palm tree. "I hid it here a few days ago," she said. "That's why I came today, to bring this back to camp so I can fix it." But I suspected the shovel was simply an excuse for showing me her world.

The third day I rowed up a coiling slough into the heart of a mangrove swamp. The tide was high, flooding the forest's mucky floor. Purple crabs peeked from niches in the above-water portion of the trees' complex root clusters. In addition to upright trunks, spindly horizontal trunks extended everywhere, supported by descending 'branches' that reached back into the muck. Together, roots, horizontal trunks, and descending branches formed a leafy matrix that covered the water to a height of ten feet. I rowed up the slough until overhanging branches interfered with my masts, then turned around. As I re-emerged, a white crane took flight, soared a single sunlit circle, then melted like a cloud, its legs jutting stiffly behind, its wingtips stretching to measure the sky.

These experiences enriched me, but I worried too much about the coast between the Gulf of Tribugá and Buenaventura to fully relax. So, early in the morning of July 2, I bade farewell and sailed from Ensenada Utria back toward Nuquí. I would reprovision there, then get it over with.

I had no way of knowing that I would run into Marta two months later on Isla Gorgona, and spend Christmas with Fabio in Bogotá. On these occasions they would tell me that, two hours after my departure from Utria, a party of men arrived in two motorboats. "They were *costeños* (coastal people)," each would say. "They wanted to know which way you had gone, and we said, 'To Bahia Solano,' instead of 'Nuquí.' They asked how much money you carried, and we said you didn't have any cash, only credit cards. Everything they asked, we tried to mislead them. They asked whether you carried a gun—we didn't know what to say about that. Then they left, and we prayed they wouldn't find you."

Had I known that Fabio and Marta had possibly just saved my life, I might have reconsidered Luis Eduardo Gonzalez's offer to carry *Squeak* and me to Buenaventura aboard his yacht. As it was, I arrived in Nuquí in midafternoon, got Alejo's permission to put *Squeak* in his outboard motor shop again, then listed the provisions I would need to reach Buenaventura, 140 miles south. Estimating it would take ten days, I bought lemons, potatoes, tomatoes, onions, rice, noodles, tomato sauce, canned meat, canned peas, bread, crackers, margarine, marmalade, oatmeal, flour, eggs, powdered milk, sugar, cooking oil, salt, chocolate bars, cookies, *aquardiente*, fishing tackle, toilet paper, lighters, and flashlight batteries. All this cost only thirty dollars worth of pesos. I also refilled my water bags with processed water from a local tuna cannery, and put together a makeshift lead line.

During the three days it took to get ready, I slept in the shop with Alejo and Juan. Once, a husky, long-haired *Paisa* stopped by to pick up a part for his motor. "I'm Lino," he said. "You should visit me on your way to Buenaventura. My place is ten miles from here, near a big rock called Terco." It sounded good: one last rest before the final stretch, the most dangerous of all due to its piracy and lack of harbors.

On July 5 I left Nuquí for good. I was a little sadder this time because I was unlikely to see Claudia, Alejo, or Juan again. The crowd that gathered wasn't as big as before, but I shook hands all around, including that of a crab the shop boy was holding in his hand. My careful good will prevailed over the crab's blind instinct to pinch—everybody laughed. Then I rowed out the mouth of the river.

Out of sight of the village, I stopped and drifted a hundred yards off a deserted beach. The sky was overcast, not too hot. I stripped down to my shorts, leaned back against the aft locker, and ate a breakfast of bread, margarine, jam, and lemonade. Then I wrote yet another poem of parting:

> Anew I stride for unknown shores
> behind me port and friends
> I lived here long enough
> that once left I call it home

Out the muddy river mouth
through green protective isles
to where the ocean impulse
rocks me in the original cradle

I awake this morning feeling
like all the rights and wrongs of the world
have melded into a single
"that's how it is"
like to have ever worried about the workings
of this great clock was a foolishness

Alone, at the ocean's feet
beyond the gaze of well-wishers
I poise, like artist's brush uplifted
ready to add an indelible flourish
to the world's great design
for where I go
that place I make more real

The design:
continent crumbling into islands
sea evaporating, to reinvade the land
in sweetwater torrents
clouded heaven mediating

"Sure."

We walked past Terco and two miles further, along uninterrupted beach. A young woman and twenty or so teenagers approached from the opposite direction, singing and swaying like Christmas carolers. "Junior high school students," said Lino. "They're out celebrating the Day of the Virgin." When the group reached us it thronged so tightly we couldn't move. They serenaded us gaily for five minutes, then moved on down the beach, never interrupting their song. We continued through a beach hamlet, where Lino exchanged many greetings, then hiked a mile inland on a well-worn trail through flat jungle.

The thermal spring seeped from an earthen bank above a large stream. A semicircular wall bulged out into the streambed, pooling the water. The pond was twenty feet across, the smell slightly mineral. We stripped, stepped in, and floated, knees flexed, toes on the bottom. The water was comfortably hot.

"If you hold your breath," said Lino, "then exhale and rest a while, then repeat, you can hold it longer each time." Sure enough, I held my breath one minute five seconds on my first attempt, one minute fifty-seven seconds on my second.

"Here goes again," I said. Stepping into a deeper part of the pool, I relaxed everything but my clamped eyelids and floated, like a dead man.

I sensed myself slowly floating about the pool. I lost my bearings, and felt the heat bubble up through me. Weird images projected onto my eyelids, as if onto a screen. The projector lay deep below, in the earth's molten core. The outside world came to seem unlikely, remote. It was always so varied, inconstant, while this was monolithic, as long-lived as a planet. How long would it take this core to cool? I was a link in the thermal chain. The oxygen in my bloodstream dropped. My lungs convulsed, I caught them, the crisis passed. It was easier now. I continued watching the hazy, orange pictures on my eyelids until something told me to stop. I lifted my head, gasped air, and checked my watch, which I'd switched onto chronometer. "Two minutes and fifty seconds!"

Lino and I relaxed emptily, our arms folded over the top of the cement wall, looking down the stream which babbled over cobbles, straight and open through the damp forest. A white crane fished nearby. Standing on one foot, he fluttered the other lightly and intermittently in the six-inch-deep water. He watched the effect, beak pointed at his foot like a cocked gun. Was he luring small fry? Brushing away silt to reveal aquatic insects? Drying the polish on his toenails?

We walked home. "Let's keep going past the house," said Lino. "There's something else I want you to see." We traversed slopes of broken rock, invaded by green succulents, and crossed wave-swept pocket beaches. On one we came upon the wreck of a fourteen-foot sailboat. Its forest green paint had nearly weathered away. The inside was full of sand.

"A Swiss man sailed this here from Portugal a year or two ago."

"It's beautiful," I said. "A perfect miniature of a Mediterranean fishing boat. Wooden keel, soft bilge, wineglass transom, heavy scantlings. It's the only foreign vessel I've seen on this coast, besides *Squeak*. Too bad the rocks have banged these holes into it."

"Yes. It wasn't meant to wash up here. The waves still reach it at full moon."

That evening, as the world grew pink, then dark, I asked, "Why are you here, Lino?"

He rested a brawny forearm on his table, sank the fingertips of the other hand into his hair, and rubbed them over his scalp—his Afro-like curls jiggled. Then he lay his hand over his forearm and sighed. "I used to live in Medellin. I was into Heavy Metal, black leather. Built me a macrobiotic sandwich shop. I was doing pretty well. One day a customer came in, skinny guy, somebody I didn't know. He sat by himself at a table. I gave him some guava juice. Then I stood in the doorway of my shop, looking out at the street, nothing in particular on my mind. I felt a blow in my lower back, heard an explosion, spun around. This guy had stood up and was pointing a gun at me. I leaped to one side just as it went off again—the bullet missed. He shot one of my customers too, then he ran out. Neither of us were badly hurt, only flesh wounds."

"Why? Why'd he shoot you?"

"I don't know," said Lino. "Never found out. Medellin's kinda fucked, but it isn't just that. It's society, everywhere." He shook his head. "I felt sick. I lost interest in everything. So I sold my business and came out here. I bought this land, built my house. Then this guy who owns land down the beach asked me to build him a house, too. That's what I'm doing now. I like my work, my place. Cholo here's my buddy." The boy beamed at his boss. "That's all. No plans."

"You're still working through it, Lino," I said. "You're making progress."

Lino pursed his lips. "Thanks," he said. Then we went to bed, he and Cholo in hammocks, I in *Squeak*.

Lino and I dove every day. I came to know the whole stretch from the Terco beach to the shipwreck beach, including a huge rock two hundred yards out. It stuck up from a sandy bottom at a depth of fifty feet, and protruded from the sea at low tide. The rock was intricately faceted, and pastel-colored from coral encrustations. Its sides fell steeply through blue water, into clefts and rounded shoulders of rock, and further, further, to rippled, drifting sand. Fan coral waved in the undulating current. Sun glinted unevenly, refracted by the sea's wavy surface. I entered a cave full of small fish making clacking sounds. I dove and dove, long and deep, reveling in the vertigo which the sheer cliffs induced in me, and in the tingly body-high caused by the inversely oscillating levels of oxygen and nitrogen in my bloodstream. Two-foot-long parrot fish nibbled the coral—their psychedelic blue-green bodies glowed as if from an internal light. Bonitos cruised in packs of silver light. Five manta rays regularly flew by, like silent birds in a tight squadron. Their bodies were mottled brown, black, and gray, with white spots overall. But small fish were most numerous: angelfish, bass, candlefish, triggerfish, many unknowns.

One day, while swimming on the surface in six feet of water, I realized I was directly over a giant stingray. The bottom was sandy. The stingray lay flat, covered with sand, indistinguishable except for the outline of its body and its eyes, which watched me. It was six feet across, six feet long. Its spear-like tail was that long again. If I settled down onto its back and sat like an Arab, I wondered, could I fly through the ocean as if on a magic carpet? What would its skin feel like? What horrible wound was he capable of inflicting? He watched me, absolutely still, as I bobbed above him. Perhaps it was a wave a little bigger than the others, that agitated me a little more, that caused him to disappear so instantly that the sand on his back stayed where it was, like a table setting when a magician pulls the cloth away. I caught only a glimpse of him, disappearing in the distance. How could such mass accelerate so rapidly? How can one creature master both stillness and speed?

Another day, while Cholo accompanied us in their dugout canoe, Lino shot a twenty-pound red snapper with his spear gun, but it wedged itself in a cave so he couldn't pull it out.

"Lend me your Hawaiian sling, Estevan," he said, on the surface between breaths. I handed it over, and went down with him. He jabbed the fish powerfully several times, but the spear's triple points couldn't grip it. He surfaced again, blew the water from his snorkel.

"Cholo, go fetch the kitchen knife!"

A half hour later he pried the monster out and slopped it, alive and covered with deep gashes, into the canoe. We took it ashore and lugged it up to the house. It swiveled its bulging eyes and worked its gills in the dry air till finally it died under Cholo's knife on the kitchen bench. Its scales were the size of guitar picks.

That afternoon, a small, erect man in his late twenties appeared in the doorway. His skin was pale, his hair crewcut.

Lino jumped up. "Pablo! What are you doing here?"

"Medellin became tiresome. You know how that is. So I thought I'd come work on my place for a few months."

"Estevan, this is Pablo, my next door neighbor. He owns the property where the wrecked sailboat is." Turning back to Pablo he said, "Go unpack. We'll visit you in a little while."

When Lino had finished the sketch he was working on, we hiked to the sailboat, then up a steep knoll to a two-story cabin with a yellow metal roof. A sign over the door said "Xtatlan." "From the book by Carlos Castañeda," said Pablo, who had been clearing the slope with a machete. "Come in."

A crude table and three chairs sat on the bare earth of the first floor. Boxes and odd items of equipment lay on the table and along the walls. The sea showed widely through the building's front openings. The rear openings looked out over the back side of the knoll, and up, over a steep opposing slope, several times higher, to the rim of the peninsula terminating in Cabo Corrientes (Cape of Currents).

"So much grows back in two months," said Pablo. "I'm clearing the slopes so as to reorder the landscape. This hill is a center of earth power."

"Why'd you spare that one tree?" I asked. "It must be a hundred meters tall." Its base was well down the knoll's west slope, yet its leafy canopy towered high above us, and was nearly as wide as it the tree was tall. Vines and parasitic plants festooned the tree's disproportionately thick trunk and its three massive, horizontal branches.

"After I'd stripped the rest of the forest it looked too much like an old giant, chained in the middle of a field. I can't kill it."

While Pablo and Lino assembled a water pump, my attention shifted to a large butterfly. The outer margins of its wings were nut brown with white specks. The inside, around the body, was crimson. A thin white line highlighted the jagged, symmetrical boundary between brown and red. I tried to capture it, but it kept escaping. That butterfly flew away, and an equally beautiful red and blue one took its place. Its colors reminded me of a two-toned '56 Chevy I used to see in my high school days.

Another day, Pablo came to examine *Squeak*. "I know nothing of sailboats except that I want one. That's why I bought the wrecked boat. Do you think it's worth saving?"

"Yes, if that's the kind of boat you want. If not, you should build one from scratch."

"What kind of boat should I build?"

"Well," I said, "when I was staying with Javier and La Negra in Morro Mico I sketched a light outboard motor launch that would be much easier for them to haul out." I showed him a tracing of the sketch. "A multi-chine sailboat could be built the same way. You'd laminate it together from cedar planks like the ones I used to build my temporary hatch cover. You wouldn't need power tools."

"Please, pursue this thought for me," he said.

I began sketching, and after several hours realized I wasn't thinking of Pablo at all, but rather of my own next boat. It was a *Squeak* large enough for two, equally light for its size, with new ideas, like a hollow keel sized to hold water containers. Not even half done with this voyage and I was already dreaming of the next! I buried the sketch in my diary and turned my attention to a better means of controlling my fishing line while trolling. I carved a spool out of a six-inch-diameter trunk of balsa Lino had given me, and attached it to *Squeak's* aft deck so I could wrap or unwrap the line with one hand while sailing.

Following local custom I went shirt-less. The cloud cover intercepted most sunlight, so my tan deepened without burning. I freed my hair from its ponytail. There was time to read, and to meet animals. For that, it was unnecessary to go outside because they came in. One day I noticed something moving on top of Lino's tape player: a 3/4-inch 'newt,' black and tan in alternating bands. It had blunt features, smooth dry skin, and big eyes. It was a perfect miniature of a foot-long adult I had found crawling in the woodwork at Morro Mico one night, and equally unafraid of me. I persuaded him to crawl onto my finger. He was so weightless I couldn't feel him. Content to sit and look around, he cocked his head like a curious spaniel, undulated his tail, and blinked his eyes. His miniscule rib cage expanded and contracted with his breathing. Another time I noticed something yellow crawling on the tree that shaded *Squeak*. It was a six-inch-long caterpillar with tall, banana-colored hairs sticking up stiffly along its back, like a Mohawk haircut.

My week at Lino's house was my final chance to savor the rocky, mountainous coastline between Punta Garachine and Cabo Corrientes. Thereafter, uninterrupted surf might prevent me from landing until I reached Buenaventura. But the old bogged-down feeling still plagued me. So much time had gone by, and so few miles covered. Was I really just putting it off? Was the fear impeding me? Even my relaxation required discipline. I told myself to trust my instinct on how long to linger, to recognize rest as preparation for work, to differentiate less between work and play if both are purposeful.

While this tug-of-war went on inside, Cholo kept me well fed, and my clothes clean. He was seventeen, gentle, with golden skin, flat face, and a tall forehead. I had often noticed a desire among the coast's young black males to take a master—a strong word, but descriptive of the more-than-economic relationship they sought. Cholo not only worked for Lino, he also lived with, followed, and learned from him. "I'm fortunate to serve a *Paisa,*" he said. "My life is better, and we have many nice things, yet I'm still here around my own people. I don't have to choose between the two."

"You work hard," I said. "You're always washing clothes, or landscaping, or preparing the fish and lobsters we catch. Sorry you have to work harder on account of me being here."

"Nonsense! That a gringo is now under my care as well gives me even greater pride!"

One evening after dinner, while we sat around his small, handmade table, Lino mentioned some design problems relating to the completion of his house. Inspired by a new idea, he started revising his plan. I was then doodling with my new boat design. The mood must have caught Cholo too, because he got out his own pencil and paper, and soon all three of us were scribbling and erasing, each absorbed in his own project.

An hour later we played show-and-tell. "Look at mine," said Cholo. It was a fanciful house: tall, complex, surrealistic. Its myriad spires leaned to the right, as if blowing in a stiff wind.

"What are you going to do with such a big house?" I asked.

"Tourism," he replied, looking wise.

"Very astute," I observed, half smiling.

Something in our exchange caused Cholo and Lino to look at each other and chuckle. Infected, I joined them in a laughter that cropped up again and again, till lost in the moodiness of the deepening night.

Lino put on a *vallenato* tape. We listened to its happy melodies and sad words, talking and falling silent at intervals. The sky was calm. On the dark gulf, an endless chain of torches snaked restlessly, left and right. "Night fishermen from Arusí," said Cholo. "They're working their nets near shore."

Cholo talked about his father, a smuggler of dutiable goods. "Once I went with my dad and his partner on a run from Panama City to Buenaventura," he said, his eyes wide with awe. "Their boat was very fast, and we never stopped. By the second day we were already at Boca Chavica, one of the mouths of the Rio San Juan. Suddenly three *Paisas* in a speedboat came out of the *boca* and attacked us!" Cholo gestured wildly to show how the boats swerved and pounded through waves. "'They want to steal our cargo!' said Papa. He tried to shake them off by driving into shallow water, but the pirates kept chasing us. Then they opened up with shotguns!" He demonstrated their pump-shoot-pump motions. "'I'll kill the sons of bitches!' yelled Papa. He gave me the wheel while he and his partner got out their machine guns. 'Okay, turn!' he said. I turned the boat around and drove straight at them. Papa and Chenco shot them full of holes. There was blood and bits of meat all over their boat! I stopped the engine, and they kept shooting holes in the boat so it would sink. 'Let's just leave the bastards here for the fish to eat,' said Papa. So we did!"

Lino had laughed appreciatively throughout Cholo's story. Now he shot me a smile, as if to warn that all may not have happened exactly as told. Given that I was bound for the same river delta, I hoped not. But it corroborated similar reports I'd heard of pirates preying on *contrabandistas*.

It was time for bed. I bid them *buenas noches* and started along the trail to the beach, lighting the way with my flashlight. There was something funny about the woods. I flicked the flashlight off and adjusted my eyes to the darkness. All around were patches of luminescence. I turned the flashlight on and off, seeking the source. The glow came from rotting wood: humus, decomposing branches, logs. The dry-rot fungi were phosphorescent.

A solar eclipse was predicted for the following day, July 11, 1991, at 2:00 P.M. I'd known about it for a long time. Now, thanks to the delays, I found myself still in that part of the globe in which the eclipse would be total. My nautical almanac mapped its track. The 130-mile-wide swath representing the zone of total eclipse started in Hawaii, arced over the eastern Pacific, and entered South America at Cabo Corrientes. I was within a few miles of the track's centerline. I decided to leave the following morning and experience the eclipse alone, off the cape. I would be the first person in South America to see it, and it would signal my departure. But another arrival changed my plans.

While Lino and I celebrated one last dive together, a bright blue dugout with yellow stripes pulled alongside. It was Javier, La Negra, Melissa, and Luciano. La Negra jumped in and snorkeled with us. In her bathing suit she was more pleasing to watch than any fish. I showed her one of my favorite spots: a small cave with two entrances, in twenty feet of water, inhabited by a big red snapper. I swam in one door and out the other, and the snapper didn't leave, because that was his home, but he paced nervously in the corner, an arm's length away.

I loved my Morro Mico friends, but the timing was awkward. They had come to Lino's house to witness the eclipse, and wanted me to stay too. To prepare for my departure I needed to withdraw into myself, but the presence of my friends yanked me outward, leaving me confused, vulnerable. I dreaded saying good-bye a second time.

Everybody was excited about the eclipse, and about an elaborate cardboard mask with a dark lens they were building. There followed a big dinner and often uproarious evening. I cuddled in a hammock with Melissa, thinking of my niece of the same name.

In the morning I launched *Squeak*, hoping to sneak away, but before I could escape, Alejo and Juan arrived in another boat.

"Where you think you're going?" yelled Alejo.

"Buenaventura!"

"Bullshit! You're staying here and watching the eclipse with us."

I was licked. "Okay. But you better have brought some cold beer."

"Don't worry. Here's one now," said Alejo, and threw me a cold bottle of Poker Beer.

We arrived at Lino's house to see Lino, Cholo, Javier, La Negra, Melissa, Luciano, and some local blacks, all clustered excitedly around the cardboard mask and a tub of water intended to provide a reflective surface on which to safely watch the sun. The atmosphere was festive, anxious, chaotic.

At 2:15 the moon began to come between ourselves and the edge of the sun corresponding to five o'clock on a dial. High-altitude overcast largely blocked our view. As this blanket of clouds drifted eastward, patches of clear sky sometimes revealed the superimposing spheres. In those moments the excitable *Paisas* cried out and jostled for their turn at the mask. The blacks were relatively composed, happy with whatever diversion the event might provide.

Just before the eclipse became total, the clouds dispersed. Protecting one eye with a dark lens from my sextant, I recorded my observations:

> 3:04: Cloud cover parting. Eclipse eighty percent complete, leaving only a downward-facing crescent, yet sky and earth have not noticeably darkened. Moon eating sun from bottom up. Excitement building.
>
> 3:09: Crescent thinning, sky clearing. Getting dark.
>
> 3:15: Only a slim, ninety-degree arc of sun remains, centered on the eleven o'clock position of the sun's circumference.
>
> 3:18: Sky and earth darker, arc a razor-thin line, getting shorter.
>
> 3:21: Arc extinguished, eclipse complete. Paisas going nuts. Moon is distinct, featureless, cobalt blue, barely big enough to cover the sun, circled by a ring of fire. The darkness compares to twilight twenty minutes after sunset. Sea sparkles darkly. Birds stop their chatter.
>
> 3:24: A short, thin arc of sun appears at five o'clock.
>
> 3:29: Arc thickens, lengthens. Getting light again.

Moon and sun diverged as slowly as they had merged. Clouds covered the sun again. The show was over. Among the watchers, frenzy gave way to contentment, like the lull after lovemaking.

"I'd have preferred less distraction," I said to Luciano, aside.

"Me too," he whispered.

While I shared a final evening with my friends, I wrote these stanzas in my diary, like an artist's quick sketches:

Luciano when he speaks
glows with manly innocence
Spanish sounds so beautiful on his tongue!

Javier: David Niven wit and charm
but his funniest quips
go too fast for me to understand

Melissa, the beauty in waiting
model's nose
moods like all kids
"Let's go eat the little crabs!" I say
"Let's walk in the woods with the wild animals!"
and I laugh at the excitement and fear in her eyes

Negra: eternal, complete
intimate with me in motherly ways
health, food, clothing
always the only woman
yet she balances all the men

Juan always talks
with headed cocked at an angle for suspense
maluca! a la lata! vacan!
wild eyes driving home the slangy words

Lino: nobody's-fool masculinity
a bit of brusqueness
learning to be a good person
seeking the seeker in himself
We knew how close to get
and what to hold back

I slept in a hammock, and was woken in the night by a damp wind. By the light of lightning flashes I found more clothing to put on, and got more sleep.

At first light I slipped the borrowed garments off. Cholo tiptoed down from the second floor. *"Suerte* (good luck)," he said, sadly.

I hurried down to the beach, ran back and forth a while to stop my shivering, and waded out into the water. It was fresh to the touch, salty, not cold. *Squeak* lay at anchor a hundred yards out, very pretty, waiting for me. I swam to her, pulled my torso up onto her stern deck, where my weight would be near the centerline, and swung my legs over into the cockpit. I took down the rain cover, raised the anchor, and rowed west as the sun rose in the east, turning the world pink and blue.

CHAPTER 15

TO BUENAVENTURA

I rowed beyond familiar landmarks to a village I thought might be Arusí. "No, Arusí is the next village down," said one of the many blacks gathered on the beach. Another tried to climb in with me, but I put him off and pulled away. Someone else got in a canoe and chased me. The gap between us slowly narrowed, but the paddler turned out to be just a kid wanting to make sure I did my buying at his grandparents' store in Arusí. There, I anchored *Squeak* in two feet of water and walked into the village with him.

His grandma and grandpa helped me replace various provisions that had been consumed at Lino's house. Then he showed me to the tiny bakery. Villagers squeezed inside with us and laughed hilariously while I sorted through the loaves to select the ten least infested with ants. "How picky!" they exclaimed. Finally, passing a little boy with a bowl of guavas (a handball-sized fruit, green on the outside, pink on the inside), I bought five for about a penny apiece.

At 9:30 A.M. I rounded Punta Arusí, hoisted sail, and tacked into a ten-knot headwind and contrary current. A pair of whales passed a half mile distant, heading the opposite direction, discernible by their black backs and misty spouts. The coast was a rugged cliff, perhaps five hundred feet tall, broken, uninhabited. In some places it was forested, in others bare stone. Jagged rocks were strewn along the shore, some big enough to be called islands. One stout pillar, protruding some twelve feet above the water, was capped by a mound of vegetation like a green ice cream cone, half-obscured by white, roosting pelicans. I wrote:

> I love wilderness more
> and for the same reason
> that I love history:
> origin, connection to long-ago lives

How did this rock look
in 1525 when Francisco Pizarro passed?
when Adam and Eve were still in the garden?
Answer: this rock *is* the garden
here before, here before, here before

God gave them this succulent bed
but it wasn't big enough
so they left it, to wound continents and oceans

I travel not to document the extinctions
but to seek the places still left
the garden that wasn't big enough
the origin

I know I'm close
when there's no trace of man
on that wild shore, nor on that sea
but me

Ahead, jutting twelve miles out into the Pacific Ocean, was Cabo Corrientes. It was the limit of the known world for many of the natives I had lived among in the Gulf of Tribugá. They regarded it as a dangerous place. Indeed, the sea got rougher, the cliffs more sheer.

At 4:30 I arrived, having averaged only a mile per hour. I sat drifting twenty or thirty yards off the very tip and admired the fierce architecture. Could I build a house on the peak that forms its extremity, I wondered? No: it was too pointy, and the razorback ridge behind, that connected it to the high plateau of the peninsula, ascended too steeply. The swells rose up as if over a shallows, but my lead line registered eighty feet—the cape dropped off as steeply underwater as it rose above.

I rounded the cape, and my fishing line suddenly snapped. The water was too deep to have caught on a rock, so it must have been a big fish. I had only that one lure, a gift from Alejo—no more fishing for now. I stopped at a slight indentation in the coastline, where the shore was a tangle of fallen palm trees. It faced wind and waves, but it was shallow and the bottom was firm sand. This would be the first test of my strategy for the following seventy-five miles of coast, to the delta of the Rio San Juan. The problem was that the coast ran due south, exposed to the west-southwest swells. I might not be able to land for a week, and if I drifted at night the northbound current would wipe out my hard-won gains. How to hold my ground while I slept?

My plan was to anchor offshore each night. According to the chart, the bottom was sand, and the coast had an exceptionally gradual seaward slope. The ten-meter depth contour averaged 3.5 miles offshore. Thus, should swells break in ten feet of water, they would do so 1.2 miles from shore. Furthermore, the shoreline from which to measure such distance would itself migrate dramatically in accordance with the tide. Since the tidal fall averaged fifteen feet, the shoreline would shift 1.8 miles seaward, and back again, twice daily. Theoretically, in order to keep sufficient water under me at low tide, I needed to anchor at least four miles out, measuring from the high water mark. Unfortunately, I had no means of knowing my position so precisely, nor did I have much anchor line.

I had only 150 feet of rode (rope and chain) worth risking my life on. Given the good holding ground and moderate winds, I thought a 1-to-4.3 depth/rode ratio should suffice, which meant I could anchor in water up to thirty-five feet deep. But if I anchored in thirty-five feet and the depth increased to fifty during the night, the anchor could drag and the wind would blow me into the surf. Conversely, if I anchored in the minimum depth of twenty feet (ten feet plus a ten-foot safety margin for rogue waves), the depth could drop to five feet during the night, and the breakers would catch me. Either way, *Squeak* would be swept into a gauntlet of surf. Each new breaker would capsize her, crush her, carry her further from safety. If *Squeak* broke up, could I swim to shore? And if I did, could I survive in that desolate jungle without any provisions?

Everything depended on my tide table, watch, and lead line. In order to anchor just seaward enough for depth at low tide to be twenty feet, I would determine how long it would be until the following low tide, then solve the following crude equation:

$$\text{depth at time of anchoring} = \left[\left(\text{\# of hours between time of anchoring and following low tide} \div 6 \text{ hours}\right) \times 15 \text{ ft.}\right] + 20 \text{ ft.}$$

That night, just inside the tip of Cabo Corrientes, I located the indicated depth with my lead line and dropped anchor. I tied the anchor line to the base of the mizzen mast, because the greater windage of the main mast caused her to ride better facing downwind. Then I boiled some potatoes and onions, careful lest the bounciness of the anchorage upset my pot. I fell asleep praying that my anchor wouldn't drag, and my rope wouldn't untie.

I weighed anchor at 6:30 A.M. For an hour I struggled futilely against wind and current. Then I noticed what looked like an oddly shaped island, out where there should have been only deep water. It was a black column, terminating in a blunt point. As I watched, it slowly sank straight down into the sea! Knowing islands rarely do that, I supposed it was a jumping whale. Later I saw them: humpbacks, perhaps the same pair as the day before. They passed inshore of me, a hundred yards away, traveling toward the cape. Every few minutes they surfaced, spouted, and sounded again, in one smooth, humpbacked motion, sometimes slapping their tails at the end. Their breaths were powerful, high-pitched, precisely valved, one second in duration.

I sailed to the base of the cape then turned south, staying close to the surf to minimize adverse current. Whenever I found myself especially close to breakers I dropped my lead to better know what constitutes minimum safe depth. The soundings ranged from fourteen to twenty-three feet. The swells were twelve feet tall, perfectly straight, perfectly parallel, two hundred yards apart. I could never surf them, as I had at Morro Mico. The sea between each pair of swells was smooth, as if the rearing waves ironed out all else. They came not quite parallel to the shoreline, so, sighting down a swell, at some point downcoast it would already be breaking. That line of snowy foam would proceed straight on to the horizon, eventually terminating on an unseen beach.

Suddenly the swells became taller, and frightfully steep—the ebbing tide had trapped me in shallow water! Now the breaking point was a mere hundred yards away down the line of the swell. To get outside the breakers I rowed desperately seaward, into the waves. Each wave tilted *Squeak's* bow up. I felt a G-force and a rush of wind as we shot up to its crest. Then *Squeak* teeter-tottered, and we cascaded down to the perfectly flat plain beyond. Adrenaline pumping, I rowed to the next ridge of water, then the next, then the next. For an hour I labored, wondering if the next wall would flatten me. To my left the walls were white thunder, under me and to my right they were blue and curling. Finally the breakpoints became more distant. When I reached safety I vowed to stay at least a quarter mile from the breakpoint, measured down the line of the swell. Still, I couldn't play it entirely safe because the further out, the stronger the contrary current. To make progress, I had to remain close ashore.

The coastal ranges I'd followed since Punta Garachine now fell away, and a low plain took their place. The map showed it extending fifty miles inland, roadless and wild. Numerous small rivers drained the plain, and terminated in mangrove-swamp estuaries. The mouths were rarely distinguishable except for their effect on the surf. Sediment issuing from the rivers made the water even shallower, causing waves to break much further out. The sight of breakers far out to sea was my sign to start angling seaward, which usually meant sailing hard on the wind or tacking. The wind came from the south until about ten A.M., then gradually veered clockwise. By three P.M. it blew steadily from the west. This pattern would hold throughout the passage. I made good use of the more favorable afternoon wind, covering nearly twenty miles that day. The weather was hot, humid, rainy.

Once I saw to seaward a thin silhouette, which became two silhouettes, then merged again. It came toward me: two tall black men standing, paddling a light dugout. They tried to intercept me, gesturing strangely. I avoided them, glad the wind was sufficient to sail away. A curious pelican also followed me. It landed in the water beside me, watched me sail away, then flew to me again, over and over. Another time I crossed a "water boundary:" a sharp delineation of brown river water and blue seawater, agitated and full of floating jungle detritus at the juncture.

At nightfall I calculated the necessary depth, and sailed seaward an hour to reach it. I anchored, threw a twig in the water, and clocked the northbound current. It took eight seconds for the current to travel one boat-length: about one knot. I turned in, and dreamt of sea avalanches. Their roar deafened me. Their tons of sunlit foam blinded and suffocated me. Their nightmarish beauty gripped me like a pain in my heart.

I crossed many more "water boundaries" the next day. They were serpentine, endless. Logs and branches formed a continuous line at the juncture, which flowed like a river in the sea. To cross them I found a weak point and crashed through. They sounded like rivers too, so tingly was the water, so charged with inexplicable wave action.

I was often within sight of the beach, and never saw a hint of man. I longed to land. My body ached from constantly balancing *Squeak*. My butt hurt from sitting, and my knees from bending. But even coming close was dangerous, because any rogue wave could shipwreck me. I kept a sharp lookout, and stood occasionally to boost my sight distance. Wherever I saw white, even for a second, I memorized that spot and went outside it. My solar plexus hurt, a near-ulcer condition I get when stressed. The breakers terrified me, but my plan was working.

Night found me about three miles off a river mouth called Boca Docampadó. Seven or eight big shrimpers were working within sight. No sooner had I anchored and boiled some vegetables when a file of them came toward me. They were towing nets by means of cables attached to spreader poles. Red-to-port and green-to-starboard navigational lights revealed their course. The wind blew vigorously from the northwest. The night was dark, the sea rough. The sound of breakers ground in my ears.

When the first shrimper was a hundred yards away I shone my flashlight at his bridge—he veered away. Fifteen minutes later the second one arrived; he too veered. But the third changed course as if to run me down. I flashed my light on and off as the gap narrowed. I grabbed my oars, but the taut anchor line make it impossible to row out of his way. I prepared to jump in the water, thinking to grab onto his net cable as he went by, when he finally swerved sharply, some thirty feet away.

That unnerved me. The shrimpers kept working back and forth. It was a lousy place to anchor, but to sail at night wouldn't be safe either. I lay down in the cabin and set my watch alarm to wake me every twenty minutes to check on the shrimpers.

At eleven o'clock a full-fledged storm hit, like the one that had capsized me near Morro Mico. To avoid the same fate, I stripped naked and got into the cockpit, quickly replacing the hatch cover. I took advantage of the pelting rain to shampoo and shave. Then I donned rain gear, curled up on my right side on the seat deck, and bailed rainwater from the footwell with my left hand, about a pint every four seconds. *Squeak* bounced like a poodle at the end of its leash. Lightning bolts lit the sky almost continuously. I shivered, and worried about the strain on the anchor line. I didn't have enough batteries to leave the flashlight on, only to signal when a shrimper got close. Dangers crowded all around: capsize, collision, lightning, surf. My skin pruned from prolonged wetness. The sound of wind and waves droned in my ears. I bailed until the storm eased at four A.M., then crawled wearily inside for a couple hours of sleep.

When I woke, sky and water were gray. The coast was a thin line on the horizon. With the hatch closed, just enough light entered through the two portholes to prepare a bowl of rolled oats. Suddenly, through the aft porthole I saw a crude wooden boat approach. I grabbed my machete. The helmsman stood on the aft deck, controlling an outboard by means of a tiller extension. The cargo consisted of several new dugout canoes, nested one inside the other. Three passengers huddled under a makeshift shelter in the bow. I opened the hatch and stuck my head out.

The helmsman twisted his hand imploringly in the air, meaning, "Where you going?"

"Buenaventura!" I yelled, waving my arm south.

"Sí! Tambien! (Yes, us too!)," he replied, and went on.

Later, a tug towing a barge went several miles out of its way to inspect me. It came alongside. Five or six black crewmen checked me out. I bummed a pair of flashlight batteries off them, then we each continued on our way.

I sailed for hours as close to the wind as possible on a starboard tack. The gap between me and shore slowly closed. Just as I was about to tack out and get more sea room, I noticed a small river mouth that appeared passable. I studied it for ten minutes. The mouth itself was too risky; at one time or another waves broke across the entire opening. The beach a quarter mile north of the mouth, however, appeared to have little surf. I dropped the sails and rowed close.

Low, brushy jungle began just behind the moderately steep beach. A black man walked by, shotgun in arm, accompanied by a small boy and a dog. Curiosity and sea-weariness impelled me toward that mysterious shore.

I battened everything down and rowed in fast, facing backward. A four-foot wave passed without surfing me—I was almost to the beach. But the next one suddenly reared up like a bear on its hind legs. I backed to a standstill, turned perpendicular to it, and held my breath. It caught me at the worst possible moment—vertical, curling. The wave flipped *Squeak* end for end like a book of matches, catapulting me into the sea. I twisted around underwater a while, then, just as at Morro Mico, found myself waist-deep in water, with *Squeak* on her side beside me. Her forward somersault had thrown her masthead-first onto the sand, yet everything was intact. I righted her and pulled her up with the next wave, then plucked my oars out of the surf and threw them onto the sand.

Damn! I had taken an unnecessary risk and now was washed up on a shore as strange as the moon. My cap and towel were gone and an oarlock socket had been damaged. The surf appeared much worse looking seaward. How would I ever get off again? My inability to leave put me at the mercy of whoever lived around there.

I was hauling my stuff up into the tall brush behind the beach when the man with the old-fashioned shotgun returned. He was short, with grotesquely callused hands. His clothing was factory-made, old and worn. His son now carried a bunch of plantains on his head. When I explained my need to get above the beach before the tide rose, they cleared a spot in the brush with their machete. A group of *monte* laborers arrived. Together we hoisted *Squeak* into the clearing. The natives seemed no different from those of Arusí or Nuquí. They said they were from Orpua, a village just inside the river mouth.

No sooner was everything moved when the man with the shotgun, Mamerto, got a better idea. "Let's take the boat around to my father's house. It's safer there, and the *chitras* aren't so bad," he said.

They all excitedly urged my consent. Again the problem of keeping control, of keeping things from getting stolen. But it made sense. So we hauled everything back down to the water and loaded up. Mamerto and I walked *Squeak* toward the mouth, wading in the shallows. The waves, though largely dissipated, slammed *Squeak* up-beach and sucked her down-beach, while between waves she often grounded out. At the mouth, Mamerto and I got in and rowed into a briny lake from which brown sloughs radiated into the surrounding mangrove swamp. We turned into the second slough on the left and stopped in front of a planked hut set ten feet from the bank. To keep me out of the rain, Mamerto helped me drag *Squeak* onto the hut's porch.

The porch took up one corner of the floor plan, leaving an L-shaped enclosure containing two small bedrooms and a kitchen. Bamboo rafters supported a roof of palm thatch. The hut sat on a narrow peninsula at the juncture of two sloughs. There was no yard, just clumps of grass, palm and other sand-loving trees, and the mangroves in the mud at the margins of the sloughs.

Neighbors came to see what was going on. Mamerto brought out his father, an erect, white-haired man named Vincente. He offered me his hand. "I'll be responsible for your welfare while you're my guest," he said, falteringly. "I was born in the year 1905. I have thirteen children and seventy-three grandchildren. Welcome to my house, señor."

I hung up my clothes to dry, then Diego, a thirteen-year-old grandson, paddled me to the village in a leaky canoe. Mangrove saplings and bamboo poles protruded from the water. We disembarked at a sawmill where I met the manager, a middle-aged mulatto named Señor Genaro. He showed me the facility: a large hall, a ramp for winching logs out of the water, a circular saw powered by a diesel engine, and a quay for loading the lumber onto boats for shipping to Buenaventura. "The principal species is *nato*," he said. "It's heavier than water, so our providers must raft it downriver with balsa logs. We make railroad ties out of it, and pallets for the coffee industry."

The village was surprisingly large. Thinking they should present me to the authorities, Diego and some other boys took me to see a pair of Spanish nuns. When these good women showed no particular interest, they took me to the house of "the inspector." This old man had no uniform or symbol of office, but he slowly leafed through my papers, jotting notes on a pad. "What you're doing isn't safe," he said. "Take the packet boat to Buenaventura." I bought some oranges from his tree, and thanked him for his advice.

The town had just received a new "water system:" large, open-topped plastic barrels with taps at the bottom. They simply caught and stored rainwater. One stood here, another there, with no apparent pattern except that all were right-side up. The barrels had been sent from the interior to stop people from drinking polluted water and contracting cholera. The kids explained this to me, but tomorrow's being Day of the Virgin of Carmen excited them far more. They took me to the church, whose walls were a lattice of cement blocks. Peeking through the holes, my friends oohed and ahed over the brightly colored papier-mâché effigies of animals and saints that would be marched through town in an annual parade.

I savored the stillness of a night on land, inside *Squeak* as usual. When the crowing cocks woke me, at dawn, Vincente came and sat by me. His old hands toyed with a bright green switch. An eight-year-old girl came out rubbing her eyes and knelt before her grandfather, who placed his hand on her head and mumbled a blessing. Then she wandered away.

I missed the parade, concentrating instead on my diary and on replacing the ruined oarlock socket with a spare I had bought in New Orleans. A lively crowd watched. Vincente sat on his stool, telling what he knew of the coast ahead. The little girl sang songs. Chickens and pigs foraged for food. The only blemish was a queasiness in my gut that obliged me to spent a lot of time squatting behind trees. Whether the microbes that now vexed me were the offspring of those that had entered by means of the ice cube in Eulalia's oat drink, or from some more recent source, I couldn't say.

In the afternoon the tide was low and the slough could be crossed on foot. My temporary hatch cover had been leaking, so I carried it to the sawmill and coated it with an oil-based paint that Genaro provided. He also gave me an old Playboy magazine. I cut out pictures and presented them as gifts to my various guides and helpers. They were a little young for the girl pictures, but they loved the motorcycle ones. I bought batteries at a hole-in-the-wall store, and hobnobbed with the people on the street. A motorboat operator said a man had been fatally ambushed in the next river mouth south, three months before. "You'd better bypass the coast," he said. "There's a slough you can follow that joins up with the north fork of the Rio San Juan. You go up the north fork, then down the south fork, back into the sea. Then you're very close to Buenaventura."

"Thanks. I might do that."

I had dinner at the sawmill with Genaro, the manager. "My company recently assigned me here," he said. "I like it, except my wife and children have to stay in Buenaventura, where the schools are better." Rain drummed on the tin roof. The hall was empty, feebly lit by a single kerosene lamp. It faced the lake through large, paneless windows, but nothing was visible through the pouring rain but a glow in the sky to the southwest.

"What's that?" I asked.

"Buenaventura—the lights of the city, reflecting off the clouds."

"Oh, I'm so close!"

When the rain stopped I walked homeward with Diego. Passing a house from which lamplight and voices emanated, we were hailed by a black man wearing shoes, dark trousers, and a white shirt.

"Come in, please, join our group!" he said. We did. The house was small and modest. "We're a committee. We investigate phenomena we find curious. We've heard about you, and wonder if you'd mind answering some questions?" He sat me on a couch beside a woman so drunk she was passing in and out of consciousness. Someone poured me a glass of clear liquor. All five "committee members" were drinking it.

"What's this?"

"Biche," he said. "From sugar cane." I tasted. It was nearly pure alcohol, with a smell and tang reminiscent of turpentine.

"Mm! Not bad!"

The woman tried to speak again, then slumped against me. Ignoring her, the well-dressed man and another gentleman questioned me keenly about the voyage, especially place names and distances. *"Que valentía! Salud*! (What courage! Cheers!)" When I left they presented me with an honorary bottle of *biche.* Months later I was still nipping occasionally off that bottle.

Diego and I continued through the dark, silent village to the innermost tip of a tiny channel. It was high tide again; we had to go by canoe. I took my shoes off and waded into the muddy water, lighting the way with my flashlight. With a series of heaves, we worked the canoe out the winding trough and paddled home.

I was ready to leave at 7:30 A.M., thankful for a rest midway between Arusí and Buenaventura. I had rejected the slough route for lack of information, but still hoped to go up the north fork. The neighbors helped me move *Squeak* to the bank. When I sat down at the oars, old Vincente shuffled alongside, reached out a trembling hand, and touched my head. "Bless you my son," he said with sweet humility. Then they all pushed me off and bade farewell.

The tide being high, the river bar was now clear. I rowed out the mouth and continued south. The wind was too light and contrary to sail. Just as well; I was less conspicuous rowing. Breakers barred Boca Togorama, first of the six mouths of the Rio San Juan. It got dark before I reached the second mouth. I'd covered fifteen miles, and had reached the bulging delta. It took two hours to row out far enough to anchor.

To take the river route would now mean backtracking, so the next day I rowed around the low islands and shallow passages that constitute the second and third mouths. When I reached jungly Isla Cacagual, the outermost part of the delta, a two-knot current forced me to anchor a hundred yards offshore and wait for something to change. Pelicans by the hundreds fished the waters around me. Canoe fishermen worked the waters further out. The sun reflected blindingly off the foam of the roaring breakers. Ahead was the breaker field of the fourth mouth. I had only to round it, and the coastline would start veering southeast, off the wind.

Fortunately, that afternoon the wind swung all the way to northwest, allowing me to sail a favorable course. I passed a rusty shrimper hauling in its net. Its unmuffled engines growled brutishly, and emitted huge billows of smoke. These shoals seemed to stretch endlessly seaward, and their outer boundary was indistinct. Finally I was round them, headed south. Huge ground swells, soon to become breakers, passed under me, one after another, from right to left. Once, looking back, I saw one break where I had just been—too close.

I had heard that the breaker field off Boca Chavica, the fifth mouth, was even bigger, so I maintained my distance from shore. This was where Cholo's father had made Swiss cheese out of the bloodthirsty pirates, but at least I had the wind aft of abeam for a change. It was four o'clock; could I round Boca Chavica before dark?

An hour later I started seeing the white of its breakers. The closer I got, the further seaward they extended. Despite my precaution, I had underestimated the size of the sandbar and was forced to sail close-hauled again to round it. It was getting dark. I skirted the outer edge of the breaker field, with a half-mile safety margin, until I approached land again. Then I started measuring the water. When I reached the proper depth for that point in the tidal cycle, I anchored and went to bed. Coastal traffic had to stay further out, so I felt relatively safe.

That night the wind continued from the northwest while a strong current flowed from the south. The two couldn't agree on how *Squeak* should lay to anchor, so they worked out a compromise whereby the wind dictated the orientation of the anchor line and the current dictated that of the boat. That is, line and boat together formed a J shape. Being sideways to the waves, *Squeak* rolled more, waking me at 10:30 P.M. I checked the anchor line. Leaning over *Squeak's* pointy stern, I saw it—the phosphorescence lit it like a laser beam. The 3/8" beam of light descended, curved to the right, and disappeared in the inky depths. I got back in bed, read a while, then wrote:

Inside *Squeak,* reading by flashlight
I sit up though the open hatch:
yes, the ocean is still here
I'm in it

Slow, dark clouds veil and unveil the halved moon
a porpoise circles; I hear his perfect breath
air-rush of pelicans overhead
white noise of breakers

The moon, when clear, sheens the rippled ball
(two kinds of ripples, one large, one small)
paving a silver path back to itself

I can't live in the sea, like the porpoise
swimming naked day to day.
My home, though hardly larger than myself
contains me, and my necessities, surprisingly numerous

Less natural than the porpoise
but more adaptive
I can do this, and other things too
I think, as I sway with the ocean
which I fear, engage, study

Opposite the moon, southeast
another light: the sky glow of Buenaventura
my objective these past six months
one, two days away?
The glow is not home
but another strange place
(visited in 1973, too long ago to remember)

As I sit, head through hatch
the breeze stirs the few hairs
not imprisoned in my ponytail
reminding me to remember myself
as a person who can be touched
not solely a proud, efficient machine of discovery

But for now to be an adventurer is enough
because now I feel good
because that glow is the light at the end of a journey
through the ocean of my potential
"ocean" not because broad
but because deep, never fully probed

Now, while my anchor tethers me
a new sound approaches: a "water boundary"
front line of warring tidal masses
it passes below me, foamy, troubled

I do not claim to know this ocean
rather it symbolizes what I don't know
this ocean that is not home, but a medium
I fear it, engage it, study it

July 19 dawned brightly. I squeezed my daily dose of lemons with a pair of pliers, and found the appetite for a breakfast of pre-cooked oats. I waited comfortably for the morning south wind to develop then sailed, slackening my sheets more and more as the wind walked slowly around the clock. I wore my long white pants and shirt to prevent sunburn. On my head I wore the straw hat I'd purchased at the Bremerton Salvation Army before leaving. That, my navy hat, and my khaki shorts were the only original items of clothing I had left. Everything else had been worn out, lost, replaced.

I passed the final mouth, Boca San Juan, about three miles out. The wind shifted to my starboard quarter and stayed there the rest of the day, steady at about ten knots. Launches passed more frequently. The old fear touched me each time, but they always just smiled and waved. I looked so small and funny, maybe even a real pirate would react the same way. Who knows?

Past the delta, the land rose, still flat. The shoreline became a cliff. A new range of coastal mountains appeared beyond the plain. I passed the opening of a sound called Bahia de Málaga, which I had often noted for its curious shape on the map. I had imagined mangrove swamps, but it looked more like a fjord. With two hours of daylight left I continued along alternating cliffs and coves. I passed a hilltop mansion and was tempted to stop in for some First World conversation, but Buenaventura drew me like a magnet.

The wind now blew from behind, for the first time since the Mississippi River. I pulled the mizzen around opposite the main and sailed "wing-on-wing." The motion was now smooth so I stood up and steered with a hand behind me. I shifted weight slightly from leg to leg, rocking *Squeak* through a forty-degree arc. Her masts rocked like metronomes. Heedless of my frolic, she barreled along without deviating her course. I enjoyed a final sea meal of crackers, peas, oranges, and cookies. Wonderful! Buenaventura!

The shore became more urbanized until I reached the sandy point at the entrance to Buenaventura Harbor. Families strolled the beach. Waves lapped gently on the gray sand. The sun was setting. Six miles northeast, at the end of the inlet, the lights of the city were coming on. I dropped sail and tied to a public pier among small fishing boats.

A crowd gathered as usual. This was not a village, however, but a satellite neighborhood known as La Bocana. Some of the people were whites or mestizos from the interior, passing their holidays in guest houses near the beach. I ate boiled clams at an open kitchen and bought a beer to go. As I passed three idlers, one motioned for me to come, a sort of heel command.

I lifted a palm, impatiently, inquisitively.

"*Venga* (come here)."

"*Por que* (why)?" I asked, standing my ground.

"Buy me one beer!" he said, in bad English. They all laughed.

I walked away, weary of such manipulators. It didn't look like a safe place to spend the night, so I climbed aboard and drifted with the incoming tide beyond reach of the electric light.

The shoreline became a gloomy cove, fringed with mangrove. Tiny flames crept through the flooded trees at the margin of the cove—some form of night fishing? How could anyone walk there? Rowing silently, without splash or clunk, I found a spot deep enough not to go aground at low tide. Sure no one had seen me, I anchored and turned in.

I woke to the sound of another boat bumping alongside. I flung open the hatch, adrenaline rushing, and beheld a nearly naked man standing in a dugout canoe. His net lay piled before him. A smoky, homemade oil lamp flickered in the canoe's bow.

"I saw you, wondered what you were," he said, wide-eyed.

"I'm anchoring here for the night."

"You shouldn't—*los atracadores* might find you."

"I'll be okay. Just don't tell anybody I'm here. Promise?"

"Sí!" he said, and left.

Too jumpy to fall back to sleep, I lit my flashlight, pulled out my dictionary, and looked up *atracador*. "Gangster, holdup man," it said. That substantiated the evil things I'd been hearing for months about Buenaventura. When I reached the city I'd have to find a safe place before dark. My original plan had been to look up some friends of Juan Uribe, my friend in Bahia Solano, but those notes had been lost in the capsize. Fortunately, Luis Eduardo Gonzalez had then given me directions to the place where he kept his own boat, at the property of a Captain Minning. "It's at the end of a slough, accessible only at high tide," he'd said. The next high would be at 10:30 A.M. I would ride the tide in, and arrive before the current reversed.

Saturday, July 20, 1991, dawned gray and drizzly. The inlet was large, with mangrove swamps and estuaries radiating in all directions. I had no chart, only sketchy instructions on how to find Captain Minning's landing. I sailed, land to port, past slough openings and defoliated hills. Ahead lay the city, on an island at the end of the inlet. The city center and port terminal occupied the west half of the island. A short bridge connected the island's east end to the mainland.

Nothing matched my memories of the place when I visited it with my brother Mike. Gray, multistory buildings jostled for space. The streets were now paved. Much of this must have been built since 1973, yet it looked ancient, decayed. A wrecked ship encumbered the waterfront. The ferry pier was crumpled and leaning, but crowded nonetheless with people bound for La Bocana via a fleet of small ferries.

I proceeded clockwise around the island, past Liberian, Panamanian, and Greek-flagged bulk freighters tied to a tall quay. By the time I saw the bridge, the channel was narrow, with mangrove swamp to my left and a line of foul shacks built over the water to my right. The shoreline bristled with rickety docks serving outboard-driven dugouts and clumsy coastal freighters. Following the directions of some boatmen, I backed out of that channel and took the next one to the right. Low, brushy mangrove lined this new channel. The water was brown.

A man in a dugout cast a circular net with a frisbee-like motion, retrieved it, and cast again. "Where's Captain Minning's landing?" I asked. He pointed to a house and ramshackle cluster of boats at the far end of the slough.

The tide was beginning to drop. Wind and drizzle had given way to a silvery, humid stillness. I rowed to the landing. A burly white man wearing a Greek fisherman's cap walked stiffly down to meet me, one hand in his pocket, the other on his hip. I introduced myself.

"I know, I know," he said in German-accented English. "Congratulations. You're absolutely mad."

"Are you Captain Minning?"

Ignoring me, he called, in Spanish, to a lanky mestizo with a handlebar mustache. "Jorge! Let's pull this thing up."

We parked *Squeak* in front of the house, under the bowsprit of a shored-up aluminum yacht.

"Have Luz fix him a bed," said the captain.

"Sí, señor." Jorge disappeared into the house.

"We'll talk later. You're tired," said Captain Minning, reverting to English. Then he climbed a flight of steps and entered an upstairs door.

A petite Indian woman beckoned me inside the downstairs apartment, past two wide-eyed little girls, to a bed in a corner of the room. Smiling timidly, she lifted the mosquito net.

"Well, I guess a siesta would feel good. *Gracias, señora."*

"A sus ordenes (At your order)," she said. I brushed my feet off and lay down. The mosquito net fell into place, bringing to a close the Pacific Ocean phase of the voyage. Weariness and relief overwhelmed me. Only later would the full impact of those six stressful months become apparent. It was the hardest thing I'd ever done. But it was worth my giddy sense of discovery, my feeling of having found a way through a land of unknown dangers and delights to a semi-civilization on the far side.

I thought back to when I had set out on the voyage. I'd had an idea of what might unfold, and a will to make it happen. But I'd always granted the voyage a measure of self-determination. It wasn't a mountain to be climbed, so much as a path to be found. So far, the path I'd found was very nearly the one I had anticipated. Now for Phase 3.

My original thought had been to sail to Tumaco, 185 miles further south.

From there I could transport *Squeak* to Puerto Asis, on the border between Colombia and Ecuador, and cross South America by the Putumayo and Amazon rivers, just as I had crossed North America by the Missouri and Mississippi. For some time, however, I'd been considering the Meta and Orinoco rivers instead. The voyage was taking much longer than expected, and the Orinoco route was shorter. I knew less about the Orinoco, and was therefore more curious about it. Finally, I was tired of rain, and had heard that the Orinoco flows through dry country. Buenaventura was the best place to begin transport to the headwaters of the Meta. The first step, after this sweet nap, would be to get a ride to Cali.

PART III
SOUTH AMERICAN RIVERS

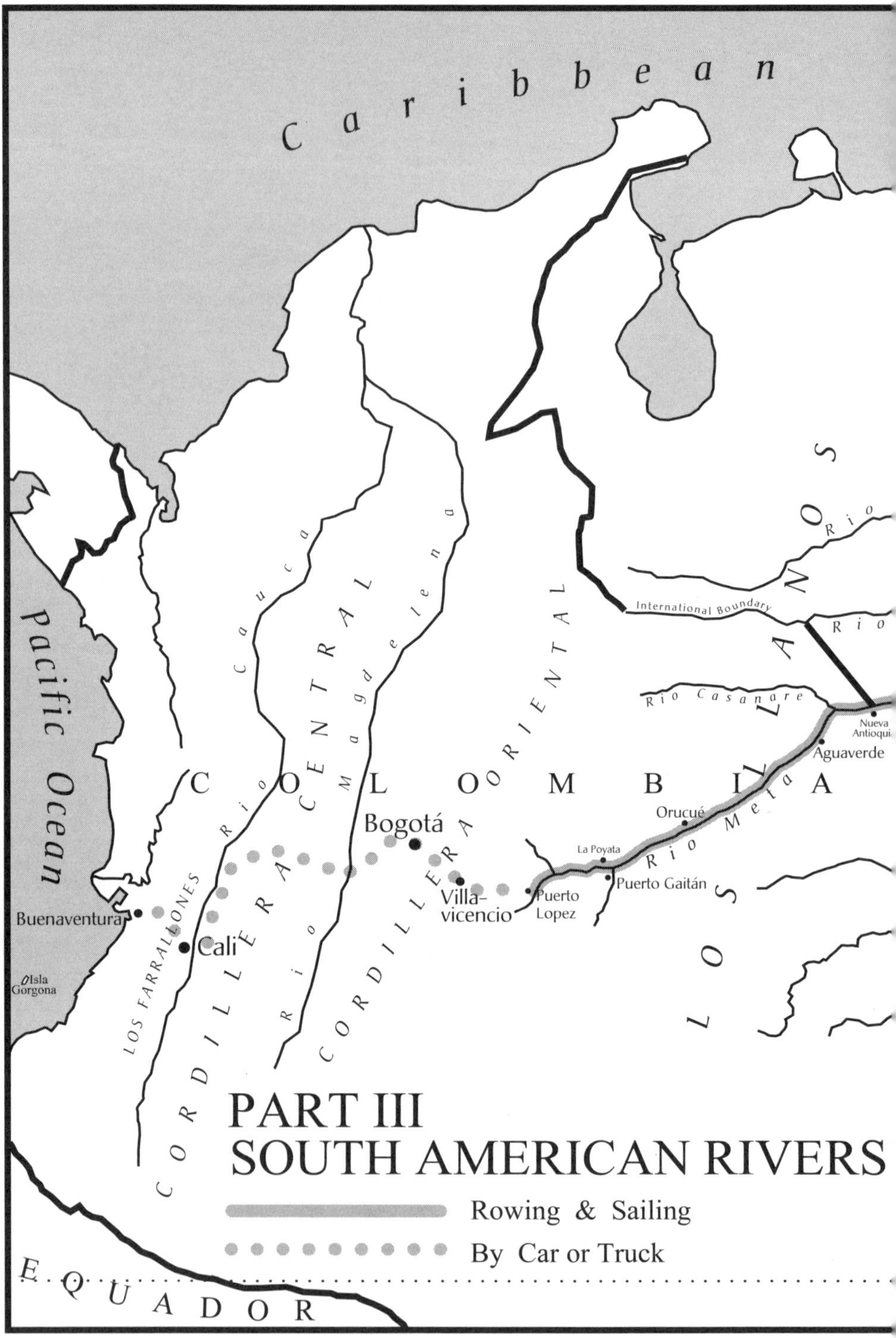

Sea
0 100 200 miles
0 100 200 300 km
N
TRINIDAD & TOBAGO
Gulf of Paria
Mouth of the Serpent
see inset
Caracas
Puerto La Cruz
Tucupita
Boca Macareo
Barrancas
GUYANA CASTLES
Ciudad Guyana
Rio Orinoco
Mapire
Mouth of Hell
Ciudad Bolívar
Apure
Arauca
Caicara
Rio Caroni
Rio Caura
El Dorado
La Urbana
VENEZUELA
Puerto Paez
International Boundary
Puerto Carreño
Puerto Ayacucho
GUYANA HIGHLANDS
LA GRAN SABANA
GUYANA
Santa Elena
COLOMBIA
Rio
Orinoco
BRAZIL
Equator
Negro
Amazon River 300 miles
Mouth of the Dragon
Port of Spain
Gulf of Paria
San Fernando
Brighton
Mouth of the Serpent
PUNTA PESCADOR

CHAPTER 16

CALI

I woke at two P.M. The walls were of cement block, painted white, moldy. A sink, counter, and table took up the front of the room. My bed and another took up the rear. Sheets had been hung from the ceiling to screen off the other bed. From this enclosure came the sound of a little girl talking to herself, perhaps playing with dolls.

I walked outside. The property lay at the tip of a small peninsula. Propellers, nets, and rusty machinery littered the grounds. Vessels lay moored at the shallow waterfront. Up the peninsula, beyond a stout fence, were slums, but the view up the inlet and to the right was of swamps and low hills.

I found Captain Minning inside the aluminum sailboat, working in the bilge. "You've got quite a collection of boats," I said.

He set a floor panel down and straightened with a grunt. "Damn these little boats. Always crouching and twisting, bad for my back." He sank heavily onto a settee. "This one I bought from Customs five years ago, for almost nothing. They confiscated it from a gringo, like you. They said he was planning to ship cocaine out, and he couldn't prove he wasn't! Ha ha for him!"

He still wore his fisherman's cap. Pinned to it, above the short brim, was a red hammer-and-sickle. "What's that pin?" I asked.

He removed his cap, frowning. "Oh, that. A Russian sea captain gave it to me. He was a big drinker! Vodka, always vodka!"

"Where you from, anyway?" I asked.

Captain Minning shrugged impatiently. "Half Colombian, half Swiss. Until last year I owned a fleet of shrimp boats. Sold them all! I'm selling the boats, the land, everything. Buying land in the Llanos. As far as I can get from the sea and still be in Colombia."

"Llanos—great plains. That's where I'm going too. I'm thinking about following the Meta River to the Orinoco, then going down it to the Atlantic side."

He laughed. "The Meta River? The mosquitoes will pick your little boat up and fly away with you!" He pantomimed it, thumbs and forefingers pinching, lifting. "You're completely mad. Even worse than Luis Eduardo said."

He looked at his watch. "I have to go downtown. Want a ride?"

"Yeah. I need to call home."

We got into his Dodge pickup, stopped to open the gate, then drove up the spine of the peninsula, through a raw expanse of dirt and squalid shacks. "Barrio Oriente," he said. Turning right we descended into the slum, crossed a putrid stream, and climbed a parallel ridge a half mile away. We turned right again on the Cali-Buenaventura highway, drove to the bridge, and entered the city proper. Traffic slowed as we skirted a parade. Firemen, policemen, and customs officials marched in clumsy phalanxes down the dusty highway. A drum and bugle corps blatted some martial hymn.

"Colombian Independence Day," said Captain Minning.

"Will the telephone office be open?"

"I think so."

He stopped at a traffic island surrounded by dingy, institutional buildings. "That's the telephone office there," he said. "I'll be staying at my house in town most the time. Jorge's my watchman. Luz is his wife. Stay as long as you want, just don't give Jorge money or anything to drink. Understand?" Then he drove away.

A half hour later, the clerk behind the counter told me my call was ready in Booth #7. I stepped in, closed the folding door, and held the receiver to my ear until my mother's voice came on the line.

"Stephen!" she gasped. "You're okay?! Oh, thank God! Where are you?"

As usual when I felt her love after some trauma, my eyes smarted with tears, but I held my voice steady. "Buenaventura, my halfway point. Did you get my letters from Nuquí?"

"Honey, we haven't heard from you since you called from that, uh, Bahee…."

"Bahia Solano. Jees, I'm sorry! Oh well, I won't be in such remote places from now on. From here I'm heading east, then north, not south anymore. I'll be back home before you know it." I told her my plans, and gave her Luis Eduardo's address in Cali.

"Do you realize your brother David's been climbing Mount McKinley?" she asked. "Your poor dad and I've been worrying about both of you at the same time!"

"Oh yeah! Did he make it to the top?"

"Yes, barely. When he got back he had to take two weeks off work, he was so weak and sick. Now he seems to have some infection in his prostate."

I paused. "Congratulate him for me. Sorry to make you worry, Mom."

She gave her little laugh. "That's okay, honey. We're proud of you, both of you…"

I spent the rest of the afternoon getting the lay of the land, walking fast, looking suspicious characters straight in the eye. T-shirts touted American football teams. The cars were mostly Japanese compacts and fifties-model Chevrolets. I bought a dysentery medicine named Tindazeb and ate lunch in a restaurant on the side of the hill. The room was dark despite large doors opened onto the street. A rat ran worriedly around the perimeter of the room, over my feet, and under a pile of junk in the corner. I didn't mind, but the owner chased after it muttering curses. My thoughts ran back to Mom, and a family horseback trip in the Pasayten Wilderness when I was five years old. We were camped by an alpine lake. I left to go exploring with David, then age seven, and became separated from him. After wandering through deep woods for hours I found my way back to camp. I swore I wouldn't cry, but nothing could hold back my tears when my frantic mother hugged me. Still I hid my tears. Why? What made David risk his health on Mt. McKinley, and me mine on the Pacific coast?

My four days with Jorge, Luz, and the girls passed quietly. They insisted on sleeping four to a bed, leaving the other bed to me. The diarrhea I'd been carrying for a week had exhausted me. Luz cooked the provisions left over from my passage, but I couldn't eat much. Why wasn't the medicine working? Then I noticed the water I had gotten at the tuna cannery in Nuquí, which I was still drinking in order to avoid the typhoid-tainted tap water, had green globules floating in it. I started drinking boiled water and soda pop like everybody else, and slowly recovered.

Monday morning, as I walked toward the highway, I paused at a stall to drink a bottle of sweet fizz. Beside me, a dog and duck fed together from a pile of garbage. A man walked past carrying a cheap vanity dresser, plastered with little mirrors.

"Is this neighborhood dangerous?" I asked the stall keeper.

"Not anymore," he answered.

"What do you mean?"

"Not long ago they rounded up all the bad ones and did away with them."

"Who did? The police?" But he didn't want to talk about it any more.

It was bureaucracy day. I got a visa stamped into my passport, and learned that my six months' worth of mail had all been "returned to sender" (a euphemism, since the senders never saw it again). Then I went to the Port Captain's office for a permit to bring *Squeak* into the country without paying import duty. They couldn't figure out what to do. While I waited a clerk took interest in me.

"You know," he said, "you're the first person to sail to Buenaventura in eighteen months. The last one was a Frenchman." He frowned, and mumbled something.

"What?"

"I said he died."

"What do you mean?"

He sighed. "Somebody snuck aboard one night and killed him. They took his outboard motor. His boat's still down on the waterfront." Later I went to see it: a wooden, gaff-rigged sloop. A year later, in the Caribbean, I would meet some friends of the unfortunate Frenchman.

The offices closed for lunch. When they reopened, at two o'clock, I was told that Customs was in charge of my permit. But nobody there knew what to do either. Each official handed me off to their superior until I found myself seated, waiting to speak to the section chief. She, a bony black woman, stood facing me behind a desk. Three men, their backs to me, were pleading for some bit of paperwork. Her replies were vague, scornful. They presented reasons—she only became more agitated, more brittle. Finally she exploded with bureaucratic invectives and waved her arms. They retreated, exposing me to her gaze. For an awful moment we stared at each other. Her eyes showed rage, weariness, desperation, fear. I nervously got up, set some papers on her desk, started to speak. She glanced down without focusing, then assaulted me with a seamless burst of reasons why my request was impossible, why it was another office's responsibility. She seemed on the point of collapse. I protested weakly and backed off, wondering what to do next.

The office closed. I rode home in a "bus" (actually a Daihatsu pickup with a canopy and benches in back), and returned in the morning to the same office. A middle-aged under-secretary, who had shown pity the day before, now sat me in a chair by her desk. When not horsing around with the other office women she pecked at a typewriter, composing her vision of a *permiso de transito*. I shared in the ladies' jokes, and pretended to feel very much at home. When noon arrived I spent an hour on a toilet in the city's only presentable hotel, then combed the banks and contraband shops for someone willing to cash a travelers check. No one would. I was down to two dollars worth of pesos.

When the office reopened my lady friend gave me her draft permit and sent me around for signatures. Twice it turned out to be wrong and she had to type a new one. The third draft, however, was found to merit stamps and signatures. At 5:30 the final blessing was given. I kissed the document, and ran out to catch a bus. On the way home I reflected on the fact that the English verbs *expect*, *hope*, and *wait* are all represented by the same verb in Spanish: *esperar*. The Latinos' inability to distinguish between those concepts seemed to say something about their approach to bureaucracy.

I asked Captain Minning about transportation to Cali, and he took me to see an American woman named Karen Rodriguez. "Her partner has an electrical appliance shop," he said. "When she's in town she's usually there." He struggled to park in front of the shop, which was on a steep hill, without dropping a wheel into a manhole whose cover was missing. He jerked the pickup to a stop and cranked the wheels hard into the curb.

A husky woman came out onto the sidewalk. Her eyes were brown, her skin tanned, her dark brown hair short and wavy with gray streaks. She bent over to address him through the window. "What's the matter, Captain, you flunk parallel parking?" Her smile was impish, her lips full and painted. She wore culottes and a heavy cotton blouse.

"Gott verdammt, Karen, if I hurt my back parking in front of your partner's shop I'll sue him." He opened his door, got out, and pecked her on the cheek. "How are you, my darling?"

"Oh, I've been worse. What's up, sweetie?"

"I brought a fellow Americano to see you. He's crazy."

"Crazy's good."

"Tell her what you're doing," said the captain.

Karen's grin widened as I told my story. She was the first native English-speaker I'd met in months—it felt novel to speak plain American again.

"Okay," I said, "I've told you what I'm doing here. Now how about you?"

"Well I have this partner, see? Colombian guy. Together we own this seventy-foot boat we use to take scuba divers out to Isla Gorgona, sometimes Malpelo, three hundred miles out. The diving trip thing's pretty much my gig." She cleared her throat. "Well, I'm driving a pickup back to Cali tomorrow. I gather you're looking for a ride?"

I smiled apologetically. "As a matter of fact, yes." We agreed she would pick me up in the morning.

Karen arrived at ten A.M. in a tiny Suzuki pickup. Jorge helped me lift *Squeak's* stern into the back and angle her bow up over the cab. I tied her down, and we were off.

Outside the city, the two-lane highway started to climb. The vegetation became ever sparser until we traversed the flank of a deep gorge. The mountains were brown and angular. The Suzuki conked out several times on the constant grade, but always started again after a rest. We passed through long tunnels of crumbly cement, crossed a divide, snaked through alpine pastures, and descended into the wide, flat valley of the Rio Cauca. Along the way we told each other our life stories. Karen had been an Air Force brat, growing up in a dozen places around the world. When she was eighteen she married, against her family's wishes, a Colombian engineering student named Hermes Rodriguez. They lived in various Latin American cities, and raised three sons. Hermes became an executive with Quaker Oats of Colombia, based in Cali. In 1986 Karen left him, but stayed in Cali. Hermes continued to share responsibility for Junior, the only boy still at home.

At three o'clock, July 24, 1991, we arrived in Cali, a compact city of over one million. The traffic was heavy, the air dusty. We had hamburgers at a fast food place, and drove around town on errands. Then she took me to the house of Luis Eduardo Gonzalez, the factory-owner who had offered me a place to stay. I had called him from Buenaventura to say I was coming. His wife, Amparo, answered the door.

"Hi, I'm Steve Ladd. Is Luis Eduardo home?"

"No."

"Didn't he tell you I'm going to be staying here?"

"No, but please come in." I was embarrassed, but she wasn't. A few minutes later I was set up in a spare bedroom, *Squeak* was in the garage, and Karen was gone.

Their five grown children lived with them. Most worked with Luis Eduardo at his camshaft bearing factory. They were serious, hospitable, well-educated. The house was full of orderly idiosyncrasies: a little courtyard pond with turtles and goldfish, a room full of sporting trophies and framed certificates. A maid washed my clothes and fed me. A stream of cousins showed up; we all sat around and watched television. They were wonderful, but it was too crowded, too intimate. I holed up in my little room, picked up a history of Colombia, and read.

Karen rescued me in the morning. Resuming our objectives of the previous day, she persuaded an American friend to cash some traveler's checks for me. Her neighbors, the Sierras, had a computer they were willing to let me use. She referred me to a Dutch carpenter who offered me the use of his shop and tools. That afternoon, as we relaxed in her fourth-floor condominium in a complex south of downtown, she invited me to stay in her vacant penthouse bedroom. I gladly accepted. In a single day Karen had provided me with everything I needed to catch up on the book, build a permanent hatch cover, and generally prepare for the next step. I estimated these tasks would take two months.

I got my things from the Gonzalez' house except *Squeak*, whom they stored in their garage. I bought new shoes, shirt, and underwear at a nearby shopping mall. The apartment was clean and secure. A live-in maid cooked and washed. I even had a bicycle. I established a daily routine of yoga on the living room carpet facing west toward the coastal mountains, then twenty minutes of laps in a little pool in the middle of the beige apartment complex.

I ate large quantities of fresh fruit for breakfast, and vegetables and carbohydrates for lunch and dinner. I worked on the book in a little cubicle at the Sierras'. The climate lent itself to shorts and T-shirts, and rains were infrequent.

I had the comfort, food, and safety I had so craved on the coast, but, far from blossoming, I spun into a depression. I had returned from the wilderness, and life felt mushy and impure. The stresses and strains I had suppressed for so long now boiled to the surface. It was hard to put in the hours I should. I watched television and read too much. I was desperately lonely for a lover.

The writing was difficult. Previous chapters had taken seven to ten days apiece, but I had never written more than one chapter at a time. Now I had five to write, and they ended up taking twenty days apiece. I was ashamed of my low productivity. To my credit, I also wrote letters, got a physical exam and a new gold crown, and overhauled my equipment. I also researched the Meta and Orinoco rivers at the public library, but didn't find much.

I biked around the city in the course of my errands. The houses were stucco-faced, two-story, joined by common walls. Neighbors visited on porches and street corners. Each neighborhood had a public square with walkways in the form of an X, a monument at the center, and poorly tended grass and palms in the four triangles. One district devoted itself entirely to low-tech automotive and machine services. Each tiny shop was highly specialized, yet had ridiculously little equipment, and that often handmade. A mestiza woman sat on the sidewalk rewrapping the armature of a generator. My bicycle got a flat, and I had the tube repaired at an outdoor "vulcanization" stand. The proprietor was a white-haired black man in a straw hat. He assembled tube, rubber patch, a plastic candy wrapper, and the remains of an electric iron all vertically in a vise, then set the looped ends of positive and negative wires onto the terminals. He put a match on the edge of the iron, and when it ignited he cooled the iron by sprinkling water on it. He repeated this cooling process with several more matches, then removed the wires, loosened the clamp, and peeled off the candy wrapper, which had prevented the patch from sticking to the iron. *Et voilà*! (The patch came unstuck two days later.)

Artisans with specially equipped bicycles brought their services to the customer: vinyl repair, shoe repair, ice cream bars. A pony dragged bamboo logs for forming cement, three logs lashed to each side of its saddle. Nothing was wasted, down to the tiniest steel scraps, which collected in the cracks in the street and were recovered by a little man who ran around bent over with a magnet. Even in the relatively modern city center, well-herded cattle grazed on the street medians and miscellaneous scraps of lawn.

The poor begged at the stoplights and walked the streets retailing pitifully small stocks of gum and cigarettes. They were the majority, but they were difficult to talk to, and they frequented the places less safe for me to go. I regarded them curiously, almost guiltily, not because I rarely gave them anything, but because I rarely took time to penetrate their ignorance and know them. They seemed to be the same poor among whom I had traveled in Asia and North Africa:

The hot donut man, the coca-cola man
my friends! why don't I look them up?
The chiclets boy, the cigarette lady,
what a party we could have!

They were all my friends
though I didn't want to buy their junky stuff
though their eyes read a different language
in the sand and stucco street
and their hawking cries grated on me
until they became indistinguishable from cricket chirps

When we meet it is only to circle each other
do a clumsy dance of wits
our bond is weak
their fingers are brown and slippery

My friends, I'll never know you
and you'll always be a mystery to me
for even your sky is different from mine
a pale, airless blue
filled with time

Cali's slums were expanding rapidly. Curious, I met with a city planner. He was a tall, good-looking man, articulate, reserved.

"Frankly, it's out of control," he said. "About half of all new development is done without any approvals or inspections. The City hasn't the money to provide roads, sewers, or water. Many of the slums are 'invasions,' that is, the poor people organize themselves and suddenly converge on a vacant tract, such as park land or church property. Nobody stops them."

To see for myself I explored Aguablanca, the largest slum. It was a raw expanse on the flats near the Cauca River. The streets were unimproved and puddled, the ditches putrid and full of trash. The homes were tiny, close-packed, of brick, sticks, or sheet metal. Continuing to the valley's edge, I climbed the hillside *invasiones* on winding paths, past the uppermost shack, and on into the wild Farrallones, as the coastal mountains are called. My goal was Christo Rey, the immense statue of Christ that overlooks the city. I reached his stone feet, anchored in a mountain spur, and arched my neck. His compassionate face profiled against the drifting clouds of late afternoon. His arms stretched straight out from his sides, to embrace the valley and its huddled masses, but his gaze was heavenward. They were in his care, yet he was only a beautiful intermediary. How many eyes looked up to Christo Rey, how many times a day, and with what love and hope?

Karen and I took a hike in another part of the Farrallones. It was a holiday, and thousands of motor scooters, cars, and buses jammed the narrow road. It seemed all of Cali was on its way to spend the day refreshing themselves in a little river that issued from the mountains. We drove along this river until the road ended, then hiked into the valley above, past the last mountain cottage, past the last holiday wayfarers, along a cool, clear stream. We penetrated the edge of the enormous wilderness that extends from the upper valleys, across the sharp divide, and down through fifty miles of steep, untracked jungle to the mangrove swamps and tidal inlets that line the coast. I longed to explore it, but that was my frustration talking, my desire for an escape from my work.

Karen and I both needed someone to talk to. It came easier for her, who regularly unburdened herself in torrents of humor and soul-searching, who had not yet found an enduring relationship to take the place of her marriage. She was an emotional furnace. All her intense past still lived with her. Her girlhood spoke to me from the hand-tinted photograph that captured her mounted on a charging mare, leaning into a corner, cherub face alight with joy, the wind in her short bangs. Her coming of age spoke to me in the life-size portrait she kept in her bedroom, wherein beauty and bearing shone through her middle-class upbringing. Opposite was a portrait of her late aunt, the self-made Peoria businesswoman who gave Karen her taste for bullfights and her ability to discern old money from new. Karen ceaselessly studied people and her own past, as if this were the only way to keep her jury-rigged life from collapsing, as if to piece it together at one end as fast as it unraveled at the other. Relations between men and women particularly obsessed her. She was cynical and frank, yet the sight of a shoe-less beggar boy lying on the pavement at a stoplight brought her to tears.

Karen was gone from Thursday to Monday on the diving trips she organized. Eleven-year-old Junior went with her. I was glad, because I was unable to develop a friendship with him, and if we crossed paths too much he might resent my presence.

To keep a low profile at home, and with hopes of meeting someone, I went out to a bar called Martyn's. I failed in the latter objective. My pen came to my hand as a cigarette comes to the hand of a smoker:

In a bar, drinking beer
like the night in Memphis eight months ago
better music
the same dilemma

Women (sigh)
to get them, try?
don't try?
try not to try?
buy? I'm...

going out and I'm not trying
going out to the bar and writing

And what'd I say the other day?
that I'm little but mean
quick to bore
worthy
Admire me for that
stop my pride from hiding

It's been so long
'twill be so new
when it comes again
is that her? is that you?

I'm going out to the bar and writing
and when the pen stops I'll go home
Because nothing detains me
because I'm free, therefore lonely
because to be able to go
is more important than going

but staying, my pride hides
I create more
it hides

The next night I went to a *salsateca* (a discotheque featuring salsa music) and met a slim, full-breasted mestiza named Sonia. Her eyes, long hair, pants and pullover were all matte black. She was proud and self-contained, a high school Spanish teacher, a painter. We danced, talked, exchanged phone numbers. At the end of the evening I bicycled home in such a rapture that I suddenly realized I'd gone thirty-five blocks too far, and had to pedal all the way back!

Sunday, August 11, I went to the home Sonia shared with her mother, father, and brother. It comprised the second and third floors of a townhouse in a quiet, Mediterranean-style neighborhood. Her old father, Don Geraldo, received me like a son. Sonia and I went up on the roof, talked, and kissed once. I had never tasted anything more sweet. She showed me her paintings, including a self-portrait in which she stood on her terrace, frowning, examining her portraitist with cool disdain, or a curiosity she couldn't express. She often lapsed into private musings, and I wondered if they were profound or shallow, but never knew. She showed me a book of romantic poetry published by an uncle. I played their piano. Don Geraldo broke out a bottle of vin rose. We drank to friendship, and the first anniversary of *Squeak's* launching in the Milk River.

In the following days Sonia and I talked for hours on the phone. My poor Spanish was not a hindrance, but only added to the intrigue, for we were quite foreign to one another. I returned to her house with roses, and we walked to the colonial church on top of the hill, the same church that showed in the background of her self-portrait. We sat overlooking the city as its lights kindled in the twilight. Lovers and children dotted the hillside. A hundred kites flew figure-eights in the sky. We agreed to be boyfriend and girlfriend. The joy of being with her promised to melt the ice that had formed in me during my struggles on the coast, after my separation from Traci.

But it didn't continue smoothly. We suffered a misunderstanding when, at the *salsateca* the following Friday, I meant to give her the poem I had written at Martyn's bar, but accidentally gave her a blank sheet of paper. Once home I discovered my error, and returned. But Sonia ignored me, drinking and dancing with another man. Speechless, I gave her the poem and left.

I didn't sleep that night, and suffered the following days while she refused to see me. I went to a party at a neighbor's house, sat surrounded by pretty Colombian girls, and threw back ten shots of *aguardiente* in the space of a half hour. Suddenly I walked out the front door, teetered to the brink of the shadowy swimming pool, and lay down on the grass. I laughed at my own absurdity, as I had in Hermann, Missouri, and a wave of relief came over me. It was good to know I was still capable of such foolishness. I hastened matters with a finger down my throat, emptying my stomach before the bulk of the alcohol could enter my blood, and went to bed.

Finally I went uninvited to her house. She said she had been angered by the blank paper, then perplexed at my leaving so abruptly after giving her the real poem, then scared by the misery I expressed over the phone. But I began to doubt everything she said. For another week I struggled for her. Her family encouraged her, but she was elusive. I took refuge in writing, and my problem took the form of a play concerning the relationship between two friends:

FERN AND TREE

Morning in the forest. The light is silvery, diffused. The air is not quite still. A bird sings in the distance. At center stage a bright fern and a beautiful tree stand side by side.

Fern to Tree: "Stop and talk."

Tree: "Stop what?"

Fern: "Stop moving."

Tree: "I'm not moving. And neither are you, Fern."

Fern: "But the breeze is blowing you. You're moving!"

Tree: "Well, yes, in that limited sense. But being moved by the wind is not really moving. And we never will move because we're, you know, plants."

Fern: "But we move, slowly: growing, reaching for light, sinking roots. And some of us lead lives that are very unusual, like trees growing on top of dead trees, or ferns growing on sheer cliffs."

Tree: "Perhaps that satisfies you, Fern. I'm glad you're happy. But I sometimes wonder what it would be like to be an animal. Their sex lives are much more interesting."

Fern: "That's the old stereotype. The whole matter of speed has been blown out of proportion. If mass were the criterion, you, Tree, would be far superior to them. And you will live longer, too."

Tree: "Unless they cut me down."

Fern: "Who?"

Tree: "The ones that walk on two legs. They have cut other forests. It's only a matter of time before they cut this one. They'll come with growling machines and..."

But Fern seemed to have stopped listening, to have slipped away to a forgotten corner of his mind. He had talked with Tree, but not about what he'd meant to talk about. And now he couldn't remember what that was. "Tree?" he murmured.

Tree: "Yes?"

Fern: "Can I talk to you?"

Tree: "Do you have my permission, or are you able?"

Fern, angrily: "Dammit, Tree, can I? Okay, if those two things are really different, just pick one or the other."

Tree: "All right. I consider the question to be whether you have my permission. Yes, you do. But that doesn't mean I'm going to make it easy for you."

Fern's anger had vanished. He hesitated again. "Think what it would be like, Tree. To really communicate, to be intimate, to . . . you know, like people."

Tree: "Yes, but it's pointless to assign human concepts to plants. Besides, ferns can't mate with trees. We're different."

Fern: "But we live in the same forest. Within your canopy you hold habitat and sustenance for a thousand beings. Look at Nature around you. We're alive too."

Tree: "Yes, but . . . what'd you want to talk about?"

Fern: "You're so romantic, Tree. And I mean that sarcastically but affectionately, like someone who isn't getting the right signals. Like someone who would like to love even in the absence of sex. Anyway, we're talking. Tree, do you love me?"

> Silence. The breeze stopped, the bird flew away. The forest would have seemed still to human ears, but down near its floor an inchworm methodically munched a succulent leaf, and high among the boughs a tattered cloud of insects hovered fretfully. Ever so slowly, a drop of dew fattened, glinted, and splashed to the steaming earth.

I sat Sonia down and read out the parts with her. She was Tree, I was Fern. She loved it, and all my wild side, but that side can't hold the forefront for long. She admired my qualities, but one doesn't fall in love with qualities. She said she wasn't good enough for me, that she was confused, that she was still involved with a previous lover. We cautiously proceeded with the friendship, but I resented her unfulfilled promises to get together. She would disappear for twenty-four hours at a time, then say she had spent the night with a girlfriend. Friday and Saturday nights she partied until dawn, Cali style, and danced to the eternal salsa music. Her fear of suffering was a good sign, for to fear love one must be capable of it. But finally my better judgment insisted I give her up.

I went looking for someone else, to the north side of town, and encountered four teenage dolls walking the sidewalk in short, tight dresses and high heels. They were so angelically erotic, they made me ache inside.

"I lack a companion," I said.

"Pick whichever of us you like best," said one of the four.

I put my arm around a sweet thing in a sky-blue dress. But what do we do now? I bought her a flower and whisked her into a high-class bar, hoping to pry her away from her three friends. But they tailed along behind, and there I sat at a candlelit table with far more sex appeal than I could afford.

"Must I buy drinks for all?" I whispered to my girl.

"Yes, or I'll leave."

"*I'm* leaving," said I, and left.

I walked until the streets began to thin out, past unfamiliar bars, past a niche in which a woman sucked a man's penis; it glistened in the shadow. I stopped in at the *salsateca* and ran into Sonia. I had sworn her off, but she squeezed a promise to visit out of me. Then I walked the rest of the way home, another four miles.

I came to Sonia's house the next day as promised. Her brother, Adolfo, showed me the street trees he raised on his bedroom terrace as part of a scheme to landscape the entire city, and photographs of "The Last Supper," a mural he had painted on the walls of an apartment he once inhabited. It depicted a medieval bacchanal, complete with Cyrillic incantations, and real insects pinned to the wall. He recounted to me the plot of a proposed movie he called "The Eclipse," concerning the birth and death of the universe, and its subsequent decline into Hell.

Sonia was holed up in her bedroom, which I never saw. Adolfo, embarrassed on her account, strove to entertain me in her stead. Finally her mother talked to her, and she emerged. She and Adolfo showed me further artworks until Adolfo said something she took as a criticism of one of her paintings, whereupon she tilted her nose up and stalked back into her room. Adolfo tried to apologize, but it was too late. The interview was over. Disgusted, I resumed forgetting her. It remained difficult for some time.

I got one last taste of the Pacific Ocean as Karen's guest on a trip to Isla Gorgona. Thursday morning, August 29, we bought produce at a public market, then drove west across the mountains. Buenaventura was still humid, still a collage of mud, trash, and wild greenery. I waited out the rest of the day aboard her boat, the *Asturias*, while the crew brought provisions aboard. We were in the waterway near the bridge, among the rickety docks. The tide slowly rose, covering acres of mud, forcing millions of brown flies to higher ground. At nine P.M., with all passengers aboard, we chugged out to sea.

The passengers were upper-class Colombian men plus a few wives and teens. The talk centered on diving spots they knew: San Andres, Aruba, Malpelo. The *Asturias* rolled and pitched in the head-on waves. The higher up in her superstructure, the more uncomfortable was the motion. She was a typical coastal freighter: wooden and massive, with water splashing in the bilge and plenty of cockroaches and rats. I slept in the hold, with the steady hum of the engine.

At dawn no land was visible. I slept again. Upon reawaking I saw Isla Gorgona: tall, compact, alone, as it must have looked to Bartolomo Ruiz, Francisco Pizarro's pilot on his final attempt to reach Peru. Ruiz discovered the island in 1527 on an advance reconnaissance while Pizarro waited at the mouth of the Rio San Juan. He named it Gorgona for the poisonous snakes which still abound there. Pizarro's first search for the Inca Empire had failed because, like me, he had sailed in the wrong season, and had stayed within sight of the coast, allowing himself to be distracted by minor tribes along the way. When Pizarro tried again it was in the dry season, and Ruiz persuaded him to sail due south from the San Juan delta. Thus they arrived in Peru.

In the centuries since, the island had become a prison, then a national park. Jungle covered all but a cluster of administrative buildings and barracks. We anchored in front of this complex at noon.

The island received visitors such as ourselves, but the main focus was on humpback whale research. I spent my three days there with a group of Colombian, U.S., and Chilean scientists, returning to the *Asturias* only to eat and sleep. They were young and genial, like the people at Ensenada Utria, and equally willing to include me in their outings. One of them, in fact, was Marta, whom I'd met in Utria, and who had since transferred to Gorgona.

First they showed me the abandoned prison. The cell blocks, industrial-scale latrines, and walled patio were crumbling and reverting to jungle. What by nature was a paradise had become a hell, and was now returning to paradise. Then we dove among the stumps of an old pier. The bottom was of coarse, yellow sand. The water was clear, blue, warm. Below were fields of what appeared to be swaying reeds, but were actually slender eels that kept their tails in holes in the sand and pulled themselves down inside as I approached. Fiendish green morays lurked in the crevices of the old pilings. The song of a distant male humpback was audible underwater: a long series of varied sounds, unique to that male. "They repeat their songs over and over, changing them slowly with time," said my friends.

We next dove at *La Montañita,* an underwater mountain of rock a mile offshore. It was invisible from the surface, but a jump overboard revealed the mountaintop thirty-five feet down. An uneven acre or so lay within free-lung range. Beyond, the flanks descended steeply into unknown depths. I dove rapidly down and up, following scuba divers as they crawled along the bottom like snails. Whenever one found something of interest he beckoned his partners, and I went down for a look, too. Yard-long red snappers huddled and paced inside stone grottos, each of which had several openings. Silver amberjacks circled tightly in a school on the mountain's flank. I joined them in their lazy spirals, working my muscles and lungs to their limits, blistering my feet inside the borrowed fins.

The high point was a whale search. We motored north of the island, then circled south, listening to whale songs with a hydrophone. The sun shone brightly on the swells. We rode standing up, carefully braced. Each of us scanned a different part of the horizon.

"*Escucho soplo!* (I hear a breath!)" said the helmsman, and picked out the white puff of a spout. We gave chase. It was a mother humpback about fifty feet long and her twenty-foot baby. We followed close alongside. They were traveling, neither stopping to play nor diving deep to feed. Their long, white lateral fins looked like wings. My scientist friends were ecstatic; they lived for these whales. The mother and child escaped us, so we latched onto a pair of males. I saw their knobby faces, blowholes, and strong backs.

The sea was calm on our return to Buenaventura. I waited aboard *Asturias* most of Monday while Karen conducted port business. On the next dock over, bare-chested blacks unloaded freshly sawn timbers from the hold of a wooden boat. On the other side old men repaired fishing nets. On the muddy track that accessed the waterfront, a young pig stopped to chew a hunk of sugar cane already sucked dry by a human. I felt restless.

My side trip to Gorgona did not cure my depression, only suppressed the symptoms. My boredom was illogical because I had work to do. But having left "the road" I had lost its discipline and stimulus. Back in Cali, I felt more strongly my travel-weariness and lack of friends. I could be lonely and tough, or soft and loved, but not lonely and soft. The writing dragged on, and my welcome at the Sierras' house wore thin. I had lost my gusto for the voyage, but I didn't want to go home either.

This slump was uncharacteristic, because I'm generally even-tempered. I rarely laugh or cry. This temperament lends itself to purposefulness, not intensity. Yet I crave intensity as much as anyone, and create it by adventuring. So far I had done so at intervals of eighteen years, with lesser challenges between. In the course of a journey I presented the paradox of a mild, well-adjusted person doing something wild.

Only once before had I experienced such an emotional discontinuity. I was hit over the head in Kansas City in 1982, and came to in a hospital with amnesia. I knew who I was, but the past three days were a blank, and my short-term memory was gone. I felt euphoric, even tried to convince the janitor to let me mop the floor. The specialists worried. Then my rational brain realized something was wrong, so I got a pad and pencil and recorded my thoughts every couple of minutes, noting the time from my watch. Each notation said something like, "I don't remember having written that last note, but surely I'll remember having written this one." Eventually I did.

Similarly, on September 6, 1991, my instinct told me to confess that:

amid wonders of nature I'm bored, only less so
bored but well-adjusted
bored, therefore boring
Yes, I flee that
leap from burning buildings
dive to the bottom of the sea

David gone to Denali, I to the path that only I can find
because who else would happen that way?
to drink from the cupped hand
'mid fading memories of love

till it's a habit
till it's a habit and I'm bored again
and I'm bored because I'm well-adjusted
and because I'm well-adjusted
it's really not a problem. Is it?

I needed to make friends. Suddenly this began to happen. I went out on a series of forgettable dates. Then, on October 4, I paired up with a rakish buddy named Alfonso to go to a big dance at the college gymnasium. We shared hits from an *aguardiente* bottle and surveyed the crowd.

"Which woman appeals most to you?" he asked.

I scanned from left to right. "The little black girl there," I said.

It seemed appropriate to inform her of her selection, so I walked over. She watched me approach, her eyes and smile drawing me like a beacon. She was Mariela, an economics student with chocolate skin and a tight afro. She was compact and spirited. We hit it off.

We proceeded to see each other two or three times a week, and my loneliness vanished. I met her after class; we joked and kissed in the shadows. I visited her village, an hour away by bus. Her home boasted a television and VCR, but the plumbing was primitive, the furniture ill-proportioned and uncomfortable. We sat in the little public square, and ambled the hedge-lined lanes that radiated into the flat countryside. Her family tried to make me feel welcome.

"Ayyy, Steve, que quieres conmigo, fea negrita? Tu no me recordarás nunca. (Oh, Steve, what do you want with me, an ugly little black woman? You will never remember me.)" She asked me such things often, partly teasing, mostly serious.

"*Muchachita mia, no te preocupes. Eres lindisima. No te olvidaré nunca.* (My little girl, don't worry. You're lovely. I'll never forget you.)"

She was honest, innocent, didn't want my money, couldn't believe I wasn't seeing anybody else, couldn't believe she was pretty. Embarrassed at her humble origins, Mariela nonetheless found the courage to bring me into her life of study, family, and friends. She dressed alluringly, as do all *Caleñas,* and gradually accepted intimacy. During my final month in Cali she came on certain afternoons to my apartment, where we made love. I wanted to really explain myself to her, to break through the barrier of our contrasting backgrounds.

She knew I would have to leave. We never discussed it. We knew it would hurt. I suspected it would hurt her more than me, and felt guilty. We could only love as well as we were able during our time together. I wrote to her:

> Mariela, there's a door—lets open it
> I'll be inside, welcoming your laughter
> will you see me?

Mariela, be brave
take the risks you think you should
your vulnerability will protect you
beauty will not cease to burn in your heart

Mariela, innocence need never be lost
though other things be found
ask me questions
don't assume you can't know me

Mariela, there's a door
shall we open it?

I gave her this, and a heart-shaped turquoise pendant I bought from one of the hippie artisans lining the Avenida Sexta. The stone was from Afghanistan, and in it I saw that country's ancient sky. Mariela reciprocated with a copy of Gibran Khalil Gibran's *El Loco*. On the back leaf I found, in her tight hand, the following. I understood her to mean she had composed it. Translated it reads:

I will pass through your life
quick as lightning
and guard in my soul
your indelible memory

and in the days of winter
when the sun hides
a light of nostalgia
will vibrate in my pupils

I will pass through your life
as fleeting as the wind
and keep hidden
your childish smile
your sweet words
of optimism and love
that fill my life
with enthusiasm and ardor

I will pass through your life
in a month of summer
and my melancholy voice
will drown in the shadow
and my thirsty lips
will die of drought

Work was easier now. I stopped going out with my other friends; they had only been a means of meeting her. At the end of day I stood on my terrace and watched the sky over the Farrallones fade from one smoky violet to another. I listened to the frequent gunshots, and wondered if any found their mark. Were those the sounds of people trying to kill each other? I listened, sleepless, to the riotous cheeping that began an hour before light, when the red-headed wrens awoke in the treetops outside my window. With Mariela's love, the universe's random sparkles gladdened me again.

On October 15 I finished drafting this chapter and started working on the boat. Heine, my Dutch missionary friend, let me use his carpentry shop. His tools were good, and his family and employees made me feel at home. Slowly, carefully, I built the hatch cover. Its large size, curved shape, and need for a perfect seal complicated the task. I also built a hasp-and-lock system, a new depth-sounding reel, a mechanism to secure the tiller in a range of positions, a strong bailing bucket, and a sea anchor. These, and lesser tasks, constituted a To Do List that reached two pages at its height, then slowly shortened. Each day I prayed that my various welcomes would last until the work was done, and looked forward to 5:15 when I would meet Mariela at the "X" we had drawn on a banister outside the university cafeteria.

On December 10 I began dealing with the financial, bureaucratic, and transportation aspects of getting to the headwaters of the Meta River. I biked ten miles across town to get my visa extended at the national security office, but a plainclothes guard with an Israeli submachine gun wouldn't let me in.

"No shorts," he barked.

I didn't want to go all the way home to change, so I walked out onto the street and found someone of my build. He wore a pair of light blue, pleated cotton trousers. "Pardon me, I need long pants in order to enter the security office. Will you rent me yours for two dollars?"

Not only was he willing, he gave me an option to buy should I become attached to them. He found a place to change and waited for me while I got my extension. The pants performed well, so I paid him another four dollars and kept them.

My enthusiasm for the voyage, which had waned during my four and a half months in Cali, built up again. Luis Eduardo, who was a pilot, gave me an aviation map of the Caribbean. That old goal from my shivery days on the Missouri and Mississippi rivers was now within my grasp. Best of all, the Orinoco would drop me off at the southeast corner of that sea, whence wind and current would favor my return to North America.

Christmas spirit was building. Each of the nine nights before Christmas, children recited stories of the Christ child in front of the nativity scene at the gate to our complex. There was much popping and splendor of fireworks.

On the *Paseo de la Virgen* I helped Heine and his family launch a hot-air *globo* (balloon). It was of brightly colored paper, a meter in diameter, powered by a wick soaking in a cup of diesel fuel. It rose rapidly and drifted north on the gentle breeze, glowing warmly in the evening sky. I followed on my bicycle, hampered by the limitations of the street system. I sought bridges across ditches, and struggled to keep up as it drifted straight and effortlessly, five hundred feet up. It was an orange harvest moon, a tiny satellite, a transcendence; and not the only one, for other people were launching them too. The wind picked up, and away I flew north, face equally uplifted and downcast, seeking routes, until it seemed I was a medium through which sky communicated with earth, or fire with darkness. It began to fall. I pedaled faster, maneuvered below it. I dumped the bike, ran through a littered no man's land, and caught it in midair before the smudgy, dying flame could ignite the gauzy paper.

My final days in Cali were colored by the passions of Garcia Lorca's poetry, which I was then reading, and by the anguish of my parting with Mariela. We trusted one another. I was her first. Still, I didn't want to marry her, and it hurt to hurt her. Of Karen I saw little. She was generally in Isla Gorgona or in Bogotá visiting a new boyfriend.

"When will you return to Cali?" asked my friends.

"If past experience is any indication, I'll be back in eighteen years," I replied.

To Karen, Luis Eduardo, the Sierras, and Heine and his people I gave the following note:

> How long, sad, and sweet is "the road"
> Its markers are you who have cared for me
>
> Lately I seem to receive more than I give
> this bothers me
> but I do each as well as I can
> I give of myself as necessary to complete my journey
> I receive of you as necessary to complete my journey

You help me to hope that what I am doing
does indeed help in some way,
is my appropriate contribution

Friendly sponsor
I wear your decal on my heart

By inquiring among the truck drivers who congregated outside the public market, I negotiated a ride to Bogotá for December 18. Mariela spent the last night with me, daring just this once to deceive her family into thinking she was at a girlfriend's house.

We said good-bye at the bus stop in the morning. Then my driver said he couldn't leave until the next day, and I made the mistake of getting this word to her. She visited me again, and it broke my heart to see her beam with joy as if having been reprieved, as if a few more hours together would be an eternity. I was unable to live in the moment so fiercely. It was an agony for me, and soon was for her, too. She helped me pack, then we walked toward the bus stop. At the second-to-the-last corner Mariela suddenly hugged me and hurried away. I watched her go, but it didn't work for me like that. I ran and caught her. Her face was dull and blank; she winced when she realized it was me.

"Mariela, I'm so sorry." We held each other and cried. It didn't do any good. The pain was unavoidable, long-lasting, and well worth her gift to me.

CHAPTER 17

OVER THE ANDES

My driver, Jaramillo, arrived at seven P.M. in his Dodge pickup to take me to Bogotá. We loaded up and took the *Autopista del Norte* out of town. He stopped at each police checkpoint and bribed the soldier a hundred pesos for not checking his truck while I dozed sitting up.

Toward midnight unaccustomed cold woke me. Flooding had blocked the main highway. We had taken a two-lane alternate route and were switch-backing up the Cordillera Central. High above shone the lights of backed-up traffic. We stopped behind the others, mostly night-traveling trucks like ourselves. I slept a while longer, then got out to warm myself up.

The jam stretched several miles to either side of the summit. A smashed tanker truck had started it, but anarchic driving habits had given it a life of its own. Upon finding their lane backed up, drivers had taken the opposing lane until met by on-coming traffic, bringing everything to a standstill. *Machismo* prevented anyone from backing up. No one exerted authority, so drivers simply shut off their engines and went to sleep. The tanker truck had long since been pushed over the edge, but the jam continued to grow.

It was Thursday night. I hoped to reach the Venezuelan embassy before they closed on Friday, get a visa, and continue to the Meta River with Jaramillo. Otherwise I would have to spend the weekend in Bogotá and arrange another truck ride. So I walked over the divide and down the far side until I found an open lead in our lane. I then worked my way back, waking up driver after driver with a yell and a slap on his door. Engines had cooled, so starting was often slow. Rigs stalled, creating further obstacles. One bruiser smirked at me and asked his comrade, "Who's the twerp giving orders?" but the men I woke generally jerked up with an expression of alarm and cranked their starters without even looking at me.

The more I cleared traffic, the more I appreciated the size and complexity of the jam. East- and westbound lanes each had three possible states: empty, flowing, and backed up. Usually one lane was empty or flowing and the other was backed up. Sometimes both lanes were empty, or both flowing, or both backed up. Time and again I cleared traffic back to our truck, thinking we could now drive unimpeded to Bogotá. Each time, before reaching the point at which I had began clearing, we were stopped by another backup. We were slowly working our way over the divide, but the jam as a whole was still growing.

I walked further than ever, to a vantage from which the highway was visible for miles. The night was dark, but the surrounding mountains were discernible: steep, rounded peaks and ridges falling away into dendritic folds. The vastness of the night contrasted with the worried tightness of the stalled vehicles, which zigzagged down into the widening valley, a string of red, orange, and white lights. It was too big for me to make much of a dent. Cold and tired, but strangely thrilled, I rode back up with a passing vehicle and fell asleep in the truck.

An hour later the sun rose and did what I never could, warming and wakening as individuals those who overnight had formed a single, torpid whole. All along the line, pockets of initiative kindled. Men shouted, signaled, collaborated. The road freed up, and we descended into the valley of the Magdelena River. We crossed the river at Girardot, and stopped at a restaurant for a lunch of fried river fish. I saw tired fields, low forests of pine and palm, horseback campesinos. The water in the gullies was bright chocolate.

At two o'clock we began to enter the city. The portal was not distinct, only the shabby, momentary edge of a growth containing eight million people. The sky was gray, the streets potholed. Jaramillo refused to penetrate the skyscrapered center, which was one big jam, so we parked in an inner-city neighborhood where he had friends. One, a skinny galoot with popping eyes named Carlos, accompanied me by bus to the Venezuelan embassy. It was already closed.

I needed a place to store *Squeak*. Fabio, the biologist I had met in Ensenada Utria, had offered to take me in at his parents' house, but the public telephones were all broken. I couldn't keep Jaramillo waiting, so we put *Squeak* in a "garage" across the street from where Carlos lived. It was a crude, partly roofed enclosure. An auto body man worked there by day, taxis parked there by night. The owner and his family lived in a hovel at the back. The garage was an abscess in the tight fabric of run-down two- and three-story brick buildings constituting the Barrio Eduardo Santos.

We put *Squeak* against the wall, in the part not sheltered, and I paid Jaramillo $200 worth of pesos. Then Carlos and Jaramillo took me to a bar next to the betting house where Carlos worked. They urged me to drink, and heartily approved when I chose *aguardiente.* They had grown up together in Cali, and were very conscious of regional origins. Pointing from table to table, they said, "Those people are *Paisas*, those are *Caleños*, those are from the Atlantic coast. Most *Bogotanos* are from other parts of the country."

"Can you tell them apart so easily?"

"Oh, it's like they're from different countries, the way they speak, dress, everything. But stay on your toes here. Bogotá has the highest murder rate in the world."

At ten thousand feet above sea level, Bogotá was also cold. It rained that night, so I brought my things inside the cabin and packed them around me. I was living aboard *Squeak* again, though our "harbor" was incongruent. I spent the weekend reviving my diary and walking the city with William, the garage owner's twenty-year-old son. The neighborhood was residential, with no stores, but many small cafes and bakeries. To the north was a sector of crowed stalls and discount shops selling clothing, electronics, and flashy furniture. "*Very* dangerous here," said William, walking fast. Further north still, at the foot of a convent-capped mountain, were colonial Santa Fe de Bogotá and the various cathedrals and palaces that make up Colombia's ceremonial center.

Monday morning, December 23, I went into the garage's foul latrine and pulled in place the scrap of corrugated steel that served as its door. I stripped, my skin goose-pimpling with cold. I piled my clean clothes in the least soiled spot, bathed with a hose, and redressed. Then I moved aside the poles that propped the garage door shut and set forth to get my visa. Simple, good-natured William insisted on accompanying me.

We went first to the fortress-like American embassy. Leaving William outside, I cut ahead of hundreds of Colombians seeking visas to the U.S. and entered the Citizen Services section. I browsed their Travel Advisories, which advised against going every place I'd been and every place I planned to go. Then I wrote my travel plans on a little card and gave it to the woman at the window. She took it to her boss, who promptly called me in.

He was a pudgy fellow, about my age, refreshingly North American. "The Llanos is largely controlled by guerrillas, you know. There's no government in there, so we don't get much hard information, but we hear about extortion kidnappings. There's a lot of cocaine labs, too. The river's probably a smuggling route. I've never heard of an American going in there." He pursed his lips worriedly. "The locals might assume you're with the embassy."

Presumably, that would be lousy for my public relations. His paranoia was contagious, but not very. I had already decided to go, so there wasn't much point in the conversation.

"Thanks for your time," I said. "I know you're just doing your job. I'll write when I get to Venezuela, if you like."

"That might be interesting, yes."

We caught another crowded bus. At the Venezuelan consulate I joined a mass of Colombians seeking visas to Venezuela. It was four hours before anyone could tell me the paperwork requirements, then the consulate closed until the twenty-sixth.

Three more days to kill. William was only too happy to help kill them, but he bored me stiff. Like the guys in Piñas, he would get drunk and play "pretend-to-speak-English." He had a habit of showing me off to the neighborhood girls, thereby improving his own status, and of making himself out to be an expert in subjects he knew nothing about. "Wait, no, let me handle this!" he would say, and I was supposed to move aside and admire his skill. His little brothers were a nightmare. They ran around the compound all day, doing what they weren't supposed to do, getting spanked, doing it again, getting spanked. I didn't pretend to take an interest in the family.

Fireworks, fireworks, fireworks. On Christmas Eve they exploded for hours as I lay in bed with a headache and thought about Mariela. How many hearts had I broken in the past twenty years? Somehow it all added up to a big sadness, all those good women, hopefully happy now with other men.

I itched and scratched; what was crawling all over me? Twenty after ten—salsa music, firecrackers, dogs barking. Fear of the river ahead, of the evil that reputedly lurks. Christmas Eve, and Fabio was supposed to have picked me up three hours ago. He's not coming.

At 10:30 he came. Bright-faced, chubby, dear Fabio! "I've been driving for hours, couldn't find the place," he said. "Bogotá's streets are confusing even to its natives." We got into his car and drove to his family home, in the Barrio Nuevo Campín.

Aside from a brief phone conversation, we hadn't spoken to each other since Ensenada Utria. Now he told me, as had Marta on Isla Gorgona, how pirates had come looking for me just after I left. Both being modest and scrupulous, the story was probably true. But I had too many future dangers to worry about past ones.

He took me into the bosom of his family. The neighborhood was upper-class: neat houses neatly lined up, a car in each garage. Educated, successful people. Fabio was the youngest of five brothers, all but one still living at home. The brothers all looked different, but all were remarkably warm and sensitive, shy with strangers, talkative and jocular among themselves. Their mom and dad presided with quiet dignity. The house was orderly, festive.

We passed unhurriedly from one phase of the Christmas celebration to another. At 11:30 they performed the final *novena* recitation. They read in turns from a little book, chanted Ave Marias, and sang in chorus, "Come, Jesus, come!" At midnight we went outside for the fireworks climax, like New Year's Eve in the States. All the neighbors were there. Then cherry wine aperitif, dinner at 1:30 A.M., and the opening of presents. There was a present under the tree for me too: chocolates that Fabio had made himself. We didn't turn in until nearly dawn.

On Christmas Day I called my sister from a pay phone in the Barrio Eduardo Santos. "I'm fine except I have fleas," I said, knowing that would strike her funny. I had finally diagnosed my itching problem, and the probable source: the couch in "the hovel," where one evening I had watched TV with William and his scruffy relatives.

On the twenty-sixth, after six hours of bureaucratic torture, I had my visa. Now to find a ride to Puerto Lopez on the Meta River, in the Llanos (Great Plains). None of my leads bore fruit until, in a gathering place for truckers in the Plaza Santa Barbara, I met an old man named Jeremiah. He had worked in Florida in the early sixties, and waxed nostalgic about the States. "Going there was *my* great adventure. I recommend you try the trucks by the stockyards. They deliver cattle from the Llanos, and return empty. The drivers will be anxious to make some money on the way back."

That night, my last in Bogotá, I was wakened from deep sleep by the sounds of a running gunfight. Dozens of shots. Weapons of various calibers, distinguishable by their reports. Shouts. They worked their way slowly through our street, past our door, westward. Then the gunshots became more distant, until a sad silence returned to the Barrio Eduardo Santos.

Saturday, December 28, I caught a taxi to the slaughterhouse stockyards. I took a seat in a restaurant patronized by truckers, ordered breakfast, and let my needs be known. The grapevine kicked in. There wasn't much traffic on weekends, but drivers came and sat down with me, one after another. They were rugged, unshaven, cowboy types. They seemed taller than they really were. The figure of 270,000 pesos was dropped, and I only smiled. The offers came down to 90,000, but they were going only to Villavicencio. I needed a driver going all the way to Puerto Lopez.

That person arrived as I was finishing breakfast. We agreed on 65,000 pesos, about $100. To get anything cheaper I'd have to wait until Monday, whereas this guy already had his motor running. So we drove to the garage and nestled *Squeak* into the pile of chaff intended to protect the flatbed from cattle hooves. As we pulled away I told William to keep the two thousand pesos he had borrowed with such emphatic assurances about paying me back. I had known all along it was a gift.

As we chugged up the Cordillera Oriental, Bogotá spread out behind me like a dusty blanket across the high plain. We passed a mountain village, green pastures, and forests of banana and willow. Peasant huts dotted the steep, uneven countryside. From the red, cut bank of the winding road grew shrubs that looked like clusters of green swords radiating from a common center.

As we descended the other side, the subalpine vastness slowly condensed into a monolithic valley through which ran a green torrent. Now we passed bush-bean plots and pig farms. We crossed bridges guarded by men with old shotguns, "to keep the guerrillas from blowing them up," my quiet driver said, crossing himself at each bridge. We stopped for lunch, and continued downward. The air became hotter, the valley narrower, more heavily forested. At 1:30 P.M. we cut out to the left, topped a low saddle, and there were the Llanos, flat as a newly risen seabed, dissolving into the eastern horizon. It was 500 miles as the crow flies to the Guyana Highlands, on the far side. I had to cross that.

We paused to repair his alternator in Villavicencio, on the shore of that once-sea, then drove another two hours due east past neatly fenced pastures and groves of large trees. A strong headwind was blowing. We drove three miles past the town of Puerto Lopez to a long bridge. Below me the Meta River ran northeast through a sandy bed. The river was 150 yards wide, slow, apparently shallow. I was at its highest navigable point accessible by truck. We paralleled the river to a likely launching spot and lowered *Squeak* down the ten-foot bank. After five months on land, she was once again in her intended medium. I tied her to a moored barge, loaded her, and rode back into town with the empty truck as darkness fell.

Nobody knew where I could provision again, so I bought a bucketful of produce and five gallons of pure water, and hired a car back to the river. Mosquitoes bit me as I arranged the cabin, squeezed in, and closed the hatch. I lay naked and sweaty for hours, full of doubts, unable to sleep in the unaccustomed heat.

CHAPTER 18

META RIVER

It was December 29, 1991. Anxious to get rid of the fleas, I bathed and washed my clothes and sleeping bag on the river bank. While my things dried I stowed gear, bundled up the sailing rig, and lashed it down horizontally to reduce wind resistance. At 10:30 I shoved off.

All day I rowed into a strong headwind, a difficult maneuver in *Squeak* due to her high freeboard. The opposition of wind and current resulted in corduroy waves that further hindered progress. Even with the favorable current I averaged only a mile per hour. The wind kept me from over-heating, but the land was wilted, and the air was hazy with heat shimmers and dust. Would it be like this all the way to the ocean, 1,200 river miles away?

Unfortunately, yes. It was summertime in the Llanos, that especially hot period from December to May, when the wind always blows from ENE, exactly opposite my line of travel. I had descended the Pacific coast in the rainy winter when I should have been there in the dry summer, and now I was descending the Meta/Orinoco in the summer when I should have been there in the winter! How could I have committed such a blunder?

All day I thought back through the events. In Cali I was unable to learn anything about the winds east of the Andes. It had occurred to me that the Llanos may be subject to the same trade winds that dominate the Caribbean, so I made the sea anchor, expecting it to pull me downstream against a headwind. Now I knew it wouldn't work. There was too little current and too much wind. Anyway, my options were limited to the Orinoco and the Amazon, and the latter probably had its own unforeseeable problems. I stopped beating myself up and settled into my new environment.

It was dry and flat, like the North American plains, but tropical in its plants and animals. It was less developed in the sense of roads and bridges, but more heavily populated. Fishermen in planked canoes, some with outboard motors, stared at me until I was out of sight. Women and children stared at me from thatched houses on the banks. They didn't wave, or move, or show emotion. They were dark but not Negroid, and wore worn-out Western clothing, no shoes. I passed a stranded barge. Seven men worked in water up to their chests trying to free her. They were laughing, as if it was great fun. I felt incapable of communicating with them.

As the day closed I sought a hidden campsite. The beaches always had people nearby, so I went until dark and camped within earshot but out of sight. Mosquitoes promptly covered me from head to foot. I employed my entire arsenal: two layers of clothes, gloves, head net, and insect repellent on wrists and ankles. It was too hot to wear all that stuff. Halfway through cooking dinner a flame sprouted from the gas cap of my Svea stove. I turned it off. The spring that holds the pressure-release valve shut had rusted out. I went into the cabin and dozens of mosquitoes came in with me; it took an hour to swat them all. Even then, the buzzing of those trying to get in through the screens on my portholes kept me awake. Outside, fishes splashed and unidentified animals emitted strange cries.

In the morning I pored over my sleeping bag, popping the last of the fleas between my nails. I went back into the river and wound back and forth through its mild meanders. I stayed to the outsides of the bends, where the cutting action dropped a ragged curtain of fallen vegetation over the bank. I stopped at the juncture of the Rio Upia and napped, prone inside the cabin, while the wind passed its midday climax. I propped the hatch to keep the sun out and scoop air in. Even so, the heat was cruel. I started again at three P.M.

The wind and glare slowly died. Lengthening shadows brought the world into focus: yellow birds, a green island on which brown and white horses ran wild. The whistling in my ears stopped, the water flattened, the dust settled out of the air. Mosquitoes came out. The setting sun created a fan of alternating pink and blue rays, so big I had to swivel to see it all. It melted into cobalt blue, then blackness with bright stars. Insects and birds made soft sounds. I drifted silently past fishermen tending pole-strung nets. There was no moon, so they couldn't see me, but they saw my flashlight when I shined ahead for snags, and wondered who I was.

"*Que es eso?* (What is that?)" one softly asked another, his words carrying over the still water.

I listened for the flowing sound of snags—trees that had been washed into the river and were sitting lengthwise on the bottom, a portion of their roots or branches showing. I compared relative densities of darkness to discern banks, and sought the silhouettes of objects coming between me and the reflection of the stars on the river. The river braided, and I blindly took this channel or that, vaguely detecting islands.

I camped around midnight, and started again when the eastern sky began to lighten. When the wind became excessive, at 8:30 A.M., I stopped on an expanse of rippled sand. A pair of dart-shaped birds, black and white with long, orange beaks, dive-bombed and screamed at me; their nest was nearby. I performed chores, slept a couple of hours, woke up groggy with heat, and resumed rowing at four P.M. Again, the wind dropped off in the afternoon. When it got dark I turned around and rowed pushing, to better see ahead. If only I had some sort of headlights this night travel could work.

It was New Year's Eve, 1991. I had resigned myself to celebrating it alone. But as I descended a small side channel, anxiously feeling for depth with my oartips, I heard music. It was like the *vallenato* I had enjoyed in the Chocó, but more intricate and impassioned. I saw a light, and maneuvered toward the steep bank. I tied, climbed up, and saw an open-air cafe/bar. The kitchen's stucco walls were painted in a simple, white and sky-blue pattern. Under a bare light bulb a dozen people were drinking beer at little tables. The men wore cowboy hats of straw or felt, the women wore festive dresses. I stepped among them, and they fixed on me.

"Is a stranger welcome here?" I asked.

There was a brief silence, then a small man with bronze skin, long eyelashes, and sharp features said, *"Sí!"*

"What is this village called?"

"La Poyata." I bought him a beer, and gained a friend. His name was Alvaro.

Only that and one other structure were visible. I went to the other, the "*discoteca.*" Under its thatched, conical roof were a twenty-foot-diameter dirt dance floor and tables at which sat some thirty people of all ages. Others stood outside a whitewashed lattice railing, in the extremities of the escaping light. Few paid me any attention until Alvaro came over and drank with me. He was a beautiful man, proud and intense as a finely plumed bird. He introduced his children, from toddlers to a son attending the university in Bogotá.

The people lost their shyness toward me. Cowboys bought me beers. Even those who became drunk maintained a certain formality, a respect for space so lacking among the people of the coast. Theirs was not the closeness of the huddled village. Rather, their faces revealed years of squinting, scanning horizons, coping with the dry blankness of the plains, which forces men to spread out to find sustenance. All wore their finest, whatever that might be, and most danced. Dust rose from their twirling, staccato steps. They embraced at forearm's length, eyes at each others feet, engrossed in the intricacy of the dance. I located myself among the prettiest girls in anticipation of the stroke of midnight, but no one kissed.

I went to bed, and rose at six A.M. Many were still partying. A young cowboy in poncho and chaps "danced" his small, skittish horse. He was wavering in the saddle, but he whirled and pranced his pony via commands invisible to my eye, with the same calm discipline that showed on the dance floor. A bottle of Poker beer waved in his hand, and *musica llanera*, as it is called, flowed from a set of cheap speakers. Dawn slowly spread over a billiard-table landscape of fenced pastures and wood lots.

Alvaro sat with six or seven comrades at the cafe/bar. "*No quiero que te vaya* (I don't want you to go)," he said, simply and vulnerably, like a child. But I had to.

To get lighting equipment I turned right at the mouth of the Rio Manacacias and worked my way ten miles upstream, but downwind, to Puerto Gaitán. Along the way, picnickers fed me roast beef, boiled yucca, and fermented corn juice. I arrived in late afternoon at a town of twenty or thirty city blocks. In the center was a plaza with a statue of a man waving his fist. It was the great Liberal leader Gaitán, whose assassination started *La Violencia*, the civil war that rocked Colombia in the forties and fifties. Puerto Gaitán was a town of cowboys, merchants, and soldiers. The stucco houses and shops were common-wall to their neighbors. They were painted in light hues, with a darker contrast band from sidewalk to calf-level. It was quiet except near the park, where several bars blasted music out onto the dirt street. While I dined in a restaurant, a young girl who was vacationing with her family introduced herself. She explained to me with words and pictures the animals in the river: pink dolphins, giant stingrays, electric eels, piranha. She also gave me local names for the water craft I had been seeing: *canoas* for the planked canoes, *falcas* for the long, roofed, outboard-powered vessels that carried passengers and cargo.

Besides normal provisions, I purchased a length of wire, a switch, and two flashlights, each accommodating three D-cell batteries. An electronics man soldered the connections while a carpenter made me a mount, which I attached to the bow by means of a bolt passing through the mast hole. On the night of January 2 I trained the headlights and got underway, anxious to try out the system.

I rowed back down the Manacacias and into the larger Meta. Still no moon. Big animals were following me, splashing and snorting—must be river dolphins. Orange eyes on the banks reflected in my headlights. I later identified these as caimans, a species of small alligator.

After experimenting with various switch positions I decided in favor of thumb activation. Without releasing the oar grips I flashed the headlights on for five seconds, once every minute or so. This was sufficient to miss the snags. The lights didn't help much in following the channel, nor had I a detailed map, but the bottom was soft, the current gentle. To judge current speed and direction I passed close by snags, pondered my movement relative to them, and studied their wakes. I kept my bearings by the stars, whose positions I determined from my compass. Whenever the depth became less than three feet my oar tips would scrape bottom; then I turned right or left depending on my sense of where the channel lay. I often ran aground on sandbars and drifted into dead-end bays. On these occasions I got out, reconnoitered by wading, and dragged *Squeak* to deeper water.

That first night out of Puerto Gaitán I navigated until midnight, then looked for shallows on which to ground out and go to sleep, but the banks were steep on both sides. The water was calm as a lake; a "snag wake" indicated only a mild current. Why not anchor? I secured the oars, opened the main hatch, got out my Danforth, and dropped it over. It sank straight down, pulling the rope rapidly through my fingers. The river was surprisingly deep.

Suddenly it caught—the rope burned through my hands! Groggy and disoriented, I gripped tight, thereby halting *Squeak's* drift. Inexplicably, the current was swift now. *Squeak* being perpendicular to the flow, the current gushed violently, threatening to capsize me. The hatch was open! I couldn't pull her sideways up to the anchor, so I stumbled desperately forward, expecting the current to throw the stern off, but my weight in the bow caused it to dig in, and pull even harder downstream. I went aft and the same thing happened to the stern. She wouldn't point up. I couldn't hold on, much less tie off. I was losing rope. I swore I wouldn't lose my trusty anchor, but the line burned through my fingers to the bitter end, and then it was gone. Damn!

As I drifted now peacefully away, I made out, some twenty feet distant, a tall, vertical bank passing swiftly by. Two hundred yards further down was a shallow side channel. I beached, bandaged my fingers, and slept.

In the morning I walked along the caving bank and looked down at the river. Between seeing the snag and dropping the anchor I had passed into a fast bend. Somewhere under all that water was my anchor, five feet of chain, and two hundred feet of braided nylon. The current was too fast to swim or row. No way to retrieve it. There wasn't much need for an anchor on the river anyway, but I would have to find one before I entered the ocean.

In the following days I refined my schedule. From five A.M. to eight A.M. I traveled. During the day I hiked, cooked, performed chores, and napped. From four P.M. to midnight I traveled again. By avoiding the river most of the day I also lowered my profile, making it less likely that word of my coming would precede me.

The river was about the size of the upper Missouri but slower, perhaps one knot on average. Recently exposed sand bars were clean, light gray sheets. Those a few feet higher supported newly sprouted grass and shrubs. Higher still, where it flooded only in winter, were silver-leafed trees that quaked like aspens, thirty-foot palms resembling giant feather dusters, and larger, broadleaf trees, airy and wide of crown.

For my night camp I had only to go lightly aground and drop the leeboards, but day camps were hard to find. I wanted a sandy bank of mild slope, on a side channel so river traffic wouldn't see me, with high ground nearby for exploration, shade, and no people around. I never got all these things. The river people had taken most of the good spots. I saw their canoes pulled up on the bank, the women's little platforms in the water for washing clothes and dishes, their thatched huts on the bank above, their line of drying clothes. Nearby would be the nets and hooked lines that fed the family. Those not so lucky as to possess a high site near the river's summertime channel lived on exposed flats in temporary camps of brushwood, plastic, and corrugated steel. The river level varied with the seasons as much as twenty-five feet, forcing these people to shift between higher and lower camps.

Dolphins followed me faithfully, usually in pairs. They jumped and sported about, but not with the speed or grace of their marine cousins. This "pink dolphin" was actually violet with pink patches on beak and belly. His forehead was bulbous, his dorsal fin long and pronounced, his body rather blubbery. His breaths were noisy and variable, perhaps doubling as a form of expression.

Something in the trees was making horrible, growling sounds that carried for a mile or more. The growls were sustained, resonant, modulating, composed of an indefinite number of voices. They sounded like lions, but were actually howling monkeys. I saw them indistinctly: black blobs in the treetops. On land, iguanas ran on their hind legs, and black, shiny-headed vultures picked over the carcasses of prehistoric-looking fish. Other notable flyers were hook-nosed hawks, pink flamingos, white herons, and turkey-sized creatures with hole-probing beaks. There were strange new species of ants. The mosquitoes obliged me to cover my feet and ankles in the evening.

My body slowly changed from that of a swimmer/bicyclist to that of a rower. Being hard, it wanted to sink when I swam in the clean, naturally turbid water. I regained my tan by revealing skin in the morning and afternoon, when the sun was less lethal. At midday I lay naked and motionless on my back in the cabin, limbs spread to maximize evaporative surface.

I slept, and dreamt I was standing in a cemetery in an old English manor. My hosts were the parents of a friend who had died; their stone mansion stood nearby. My friend was buried in the cemetery, and from his grave, through lovely lawns and trees, the sea was visible. I needed to return to *Squeak*, away across that sea, but where had I left her? Mexico? Argentina? I saw a stylized world in brightly colored maps. I was without family or friends. I didn't question the need to go back and complete the voyage, but I felt strange, like my life was a lifeless work of art, an eternity on a mountain top.

I awoke, drugged with heat, and clawed my way out of a painful stupor. I opened the top and the sun blazed in, as if I had opened the door to a furnace. I collapsed into the river, soaking the soothing coolness in through every wakened pore.

What was I doing there? Where was the environmental good deed I contemplated in Culbertson, Montana? Where was the fluke of fate that would sidetrack me, like Indiana Jones, into ever-higher planes of adventure? But I already knew: it doesn't get any better than this, the voyage itself. I can best honor Earth by grabbing her by the horns. Indiana Jones isn't real, I am. I was doing what I do best: hard travel where the requirements constantly change. My medium was the world at large, and the world, thank God, is still largely wild.

That night I approached the town of Orucué. The glow in the sky ahead meant it had electric lights. While I rowed toward this convenient beacon, someone flashed a flashlight at me from the low bank to my right. Pulling over, I made out a man and five children.

"We're stranded on this island," said the man. "Please, give this one a ride to Orucué so he can come back for us in a canoe." He indicated the tallest boy.

"One of the smaller ones," I said, afraid he might capsize me.

"But this one is nothing!" said the man, shining his flashlight up and down a scrawny frame.

"Okay, but you have to sit still." I sat the boy on the hatch cover and took him to the Orucué boat landing, a mile further on the left bank. While I made up my bed, he pulled a canoe into the water and returned for his family.

In the morning, the once-stranded man came to me with a sack of plantains and lemons. He was a dark, self-effacing campesino named Pedro. "For you," he said. "Please, I will be your guide." Orucué was the size of Puerto Gaitán, but the economy here was agricultural. Pedro led me to the people capable of helping me improve the headlight system and repair my stove. These tasks took two days. Once the townspeople discovered I was friendly they mobbed me with questions. The slightest technological knick-knack fascinated them, like my candle-lantern or my collapsible water containers. They wanted to know how much everything cost. Pedro too was curious, but circumspect. A pained look in his eye told me he was covetous; my relative wealth aroused his discontent.

Poverty didn't embarrass Pedro's wife, however. She boiled drinking water for me, and on the second afternoon invited me to their house for a horrid dinner of white rice, white bread, and fried dough. Afterward she sat me down with six female relatives, mostly unmarried sisters.

"Do you like any of them?" she asked.

"Oh yes, very pretty!" I said, then escaped, from them and all the village's prying eyes and cloying sentiments. The sun was just setting as I pushed into the river. When it had carried me around the first bend I felt again the delicious freedom of the prairie, at the interface between hot and cool, dry and wet. I stood rejoicing atop my sturdy new hatch cover, balanced as if on a log, and drifted. I reminded myself:

to go, and pick a star to return by

to say good-bye a thousand times
then say hello to myself but once

to carry the burrs on my pantlegs
harmless hitchhikers
as others have carried me

A skin infection on my nose came and went. Lice and ticks found their way onto my shores during my walks in the dry woods; I picked them off. As I zigged and zagged with the river, brown-skinned families stood frozen on the banks as if posing for portraits: wild-haired toddlers, mothers with sagging breasts, men risen from their shady hammocks. Dogs, chickens, and pigs roamed their homesteads. Evening revealed a newborn moon, which lingered an hour or two, then followed the sun to bed. Fox bats swooped in the darkness. A bird cried out as if being raped. I rowed toward a constellation I dubbed The Basketball Player because he appeared to jump higher and higher into the northeast sky. Others rose below; I followed them too. Last to rise, a little to my left, was the Big Dipper. It pointed, upside down, to a North Star that remained hidden below the horizon. I had food, water, and batteries for a week.

According to the map, I passed the mouth of a major tributary every day or two, but it was difficult to distinguish them from the various channels of the braided Meta, and darkness often obscured their mouths. The tributaries originating in the Andes had some flow; the Meta grew accordingly. The streams originating in the Llanos were dry. Their mouths were often perched five or ten feet up a cut bank, revealing powerful, U-shaped channels in perfect cross section. The Meta and some of its tributaries formed the boundaries separating Colombia's various *departamentos*, or states. Thus, the Department of Meta, on the right bank, gave way to that of the Vichada, and the Department of Casanare, on the left, gave way to the Arauca.

I was averaging twenty-five miles per day. Light bulbs went out; I replaced them. Switches malfunctioned, I fixed them. Oarlocks squeaked; I greased them. Night gave way to day, and day to night—

> Sun sets, and they who hunt at night rise
> Wind sleeps—voices waken
>
> River nibbles, nibbles
> a tree falls
>
> Mariela, I'm a sunset away
> yours is the same new moon
>
> grow, Moon, grow
> reflect me the sun

On the evening of the seventh I asked a man in a canoe where Santa Rosalia was, and he pointed out a landing with a moored *falca.* It took ten minutes to walk into the village. It was laid out in blocks and disproportionately wide streets. The buildings were long and continuous, with inner courtyards. All was dark except for a few establishments with generators running. A horse-drawn wagon rattled past. I entered a tavern lit by a single candle and sat at a tiny table of crudely planed wood, painted dark blue. "*Cerveza, por favor* (Beer, please)." Outside, under a dangling light bulb, two men were shooting dice and wagering five-thousand-peso bills. Teenagers gathered around, watching.

In the morning I helped six men overturn the *falca* so the bottom could be caulked, then got underway. A tugboat pushing a roofed barge soon overtook me. A speedboat ran ahead of the barge checking depth with a pole. Its driver told me to go and catch a free tow. I did so, but it proved more convenient to pull *Squeak* up onto the barge.

I was a guest of *La Claudia* of Puerto Lopez, bound for Puerto Carreño with a load of telephone poles, cement blocks, fertilizer, rice, bottled pop, potatoes, office furniture, etc. She had a compliment of twelve crewmembers and several wives and children. I joined the off watch for beans, rice, soup, and fried fish in the kitchen next to the two big Detroit Diesels. I visited with the pilot in his booth on the upper deck, and surveyed the river and the dusty, flat forest on either side. The reconnaissance boat driver who had invited me became my main buddy. He was a rakish *Paisa* with wavy black hair and a strong mouth and chin. His flamboyance and light skin distinguished him from the darker *llaneros.* We lounged together in a corner of the barge, he reclining on a dentist's chair destined for a clinic in Puerto Carreño, I making

Velcro fasteners to help hold my mosquito net in place over *Squeak's* hatch.

"Here! Don't tell anyone," he said, and toggled aside a bit of wooden crating. He reached in and pulled out a packet of sweet fruit paste.

We anchored by night and sought out the deep water by day. With the barge's five-foot draft, *La Claudia* was barely able to get down the river. A crewman always stood at each of the two forward corners of the barge sounding with long poles. If they touched bottom they raised the pole up where the pilot could see it, and marked the water level with the other hand. When we ran aground they released the barge and pushed it with *La Claudia* from various angles to free it.

We scraped along steep, sandy banks when necessary to stay in the deep channel. In doing so we once caught a three-foot-long turtle-like creature called a *mata mata* by pulling him from the bank onto the deck. His shell was covered with short spikes. His head was flat, triangular in plan view, with teensy eyes close together near the nose. His extremities were powerful, heavily scaled, nonretractile. I teased him with a strap and he lunged like lightning. Another day the *Paisa* shot a *chinguia*. It was a rodent the size of a hog, with coarse, chestnut hair, hoofed feet, stubby tail, and a head like a beaver. The *Paisa* lifted its hind leg and pressed down on a bulge near the anus. A skinless penis snaked out of a little hole. "*Macho* (male)," he said. We ate the creature's meat for two days.

On the morning of January 10 we arrived at the village of Aguaverde, where I borrowed a horse to explore the countryside. Beyond the corridor of riverine forest stretched a grassland studded with termite mounds. The horse's high spirit was wasted on me; he wanted to trot but I found the jackhammer effect too painful. His full run was tolerable in spurts.

I had no particular goal, so I accompanied a portly *llanera* woman to a ranch where she served as cook. It was noon, and a half dozen cowhands lay sprawled on the shady porch. Their feet were grotesquely callused from a lifetime of going barefoot, and most had teeth missing. While I relaxed with them, a thirty-ish woman with pale, freckled skin and short red hair rode in. Her body was gangly, but she rode effortlessly without reins. She stabled her horse and entered the house without speaking.

A husky man with a full, gray beard came out onto the porch. "Hello, I am Lothar, the owner," he said in English. "Welcome to Rancho San Antonio." Lothar said he lived in Munich, but was currently conducting his semi-annual inspection of his ranch and its thousand head of cattle and horses. He had with him three Bavarian guests: a middle-aged couple on vacation, and the silent woman I had just seen. "Johanna is here trying to decide whether to buy the adjoining ranch. She has just returned from an inspection. If you join us for dinner you can meet her."

I returned my horse to Aguaverde, then walked back to Rancho San Antonio in the evening. The cook had set a table on the bluff overlooking the river. I joined the four Germans there. "Back home I am president of a university," said Lothar, "but Germany is too crowded now. I bought Rancho San Antonio eight years ago. I hope some day to move here permanently."

"And what does Johanna do in Germany?" I asked. The woman might have been mistaken for a young man but for her breasts, which were round as apples, and which curved upward at the nipple.

"Johanna tames horses for a living. Isn't that so, Johanna?" said Lothar.

She had glanced at me during dinner but had spoken only German. Now she turned toward me, hesitantly. "Yes, I own a farm near to Munich. There I live alone with my animals. My farm I sell for much money. Here land is very, you say cheap? Yes. For one hectare in Germany I buy one hundred hectares in Colombia. The people here I do not understand, but I know very well animals."

Her English was limited. She hadn't come there to meet a man, perhaps didn't like men, but she seemed lonely. Everyone went to bed, she in a hammock a little removed from the others. Kneeling, I rocked her, pressing lightly with the fingertips of one hand on her waist at the completion of each swing. We didn't speak. I rocked her gently, and felt her eyes on me. The new moon twinkled on the river and faintly lit our semi-enclosed sleeping quarters. It was the moon the cow jumped over, the Crescent of Islam, the Cheshire cat's grin. It worked its eternal magic on us. Without knowing exactly why, I advanced the timing of my taps, so that each press of my fingertips decelerated her, ever so slightly, until she came to a stop. She hadn't moved. Her face was toward me, but it was too dark to see her expression. I leaned slowly, slowly over and kissed her. Her lips sustained contact with mine for a second then broke into a gasp. She turned her head away, and back again.

"Better we sleep now, no?" she whispered, tensely.

I got into the hammock beside hers. I stretched out my hand, and hers met it in the darkness. Our disembodied hands acquainted, caressed, marveled, like birds courting in midair.

I returned in the morning to Aguaverde. Out-of-work cowboys idled in the sleepy streets as the crew of *La Claudia* prepared to unload the concrete telephone poles. They had no weight-handling equipment, so the twelve of us tied on wooden crosspieces, lifted in pairs, and sweated them up a ramped bank. I took us an hour to move seven of the poles. Only seventy more to go!

It wasn't fun anymore, so I got the *Paisa* to help me throw *Squeak* into the water. I rowed down to Rancho San Antonio and parked in a convenient nook surrounded by low dunes.

That night, after the others had gone to sleep, Johanna and I walked to a hammock she had slung between two trees. "We stay only friends, yes?" she asked. Her voice, already unnatural in English, quavered with emotion.

"No." I sat down on the grass beside the hammock, my hand still holding hers. "Come," I said.

We made love. Johanna tried to enjoy it. She sought a rhythm to match mine, then gave up and simply submitted.

"You will not tell the others, okay?" she beseeched.

"Don't worry."

"It is the first time I am with a man since three years," she said. "This thing with the man I cannot do."

"Why? What's the matter?"

She pulled her pants on, buttoned her shirt. Her shoulders hunched forward, her eyes stared into the darkness. She didn't respond to my caresses anymore.

"When I am very little a man, you say rape? He rape me."

I couldn't comfort her. Her repugnance outweighed her need for love. "I'm sorry. I understand now. Let me be your friend." But she didn't want me to sleep beside her.

Johanna refused to be alone with me the next day. She didn't want to struggle with the stupid English anymore. Lothar and the couple accommodated her by speaking German at the table, which left me out. Lothar remained warm to me, but Johanna was an old friend. Her needs came first. He didn't ask me to leave, but he didn't encourage me to stay either.

I drew away from the group but stayed at my campsite another couple days doing chores, sorting out feelings. I lay writing inside *Squeak* through the blistery midday. Windblown sand pelted against her hull. I daydreamed of descending the Nile River, or a great river I had heard of in Somalia, which never quite reaches the sea, but vanishes into a marshy wasteland. The hatch was propped slightly open; a thin strip of sunlight lay like a burning string from my left breast to my left foot. I propped my clothes bag under my head, and my pack under my buttocks to keep me from sliding into the belly of the boat, because *Squeak* was parked with her bow high.

An enormous iguana entered my peripheral vision through the starboard porthole. He's twelve feet away, patrolling the river's edge, working his way upstream. He doesn't see me. I silently lift the top and raise my head until our eyes meet. He freezes, stares. He lowers his head an inch, severing eye contact. I raise mine an inch, re-establishing it. He crouches more, I raise more. I move to get my notebook, he runs away.

From my campsite the view across the Meta was of four thin layers and one infinite one: river, sand, grass, trees, sky. Clouds came, then dusk.

At Rancho San Antonio, Colombia, 1/12/92

Heat lightning shifted and shimmered silently. I slept, and dreamt of a high school reunion. People I can't visualize anymore when awake came up and talked to me. Joe Murray, still up to no good. Robin Hammond—I didn't recognize her at first, then suddenly remembered I had played with her even before kindergarten. I woke up, my face wet with tears. It was jolting to remember where I was, in a place my childhood friends would never have heard of. I had recently missed my twentieth high school reunion. Did anyone miss me?

In the morning I saw that my cap had blown away. Without it my face would burn off, so I walked to Aguaverde once more. I crossed low areas which had been trampled by cattle when muddy and had subsequently dried, leaving tedious pockmarks. Five riders stood in profile on the horizon wearing long-sleeved shirts in bright solids: white, green, tan, and blue, from left to right. I followed the river bank, and an iguana suddenly landed in front of me with a thud, eyed me, and scrambled away. It was the same fellow I had stared down the day before. I looked up into the tree he had fallen from and saw a large bird's nest. He was hunting eggs.

Neither of the two stores had any caps, so I asked around for a used one. A brown-skinned cowboy took me to his house. He was old, but still stood straight, proud, impassive. He produced a denim baseball cap, so worn that only the inner white threads showed in spots, but functional. I paid him five hundred pesos. He was pleased.

"You are going downriver?" he asked.

"Yes. Why?"

"The guerrillas may stop you."

"So?"

"They dispense justice. If they catch a man who has stolen a horse they shoot him. If they stop you—tell them I am a friend of yours. They will let you go."

"Maybe they won't believe me. Please, write it in my notebook. Say I am your friend, and put the date."

He appeared taken aback, perhaps self-conscious about his schooling, but he took my notebook and pen and scrawled: "*Yo soy amigo de Guiano. 13 Enero, 1992* (I am a friend of Guiano. January 13, 1992)."

At *La Claudia* the men were still laboring over the concrete poles. "See you in Puerto Carreño!" I said. I walked back to Rancho San Antonio, took leave of the Germans, and departed at dusk. The moon was half full and didn't set until midnight. I didn't need the headlights anymore.

Two days out from San Antonio I reached Nueva Antioquia, on the south bank. It was the last place to buy provisions before Puerto Carreño, at the mouth of the Meta. It had only one store and one woman willing to cook meals, but that was enough. I bought Quaker oatmeal, sugar, potatoes, and plantains. When lunch was ready I ate it in the woman's courtyard. Two men in a room behind me played harp and guitar, the traditional Llanos instruments. The music floated from an open window and twisted away in the wind. I looked at my map. The south bank would remain Colombian territory until I reached the mouth of the Meta, but the north bank would become part of Venezuela a few miles downstream from Nueva Antioquia. I had been in Colombia nine months, three times longer than expected. How long would I be in Venezuela? What would the Venezuelans be like?

My first impression was not good. That night I approached a settlement on the Venezuelan side. There were lights, so I thought there might be a restaurant. As I nudged onto the bank, a voice yelled, *"Avance con los manos en alto!"* I saw the man was pointing a submachine gun at me and realized the words meant, "Come forward with your hands up!" Others streamed over the bank, some in battle fatigues, others in white shorts and T-shirts, all heavily armed.

I had stumbled onto a Venezuelan naval base. Two of them searched *Squeak* while a lieutenant questioned me. He calmed down when he saw my American passport.

"It is prohibited to navigate at night."

"I have no choice. The wind is too strong during the day."

The men had found my hunting knife and machete. "Sir! Weapons!" The lieutenant made a gesture of unconcern.

"*Americano*, you may put your belongings back in order. Be very careful. The Colombian guerrillas are here. Sometimes they come to Venezuelan soil. It is a bad situation."

"What do they look like?"

"Like you or me," he shrugged.

"Are they armed?"

"Oh yes, big guns," he said impressively, holding his hands wide apart. His men chuckled, but it wasn't entirely a joke.

"Good luck," he said as I pulled back into the river. Seconds later I was alone again in the darkness. The world seemed a more dangerous place now. I was torn between fear and curiosity about these mysterious bogeymen, *los guerrilleros.*

The final two hundred miles of the Meta River were the most remote. River traffic was slight. I saw no villages, and few signs of agriculture or ranching, but men still fed their families from the river. They stretched nets between poles, cast nets from their boats, towed hooks, or tied hooked lines to snags or anchored floats.

On January 16 a man driving a canoe with a forty-horse Yamaha pulled alongside. "Hey! I'll tow you."

"Thanks, but I don't need it."

"Come on! Why not?"

I smelled rum on his breath, but was curious about him and his two passengers, a married couple. "Okay, but slow, understand? Slow."

"Yes, I'll go very slow."

We tied a line, I got into his boat, and he zoomed off like a bat out of hell. *Squeak* squatted at the stern until her leeboard rubstrakes (horizontal fins for holding the leeboards out to either side) half-submerged, then she rode them like water skis, straight as an arrow. I expected the handles to break off any second, but the man's recklessness immobilized me. Disaster threatened, and the slightest move on my part could trigger it. The driver was roaring drunk, but the husband and wife were sober and detached. He wore a suit and leather shoes. She was barefoot but wore a long black skirt, blouse, jacket, scarf, and silver jewelry. Their apparel was travel-worn and archaic, like what I imagined a gypsy bride and groom would wear. The woman, I couldn't help noticing, was as darkly beautiful as a gypsy princess. A half-hidden smile suggested that she returned my curiosity.

Thirty minutes later, the driver turned and rammed into the bank at a speed sufficient to fully beach his canoe. *Squeak* came whipping around behind, aiming straight for another boat already on the bank. Its outboard motor was cocked up—*Squeak's* bow was about to smash into its upturned propeller! I dove into the water and positioned myself just in time to deflect *Squeak* from the collision. My rash motorist never even noticed. Upon touchdown he and the male passenger had jumped out and hustled into the woods to visit whoever was there.

It was just getting dark. I stepped back onto the canoe to untie my line, and the pretty wife approached me.

"You're going?"

"The man's crazy. I want nothing to do with him."

Her eyes smiled accessibly, and a shot of lust mingled with the adrenaline still coursing in my veins.

"*Adios, entonces?* (Good-bye, then?)" she asked.

"*Sí, señora, adios.*" I rowed quickly away, staying close to the bank, where the shadows of the overhanging trees would hide me. Five minutes later I heard the Yamaha start up and speed away into the darkness.

At dawn on the eighteenth I was sleeping on a vast sand bar when a "Halloo!" woke me. I looked out and saw a goofy-looking fellow standing beside me with an old, single-barreled shotgun. His hat had once been a high-crowned felt sombrero, but now it was mostly holes. Amazingly, it still stood upright on his head. His pants matched his hat.

"I's just out a-huntin' an' saw this hyar boat, curious-like," he said, as well as I can translate his rustic dialect.

"Dat gun use to belong to yo' granpappy?" I asked, copying his speech to the best of my ability.

"Shucks, still puts meat on the table," he grinned.

He seemed harmless, but word of strangers spreads quickly, so I moved further down the river to complete my sleep.

That night while I rowed, someone approached in a canoe going upstream. *Musica llanera* blared from a radio. It mingled with the whine of the motor, carrying for miles over the quiet water. The rhythm was tight and fast, the chords minor, the progression repetitious. A female voice sang passionately, fluidly, in endless variations. I moved to one side. They passed without seeing me.

The wind now began before dawn. I skipped the morning run and traveled from dusk until the moon set, which occurred an hour later each night. The river was at its largest, and snags were less common. These factors, plus the moon, allowed me to row pulling, looking over my shoulder every ten or twenty strokes.

Sometimes the river ran straight between treed banks a half mile apart. In those stretches the depth was good throughout. Eventually the breadth would widen to a mile or more, which meant shallows, low islands, and the initiation of a mild meander. Where the river divided into channels, only one generally had sufficient depth. The land was so flat and vast that even in daylight it might be difficult to tell which way to go. In moonlight I could only guess. I found myself in dead ends, and had to back-track. To determine which way the current was flowing I probed the bottom with a stick. I then aligned *Squeak* with the current and rowed. It was usually fastest to one side or the other, but staying in the middle had less risk of getting corralled.

Shallow water slowed me down, in three degrees of severity. In less than three feet I was restricted in the depth to which I could immerse my oars. In less than eighteen inches *Squeak's* wake rose up the way a swell rises over a sand bar; the wake acted as a brake. In less than eight inches *Squeak's* keel dragged.

If the water was shallow and without current, it meant I was in a bay or disconnected channel. If it was shallow with current then I was on a sheet flow which would eventually empty back into the main channel by spilling over a steep underwater bank. This drop-off was visible as a line of disturbed water more or less perpendicular to flow. This line in the water was a good sign because it meant deeper water lay on the far side. Another type of water disturbance was neutral: the boils that sometimes lifted and squirreled me around but did no harm. Other disturbances were bad, such as the rock ledges I was beginning to see. I'd heard rumors of rapids and whirlpools, so I always backstroked and studied questionable water patterns before continuing.

The nights were cool and tranquil. It was an endless pleasure to row "with long legs" through the glassy water. Thanks to the moon, my average shot up to fifty miles per day. Every night the moon got bigger, and set later. The semi-darkness affected my perception of the country. Colors did not exist, but the play of moonlight on water, sand, and vegetation was exquisite. Trees seemed abstract, idealized. Flaws didn't show. Subtleties of shadow piqued my imagination as I ghosted by the wild banks. I surprised watering *chinguia,* and caught them in the beam of my flashlight as they stampeded diagonally up the steep bank. The calls of the nocturnal animals formed a mercurial symphony—sometimes soothing background music, other times like an orgy at the zoo. Sand calved off the bank like bergs from a glacier. My faithful dolphin friends were never far away. They left me when I entered shallows only to startle the daylights out of me later with a big, close splash. The stars rose in the east and marched straight up to the zenith, just as the sun did by day. Falling stars were commonplace. I never saw airplane lights. Whimsical in the long night, I practiced boating maneuvers. I determined that it took me six strokes to get up to full speed from a dead stop, and it took twenty-eight seconds to execute a 360-degree turn at full speed. I perfected my stroke, savoring the tight, clean "snitch" of my oars as they re-entered the water every two seconds.

It seemed a different world by day. Whitecaps furrowed the river. The wind was hot and dusty. It was tough to sleep in the furnace-like heat, but my reversed camping schedule had advantages. Chores were easier in daylight, like cooking, washing, and dispensing water from my five-gallon bag to my day bottles. If I couldn't sleep, at least I could read, write, swim, and explore. And my schedule made it less likely that the guerrillas would see me. Sometimes I camped at the edge of featureless sand flats, sometimes in the lee of dunes, sometimes in backwater basins barely large enough for *Squeak*. Some camps were on the mainland, others on islands. The further my campsite was from the main channel and signs of habitation, the safer I felt.

On January 19, I pulled into the river as the sun set astern and the full moon rose ahead. The river now flowed due east. At seven P.M. I noticed the river was relatively narrow, yet slow, and deduced that it must be deep. I dropped my lead line: forty-four feet. I was drowsy, so I grounded in a mess of small, stranded trees, emptied the cabin into the cockpit, set my wristwatch alarm, and lay down.

I got underway again at eleven P.M. My body, fooled into thinking it had gotten a full night's sleep, never got tired again. Toward morning I saw lights on the Venezuelan bank. The eastern sky began to brighten, profiling dark mountains: the Guyana Massif. The river became unusually turbulent, the banks fell away, a vast openness approached. It wasn't just another widening of the river.

I stopped on the right side, climbed a sand bank, and sat facing east. The Meta River, with whom I had traveled 620 miles, ran another half mile, turbulently, through a delta of low sand spits, into a wide valley. Through that valley the Orinoco River, still indistinct, flowed from right to left. Beyond, the foothills of the Guyana Highlands were taking on color and texture below the yellow-pink brightness that marked where the sun was about to rise. To my left, streetlights still burning, was the Venezuelan border town of Puerto Paez. The Puerto Carreño waterfront was visible a mile up the Orinoco, to my right. Behind, the moon was setting. Thank you, moon.

For months Puerto Carreño had been an abstraction on a map, a destination I could not be sure of reaching. Now I saw it. Like Buenaventura it was a critical milestone, because I had crossed an especially remote region. Bridging this gap had engaged all of me. My analytical brain had judged the distances and calculated the forces. My intuitive brain had danced with the river until we interpenetrated, just as running wolves become a pack, or a hawk is one with the wind. The interpenetration wasn't total, but even if slight it might alter consciousness, just as a meditator who only marginally empties his or her mind may experience relaxation.

Night after night I had plumbed external and internal depths. This semi-hypnotic state intensified the emotions that welled up upon reaching the mouth of the Meta River. Those emotions were relief from fear, awe of nature, and a rarefied joy.

CHAPTER 19

ORINOCO RIVER TO CAICARA

I savored the completion of another phase of the journey, then dropped down through whirls and boils into the Orinoco River. It was the same greenish brown, but much clearer. The Meta's momentum caused the mixing of waters to bulge well out into the mile-wide Orinoco. All along the water boundary dolphins were gobbling up fish, and fish were jumping out of the water to escape them.

Overnight the landscape had radically altered. Huge domes of ancient bedrock protruded from the plain like half-buried bowling balls. Those with one flank in the river were chalky to a height of forty feet, representing the winter high-water mark. Above this line they were dark gray. Their surfaces were smooth in large scale, rough up close—easy to climb, but bad to take a fall on. I paused beside a cluster of such spheres to change into my good six-dollar pants, then rowed into Puerto Carreño craving beer, other people's cooking, and new friends.

The waterfront was busy with tugboats and small craft. The shore was moderately sloping, of sand and dry silt, vegetated in spots. A boat was piling what looked like crocodile skins into the back of a truck, but they turned out to be huge dried fish. I pulled *Squeak* up beside the Colombian naval base, which consisted of a gunboat moored to a barge cabled perpendicular to the shoreline, like a pier. Steps led to the top of the quay, along which ran a waterfront boulevard. The town's topography was a mix of lumpy bedrock, red-soiled flats, and swamp. A sugar loaf towered over the settlement, giving it the aspect of a miniature Rio de Janeiro. On top, statues of Jesus Christ and a revolutionary war hero competed for attention with a modern art sculpture, a communications tower, and a water treatment plant. It was becoming quite cluttered up there.

The streets were paved! Being the capital of the Department of Vichada,

Puerto Carreño had several government buildings. The hardware stores sold fishing hooks nearly as large as those used to lift bales of hay. Such hooks must have caught those dried monsters I saw on the bank. The bar with the red light bulbs outside was the brothel—logical. The restaurants ranged from upscale to Third World Funky, mostly the latter.

I picked up mail, and met the official in charge of river navigation. He showed me with maps how I could ascend the Orinoco, get transport around a series of rapids, continue up a tributary, make a twenty-mile land crossing, and end up on the Rio Negro, which feeds the Amazon. I was tempted. It would be easier, in the short term at least, than to descend the Orinoco against the wind. But it would add maybe another year to the voyage. Another time. (In 2012 Ginny and I would reach the Amazon via a similar route.)

The town didn't have electricity, much less a computer to write on, so I focused on another problem. The seat deck, on which I sat to row pulling, and which consists of two veneers glued in an arch, was cracking transversely, with the grain. It needed reinforcement, so I glued a patch of thin plywood to its underside with a bedding of thickened epoxy, pressing it up into place with props set against the cabin sole. Meanwhile I looked for pretty women, and found four. The first was married. I got a date with the second, but she turned out to be a prostitute. So was the third. The fourth was too young to seriously consider. Somehow, that summed up sexual relations in Latin America.

Everybody came down to the boat and checked me out. Some acted buddy-buddy in hopes of scoring something off me.

"Please, won't you give me your backpack as a memento to remember you by?" whined a sailor.

"Nice try, amigo," I thought, and pretended not to hear him.

Others were sincere. On January 22, 1992, a vacationing businessman named Luis insisted I accompany him to a bar on the esplanade. There he introduced me to his companions, all from Bucaramanga, all fifty-ish, in their second childhood. They were there for a few days to sportfish in the Orinoco. They bought me drinks for three hours, reveling in the sense of adventure they got from just sitting with me, glowing in the rapture of rugged, male companionship. "To the gringo's balls!" they toasted.

Luis and I met again that evening to drink beer. He was a good six-foot-four, big around the waist, dressed in elegant sandals, shorts, and sports shirt left untucked. He looked orthodox but his hormones were those of a teenager.

"*Hola,*" I said, too faintheartedly for him.

"*Hola?*" he echoed, with mock effeminacy. "*Que clase de saludo es? Hijeputa, 'mano, somos amigos o que?* (What kind of greeting is that? Sonuvabitch, bro', we friends or what?)" He led me to a decent restaurant next door to the brothel, but before entering pulled me into some shadows. There he fumbled in the breast pocket of his shirt, produced a marijuana cigarette, lit it up, and puffed voraciously. "My friends say I'm smoking too much weed. Fuck 'em. What do they know?"

The restaurant was open to the street, with seven or eight tables. We sat down, and Luis launched into a dissertation on the various ways to say "stoned," followed by a selection of pithy salutations sure to demonstrate one's cool with the brothers, or catch the eye of a woman. Our food came. I ate mine slowly, as always. Luis shoveled his down, seemingly without breathing.

He had cleaned his plate and was drawing on his beer when two nicely dressed whores came in, sat at the table behind me, and ordered dinner. The one facing us was a buxom brunette in a low-cut, fuchsia dress. Luis's Adam's apple stopped its up-and-down motion. He set his beer down and gazed at her. A tremor passed through him. He knitted his eyebrows, then lifted them, sufferingly. His eyes took on a faraway look. His mouth opened and rounded slightly. Then he must have caught her eye, because he pursed his lips and blew a long, lingering kiss. He looked like a condemned man bidding farewell to his sweetheart.

Luis and his buddies flew back to Bucaramanga on the 24th. A *casa de cambio* exchanged my leftover pesos for bolívares at a ratio of 10.2 to 1. Then I pushed off and rowed a couple miles past the mouth of the Meta to the Puerto Paez landing. I arrived at what I thought was five o'clock on a Friday, but I had just crossed a time zone. It was now six o'clock, and the immigration office wasn't due to reopen until Monday.

The landing was both a *Guardia Nacional* post and a terminal for ferrying vehicles across the river. At the landing were a Frenchman about my age named Gerard and a beautiful German named Annette. They were travelers who had just ridden down from Puerto Ayacucho, on the upper Orinoco, with a burly Venezuelan named Pedro. At the latter's invitation I got into his Chevy pickup and rode with them the two miles into town, where we stopped at the only restaurant.

Gerard was of medium build, strong, with slicked-back, ebony hair and dark complexion, the son of a Vietnamese man and an Italian woman. He crewed on yachts for a living. He was easygoing, playful, always looking for the humor in things. When there wasn't any he made up his own little jokes and laughed at them. Annette was twenty-eight, a model turned fashion photographer, blond, with a clear, straight, Aryan face. They spoke Italian together but English with me, Annette fluently, Gerard not well but unashamedly. Their clothing was plain and appropriate, like they had shopped at a Banana Republic store.

Our host, Pedro, was a big, excitable man in jeans and jean shirt, open at the neck to reveal a hairy chest and gold necklace. I didn't get to talk to him very long because soon after our arrival three policemen came into the restaurant to arrest him. Pedro was stunned. "No, this is impossible, leave me alone!" He resisted. The cops were reluctant to use force. For five minutes they argued and tugged, pushed and pulled, on the brink of violence. Pedro slowly gave way, and they dragged him into the slammer across the street. They put him in the cell facing us, where he shook the bars and wailed in a mixture of anger, shame, and despair at being separated from us, his new friends. Meanwhile, our dinners came, and we ate them. Poor Pedro was great entertainment.

We never found out why he was jailed, only that it was for seventy-two hours, that it had been ordered by the commander of the local army garrison, and that there was a hint of a triangle involving these two men and Pedro's wife. The latter arrived, a small, self-assured woman. We all consoled Pedro from the sidewalk outside his window. Then Pedro passed her the truck keys and we went to their house to sleep.

On Saturday I found the immigration officer's house and paid him 100 bolívares ($1.50) to stamp my passport on his day off. I didn't feel like being alone yet, so I took Gerard and Annette to see the Meta River. We walked to the far side of town, crossed some dry channels, and found a steep bank a little above the mouth. I went in first. "The water's fine!"

I looked back up and there was Annette, naked, her perfect body glowing in the sun. She was taking her time coming down the sandy bank, unconcerned that two men were just then passing by in a canoe.

"You're the first naked blonde these guys have ever seen," I said, cringing at the thought of the damage being done in their poor minds by the sight of such forbidden fruit. Bad enough what it was doing to my own.

At the base of the bank was a bench of wet clay. Gerard and I threw mud balls at each other while Annette daubed her pubic hair and laughed at how funny it looked. I heaped mud on top of my head, then poured sand on top of that. Annette got up close and took a picture of the pattern created by hair, mud, and sand.

In the afternoon we took a walk in the countryside, where we discovered a tamarind tree. Its fruit was a legume too sweet to resist yet so sour I puckered involuntarily. In the evening we sat on the curb, guzzled the street vendor's cheap pop, and ate her greasy meat pastries. We interacted with even the least interesting people on the street, including a self-important young frontier guard, whom we taught how to say "Give me your passport!" in six languages. Gerard spoke no Spanish, but this didn't slow him down. He just tried out French and Italian words until he found one that worked. Meanwhile I ruminated with Annette. "How strange to meet fellow travelers after so long with only the local people. I like you and Gerard. You make me realize how lonely I've been."

"We like you too."

"Where you going from here," I asked.

"I'm en route to Miami to work in the fashion industry, but it's turning out to be a very circuitous route. I crossed the Atlantic aboard a yacht that needed to be delivered to a new owner. That's how I met Gerard. He was a member of the crew. We became lovers, and when we got to Martinique he said, 'Let's go to Venezuela.' 'Why not?' I said. He doesn't have anyplace he has to be, so from Puerto Ayacucho he wanted to continue up the river to Brazil, but I told him no. I'm supposed to be in Miami in two weeks and I still don't know how I'm going to get there. I like it here very much also, but I don't have time to enjoy it, so what's the point? Now there's no bus out of here until Monday. I'm feeling more and more frustrated."

"Do you think you and Gerard will stay together?"

"No, of course not. He knows very well this is just temporary between us. I have a husband in Germany, though I'd rather forget about him, and about Germany too. It's all shit there now, with this stupid unification."

"Then why don't you stay with Gerard?"

"Because the man I love lives on a sailboat in Key West. He's an artist, very reclusive. States is where I want to live now. Gerard won't go all the way to States with me."

This jolted me. "Jeez, I can see how you might be unfaithful to your husband if you're separated from him, but if Gerard isn't who you love either…"

"Don't bother trying to figure me out. None of the usual rules seem to apply to me. All my life I've lived too fast. You want a shock? I was even addicted to heroin for six months when I lived in Venice. I got past it. What's important is that we have the courage to live freely. For this I admire you very much."

The parallel to Traci dawned on me. What a coincidence I should fall for two confused, unattainable, free-lance photographers in the same voyage.

"You're a beautiful woman. Hope you don't mind if I look at you now and then."

"Go ahead, everybody else does. But I only want the men I can't have."

It was late, yet the northeast wind still blew unchecked. How was I going to get down the river with the wind wailing twenty-four hours a day? My only map of the region ahead was a tracing I had taken from Gerard's road map of Venezuela. Information was scarce. I worried about the navigation, but I worried more about the good-bye that was coming up fast.

Sunday we got up a little expedition. Low in the water from the extra weight, *Squeak* carried the three of us across the Orinoco and a little upstream to where a sandy beach, a network of lagoons, and a pile of rocky knolls came together. Stripping to shorts and tennis shoes, we swam across a lagoon to a protruding knoll and scaled it. On top, perhaps two hundred feet above the river, I found a tiny jawbone with sharp teeth. Gerard found a similar fragment some yards away. We held them together—they fit. From the same, long-dead creature. "A new species!" Annette said. We laughed.

The far side of the knoll was splintered. The newer fractures could have been neatly reassembled, but the older fractures had been rounded by time to create car- and house-sized boulders. We crawled down into crevices which sloped and curved at odd angles. The air was cool and damp, the light filtered. Bats fluttered and crawled on the walls. At the bottom was a pool. I dropped down to it, wet my hands, and dampened my face. Looking back, I noticed that to one side of the crevice I had descended was a narrow shaft that led up and away, then curved in the direction of my friends. Silently, I climbed up through it. At its narrowest there wasn't room to crawl, so I wiggled like a snake until I found myself directly behind Gerard. He was on his haunches, facing the other way. He and Annette were examining something on the wall. They hadn't heard me. I reached out and snapped the elastic band in Gerard's briefs. He gave a start and bumped his head on the ceiling. We laughed, then they became serious again.

"Look," said Annette. It was an Indian petroglyph of a sailing ship, carved low on the wall.

"Did the Spaniards sail up the river this far?" murmured Gerard.

"Yes," I said. "About four hundred years ago."

We rowed back after dark, Annette sleeping curled up in the cabin, I pulling the oars. Gerard sat facing me and pushed the oars for extra propulsion. His face was so close in the little cockpit, I had to take care not to punch him in the chin with each stroke. It was more difficult rowing against the wind and with the current than vice versa, but Gerard knew how to handle himself, how to help a skipper without contesting his command.

"What is it about the sea and about boats, Steve? All my life I am a slave to them. Never to women, only to boats."

"Tell me about your boats, Gerard."

"I have built them. I have owned them. I have wrecked them. It's a sad story!" he chuckled.

"Tell me anyway."

"When we are youngest is when we are the best. When I am still very young I build a boat in Tahiti and sail it to France alone. Nothing I do since then is so—important, big in my heart. So big it is hurting."

"I know what you mean."

"That boat she dies, and I have many others. Now I only sail for other people, on their boats. It is a job for me. But in France, on the Canal du Midi, I am building another. I would like for you to see it sometime. I would like to sail with you."

"I'd like that too. You love the sea, like another Frenchman I met once, in Panama. His name was Michel."

I walked back to town with them for dinner and beers. When the restaurant closed we walked the dusty road to where our paths split, theirs to Pedro's house, mine to the landing. It was Sunday night. A bus would take them to San Fernando de Apure in the morning. *Don't cry until they're gone,* I told myself.

We joined in a three-way hug that rocked, squeezed tighter, lingered. Then we split. They left together, I alone. I jogged back to the landing, wiping the stinging tears from my cheeks. When I got back to *Squeak* the moon hadn't risen and the wind hadn't stopped blowing. Might as well wait till morning.

It was January 27. "Watch out for the rapids!" yelled Pedro as I rowed past the ferry terminal. He had just gotten out of jail and was on his way back upriver.

I made painfully slow progress until ten o'clock, when the waves got too big. At two o'clock I started again, and passed the cataract. It was majestic in its size, and in the complexity of the rocks it gushed through, but not difficult.

The river was well channelized, snag-free, slow. There still wasn't much river traffic, nor was it more heavily populated than the Meta. The people seemed to have more Indian blood, or a different kind of Indian blood. Their features were sharper, and some had a Negroid frizz in their hair. Their dialect was different; they had different names for all the fruits, for example. They stared the same way the Colombians had.

The hills east of the river were of ancient stone. They fell off as I proceeded north, but other, lesser ranges appeared in their place. Collectively they made up the northwest fringe of the Guyana Massif. Mesquite grew wherever soil had formed. In the gaps between the ranges the land was flat and scrubby. West of the river stretched the Venezuelan Llanos.

As I traveled, the orientation of the Highlands' foot slowly veered from north to east. The river trended accordingly. It was as if the Llanos, in addition to their infinitesimal seaward tilt, had another that kept the river pegged to the toe of the Guyana Highlands rather than flowing down the middle of the plains. I camped behind rocks or on deserted sand flats, cooking potatoes, carrots, beets, or noodles. I tried night travel, but the moon phase was against me. By the third day I had developed a new schedule based on sailing by day.

Sailing hadn't worked in the Meta because the deep water wasn't wide enough to tack, but here I had five or ten minutes before the leeboard would start to scrape sand. The river flowed northeast while I tacked north, then east, then north, then east. It was slow and rough, but the fastest alternative. In the morning and late afternoon the wind blew at ten to fifteen knots, which *Squeak* could handle under full sail. In the middle of the day I had to reef, and let go the mainsheet occasionally to reduce heel. The wind was steady away from the hills, gusty near them. The waves pounded *Squeak* and sapped her momentum. Where the current was strong it was too rough to navigate, so I stuck to the side with less current.

On January 29 I passed a large bauxite-shipping terminal serving a mine someplace up in the hills. From there on the channel was marked with lighted buoys. Late that afternoon I pulled into a tiny cove. It was of a type which provided me with most of my campsites during this phase.

I dubbed them "fjords." Wherever a dry channel branched off from the main channel, the shoreline was irregular and fluted. These flutings were the result of waves in the sand of the dry channel bed. These dunes ran perpendicular to the axis of the dry bed. In filling the voids, the river created a shoreline like that of Norway in miniature. The typical fjord was ten feet wide, fifty yards long, and a foot deep. It branched off at an angle 120° to the flow of the actual river. It had a steep, four-foot bank on the upstream side and a sandy flat on the downstream side. The dry channels being numerous and wide, I had plenty of fjords to pick from. Those near the middle of a dry channel were well removed from human habitations. Only *Squeak's* masts showed above the dune, so I was partly hidden from the river, too.

A nearby dome attracted my attention. I had an hour before sunset, so I trekked across a half mile of sand to its foot and crossed a narrow, moat-like lagoon. The rock, as I verified later from navigational charts, was six hundred feet tall. Like the smaller one I had climbed with my friends near Puerto Paez, it was steep enough to be exciting, but gave good grip. Parts of the rock were bare, others had a skin of soil in which cactus and thorny shrubs sprouted yellow and purple flowers. Lizards the same gray as the rock darted into cracks at my approach.

The rock lay at the northwestern tip of a subrange I'd spent the entire day approaching. A similar band of hills was now visible to the northeast. Seemingly straight down was the flat I had just walked across. Beyond that was the river, wide and braided. Some of the secondary channels were running, some had standing water, others were dry. The dry channel in which *Squeak* was parked stretched eight miles before rejoining the main channel. In winter the land between them would be an island one to two miles wide. Ah, to see this then! Farther away were ancient meanders, now elongated lakes, that still served as supplementary channels in the big floods. Beyond that, a sea of low, mangy forest stretched to the setting sun, dipping at the edges with the curvature of the earth. In the middle, barely discernible, was *Squeak*, in her fjord in the sand.

I stayed put the next day. While I was busy with some chore, my nearest neighbor appeared with his four boys and five dogs. They had just caught four small iguanas. They carried them by their tails, their heads crushed and bleeding.

I later went for a walk with the oldest boy to a summer camp where some relatives were staying. Three men gambled at cards while children played on the outskirts, a woman messed with the pots, and a baby slept in a hammock. Flies buzzed on the litter-strewn sand. The wind flapped madly in the disintegrating plastic that served as walls.

The boy then took me to his own home, where his father was scaling and cleaning the fish he'd caught in his net that day. He tossed the scraps to the dogs, cats, pigs, and chickens that milled about, making sure the small and weak got their share. One fish was a four-foot-long speckled catfish with a broad, hard, flat skull. He also had smaller catfish, each with four "whiskers" half the length of their body, and piranha, three or four pounds each, highly prized for their flesh.

We went back to *Squeak* along a bank grown over with mangrove-like brush, wading whenever it extended into the water. Twenty feet ahead a six-foot crocodile slipped down into the water and sank. "They eat people," said the boy, matter-of-factly, and skirted to higher ground.

When I fought the river again, the wind quickly built until spray was heavy over the windward gunwale. Even reefed she leaned too far. Heavy water came over the lee gunwale if I didn't loosen the sheet fast enough. Bang! bang! came the waves. It was more like whitewater rafting than sailing. The chill of the wind overpowered the heat of the sun, so I put on my rain jacket. Feet and groin were constantly wet, causing fungal rash. At eleven o'clock a wave flooded the cockpit. The gain wasn't worth the risk, so I bailed the water out, went to the nearest fjord, and waited till midafternoon. The sand was littered with the bones of armor-plated, exoskeletal fish.

In the following days I identified the point at which there was too much wind by a reddish haze that developed over the sand flats. I was down to twenty miles per day. Fortunately, I was able to provision in the village of La Urbana. The watermelon, oranges, bananas, and tomatoes boosted my morale. I marked my progress by the clusters of hills I passed every ten miles or so on the right bank.

One day I took my siesta in a lagoon at the foot of an isolated hill of broken rock. After napping I walked toward the hill, but the mangrove-like brush blocked my path. While I looked for a way through, two dogs timidly approached. A little further was a third dog, surrounded by vultures that flew away at my approach. He was still alive and conscious, breathing rapidly and shallowly. He was nothing but skin and bones. The hide on his neck was missing, the flesh rotten and crawling with maggots. The remains of a rope were still tied around the putrid neck. He lifted his eyes at me. His tail tapped the sand feebly. I felt sick. He needed to be put away, but there weren't any rocks around. My machete . . . But the idea of chopping through that rotten neck was too disgusting. "Sorry, not my job."

Still intent on climbing the hill, I got into *Squeak* and rowed to a beach on its further side. The two healthy dogs, perhaps abandoned by the same owner who had abused the dying one, swam desperately after me. This new beach smelled of something that had been dead for some time; I didn't want to know what it was. Machete in hand, I climbed up through the heat and cactus, boulder to boulder, ledge to ledge, watching for thorns, snakes, people. The dogs stuck to me like glue. From the top I saw the next hill, but couldn't tell to which side of it the river passed. I saw signs of man: a patch of agriculture on an island downstream, the remains of a hut, cattle paths running through tinder-brush trees, a smoke in the distance. Objectively, this landscape was similar to that of the other dome, but now it looked dried out, dead, sinister. How old *was* this crag, this island in a sea of sand and silt?

Jumpy from head to toe, I hustled back down to *Squeak* and shoved off. What a relief to be gone from there! Fido and Rover swam along behind, whining. The last I saw of their two little heads, they still hadn't given up.

At sunset I camped near the mouth of the Rio Apure, the Orinoco's last tributary originating in the Andes. I had left the Llanos. From here on the Orinoco flows through the immense valley that separates the Guyana Highlands from the coastal ranges. The next night, February 3, I pulled *Squeak* up on a filthy waterfront among a profusion of dugouts and roofed, steel passenger launches. I had reached the town of Caicara.

I woke up the following morning to the sound of people discussing me. "He's gotta be a filthy rich gringo to have a boat like that," someone said.

I sat up so they could get a better look at me. Some left, but a man with wiry gray hair and mustache kept studying *Squeak* from all angles. He stroked his stubbly chin, squinted first one eye, then the other. His skin was light brown, his frame gaunt, erect. When conversation rekindled he stole the show, interpreting my boat for those in the audience not blessed with his powers of observation. He rapped *Squeak's* wooden hull with his knuckles. "Pure fiberglass!" he said, admiringly. Someone asked what the big, flat things on the sides were (my leeboards) and he said, "Oh, those are his spare oars. This baby don't got no motor, you know." His gestures were eloquent, complex. He pointed at things by lifting his chin and puckering his lips in the indicated direction. To make a point, he took a diagonal stance, shifted forward, jutted his chin, and nailed his victim with a sparkling gray eye while brandishing his index finger like a sword. If the effect was good he reiterated with variations. Whenever he got a laugh he drooped his knees, hunched his shoulders, threw up a supplicating, limp-wristed palm, and grinned slyly, revealing white, gold, and missing teeth.

When I stood to pull my shirt on he lost his composure, shrank back.

"Buenos dias," I said.

He grinned and presented himself. *"Bienvenidos,* meester! The name's Emilio, but everyone calls me El Maraycucho because I come from Maracay."

"Pleased to meet you. Say, can you tell me where I can buy fruit and bread?"

"Hey! You can come with me. Over here."

We got into his decrepit Toyota Land Cruiser pickup. We spoke Spanish, but he threw out a few English witticisms to show how cosmopolitan he was.

"My friend, fuckie fuckie?" he leered when we passed an attractive woman.

I didn't react.

"Yeees, good!"

Caicara was a dull town, but relatively blessed with conveniences. Houses of stucco-faced cement block lined the concrete streets. The cars were mostly full-sized American autos and pickups. The water was drinkable. There were a post office, telephone office, and stores where I could buy dental floss, flashlight bulbs, a T-shirt. The economy was based on the diamond, gold, and bauxite mines located a few hours south by Land Cruiser or bus.

Emilio found a teacher at the local junior college who was willing to rent his personal computer to me. "You're going to be around a while now, Steve," Emilio said. "You'll need a safer place to stay than the waterfront. Come over to my place. I'll fix you up." So we loaded *Squeak* into the back of his pickup and hauled her across town to his hovel.

"You might as well sleep inside with me, eh, Steve?" he crooned, but it was another cement box without windows, full of cockroaches and rodents, like Eulalia's place back in Nuquí.

"No thanks, I'll sleep in the boat," I said, and dragged *Squeak* around back, where there were shade trees, an outdoor faucet for bathing, and a vacant lot for a bathroom. Garbage disposal consisted of a quick chuck in the weeds. I even had for a neighbor an old gray and white cat that reminded me of the original Squeak. What more could I ask for?

My new routine began at dawn with a twenty-minute jog on the dirt road that separated the town's backside from the adjoining swamps. The people were dumping their garbage there as if to build a defensive wall. Skinny dogs harassed me the whole way, all variations on the same mutt theme. I kept my hands full of rocks, and taught them to keep their distance.

The college professor set up the computer on the second floor terrace of an abandoned theater he owned. I went to work. The wind blew my diskettes on the floor and rattled the tin roofing, but at least it was cool. Rats rampaged among the spilt film reels in the trashed-out projector room adjoining my work site. Across the street a parrot and a dog barked all day, the former presumably imitating the latter. I ate in restaurants, paying about $1.80 per meal.

Not much else went on. One day, on the wall at Emilio's house, a gecko ran down a big cockroach then stopped still, hairy legs and antennae protruding from its mouth. The roach suddenly wriggled free, scurried a few feet, and froze. Another long pause. The gecko burst into life and caught him again, and froze. Over and over they repeated the sequence, like electric toys whose switches were malfunctioning. Another day rebellious air force colonels bombed the presidential palace up in Caracas. That gave people something to talk about for awhile. (One of them later became president: Hugo Chavez.) The local men played an indecipherable game somewhere between bowling and shuffleboard: opposing teams taking turns throwing grapefruit-sized cement balls in a dirt enclosure. The faithful attended Mass, mostly women and girls dressed up like it was a fashion contest. Indians with Dutch Boy hairdos and orange loincloths came into town and walked around all day, looking at the window displays and theater posters, never uttering a word.

One day Emilio showed me the original town site, on a point formed by a bend in the river. The rocks on what had been its waterfront had ancient carvings on them, one of concentric circles and radiating arrows, another the torso of a person with fantastically large ears. Little remained of the colonial settlement but a series of pits which went down through ten feet of sand, then at least ten feet of bedrock. Groundwater obscured whatever was below that. Emilio explained. "An old guy who used to live in town spent twenty years digging them holes. What a crazy old fox he was! He was looking for a golden treasure the Spaniards buried around here. Sunk these shafts forty feet deep then connected them up at the bottom with a long tunnel." Emilio became more animated, and probably more imaginative, as he detailed the old man's tribulations. "He found the rudder from a Spanish galleon and was a hair's breadth from the treasure when a big rock fell with a

CRASH and blocked the entrance, almost killing him! Well, even dynamite couldn't blow that boulder loose." As Emilio tapered the story off, the fire in his eyes burned down to a rosy glow. Finally he cocked his head in admiration. "Yessir! What a crazy old coot that Chapo was. Could have been the richest man in Venezuela but instead he died a pauper."

"Sounds like you, Emilio."

His eyes became wistful, his hand squeezed my shoulder. "Destiny, Steve. Be ready for it. You're still young."

Emilio required a lot of humoring. When we worked together, hanging a shower screen or tinkering with his truck's wiring, he treated me like a beloved, five-year-old son. I was supposed to stand by, study his Mickey Mouse techniques, and await instructions. Later on his prostate gland went bad and he lost his spunk. He didn't have much money, so I paid the bill when we ate out together. At night he locked himself up in the house and left all three light bulbs burning. Afraid to sleep alone, he kept trying to talk me into coming inside with him. "Got a hammock here for you, Steve. It's *reeeal* comfy. Go ahead, just lay here and read awhile, see what you think."

Once, while we were busy with something in his "house," an attractive young couple pulled up in a car. Emilio was stunned. "Why it's my daughter, Rosalia, by my second wife! That must be her husband!"

He hurried out to greet them, hoping, I surmised, that the meeting could take place outside.

"But Papa, I want to see where you live!" There was no escape, so he showed them into the cement cubicle. I got up from where I was sitting on the floor. Introductions were made. He had no chairs to offer them. Emilio blushed with shame, and hid it by gushing out, as charmingly as possible, his surprise, his affection for her, his congratulations. The daughter answered his questions, glanced around. I expected a grimace, but she stood on her toes and kissed his forehead.

"Oh, Papa." She smiled. "When are you ever going to settle down?"

Emilio beamed with pride, as if he could hardly believe she was his.

Soon after Emilio drove down to the mining territory to see a doctor about his prostate. On February 24, when my writing was complete, he still hadn't returned, so I signed a copy of the poem I had written for my benefactors in Cali and stuck in his door jamb. Then I paid a stranger a bottle of rum to haul *Squeak* and me to the muddy waterfront. A hundred eyes were on us as we sailed from town.

CHAPTER 20

TO THE MOUTH OF THE SERPENT

Having stayed in Caicara longer than planned, I felt a rush of freedom watching it recede. "Ha ha! you can't follow me!"

The wind was still strong from ahead, but now I kept a five-gallon water bag on the seat deck as ballast, and shifted it along with my own weight to the new windward side at each tack. This reduced the need to reef, and allowed me to sail even in midday. At dusk the wind stopped, and I rowed into the moonless night, navigating by the red- and green-lighted buoys that marked the channel every two or three miles. In Caicara the agency in charge of river navigation had given me a set of thirty-nine detailed charts. These relieved me of the worry of finding a campsite in the dark. They were all there: stippled patterns representing sand exposed at low water. I also used them to find the best way around islands, and to locate villages. Knowing in advance where I could reprovision, I traveled lighter, with less reserve food.

Each day I got underway early. The wind whistled. Slop and spray were heavy. I wore cap, sunglasses, and rain jacket, nothing from the waist down—my scrotum required constant ventilation not to rash. The river averaged a mile wide. Rock piles posed hazards, but the bottom was mostly sand. Random hills of desiccated forest rose to either side. The banks grew to twenty-five feet in height. Fields of cotton and corn edged some of them, and from these field laborers called down to me. I rarely understood them.

Tacking upwind while drifting downstream, my keel was always at an angle to my course over the bottom. I tacked as close to the bank as possible, often scraping a leeboard before pushing the tiller over, shifting weight, and rotating the bill of my cap to shade my face in the new exposure. My tiller hand learned to keep the optimum point of sail by recognizing how the air felt on my skin when the bow was forty-five degrees off the wind. After a year and a half I was still learning how to sail her, becoming more confident.

I set the tiller in just the right notch of the comb-like holder I'd made in Cali, and she continued plowing forward while I clambered about, balancing her with my bare feet. I was even learning more about my Svea stove, which I'd had for sixteen years, like that it started easier with its tank all the way full.

The dolphins were now pink over as much as half their bodies. They cavorted around *Squeak* in tight bundles of two or three. They tacked when *Squeak* tacked. They calmed along with her when her sails fell slack, and perked up again when a new gust sent her flying. Sometimes they lay on the surface breathing and snorting for a few seconds, their bulbous foreheads and dorsal fins prominent, then sank. Other times they breached and dove in a single, powerful motion. They swam underneath and thumped *Squeak's* belly. When I pulled her into a cove for the night, they splashed about languidly just outside, as if waiting for her to come out and play. While mottled pink dolphins followed in the river, hot pink flamingos flew overhead, like flames in the sky. Another species of bird skimmed the surface with long, drooping beaks, always in pairs.

The land was surrealistically beautiful. I replaced a parted leeboard control line on an isle shaped like a collage of boomerangs, nowhere more than six inches high. I camped in a cove at the mouth of the Rio Caura, which rises from the Guyana Highlands, and listened, still, while a man and boy paddled by in a canoe. They were probably returning to their home up the Caura from a day in the nearby town of Mapire. The sky was just then sinking into full darkness. They didn't see me, and I saw them only when I didn't look directly at them—a slightly denser darkness than the star-reflecting river. They talked a bit, in serene tones, of everyday things. Their voices were beautiful as the songs of birds. Living close to nature, they appreciated its beauty. They were happy.

I stopped at Mapire, on a plateau on the left bank, and helped a bent old man carry his fish up to the market. He never looked at me or spoke. I walked the rows of whitewashed houses with sky blue doors and shimmering pavements, all in a neat grid that clashed with the jaggedness of the cliff's edge, where streets fell off into nothingness. There was a park with a statueless pedestal in its crisscrossed center. A road ran out past the cemetery to the rest of the world. I passed a small, decaying house with thick, uneven, mud-and-wattle walls, rounded at the corners and recessed at doors and windows. I imagined myself fixing it up and living there, where nothing ever happens, and where nobody says hello or thank you, because it's too hot.

I averaged thirty-five miles per day, past low islands with names like Tucuragua, Canasto, La Gaviota. I tacked tightly through the "Mouth of Hell," where the river squeezed through a band of knolls. Jagged rocks constricted the channel to a mere hundred meters in width, obliging the river to run fast and scour its bed a full fifty meters deep. It could well be hellish in winter, with the river forty feet higher and ten times the volume!

I sailed through a covey of pale green butterflies jigging in the air. They parted and streamed over me like delicate foliage. I sang to myself, or joked, or daydreamed, anything to relieve the monotony. The word "inexorable" repeated in my mind like a mantra because that's what *Squeak* was, unstoppable. The sun set, and I sailed in a lee calm along a shoreline which, from foreshortening and failing light, appeared smooth and unbroken, but was really a sawtooth of "fjords." I sliced in and penetrated a long, deep fold, grounding at its very tip, hidden and intimate, sails still up and pulling. I lay down, and bubbles squirming up through the algae-covered sand under *Squeak's* hull made me think my stomach was growling, which made me think I was hungry, but I wasn't. I dreamt of Annette, and on waking wrote it down:

> I knew where she slept, in a cocoon in the desert sand, so young and blond and electric, for I'd lain with her there before. But we were friends, not lovers (yet!).
>
> "See you at the Christmas party tonight," she said, but I didn't go.
>
> Instead, I returned to her cocoon late that night. She was alone. I got in with her and wrote this, with this pen, on the clear, thin membrane that separated us, on her body, down her flank, thigh, the ink not quite sticking to the membrane but registering on her flesh, which furrowed and whitened under the ball-point, recording me, not for long, but vividly. I was gentle, but I had a lot to say. She woke from deep sleep and groped me through the membrane, for we were lying alongside, pressing as I wrote.
>
> "Steve," she said, a touch of warmth, of reproach.
>
> "Couldn't make out which of all those beautiful male bodies it was?"
>
> "Why didn't you come to the party?"
>
> "I didn't want to compete with the others. If I found you alone, fine, if not, fine." I smiled, and the puff of exhalation through nose and mouth that serves as my laughter puffed into her hair. "I was lucky."
>
> "Yes, you were."

On March 3 gusts forced me to reef early in the day. All morning I rode *Squeak* as I had once ridden a bad horse—popping at the pelvis to absorb the shocks. I steered into the wind in order to take the steepest waves head-on. A high suspension bridge appeared in the distance: Puente Angostura, the only bridge on the entire Orinoco River. I stopped on a bar of bronze quartz sand to bathe, for Ciudad Bolívar was now visible just beyond the bridge: a city on a hill in a bend of the river, with ramparts and white towers.

I reached the S-shaped *angostura*, or narrows. The wind clashed with the strong current, creating waves of fearful height. They stood in rows reaching from bank to bank. *Squeak* banged over them like knuckles scraping over a washboard. She thrashed too much to go forward through the water, but I was able to maintain proper channel position while the current carried us through. Again, *Squeak's* capability amazed me.

As the sun set behind me I tacked under the tall, white bridge and looked for a landing. The city lay before me on the right bank, where the river bends left then right around the rocky hill that the Spaniards had chosen for their town site. But the steepness of the hill was accentuated by the stone facings of an ancient fortification. Access to the city would only be possible further downstream, where the bank dropped low.

Then I noticed a sky-high wall of white haze about a mile ahead. It was advancing on me with unearthly warp speed, eating the world, blotting out land and sky! I immediately tightened the mizzensheet and released the main (those cleats being on the tiller), then leaped forward and jerked the main halyard from its clamcleat at the base of the mast. The squall exploded on me before I could set the topping lift. The unsupported boom and sail tripped in the water as *Squeak* careened and drove backward. I clung to the cabin top, struggling for balance. *Squeak* and I were like a tumbleweed blowing across the water. The noise was deafening. The mainsail, now trailing in the water, could only be hauled in by unshipping the boom, which I did, losing my mainsheet in the process. I let fly the mizzen sheet, and the greater windage of the bare mainmast threw her bow downwind. She was flying at hull speed. The waves grew within a minute or two to about ten feet. I felt the beginning of a surfing motion on their steep faces. Eventually I would either capsize or crash into a bank. The shore was rocky except for a sand spit extending from a small island downwind and to my left. I sat facing forward and readied the oars—they felt fragile and impotent in that environment. I was able to alter *Squeak's* course only a few degrees from the flow of the wind, with little control, but it was enough to slip into the lee of the spit and beach on the island.

Now that I was safe the fury of the storm was beautiful. The sky was breaking up into tracts of white, gray, and cobalt that jostled like crushing icebergs in a river, and blackened as the last sunglow drained from the sky. The city lights blazed warmly a quarter mile away. The whining wind carried wafts of music and laughter.

In the morning I rowed past the rampart, past the dirt landing where fishermen displayed their nightly catch among a tumult of buyers and street urchins, to a marina with a gas dock. It felt good to be among people. I had breakfast in a riverside public market, and walked toward the center of town along the rampart, fifty feet above the river. The city boasted ornamental streetlights and handsome shade trees. In Cali or Bogotá a policeman was lucky to ride a dirt bike; here they drove brand-new Jeeps. Blocks of two-story shops in antiquated styles looked out over promenade and river.

The hill on which the town stood consisted of gnarled red rock. One early builder had found this rock too hard to cut away, so he left random knobs projecting from his plaza floor and foundation walls.

"Interesting, isn't it?" I said to a tall, blond man puzzling over the same sight.

"Yes, very. Are you also traveling?"

He was a soft-spoken German named Richard. Both being avid walkers, we finished our tour of the waterfront together and continued through the winding residential streets leading to the Spanish colonial administrative buildings on top of the hill. It was carnival time, and kids were in the streets throwing water and squirting hoses at each other. We got our share of good-natured dousings. One youngster ran up and smeared lampblack on Richard's bare arms. He laughed wholeheartedly, and wore the soot like a badge of honor the rest of the day.

Richard and I spent the next three days walking together. He was one of many travelers, mostly young Germans, passing through Ciudad Bolívar on their way to *La Gran Sabana*, a high savanna from which rise the inaccessible mesas called *tepuys*. Most traveled as ironclad couples or in groups of four or five, but Richard always traveled alone, hence our affinity. I missed him when he left.

It was impractical to work on *Squeak* at the dock, so the people at the nearby *Club Nautico Orinoco* situated me in their boatyard under the life-saving shade of a big tree. There I worked on rigging, recoated worn parts of the hull with epoxy, and rebuilt the skeg, which had rotted at the lower rudder attachment.

Ciudad Bolívar treated me like royalty. Club members bought me dinners and drinks. Television and radio crews interviewed me. An anchor was found to replace the one I lost on the Meta. The club president said I was fulfilling his dream, which he would now live through me, and launched into an orgy of generous offers of support, which became increasingly fantastic as he saw I was disinclined to accept any of them. On the other end of the social scale, the night watchman, a gaunt man with haunted eyes, hung around me like a lost puppy, begging me to tell him he was a good person despite being a *basuco* addict. But my least expected accolade came from a U.S. Marine Corps major I bumped into on the dock one day. He was the perfect warrior: tall, strong, quick. He fired a few pointed questions at me, then ducked back into his chartered fishing boat. He returned an instant later and stuffed fifty dollars into my hand. "The Venezuelans say good things about you," he said, and marched off. I learned later that he was attached to the U.S. embassy.

My work was nearly finished when, on March 14, I met a German named Sigi. He was traveling from Alaska to Tierra del Fuego in a specially equipped Nissan Patrol, and invited me to come along on a side trip to *La Gran Sabana.* I was dissatisfied with my progress, but I accepted in order to see the country beyond the river corridor.

We drove east through dry, undulating land to the awesome cataract where the Rio Caroní smashes down through a complex of ledges three miles above its confluence with the Orinoco. We passed through Ciudad Guyana, a new city of superblocks and long, sterile parkways, then drove south for two days through progressively higher, lusher land. At the town of El Dorado we entered the gold fields. Barge-mounted dredges worked the river beds. People of lower means panned along the banks. The town itself consisted of little more than a roomy main intersection where one could sit at a table and take in the activity of the food stalls, second-floor hotels, and the assay and gold-buying shops.

Next we climbed a long incline onto *La Gran Sabana*, a vast, irregular plain of tall grasses and palm groves. As we continued south *tepuys* appeared to the southeast, particularly Mount Roraima, which inspired Sir Arthur Conan Doyle's *The Lost World.* From the highway I could only imagine what it was like on top, three thousand feet higher. Cliffs ringed it. Rain clouds draped its flat top. Waterfalls of fantastic height fell off these *tepuys*, and over abrupt discontinuities in the floor of the savanna.

Sigi was docile, somber, Nordicly deadpan. He had traveled ruggedly in his youth, then worked two jobs at once for fifteen years saving money for this trip. Yet he didn't seem to be enjoying himself. He clung to the comfort of his vehicle and didn't want to hike or leave the paved road. He performed long morning rituals with coffee, cigarettes, and news from the Voice of Germany. He was quick to criticize the Venezuelans for their laziness, their rudeness, their slowness to make him a cup of coffee. He pinched his pennies even worse than I did. He got occasional snatches of joy, then quickly fell back into some private misery.

We drove all the way to the Brazilian border, and even crossed over, stopping just short of a checkpoint. Brazil looked no different from Venezuela, of course—grassland, broadleaf groves, sharp hillocks. We were at the end of the line, with nothing left to do but head back the way we had come.

I was bored of being a passenger. It was nice to sip a cool drink and take a nap whenever I wanted, but the inactivity blunted me. As we drove back to Ciudad Bolívar I dreaded our farewell. We got along fine, but our spititual weaknesses were too similar. I knew I wouldn't know what to say. In the event, Sigi handled it well. When I got out of the car with my pack he walked around, took my hand, looked me straight in the face, and smiled. His blue eyes were suddenly steady, as if he had steeled himself for this moment. They flared unknowably. I interpret his gesture as an access of courage.

"Good luck with your voyage, Steve."

"Good luck with yours. Thanks!" He drove away, and emotion flooded over me: relief at being free of his sadness, and angst at resuming my own lonesome road.

But travel that is true to the heart is a salve that always heals, sometimes the same wound over and over. So it was that a few days later, on March 25, I cast off from the *Club Nautico Orinoco.* Any cloudiness of spirit was soon dispelled in the heat of the sun and the cool river spray.

My first stop was at the farm of two unmarried brothers, Abismael and Rafael. During my stay in Ciudad Bolívar these calm, clean-limbed young men had come into town every morning with a canoe full of watermelons. Always they insisted I eat one with them as they waited for the pickup truck to come and buy their crop. Now I found their riverside field by the description they had given me, and joined their small band.

With them were several hired hands, too shy to speak. I worked with them for an hour, ferreting out tomatoes ripe enough to take to town the next day. At dusk we dove in the river, then retired to the bamboo-and-thatch hut where they hung their hammocks. "In a few months this entire area will be under twelve feet of water," said Abismael, the elder. "We can never build a real building, but each spring the waters subside to reveal six inches of fertile new mud. The mud cracks as it dries, and cries out for seed."

We boiled soup and fried dough over an open fire, and ate standing. Their campfire method was new to me: they dug three furrows in the ground radiating from a common center, like a Y, and placed a log in each furrow. They then kindled a fire at the intersection and nudged the logs toward the center as they burned away. All the while Abismael and Rafael pelted me with questions about America.

"How much do you earn in a day?"

"Does it snow where you live? Oh, how I would like to see that."

I explained my gear and strategies to them. They were uneducated but intelligent, curious. Without complaining of their lot they demonstrated a deep craving for broader horizons.

Abismael left for town before dawn. When Rafael saw me preparing to leave he was distraught. "But we thought you would stay longer! Please don't go yet. At least wait until my brother comes back."

"I'm sorry, Rafael. Another time, yes, but I've been so long in Ciudad Bolívar. I feel I must go."

He frowned. "Wait then."

He rushed to his field. He and a worker came back loaded with watermelons and tomatoes.

"Rafael, I can't stow all that!" I protested. "Okay, three watermelons and one sack of tomatoes, no more!"

"They are at varying stages of ripeness," he noted, "so they will feed you for several days. God be with you."

"And with you."

Their generosity humbled me, but when had I not had much to be thankful for? People cared for me. The adverse wind never changed direction, but now it sometimes slowed or even stopped. It still didn't rain, but the sky was often cloudy. The days were still hot, but at night I often had to crawl into my sleeping bag. The river was still low, but rising. Winter was coming. The river would swell, and already it was so big that, where it ran straight, no land was visible on the horizon.

Traffic was no greater than back on the upper Meta. I lunched on a paisley-shaped islet and walked its perimeter, sketching in my notebook the pattern formed by dry sand (tan), wet sand (brown), submerged sand (blue-brown), and deep water. I found a blue-eyed frog stowed away in my bailer bucket, and waited until close ashore to shake him into the water, but he latched onto my oar and climbed back aboard. I tried to brush him off; he jumped onto my forearm. "If you're that attached to me, then by all means, make yourself at home," I said. He kept me company for several days. In contrast, I never did warm up to a colony of poor little black ants that had ridden with me all the way from Caicara. These I hunted down to the last man, mopping them up with my towel and rinsing them off in the river.

I continued past Ciudad Guyana's massive steel mills, and past the mouth of the Rio Caroní, whose black waters mixed but reluctantly with the green of the Orinoco. Ocean freighters plied the combined river, which was three miles wide. Each tack was a half-hour battle against waves and heavy spray. The sun burnt sores in my nose and lip, so I wrapped my face with cotton cloth, and sailed fully swathed to the Guyana Castles, gateway to the delta. They were stone fortifications, one on a lower hill, the other on a taller hill behind, each armed with a handful of ancient cannons. The Spanish had built them in the seventeenth century to repel the English, Dutch, and French invaders who pillaged their settlements, challenged their claim to the Orinoco basin, and searched for the legendary El Dorado (not to be confused with the trifling town I had recently visited). Even Sir Walter Raleigh succumbed to this myth's allure, forcing his way through in 1595. Such expeditions generally led to death and despair in the wilds between the Orinoco and Amazon rivers, for though the gold was real, there was no city built of it.

The river now broke up into islands and distributaries. Thick vegetation grew right down to the water. Coconut palms and pelicans hinted of the sea. That night, as I slept grounded in a slough opening, the water slowly drained away and came back again. It was the tidal effect of the Atlantic Ocean.

At noon, March 29, I landed at the town of Barrancas, the last place to buy provisions before Trinidad. The waterfront was foul with mud and wreckage. Fishermen unloaded their catch while Guyanese smugglers loaded their larger, decked craft with Venezuelan goods for resale on the black market in Georgetown. As I considered how to tie up, a fully laden freighter came down the narrow channel. "We must pull your boat up higher!" urged the boys clustered around me. We did so just as it drew abreast, seventy-five yards offshore. The water along the landing suddenly drained away as the river level dropped eight feet and boats flew wildly around on their anchors. The ship's stern passed, and just as suddenly the river rose in a torrent of waves and debris. *Squeak* was buffeted, but my little friends helped me hang on to her. Then we carried her a little higher, turned her perpendicular to the fall line, and put a rock under the downhill skidder to level her. My ankle bled where a piece of jagged steel, swirling in the maelstrom, had grazed me.

Typical of the Guyanese boats was a wooden cargo-carrier powered by three Suzuki outboards. Its owner introduced himself, a heavyset, bearded man named Ramon. "I've come from the Rio Amacuro to sell a crop of plantains and ginger. I know the town well. If you like, I'll show you the best places to provision." He spoke English slowly and clearly, with a Caribbean accent. Pleased to have such polite company, I followed him up over broken concrete to street level, where idlers surveyed the river and vendors sold ice cream and mangos. Ramon took me to dry goods shops kept by fellow Guyanese. Some of his compatriots were black, some white, some brown. All were hospitable, and spoke charming English: *chap* for a male person and *le's we go!* for *let's go!* We ended the day at a Guyanese restaurant. After our afternoon meal the proprietor invited us into the back room, where we sat on a couch and watched a Rodney Dangerfield movie with his family. To combat the heavy heat, Ramon and I drained five cold beers apiece.

In the morning I requested clearance to leave the country, and ended up having to go to Tucupita, an hour's ride by bus. It was a larger city, similarly flat and steamy, on another of the river's twenty-odd major distributaries. The open, cement-lined culverts bordering its streets were full of trash and algae. Empty Washington State apple boxes lay discarded under a bridge. The air smelled of garbage, stagnant water, and fresh fruit. After a day of running between the offices of Immigration, Harbormaster, Customs, and National Guard, I had all the paperwork I needed, and probably more, to exit Venezuela by way of the Boca Macareo and cross over to Trinidad. My route would take me through 150 miles of remote, swampy delta.

Outside Barrancas I left the main channel of the river, turning left then right as the river progressively splintered. The width was now a thousand yards. The current became stronger. It lessened with the rising tide but never stopped or changed direction. My course now trending north-northeast, I faced directly into the wind less often, reducing the need to tack. The banks became lower. Tidal fall became more pronounced. There was less agriculture, more forest, and the familiar sound of howling monkeys. On the upper Meta it had reminded me of lions. Now it reminded me of a car on a distant highway: that dreamy sound caused more by airstream and tires on pavement than by the motor.

There was no longer any shelving sand to sleep on, so I entered a slough fringed with drowned trees and swamp grass. Herons squawked and flew away like pterodactyls. I rowed as far in as I could get, lifting and folding my oars to clear the stumps and tilting *Squeak* to clear her masts of the overhanging branches. Following Ramon's advice, I prepared dinner, got in the cabin, and put up the screen early. At exactly sunset mosquitoes blanketed my net, causing a buzz that permeated the cabin. I had left my water bottle outside—no way to get it now. Mayflies performed a bizarre mating dance on the screen eighteen inches above my face, until ants cut them up and hauled away the pieces. A green grasshopper methodically devoured an overhanging blade of grass. As it got dark, creatures started clattering and squirming around *Squeak's* hull. A bat collided with the topping lift, thrumming it like a bass guitar. Tiny birds sang in the reeds.

At midnight the mosquitoes seemed to be asleep, so I popped out with a flashlight. All up and down the slough were glowing red eyes, the nearest some fifteen feet away on a patch of exposed mud. They were small, harmless caimans such as I had been seeing since Puerto Gaitán, though never this close.

Back on the river, parasitic succulents festooned the bigger trees. The banks were wild bouquets. I maneuvered against a wall of vegetation to capture a cluster of orange, orchid-like flowers. While I held myself in place a small snake wound through the slender, brown vines, which he imitated in shape and color, except that his head was sharply triangular and a red tongue flashed through the aperture in his closed mouth. He was hunting something small, not me.

Another time I stopped at a path. It led to a small patch that had been cultivated but was now growing over with a twenty-foot-tall grass which the natives sometimes used as poles for setting nets in the river. Another path faded away in a dense thicket of wild banana trees. Biological diversity was apparent in the number of winged bloodsuckers too. In addition to the usual mosquito, I now was plagued with no-see-ums, a big gray fly, a fly with iridescent green eyes, and a black fly whose wings were black for two-thirds their length, then clear. As each learned better ways to bite me through my armor of clothing and repellent, I learned better techniques for creaming them with my fly swatter.

My river charts didn't cover the delta, so I was back to using a road map. It was accurate with respect to channels, but not villages; it showed three on my route, none of which I ever saw, and it did not show the one village I came to. The channel had been dredged in the fifties, and this village was built on top of the spoils to avoid flooding. It had a school, water pump, electric plant, and a field of ripe honeydew melons. I bought three.

Beyond this I saw only Indians. I approached a homestead of four or five pole-frame structures with roofs of thatched leaves. A dozen of them watched me, from babes-in-arms to ancients. They murmured with excitement as I sailed right up and plowed into the bank at their feet. They were handsome people, short and square, with sharp cheekbones and broad foreheads. They had curly black hair, which the women wore long and loose. The men's attire was not distinctive, but the women and girls wore full print dresses and necklaces, bracelets, and anklets made of plastic beads. The Indians frowned with perplexity, and smiled spontaneously, never from politeness. Some of the men knew Spanish, but among themselves they spoke a native tongue which was identified to me as *Guarau.* They had no foodstuffs to sell, not even yucca or banana, probably because they were hunters and gatherers, not farmers.

I rounded another bend, and a dugout intercepted me. Kneeling in the bow, reaching out over the water, was a girl of five or six. In her hands she cupped a small, green parrot. Her blue and red dress was immaculate. Her hair was smoothly parted. She smiled sweetly but stiffly, as if taking part in a religious enactment. Behind her, a standing man in white shorts propelled the canoe with a long, dagger-like paddle. His strokes were solemn, measured. He lifted his paddle—I released my sheets. Our boats coasted together. No one spoke. When we were a few yards apart I shook my head in polite refusal, then gathered my sheets back in. For a long time they watched me recede, then they turned around and headed back toward the wild glade that probably hid their home.

They had hoped I would buy the parrot. That the Indians earned money by capturing animals was substantiated at another hamlet, where pitiful little monkeys were held captive. They pursed their lips and squealed with fright when I approached. "Men come from Trinidad to buy," the Indians said.

The channel divided and rejoined. Its shorelines were smooth, green walls. The current now reversed with rising tide, but the ebb was stronger and lasted longer. Rafts of water hyacinth with swollen leaf stalks and lavender flowers flowed one way, then the other. My final night in the delta, I pulled into a slough so small I could penetrate only about ten feet. I tied bow and stern to plants like giant asparagus that grew up out of the water on either side.

I woke later to the sensation of *Squeak* tipping. The water level had dropped a meter, bringing *Squeak* to rest on the trunks of fallen "giant asparagus trees" that spanned the slough at odd slopes. They had been submerged at high tide, but now *Squeak* was precariously perched. I was afraid to move, so I simply went back to sleep and hoped *Squeak* wouldn't fall into the water before it rose again.

At first light the sound of voices speaking *Guarau* woke me. It was a man and woman in a dugout barely wider than their hips. The woman was directing, something that would never happen among Hispanics. I realized they wanted to get by. *Squeak* was afloat again, so I moved to one side.

"What are you looking for?" I asked in Spanish as they squeezed past.

"Parrot," said the man. I longed to go with them and explore that watery path, because the jungle is impassable on foot, but I was afraid to leave *Squeak* unattended.

All that day the channel angled increasingly north, then west of north, bringing the wind behind me. The passage slowly widened. At 3:15 a distant gap opened between the left and right banks. Water on the horizon: the ocean! The gap widened until I was sailing out onto a large bay rimmed with mangrove. No land was visible, only a wall of shiny leaves, supported by a dense, unfathomable matrix of stalks and branches rising up out of the water. There would be no going ashore. A handful of crude dwellings sat on poles in the bay near the mangrove's edge.

I continued northwest, with mangrove on my right, and anchored just short of the last house. Beyond that was Punta Pescador, from whence I would cross to Trinidad.

I was as relieved and excited as at any of the previous milestones, but I was also scared. My experience on the Pacific was grueling, but at least there the sea was never very rough nor the wind very strong. Now I would contend with the boisterous northeast trade winds. A crossing of the Mouth of the Serpent—southern entrance to the Gulf of Paria—would serve as my initiation. I'd been hearing horror stories about how rough it gets since Ciudad Bolívar.

I felt exposed and precarious, with only a six-millimeter nylon line fixing me to the face of the earth. The currents were strong and erratic, and there was risk of being run down by one of the fishing vessels working the bay. The absence of solid land made me uneasy. The sea pulsed ominously even here, in this sheltered extremity of the Atlantic.

I wasn't calm, but the sky was. After four days in the close jungle it loomed very large. The sun set. Clouds blocked all but a few stars. *Squeak* bobbed underneath me. I remembered what it was like to sleep on the sea.

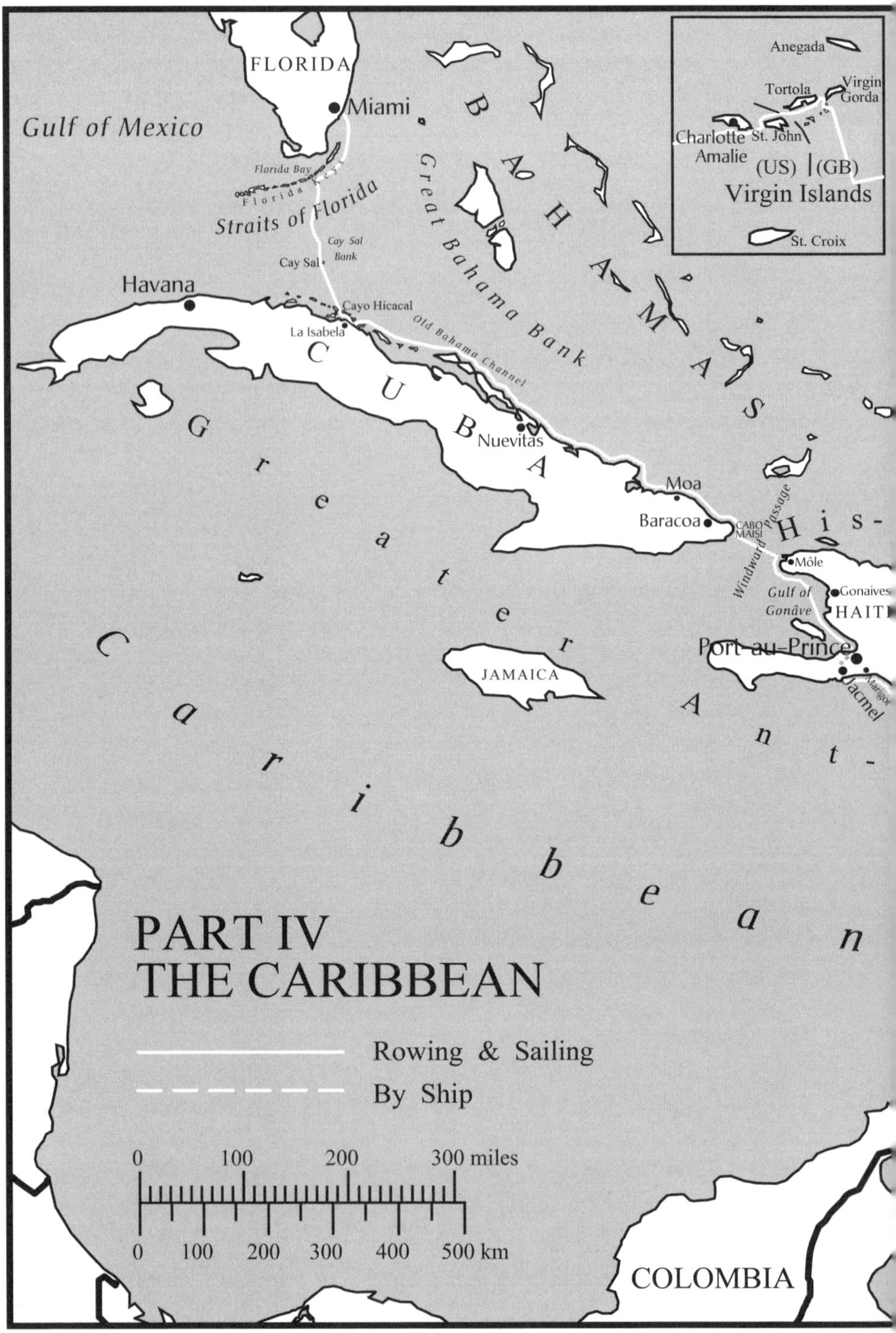
PART IV
THE CARIBBEAN
Rowing & Sailing
By Ship
0 100 200 300 miles
0 100 200 300 400 500 km
FLORIDA
Miami
Gulf of Mexico
Florida Bay
Florida Keys
Straits of Florida
Cay Sal Bank
Cay Sal
Great Bahama Bank
BAHAMAS
Havana
Cayo Hicacal
La Isabela
Old Bahama Channel
CUBA
Nuevitas
Moa
Baracoa
CABO MAISÍ
Windward Passage
His-
Môle
Gulf of Gonâve
Gonaives
HAITI
Port-au-Prince
Jacmel
Marigot
JAMAICA
Greater Ant-
Caribbean
COLOMBIA
Anegada
Tortola
Virgin Gorda
Charlotte Amalie
St. John
(US)
(GB)
Virgin Islands
St. Croix

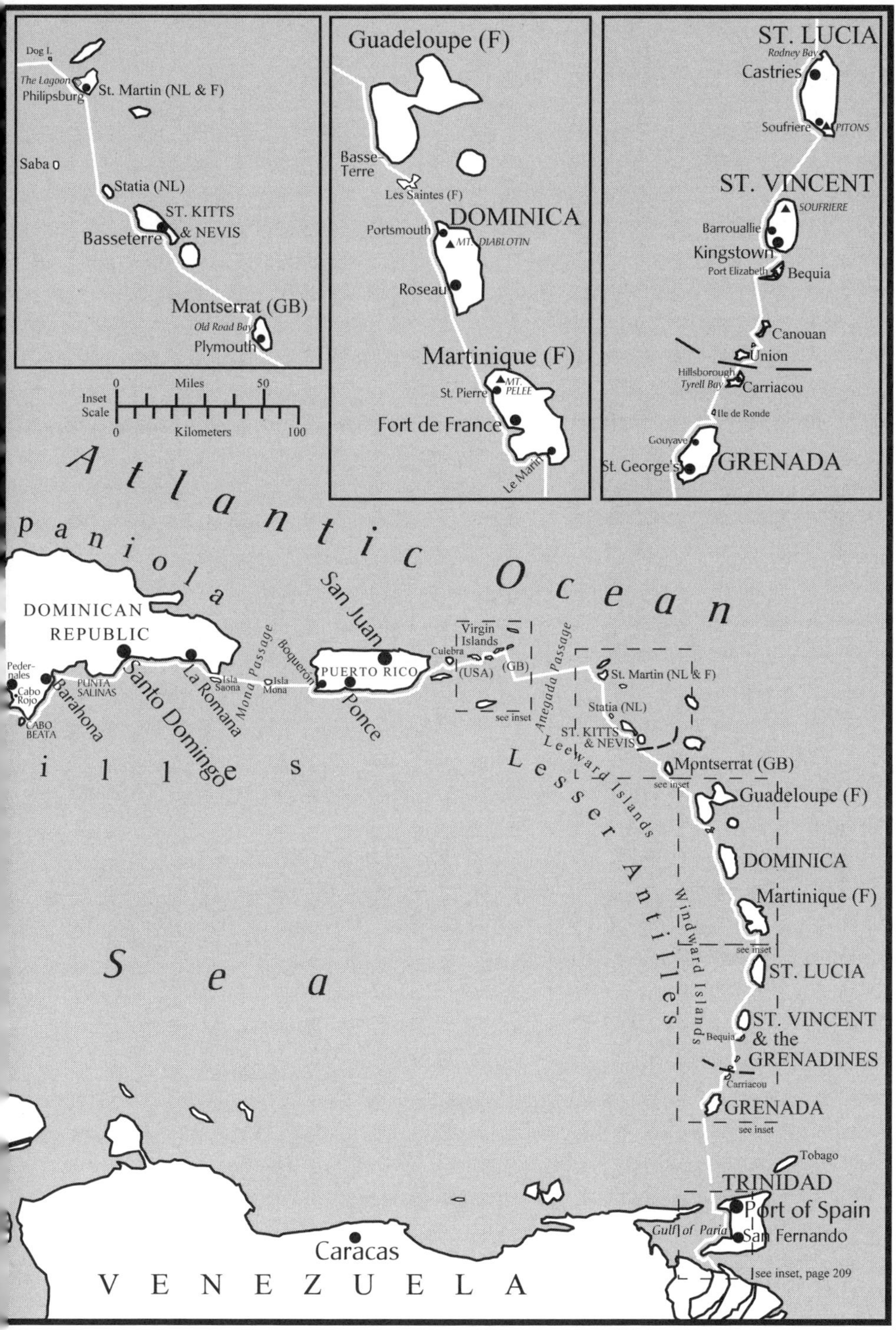

Dog I.
The Lagoon
Philipsburg
St. Martin (NL & F)
Saba
Statia (NL)
ST. KITTS & NEVIS
Basseterre
Montserrat (GB)
Old Road Bay
Plymouth
Guadeloupe (F)
Basse-Terre
Les Saintes (F)
DOMINICA
Portsmouth
MT. DIABLOTIN
Roseau
Martinique (F)
St. Pierre
MT. PELEE
Fort de France
Le Marin
ST. LUCIA
Rodney Bay
Castries
Soufriere
PITONS
ST. VINCENT
SOUFRIERE
Barrouallie
Kingstown
Port Elizabeth
Bequia
Canouan
Union
Hillsborough
Tyrell Bay
Carriacou
Ile de Ronde
Gouyave
St. George's
GRENADA
Inset Scale
0 Miles 50
0 Kilometers 100
Atlantic Ocean
Hispaniola
DOMINICAN REPUBLIC
Pedernales
Cabo Rojo
CABO BEATA
Barahona
PUNTA SALINAS
Santo Domingo
La Romana
Isla Saona
Mona Passage
Isla Mona
Boquerón
San Juan
PUERTO RICO
Ponce
Culebra
Virgin Islands
(USA)
(GB)
see inset
Anegada Passage
St. Martin (NL & F)
Statia (NL)
ST. KITTS & NEVIS
Montserrat (GB)
see inset
Leeward Islands
Lesser Antilles
Guadeloupe (F)
DOMINICA
Martinique (F)
see inset
ST. LUCIA
ST. VINCENT & the GRENADINES
Bequia
Carriacou
GRENADA
see inset
Windward Islands
Antilles
Caribbean Sea
Tobago
TRINIDAD
Port of Spain
Gulf of Paria
San Fernando
see inset, page 209
Caracas
VENEZUELA

CHAPTER 21

TRINIDAD

April 5, 1992, dawned bright and wide. The delta edge curved in a vast, flat arc. North, the hills of Trinidad shimmered in pale blues. There was no reason to wait, no further preparation possible.

I pulled in the anchor line, straining against the tidal race which stretched it stiff as a rod, and rose sail to a following breeze. *Squeak* bubbled through the water like a lass with lifted skirts. Passing the last house, my *buenos dias* brought no response from an Indian woman with tousled hair in a worn, indigo dress. She squatted alone on a bamboo platform over the water, preparing food. Her hands stopped as I passed. She was an aboriginal beauty, fearful of strangers. The coldness in her eyes burned like a question mark as she receded from my field of vision. She was my last contact with South America.

I passed islets of mounded vegetation dotted with white birds, then Punta Pescador itself, a wilderness of storm-scarred mangrove. Now *Squeak* nosed into the white-capped furrows of the Mouth of the Serpent, the pass separating Venezuela from Trinidad, and the Gulf of Paria from the Atlantic. I steered 330° magnetic, compensating for twelve degrees west variation, and hoped my timing was right with respect to currents. Wind from the southeast—good. I was anxious to reach the far shore, twelve miles away.

The wind freshened, motion became sharp. A fleet of seiners complicated navigation. I heaved to and shortened sail. When I returned to the tiller, *Squeak* failed to respond. I looked astern and saw the rudder blade fluttering in the wake, connected only by its tip-up and tip-down control lines. While *Squeak* was hove to and drifting backwards the blade had cocked hard and severed where it exits its fork. What a time to break!

I cut the blade free and steered her through the seiners with the port oar. The stress on the oar and oarlock was too high to carry on like that, so I roughly balanced her to my course by dropping the port leeboard, luffing the mizzen, and over-sheeting the main. Now she could be steered with very little rudder force. This minimal steerage I supplied by tilting the tiller up out of the way and sitting on the stern deck, thus shifting my weight aft and submerging the rudder fork's parallel, 7" x 8" plywood plates. *Squeak* responded to her tiller again, enough to keep her heading more or less the right direction. It was difficult to steer with the tiller running up my spine, behind me, so I tied a loop into the center of a line, placed the loop over the tiller, and steered by pulling the ends.

The wind blew at about twenty knots. The six-foot waves rolled along at half that speed. They overtook *Squeak,* tipping her bow-down, then stern-down, then marching on ahead. I lowered the main and sailed under mizzen alone, sitting high on my perch, feet braced on opposite sides of the cockpit. South America melted away behind me. The tidal current was in my favor, or the sea would have been rougher. I forgot my fears and enjoyed the sail.

Trinidad's south coast loomed rapidly: a narrow beach backed by coconut forests and low hills. So far so good. Now I steered west, parallel to the shore. At noon I rounded Punta de Arenal. The water inside the Gulf of Paria was calm.

At a beach just around the corner, a half dozen blacks and East Indians bathed lazily in the sea. They faced seaward, half floating, half standing, knees bent, heads and shoulders above water. Each held a yellow-labeled beer bottle. On seeing me they widened their eyes and smiled.

I addressed them in English. "Hi! My rudder's broken. I know it's not a port of entry, but do you think I can fix it here?"

They looked at each other. "Sure, go ahead!" One scampered to a paper sack on the beach. "Welcome to Trinidad," he said, handing me a beer with a bright yellow "Carib" label. Their manners and speech were similar to the Guyanese I had met in Barrancas.

I had landed at the main house of a coconut plantation. A caretaker showed me to a barn where I found a suitable scrap of wood. Sitting under a big tree I shaped it into a temporary rudder blade. The shade and absence of stinging insects were so delicious I stayed until the stars came out, and slept by the gently surging sea.

The next day I coasted up the panhandle of Trinidad. The water was blue-green, the land sandy and flat. Antique stonework drained what had once been marsh. The village of Bonasse displayed homes, vehicles, and infrastructure of high standard. I stopped to clear customs, and a troop of Coast Guardsmen came and searched *Squeak* under the supervision of a prim and proper commander.

"I see you've been to Colombia," he noted, eyebrows arched. He was thumbing through the entry and exit stamps in my passport. His men poked through my intricately packed gear like well-behaved schoolchildren dismantling their first Rubiks Cube.

A half hour later, eyebrows relaxed, the commander asked, "Can we get you anything?"

"Well, some fruit would be nice."

"Some oranges," he said to an underling. The man ran off. "While we wait, would you like some tea?"

"Sure," I said, and passed an hour with them in their new facility on a green hillside overlooking the bay. It was pastel, beautifully designed, well-fitted to its site. After fourteen months in Latin America, Trinidad was a pleasant culture shock.

Leaving my hosts I tacked all afternoon, through oil platforms and pipeline piers, to a cove near the town of Brighton. Laughter and calypso music floated out from a neatly manicured park at its head. I dropped sail and gently rowed among families, lovers, teenagers, black and East Indian. It was a Hindu holiday, made a national holiday by the government. All lolled and larked in the calm, clear, waist-deep water. They were too content to be much excited by the stranger among them, close yet untouchable, like a horseman amid foot soldiers. At dark I anchored three hundred yards out in five feet of water. Then I swam a little, and lay naked in bed, hatch open. The reverberating music soothed me into a sleep full of African horns and sparkling steel drums.

In the morning, machete-wielding laborers on shore pointed out the decrepit Brighton pier. It was supposed to be a port of entry. A hand-painted, black-on-white sign announced "Customs and Excise," but the fellow inside the shack was lounging in his shorts. "Ships don't stop here anymore," he said. "Do' have no stamps or forms. I's here jes in case."

"Of what?" I wondered, as I cut across San Fernando Anchorage in burning sun and light winds. I placed the tiller in one of the comb's notches and napped. In such conditions it was pleasant to be far from land. From my watch and triangulated fixes I calculated speed: 3.3 knots, 3.4 knots, 4.7 knots. Upon reaching the oil refinery complex around Pointe-a-Pierre I veered north and cruised along a shore too shallow to get close. The mountain range that runs across the north end of the island slowly stood out, a shade darker than the blue sky.

The coastline became swampy as I approached Port of Spain, the capital. I passed the mouth of a small river and dragged rudder through a shoal of watery muck that smelled of ammonia. I entered the harbor of a small city with a working waterfront, modern buildings sprouting from a compact downtown, and poor neighborhoods spreading over foothills. Listing wrecks cluttered the shallow roadstead. A hodgepodge of wharves teemed with small freighters of steel or brightly painted wood, some with gaff-headed sailing rigs.

It was dusk. The crew of the *Sabita*, a sixty-foot Guyanese cargo boat, suggested I tie alongside for the night. I did, and shared their homely meal of spicy chicken necks and unleavened bread. As I sat with the engineer and cook in the pilothouse a cockroach kept walking onto my plate as if wanting to be eaten. Better to tolerate him than bash him with my spoon. "We bring plantains and pineapples from Guyana and go back with milk and mattress material," they said. I felt proud to be counted a seaman among such good, simple men. Merry blacks roamed the docks, some bearded, some with voluminous dreadlocks tucked into knitted wool caps.

"Mo'nin, mo'nin, mo'nin, ma boys, sun shinin' bright!" beamed the cook of the *Sabita* at first light. His reveille roused me too. I cleared customs, bade farewell, and sailed to the Trinidad & Tobago Yacht Club, five miles west of town.

As I rounded the TTYC jetty, a lank Brit with thick blond hair and beard watched me from aboard a ketch-rigged fishing boat made into a home. "Raft up next to me if you want," he said. Tony worked on yachts, earning just enough to support his wife and their two towheads. He was a shipwright in the old tradition, a taciturn man with clipped humor.

Tony and Penny didn't mix much with the other people at the yacht club: retired American live-aboards, swinging young nomads of various nationalities, and wealthy, mostly white, Trinidadian sportfishermen. The latter group controlled the club. They must have admired my spunk, because the manager told me, "Mr. Ladd, the subject of your arrival came up at our board meeting last night, and it was agreed we can't possibly charge you moorage." I picked my spot: a *Squeak*-sized concrete slab high and dry on the jetty walkway. Showers, library, and bar were at my disposal. Across the coastwise highway, at the foot of green mountains, were a modern supermarket and fast-food restaurant. Ouch—the prices were high! I borrowed a laptop computer from a fellow yachtsman and caught up on my writing in the air-conditioned conference room. The staid American retirees invited me over for drinks and mused over my eccentricity.

To get downtown I took a "maxi-taxi"—a brand-new, fourteen-seat van. Stylish adornments hung from its ceiling, and rap blared from a high-tech sound system. Outside, a gingerbready Victorianism enlivened the otherwise bland architecture. White paint peeled from wood in ragged flakes. Moralistic slogans emblazoned the walls: "Respect our women!" "Educate the children!" "Love your country and culture!" In the office district an East Indian woman in lipstick and high heels clicked by with studied grace. At

Independence Square a vendor hacked a hole in a coconut so I could drink the juice inside.

A young black intercepted me. "Hello friend! American? German? Whatcha looking for?" He grabbed my hand and shook it, falling into step beside me. "I always like to help out foreigners. Where you going?"

"To get something to eat, but I don't need any help."

"I'll show you a good place. Dis way," he said, pointing.

When we arrived at a Chinese restaurant I said, "Thanks. Now if you don't mind, I prefer to eat alone."

Despite my protests he came in and sat down with me. "Geez, I real embarrass to say this, but my car's outta gas on the other side of town. Can you loan me a few dollars?"

"No."

"You do' understand..."

"No!"

He got up, spoke with the waitress, and joined me at my table a minute later. "I ordered sometin' for myself. I'll pay for it."

"Fine with me."

The waitress came over, looking skeptical. "He say you going to pay for him too. Are you?"

I glared at my companion.

"Mmmrr," he growled, and stalked out the door.

As in Panama, the yacht club was an island of collegial hospitality. A tiny, dark-skinned woman working at the bar asked me out to a dance. There she proceeded to rub her bottom against my loins, back arched, hands over her head, elbows out. "This is how we dance the calypso," she said. I danced as did the other men, attentively behind her. She claimed to be of mixed Saudi and Moroccan origin, but she looked more like a starving Ethiopian. She had been stranded there long before by a departing yacht and knew everyone. She showed me around town, flitting like a sparrow among the street characters she'd met during the recent carnival.

We lunched at a consortium of kitchens sharing a common hall. The dishes were foreign to me: callaloo, dasheen, roti. We were joined by Daniel, a devilishly handsome French art director for cinema in his fifties. He lived aboard an ancient Dutch East Indiaman that looked more like a museum than a yacht. Daniel raved about Trinidad—the David Rudder concert, the new play at Stollmeyer Castle, the pretty girl he'd met at Maracas Beach that day. "Ah, she was so sex*y*," he said, accent on the second syllable. His life was a whirlwind of art events and bohemian social engagements. At a dinner party on his magnificent ship I met a Parisian fashion designer, a Venezuelan film director, and a Trinidadian actress. They were fascinating, but, much as I would have liked, I couldn't match their jet-set lifestyle.

A footloose French girl named Michelle frequented the yacht club, looking for a boat to crew on. Her pixie grin appealed to me—a total face-brightening, eyebrows popping with mirth—so I asked her out to a movie. Downtown, we gobbled up a goat-and-pumpkin roti—kind of like a burrito—and arrived at the Globe Theater just as *Hook* was starting.

Sated with Hollywood goo, we spilled out into the damp streets and ended up in a second-story "recreation club," or bar. I went to the head.

When I re-emerged Michelle's eyes were on me. She was not smiling now. She was looking full at me, just a straight gaze, equally inward and outward. I imagined that is how she would look at me were we a couple—habituated concern, connection. I wanted it to be so. I liked it that she looked at me that way, and not just with the pixie mask, her face for strangers.

I told her this, and her brown eyes pleaded for understanding. She confessed, with more passion than guilt, that she was coming down from two months of smoking crack in the Port of Spain underworld. She described labyrinths of ecstasy and betrayal, and her fascination with the pipe. She mimicked the many techniques for maximizing the drug's effect, her hands frantic with remembered pleasure. Brotherly group highs had degenerated into dens of sloth and distrust, until her best friend stole her remaining money, and self-preservation told her it was time to pull out. She'd been clean for ten days. Her grin was real, but there was more to the story.

Back outside, streetlights sparkled on the grimy pavement. I stopped her close and kissed her. "Did you think to screw me tonight, Steve?" she laughed. But it was all a tease, a joke. We considered becoming lovers, but she left for Antigua two days later with a Swedish guy. Michelle might have stayed with me, but how would we have lived? *Squeak* was too small.

A new mega-yacht motored in. Its swarthy young captain tossed orders to his new neighbors as they helped him back up to the jetty. "Tie it off further back! No, further!" Josef was like a twenty-four-year-old Humphrey Bogart, only Israeli. His mate, a twenty-eight-year-old French Jewess named Miriam, could have passed for Sophia Loren. They dominated every conversation, and constantly fought between themselves in Hebrew. He was tough and provincial, she warm and cosmopolitan. They became my closest friends. Many were the hours we spent comfortably together on their *Lady Dorothy*.

I was camping around *Squeak* more than living in her. I chopped vegetables on the lip of a palm tree planter, washed clothes at the faucet, and read under the lampposts illuminating the jetty walkway. Each morning I swam a mile in the murky water outside the basin, where eel grass, nine-point starfish, and sunken garbage broke the sandy monotony. A pair of yellow-breasted finches alternately built and dismantled a nest atop a nearby piling.

Pelicans dove for fish in sudden, headlong splashes. The afternoon southeast wind sometimes spattered me with spray as waves broke on the jagged riprap, but the air was welcome on muggy nights. Then the rainy season fell like a curtain, and the tarp I had erected for shade did its feeble best against pelting rain.

The work was taking too long. I felt quiet and humorless. My first impression, that it was easy to meet women there, proved mistaken. Desperately bored, I went to a disco where the bass vibrated the floor so badly it caused the unsmiling masses to jiggle around, or maybe they were dancing. "I could be here a thousand years and not meet anybody," I muttered, and left.

Walking home, I passed a delicious strip of lawn. "I'll lie here for just a minute," I thought.

The next thing I knew a starchy policewoman was standing over me, barking in my face. "What you doing sleeping in front of the police station? You drunk or what? Wait one minute. You not going anywhere in that condition!" I wasn't particularly smashed, but she ordered a passing patrol car to take me home. They eventually did, but not until they had cruised all over town looking for some suspect, even stopping in front of the disco I had just left. I wilted with embarrassment as everybody strained their necks to gawk at the busted white guy in the back seat.

On May 8 I shifted to boat work. I built a permanent rudder blade from a board of chocolate mahogany, replaced the bicycle inner tube that seals the aft locker, and traded my full-sized sextant, which I'd never used, for a small, plastic one. I installed partial thwarts to stiffen the gunwales, and acquired a hand-held VHF radio, signaling mirror, flares, and binoculars, all secondhand.

I longed to leave, and said so to Daniel the Frenchman.

"But Steve, Trinidad is paradise! You must at least allow me to drive you around the island before you go!" And so he did, past schoolyards full of white-bloused girls with their hair in scalp-revealing cornrows, to the old sugar mill, the radio station where the blue Caribbean and muddier Gulf of Paria were simultaneously visible, and through the brown-peopled central plains. He showed me the *pui* tree, blooming like Scotch broom, also the breadfruit and cocoa trees. Timeworn gingerbread houses still stood, the sugar plantations they once commanded long since subdivided and developed. Hindus burned a coffined body on a pyre at the bank of a small, slow river. The countryside was rural yet densely built along the roads. Prosperous East Indians were building modern homes among the clapboard shacks they had grown up in.

Finally the boat work was done. On the dawn of May 26 I rowed out of the yacht club. The only person up was Tony, the shipwright who had greeted me six weeks before. "Good luck," he said, quiet so as not to wake anyone.

Tony knew I had decided to follow the Caribbean islands to Florida. My talks with yachtsmen had convinced me it would be better than following the coast of South and Central America. But the eighty-mile crossing to Grenada remained a sticking point. The adverse winds and currents would probably thwart any attempt to cross it on my own—the very thought of it terrified me. So I rowed back downtown and combed the rough-and-tumble waterfront for a ship to give me a ride. Ultimately I introduced myself to a tall Norwegian operating a passenger-and-cargo ship between Trinidad and St. Vincent. I showed him a picture of *Squeak* and explained myself. He had no questions. "We're leaving the day after tomorrow for St. Vincent. We're not stopping in Grenada, but I can drop you off a few miles offshore if you like."

"That'd be great, thanks."

This stroke of luck caused a problem with an official on the first floor of the customs building: "But sir, your vessel entered Trinidad as a yacht. We need to issue you a clearance to show that the yacht did not remain illegally in our country. Besides, you'll need the clearance for the officials in Grenada. But now you say your boat will exit Trinidad as personal baggage aboard a ship. You know, we don't give clearances for baggage." He referred me to his superior on the second floor, who referred me to someone even higher up. Ultimately I had the division chief on the fifth floor scratching his head. He studied the matter from all angles then concluded, "Okay, look, your *Squeak* is both a yacht *and* baggage." He boldly signed a paper to that effect, and the road was cleared.

At the appointed time I rowed alongside the *Windward* of St. Vincent, jumped in the water, and passed its slings under *Squeak's* hull. They hoisted us up onto the main deck, twenty-five feet above sea level.

As we steamed past the yacht club I called them up on my new VHF.

"TTYC, Sheila speaking, over." Sheila was the bar manager.

"Sheila, this is Steve of the *Squeak*. Do you see that ship going past right now? Over."

"Yes, Steve, why? Over."

"*Squeak* and I are on it. They're taking me to Grenada. Could you please tell my friends? You know who they are. Over."

"Will do, Steve, and you come again soon now. Over and out."

CHAPTER 22

GRENADA

At dusk we exited the Mouth of the Dragon, where the intermittently submerged mountain range spanning Venezuela's Paria Peninsula and northern Trinidad outlines a series of gaps like missing teeth. Venus emerged. The ship rolled. A woman screamed with fear and seasickness. Her children wailed hysterically. The captain chuckled. "Do you hear what that woman is screaming? 'I go dead! I go dead!' Really, these people."

The *Windward* was clean. Captain Tore Torsteinson had purchased her and sailed her from Norway only four months before. A tall, well-mannered man, he hosted me to a homely meal with him and his crew. His father was there too, a white-haired gentleman who never spoke. Tore had the six-to-midnight watch and would personally supervise *Squeak's* unloading. I paid my freight by repairing broken chairs with epoxy and clamps, then got some sleep on a settee on the passenger deck.

Someone woke me at 11:00 P.M. I rigged *Squeak* for sea, then joined Tore in the dark bridge. It was full of luminous screens and electronic readouts. The radio crackled softly. The lights of Grenada were visible. "You see these two red beacons?" asked Tore. "Line them up to enter the harbor."

Three miles off the entrance to St. George's, Tore stopped the engines. "Good luck," he said. Then I got in *Squeak* and a deckhand lowered us softly into the water. I opened the hook's spring-loaded catch and pulled off two looped ends, releasing the sling. Tore gunned his engines. The *Windward* was gone before I could get my oars in the water.

Here, in the lee of the island, the sea was calm. I rowed leisurely through the soft darkness, neither warm nor cold, and entered a small harbor surrounded by a town built on tall hills. A single car drove through the deserted streets, its headlights waving haphazardly into space. The harbor split into two lobes: the Carenage, to north, and the Lagoon, to south. I pulled into the

Lagoon and tied to an old piling at one A.M. on May 29.

In the morning I explored the harbor. Fort George's stone ramparts dominated the entrance from its hill on the north side of the pincer-like opening. The Carenage was the traditional, deep-water harbor. There, brightly painted wooden boats lay tied to iron bollards along a waterfront of elegant Georgian warehouses. A town about a square kilometer in area sloped into the Carenage like a funnel. From Fort George the skyline dipped and rose in a clockwise panorama of church steeples and red tile roofs to lofty, green hills bristling with defunct fortifications, around the shallower, less developed Lagoon, to the hill at the south side of the opening, where stood the ruins of a luxury hotel, burned during the reign of the People's Revolutionary Government in the early 1980s.

I cleared customs at the marina in the Lagoon and hitched a ride downtown, a mile and a half away around the harbor. I walked up to the brow of the hill and bought Eastern Caribbean dollars at Barclay's Bank. A policeman in a blue uniform with red trim directed traffic through an intersection of narrow streets curved and sloped at odd angles. I visited Fort George, and saw where socialist prime minister Maurice Bishop and his followers were massacred by a rebel faction in 1983, prompting the U.S.-led military intervention. "All Grenadians appreciated the rescue operation," a high school student told me, "because it allowed us to overthrow the rebels and avenge the death of Maurice Bishop, our martyr." The new government abandoned socialism.

I longed to travel, but since leaving the Trinidad Yacht Club two of *Squeak's* handles had broken off, an oarlock socket had distorted, and the forward deck had cracked at the edge of the hatch. Facing up to a stay of some duration, I combed the Lagoon for a place to work sheltered from the white rain squalls that rolled down over the hills every couple of hours. Finally the owner of the marina fuel dock permitted me to work in his shop. After a week of repairs I borrowed a laptop and started Chapter 21. Meanwhile I walked the waterfront streets and suffered the hard sells and persistent begging. "What you looking for?" a young tough demanded. When I told him he said, "Gimme a dollar, I'll tell ya." But even the toughest of them exchanged a friendly "All right," the all-purpose greeting. I bought a bottle of cheap, 158-proof rum and hosted the young Grenadians who hung around the marina, earning a roof over their heads by looking after boats for their North American masters.

I heard about something call a "hash," and went. Twenty people of all ages, mostly expatriated Americans and Europeans, showed up at three in the afternoon at a dock on the south coast, where we took a boat to nearby Hog Island. The course chairman announced the rules: "Follow the mounds of shredded paper. They're spaced at intervals of fifty to a hundred yards. Wherever the trail splits in two, determine which one is the true trail . Keep following until you complete a circle and return to the point of beginning. Alright? On your mark, get set, GO!" We ran in a pack. With each new mark the leader shouted, "On, on!" When he encountered a dead end it was "On back!" Whoever took over when the first leader was sidetracked yelled these same words to assist those behind him, the sport being cooperative. We ran along beaches, through thorny brush and mangrove, returning to the start about an hour later. I hounded after the others and sometimes blazed trail, pondering over the sketchy signs.

Through this outdoorsy bunch I met the local Peace Corps workers, particularly Meg, a forester from Athens, Georgia. The following afternoon I climbed the three hundred cobbled steps leading to her plank house atop Cooper Hill, facing west over the Carenage. Up here decent homes and weatherworn shacks intermingled. Above the dipping ridge that ran from Fort George to the Parliament Building the Caribbean was visible: a measured cup of silvery sea above a red roof line. Inside, Utne Reader and National Geographic lay on the coffee table. Pressed leaves and family snapshots hung from the wall.

Meg was two inches taller than I, with lovely legs, dark, curly hair, blue-framed glasses, and a honey-voiced grace. I returned the following evening, and many times thereafter. We talked about the Third World and the environment, listened to Nanci Griffith on her CD player, bathed at Grand Anse beach. We went out to a bamboo nightclub where amateur musicians interpreted Grenadian folk songs. A drunk danced for us: threw his shoulders back, ground his pelvis, tugged his shirt up and rubbed his chest, then fell into a chair. He was a parody of seduction. Meg cooked me dinner on my thirty-ninth birthday. We slept soundly together through the barking of dogs and crowing of roosters. She lay on her back in the morning light, and the pulse in her neck was like a ticking clock; I kissed it quick to keep the time from running out. We made a pancake map of the world, and ate it. Meg went to work, and I wrote on her dining room table with white drapes drifting like ghosts in the corner of my eye. Conch blasts drifted up from the Carenage and rolled around the natural amphitheater of the upper slopes—a fresh catch of fish was selling.

"Steve, I want to go out in *Squeak*," she said, so Saturday morning we rowed out the harbor opening. Sky and sea were gray. "Honey, let's go inside together," she said. I set the oars down. We carefully fitted ourselves into the cabin, I on top. It was actually quite comfortable. We closed the hatch cover. A storm swept over us. Rain pounded. The wind blew us out, past a pair of anchored ships, toward Panama. Sweat ran from our locked bodies. Moisture condensed on the fir walls that held us like a womb. We were a drifting pod.

Meg and I were playmates in the sea. We combed the shallow, rock-and-coral reefs, or cradled one another in weightless, waist-deep shallows. Black youngsters with shockingly white grins played around us like anxious pups in the beach sand. After many twists of fate I had finally arrived at the Caribbean. This was the cool blueness at the center of my voyage. This was rest, reward, and the final test of my strength. I had always been near land in the rivers and in the calmer, equatorial Pacific. The goddess of this sea, I knew, carried a dove in one hand and a thunderbolt in the other.

On June 27 time did run out. My one-month visa had nearly expired. The book was up to date. Another good-bye loomed, this time from a mature woman who, I hoped, could part gracefully. A final night in her house. Another morning—

> of love, and oranges sectioned
> clear sweet juice escaping in tiny bursts
>
> play again, honey, that Sweet Dreams song
> that already tags this new slot
> in the archives of my heart

That weekend Meg accompanied me to the jumping-off point at the north end of the island. The weather was unsettled as we sailed out the harbor and around Grenada's rocky, leeward bulge. It was a nation in miniature, only twenty miles long, and its inhabitants cherished each hollow and hamlet. Snorkeling on Moliniere Reef we found an ancient cannon among the calved rock. We passed Gouyave and Victoria, seaside villages of stone and steeple dwarfed by misty mountains. The annual Fishermen's Birthday Party was underway. Caribbean rhythms blasted from portable speakers where beer-drinking youths crowded a small beach. We needed our own patch of sand, and finally found one—just enough room between high water and foot of cliff to pitch Meg's tent.

The next day we rounded the island, exposing ourselves to the full force of wind and waves. The cockpit was small for two, but Meg ably coordinated her motions with mine. We tacked past the Sauteurs cliff, where the last of the Carib Indians leaped to their deaths to evade the muskets and swords of the French at the end of their long war. Our goal was a sandy atoll Meg knew, northeast of Grenada, but would we make it before nightfall? Sailing past off-lying Sugarloaf Island we encountered monstrous, lemon-meringue seas, caused by a superimposition of two swell patterns in the presence of a strong tidal rip. The waves were squirting, pyramidal, twelve feet tall. They batted *Squeak* about like a badminton birdie. We held on.

"Interesting," I noted, with studied calm. *Squeak* hadn't swamped yet, but it could happen at any moment.

"Steve, can't we get out of here?" asked Meg, controlling her tension.

"Alright, but where to?" Breakers spanned the gap between lofty Sugarloaf Island and the mainland. The beach at Sauteurs was similarly barred. It would be dark in an hour.

Fortunately, one empty stretch of beach was relatively calm. Remembering the fiasco at Orpua, I left *Squeak* with Meg and swam to shore, studying the surf. It was doable, so I swam back, lashed *Squeak's* vulnerable oars, and swam her in, stern-first so waves couldn't slam the rudder over. We then pitched camp at the forest's edge, dipped our feet in a bucket of water to wash off the sand, and retired to our tent, onto the single bedsheet that constituted our bedding. My candle lantern swayed gently in the peak of the tent, swirling the circle of its downward-cast shadow over us.

We thought we were alone, but in the morning Meg's snorkeling gear was missing, including her prescription mask. It was a poor way to begin our last day together. Besides, I was anxious about the rough, windward crossing ahead, the first of several I would undergo before the islands curved to the north, then west.

From our little camp I surveyed the scattering of rocky islands to north and northeast that make up the Grenadines. Wave after wave of rain hampered our efforts to dry clothing and sort through equipment. It took me a frustrating hour to determine magnetic course where true course is 20° and variation is 13° West. (The answer is 33°. West variations are added, east variations are subtracted.) Adjusting for current, I'd have to sail as close as possible to the east wind to fetch Ile de Ronde, where I intended to rest before continuing to Carriacou. I practiced with my signaling mirror, and spoke a passing yacht with my VHF.

The sadness of the good-bye combined with fear to make me queasy. I admired the way Meg balanced woman's conflicting urges to follow her man and to find her own path. I would miss her, but more than that I craved the solitary trial that awaited me.

Meg and Steve, northern tip of Grenada, 6/29/92

CHAPTER 23

THE GRENADINES

At four in the afternoon of June 29, 1992, Meg helped me launch from our beach on the north end of Grenada. She then hiked homeward on a forest trail while I sought a gap in the breakers veiling nearby Levera Bay, between Grenada and Sugarloaf Island. I hoped to spend the night there, and leave in the morning without the risk and delay of a solo beach launch. Swells broke occasionally across part of the entrance, necessitating close mental mapping. The breakers were tall and deafening, like those on the Pacific coast, but I found the gap. My new refuge was exposed to wind and current but sealed against waves.

Sugarloaf Island, a cone-shaped extrusion, was deserted. The mainland opposite was a freshwater swamp. The crystalline water of Levera Bay ranged from the sugary white of its coral sand, at its shallowest, through all the intensities of blue. Green sea turtles glided downward or upward in gentle trajectories. It was a good place to be newly alone. I set my watch to BBC Radio's time signal and slept but little as the wind howled through my rigging.

The crossing to Ile de Ronde is only five miles wide, but otherwise typifies the challenge posed by a northward route through the Windward Islands, southern half of the Lesser Antilles. The Windwards, from Grenada to Martinique, are misnamed in that they lie leeward of the so-called Leewards, which stretch from Dominica to the Virgins. The Lesser Antilles as a whole are shaped like a drawn bow pointing east-northeast into the prevailing axis of the Northeast Trades. Island-to-island bearings gradually decrease from northeast, leaving Grenada, to west, arriving at Puerto Rico. Thus, the crossings are hard on the wind at first, then come further and further off the wind.

The Lesser Antilles are a vast sieve through which the Equatorial Current filters to reach the Caribbean, where its inflow balances outflow via the

Gulf Stream. The current accelerates in the relatively shallow channels, reaching velocities of three knots. The tide rises and falls only about a foot, but this is sufficient to cause the current in the channels to stop and sometimes reverse its westerly flow twice daily. The seas alternate between more and less rough, on the same cycle. There are no tide books, but local fishermen keep the cycle in their heads.

That morning I didn't know the tidal cycle, only that I must point as high as possible and carry as much sail as possible without taking water into the cockpit faster than I could bail. I could never row against such wind and current; if I lost sailpower I would swiftly drift into the central Caribbean. Against that eventuality I carried food, water, celestial navigation equipment, and devices for attracting the attention of ships and planes.

At first light I took on five gallons of seawater ballast. Leaving the bay, I was relieved to see that the "lemon meringue" condition was not in effect. The wind was twenty knots. I beat steadily on the starboard tack, aiming northeast into the Atlantic. Due to current my actual track was due north. Good enough—it was still only 8:30 when I entered the lee of uninhabited Ile de Ronde, where I spent the day spearfishing and cooking. It was a hilly isle of fallen rocks and low trees, the first of the Grenadines. Up to Carriacou they belong to Grenada, beyond that they are part of St. Vincent and the Grenadines. Both nations are former British colonies, and use the Eastern Caribbean Dollar.

The sail from there to Carriacou, though only eight miles, is one of the toughest in the West Indies. I started by passing through the lee of Kick 'Em Jenny Island, another bleak sugar loaf, then held to NNE by the compass. The waves became violent and confused. One broke over the windward gunwale, filling the cockpit. I bailed it out. In deeper water the seas were more regular, but the motion was intense. Each new wave was a collision, an explosion of salt water that stung my eyes and mouth. The wind chilled me, despite a sun that burned through flying clouds. Even reefed and counterbalanced with ten gallons of water, *Squeak* heeled so much I had to bail continuously. Slowly I zigzagged toward my goal. The port tacks were longer, being more directly into the current. I passed a fleet of wooden fishing sloops, of low freeboard, with sloping transom, small deckhouse, and bright paint. A man at the stern fished by hand line with a long, up-and-down motion, hook just off the bottom in twenty-five fathoms.

The sea calmed as I entered Carriacou's wind shadow and tacked into Tyrell Bay, at its southwest end. It was midafternoon. The hills roundabout were each of a unique size and shape: a round knoll, a ridge, a slanting peak. I beached in front of Pizzeria L'Aquilone and was treated to a shower by its proprietors, then bought sandwich makings at a general merchandise store and ate ravenously. I was relieved—*Squeak* and I had proven ourselves capable of the rough, windward crossings that faced us.

Tyrell Bay, being hurricane-safe and relatively undeveloped, was a mecca for North American and European yachtsmen. Some popped in and out, others stayed. Charter boat people cruised a couple of weeks then returned home before their stress levels had had time to fade. In their faces I saw legal briefs and rush-hour traffic. They glimpsed freedom, yet returned to materialism and conventional responsibility—why? Meanwhile, the live-aboards shifted north and south with the seasons and learned to live with less. Friends reunited in various places, building a sense of community, a network of nonconformists. They went back home for family emergencies, worked to make money wherever it was legal, got bogged down with boat problems, grew frustrated with the commercialization that had poisoned their favorite paradises. A few would take the leap across the Pacific, or already had. They were loving couples and ex-lovers, children and grandparents. They were white-haired Scandinavian gentlemen and boisterous young Californians, eccentric English single-handers with trick knees, and Italians in flowery pantaloons.

I played the social butterfly for a day, rowing from one boat to the next. The *Freedom Rose* was there, the last commercial sailing freighter in the Windwards, and the *Sara Munro,* a Scottish fishing ketch once owned by Winston Churchill, that had helped evacuate British soldiers from Dunkirk. Each received me with gusto. It was fun, but it was a high that picked me up then dropped me down with a fuzziness of purpose. I couldn't just hang out. My self-worth depended on progress—miles sailed, repairs completed, pages written. The same Puritan work ethic that drove the charter boaters drove me too, but in a different direction.

I went to a small boatyard that an Italian husband and Swedish wife had built over the past few years. The yard nested among palms and manchineels: shore trees whose fruit is a poisonous green "apple." Local carpenters were rehanging a rudder on a wooden cargo carrier. A blond Wisconsin kid made me a set of aluminum brackets to reinforce *Squeak's* handles. A French couple, who built aluminum dinghies up the dirt track behind the yard, cut me some backing plates. They wouldn't take any money.

Port towns are of two sorts: those in which the first row of buildings are directly on the shore, and those in which they are set back behind a waterfront street. Sleepy little Hillsborough, around a headland from Tyrell Bay, was of the former plan, but shifting toward the latter. That is, a line of storefronts robbed the street of sea views, but the buildings were empty, their backsides torn off in a storm. With time, the façades too would wash away. The local dudes who hung out amid these ruins did not question this recasting of their town. "Hey, how's it goin'? Yeah, all right," they crooned as I walked by, and hit me up for change if I paid any attention.

That night I anchored in a cove at Carriacou's north end, ready to cross to Union Island in the morning. A new country faced me across that narrow channel: St. Vincent and the Grenadines. Disinclined to cook, I gorged on mangoes and oranges, and retired early.

> Gray dawn, gunmetal sea: test me
> hand: be quick to loosen the sheet—it wants to jam
>
> The Grenadines: a rippling dragon half out of water
> an emerald roller-coaster of hills
>
> The wind twists like a swallow, I with it
> the sea jumps like a porpoise, I with it

At tiny Union Island I cleared customs. While provisioning I ran into two men and a woman who reminded me of a night in Panama, when I had watched a dinghy approach from over a dark harbor. Its sweeps had caught the city-glow, pacing with a distinct gait—slow, almost jerky. A tall, thin man with long silver hair had beached his boat and walked up to me, also a short, bald man with graying beard and a cheery woman of pleasant figure. Americans Lon and Norm had struck me as an aging-hippie Mutt and Jeff. They were both career Navy men turned bikers, philosophy professors, retired sea rebels. They were Levi-and-cowboy-boot men, with saggy mustaches. German Haika had joined Lon some years before, adding a welcome feminine touch.

Now I remembered Lon by his voice: a deep, rich bass that zeroed in slowly and reflectively, each sentence a search for meanings, usually ending in humor.

"You're from Chicago, right?" I asked Lon, to peg him.

"Why, yes. Oh that's right, we met in—Colón?"

I spent the evening on their boat. Haika served rum with nutmeg syrup and a macaroni dish. She wore only a midriff-high sarong. Her full, smooth breasts were lovely in the light of the quarter moon that shone over Union's jagged skyline.

From there it was an hour's sail to Mayreau and the Tobago Cays. I worked to windward over the reefs, scraping leeboards on the brain and staghorn coral heads, past an islet with conch shells mounded high all along its shoreline. I pulled up at a fishermen's camp on tiny Baradal. They were young guys from Union and Bequia, diving for lobster and spearfishing from a plywood runabout named *Suck My Dick,* with the sign of the spurting penis. Forty yachts lay in the shelter of all-encompassing Horse Shoe Reef, and this was the off season! A mega-catamaran full of Bermuda-clad tourists arrived. They snapped pictures of water, palm tree, me. I answered the same questions over and over, repeating to myself, *they're not stupid questions; they deserve a serious response.* To escape, I swam through massive vase sponges to the reef, where parrotfish munched coral, brown tweed midgetfish hovered near their niches, and a spotted eel slithered through tendrils of filter feeders. The shallowness was claustrophobic, but surf breaking over the outer row of coral heads barred the way to deep water.

In the morning I turned down a tow from a swaggering charter boat skipper who doubted I could make it to Bequia. I crossed over to Canouan, and stopped at another fishing camp. Why spend a half hour pulling up on a deserted beach when all these strong men were happy to pull me up in a single heave? We shared an intimacy with small boats, theirs being carvel-planked double-enders with choice of sail, oar, or outboard motor. The older men were quieter and worked harder, mending nets on a natural seat formed by the roots of a palm tree, or cooking supper in a smoke-smeared hut of corrugated steel. Bits of plastic rubbish lay mixed into the sand. Worn clothing hung on lines. Gulls cawed. A bleary transistor radio churned out old Bob Marley hits.

I arranged a better way to stow my oars in rough water—oarlocks in their sockets, blades lashed to foredeck—then climbed for a view of tomorrow's crossing. I hiked a flinty, newly carved road. Doves cooed. The air smelled of bark, sap, petals, leaves. A breeze moderated the heat. Soft surf sounds drifted up from the white-rimmed shore. In this, the 500th anniversary of Columbus's first voyage, the New World remained a lush discovery.

I scanned the crossing with my binoculars from a viewpoint five hundred feet up. The area of concentrated wind and tide rips just north of the island was the most hazardous. Five miles out was minuscule Petit Canouan, then Mustique, then Bequia, fifteen miles north-northeast.

The tide was in my favor in the morning as I passed just alee of Petit Canouan and plowed on, sheets hard in. *Squeak's* wake bubbled. She pitched and yawed. The waves had had plenty of time to regularize while rolling in from North Africa, yet they retained an irreducible element of chaos. They weren't distinct entities so much as shifts in the film of kinetic energy that covers the Earth's oceans. It became clear I would easily fetch Bequia, so I eased the sheets, picking up a half knot, a knot. I passed through the gap between Isle A Quatre and Pigeon Island, cooking now through sheltered water, wind on the starboard quarter.

A dive boat pulled up. "Where you coming from?"

"Seattle, Washington!"

Confused looks.

"Se - at - tle - Wa - shing - ton!"

Dawning recognition, thumbs up, faces that shrank as the launch sped away.

I sailed round the southwest tip of Bequia, and up, in four long, biting tacks, into Admiralty Bay. The charter skipper who had offered me a tow was just then on his way out the harbor. "Guess you showed me!" he yelled, and threw me a can of cold beer as we passed.

At the head of the bay lay the town of Port Elizabeth. Yachts filled the anchorage. Trading sloops lay close ashore, their bow lines tied to palm and almond trees, stern lines holding them off. A crowd of people helped me pull *Squeak* up under a tree. I rinsed the salt off me with a bag of drinking water, shaved, and hung up gear to dry—everything was wet from a leak through the mast hole. Retired sea captains introduced themselves, nearly white men whose accents were a different West Indian from that of the predominant blacks. The latter were laid-back, jive.

"Yellow de boat?" one asked.

(I took this to mean, "You alone on the boat?") "That's right."

"You from States?"

"Yeah."

"How many days take you come here?"

"Two years."

Startled looks, laughter.

The shady beach was the town's most public spot. A new concrete street paralleled it. Flowers grew in the median. Most of the Caribbean Gothic homes of decayed gingerbread had been replaced by tourist shops and offices of bland cement-work. The "buses," actually small vans, were new and classy, with pencil-thin gold trim, white mags, and custom upholstery. I stopped in at Grenadines Yachting and Equipment and flirted with the clerk, a local girl with green eyes and silver braces on her teeth.

I woke the next morning staring up at coconuts hanging thirty feet over my face. If one fell that could really hurt! In a gap between rainstorms I renewed the mainsheet block's lashing to the rudder head. Among my observers was one Andy Mitchell, who offered the use of a nearby covered work space. I gladly accepted.

Andy presided over a warren of small businesses offering rooms for rent, bicycle rentals, boat refinishing, and commissioned art sales. My cubbyhole was a semi-enclosure in the midst of this. To my right, employees were spray-painting a runabout robin's-egg blue under a roof supported by four posts. To my left was a ramshackle bungalow, unoccupied except for a grimy kitchen, where Andy cooked for himself and his bedridden father. Across a crowded courtyard lay the main house. Altogether it was a drab accumulation of add-ons. Andy was in his thirties, a mixed blood with Michael Jackson hair and a thin-lipped smile. He was an ambitious businessman with friends and enemies, hangers-on and detractors.

It may seem I spent a lot of time repairing *Squeak*, and it seemed that way to me too. *Squeak* is intentionally light, and it's hard to be both light and strong. I was still working out bugs in her design, and subjecting her to a lot of wear and tear. Now the mast hole needed rebuilding, stress points needed to be reinforced to withstand the greater rigors of the open sea, and she needed a stowage system able to keep my gear dry. Most of all I dreaded sanding off the skin blemishes that now covered her thin, wooden hull, and applying a layer of fiberglass. But seaworthiness and *Squeak's* long-term viability demanded it.

I hated the thought of another long stretching-out of time frames, of nephews and nieces growing up without me, and parents getting old. But better to get home late than never. Besides, where else would I find free work space and access to boat-building materials? I realized now that the Caribbean phase of the voyage would be the longest of all. The traveler's checks I'd left home with were all gone, but Mom said I still had five thousand dollars in the bank, and sent me a credit card so I could get cash advances. "See it through to its natural conclusion," wrote my brother Mike, meaning the family accepted my prolonged absence. So I cleaned and built shelves in the bungalow to make it habitable, moved in, and settled down to work.

For spice I saw Charmaine, the green-eyed clerk at the marine supply store. She was in her mid-twenties, with long brown hair, handsome manners, and a plump bottom. Specks of dark tan dappled her otherwise Caucasian face. Charmaine didn't interest me romantically, but was a good companion. She introduced me to the Mount Pleasant community, a hilltop area settled by the Jacob, Leslie, Gooding, and Davis families, of Scottish and African ancestry. "My granny told me," she said, "that long ago a slave ship was passing Bequia, see? And some of the darkies was sick, so they throwed them overboard, and they washed up in Hope Bay. But they got better, and then some Scottish planters come here from Barbados, and they marry with the people that was here and they move to the mountain, because here the breeze is good and the mosquitoes don't reach us." The hilltop people subsequently intermarried, and built a social distance between themselves and the blacks of the lowland.

For as long as they could remember, Mount Pleasant women had been industrious, reliable housewives, and their men had been seamen. The older men had begun their careers in the days of pure sail, ranging from Guyana to the Gulf Coast in Bequia-built schooners up to 160 feet long. I listened rapturously as they reminisced about such-and-such vessel, how she handled, and to what end she had come. Most were eventually lost at sea, some with their cargoes, some with their men. Then came auxiliary engines, then masts and sails disappeared altogether in the larger craft. Now Charmaine's father, Errol, worked as an engineer for a shipping line based in Florida. He spent months at sea alternating with months at home waiting to be called up.

New England whalers used to base themselves in Bequia. Their whaleboats became the pattern for the Bequia boat, such as I had first seen at the fishing camp on Canouan. She was ten to twenty feet long, open, the shape of a wineglass in cross section. A spritsail and jib propelled her, sandbags kept her upright. Friendship Bay and Paget Farm, on the south of the island, were home to many such boats. From these centers Bequians ranged all over the Grenadines, fishing by techniques that varied with the season. They still harvested an occasional humpback whale the old-fashioned way, with oars and harpoons, and honed their sailing skills with an annual regatta.

Charmaine was girlish, stubborn, ultimately generous and heartwarming. The only thing I ever saw her read was *True Romance* magazine. I could be silly with her. She begged me to blabber in the hick slang my friends and I had joked around with as kids, or give my impression of a pink dolphin. When she got off work we walked past the cemetery, up trails only the locals know, to the pot-holed upper road, where it was a different world: open meadow, the sea so far below yet the horizon seemingly at eye level, so the blueness of the sea stood up like a wall. At dusk people gathered along that road, always the same people at the same places, standing or sitting in their driveways, talking or silent, playing dominoes on a little table in the middle of a barren heath, listening to country western from a transistor radio. In the distance, from left to right, were the barren crags of uninhabited Battowia and Baliceaux, Mustique (where Princess Margaret, Mick Jagger, and Sophia Loren had homes), distant Canouan, and nearby Petit Nevis and Ile A Quatre. On Mount Pleasant the sea was behind every unconscious thought. It was so big outside that it came inside too. At night the sea shimmered under the moon with horizontal brush strokes of dancing silver. The shimmering began close, just at the foot of the mountain, yet stretched so far away it made me ache inside.

Charmaine was one with that backdrop. She was a sphinx, a waiting damsel. She stood there on her hill, facing wind and rising moon, hair blowing, a faraway look in her eyes, barely conscious, a beautiful animal. The sea was a vacuum, sucking her dry of imagination.

I teased her too hard about her accent, in which a Scottish twang seemed to persist. She wouldn't speak to me for days. I tried to discuss something interesting or get her to go for a hike, and she would calm me down as if I were an overactive child, or bake me a cake. I let her have her way, going with her and her people to the beach on Sundays though I needed to work. Charmaine and her little nieces and nephews liked having me there, a grown-up who could play like a kid. Everyone bathed in the sea for hours. "The sun *hot*, mon," they would say, languorously. Then lunch would be ready, a stew of fish, plantain, dumplings, dasheen and breadfruit. Everyone was jolly, and made me feel a part of it.

Evenings at Charmaine's house were a blend of banality and spontaneous joy. Mom and Dad, Charmaine and I, little sister, and a cousin or two watched made-for-TV movies, bingo, West Indian news and sports. Bored stiff, I crossed back over the mountain's hump and descended its seven hundred vertical feet on a switchback road full of ruts and rotting mangoes. The lights of Port Elizabeth and dozens of yachts shone below. The mountainside was calm, forested. A dog barked at me as I passed, forgot why he had started barking, and kept on through sheer momentum.

I sat under the almond tree with Nawly, the island's unofficial historian. One could listen to him, but not talk to him, and he wasn't even an old man yet. With his words in mind I explored cliff-side copses, forested hills, little valleys growing peas, corn, coconuts. I pictured how they used to be. The trees were not tall, the original species gone and long forgotten. Back then it was all sugar cane and slave labor, intensive, big money, until the soil tired out. Now new houses and businesses were springing up all over—an airport had been completed some months before. Still, everything was on a human scale: plots, lanes, culverts, footpaths.

Charmaine's favorite walk was down through the steep heath and wind-matted trees to Hope Bay, at the foot of Mount Pleasant, on the Atlantic side. Nobody lived there anymore, but cows grazed in the coconut grove behind the pounding surf. We walked out onto the rocks looking for shells— her bare feet were tougher than mine. We walked part way back, to a cliff overlooking the sea, and saw a rainstorm coming, ten minutes away, like a mile-high jellyfish, gray outside, black inside, dragging tentacles of rain. It seemed it might pass to the north of us. Then the rain hit and we hugged together under a gnome-like tree, in an old orchard, protected, until the tree became saturated and big drops rained down our necks, wetting our T-shirts and heads. We shivered and laughed. The rain stopped, but night now settled, the sky dynamic with lighter and darker masses of cloud. We continued up past the prime minister's house, where on another day Charmaine had thrown the dog into the pond, laughing like a child, and the dog liked it and jumped in again and again. We continued, up the lane that has all the hill people's names autographed in the cement. She pointed everybody out. When we finally reached her home, Errol was quietly cupping water onto uncured cement posts to keep them from cracking. A goat bleated. Callaloo soup, a sort of spinach with cream and spices, waited for us on the stove.

People I had met in Port of Spain, St. George's, and Tyrell Bay passed through. I was one of the sights, part of the lore. A tourist saw *Squeak* in the shop and came back the next day saying she had dreamt she went down into *Squeak's* cabin, and suddenly it was a big ship, with secret passages leading to dungeons full of bizarre machinery. *Squeak* was upside down for a long time, and the old fishermen, seeing her, said she had the shape of a whale. Rumors went around that I was crazy, or running from the law, or "doing it on a bet." The immigration official suspected me of engaging in business without a work permit.

It was important to me that I not be confused with the pale Americans who rode in on cruise ships or stayed in the guest houses, and that made me wonder, would life be a comedown after the voyage? My antsiness made me a breeding ground for such doubts, but the boat work renewed my pride in *Squeak*, and my enthusiasm for sailing her. The boatwork was a long succession of nit-picky, painstaking tasks: little epoxy coatings, tedious arrangements for holding parts in place while bonds cured, cutting out specks of rot with a pocketknife, and sanding, sanding, the worst of all. But I enjoyed the design aspects: the direction and magnitude of loads, weight-to-strength ratios, abrasion resistance, and the need in certain cases for compactness, leading to metals rather than wood. In the handles alone I now had a combination of fir, hardwood, epoxy, two fillers, fiberglass cloth, polyurethane, aluminum, and stainless steel fasteners.

The flies were a nuisance, especially on the days when the public works crew gathered up the garbage at the dump site on the waterfront across from Andy's, forcing the flies to seek new homes. The hired hand who lived in the cubicle across the courtyard from me went on a binge every few days. He'd drink strong rum, stumble around, and rave, "Don' fuck wid me, ya mudda cunt!" then collapse in a corner. He was big, but old.

I treated myself to afternoons off, and hiked, snorkeling gear in my day pack, along road and leafy track to the various bays: Rocky, Princess Margaret, Lower, Friendship, Ravine, Hope, even Anse Chemin on the island's wild north end. I squirmed through underwater caves and worked my way along precipitous, wave-crashed shores, where schools of small fry fluttered like flags in the turbulence, and spume veiled the dangerous rocks. I dove under the spume to get closer to the cliff face, and examined the surface chaos from below, surging violently but predictably with the swells. On the way home I filled my rucksack with ripe mangoes, fallen unwanted from the trees. I paused in the cemetery as the sun's rays grew long, and sketched it with my words:

acre of roughage, stem and stalk
orange and violet sparks, green swells
semiwild, flowering

the tombstones: not crowded
not well tended, not forgotten
the great jagaweeli tree in the east corner
a vast leafy warren

hey goat
does the grass taste better
here, in the Port Elizabeth cemetery?

One of my friends in Bequia was a huge Swede named Thomas with curly blond hair and blue eyes. "Hey, Steve," he said. "I'm entering my boat in the Carriacou Annual Regatta. Want to crew for me?" I agreed because it would allow me to see Meg again. We sailed on Friday, July 31. His sloop being fast, and the wind favorable in this direction, we covered in five hours what had taken me five days.

That night, sleepy little Hillsborough teemed with carnival-goers from all over the Windwards. As Thomas and I sat in a crowded rum shop near the dock an Irish seaman came in, inebriated. "Move aside, mate, it's a Master Mariner you're looking at!" He boasted his rank, over and over, and scanned the room for someone willing to return his gaze. I didn't, but Thomas did.

My friend was a teddy bear inside, but outside he was a husky man with a booming, center-stage voice. Rowdies often targeted him as a worthy opponent—it was his curse. Now the Master Mariner's eyes latched onto him. A sadistic smile grew on his face, as if to say, "Ah, here's someone I can exchange body blows with!" He needled Thomas, subtly at first, like it might all turn out to be a manly joke, then nastily.

"Oh shit," Thomas whispered, squirming on his stool.

The drunk worked himself up. "*You're* not a Master Mariner. I say *you're* not a Master Mariner! You're a fucking fraud! *Fuck off!*" He got up and lurched toward Thomas and me, but two burly bouncers had their eyes on him. Harnessing his own momentum, they spun him neatly around and deposited him outside the door. There, he presumably took a breath of air and forgot all about it, because we didn't see him again.

Meg arrived the following afternoon on the inter-island boat from Grenada. We reacquainted over a salty conch stew at a cafe by the pier. Again, it was her height that most struck me.

"Whoa, so much woman!" I said, our hands touching across the table.

"And every inch of you is so—earnest."

Meg blushed. "Lotta woman for a lotta man."

By night the streets were full again, especially in the canyons formed by massive banks of speakers. They played the same hit songs over and over: "Murder She Wrote," "If you Can't Find a Woman," "Jump." In the canyons, the people danced so tightly it was tough to get through, and impossible for Meg not to be fondled by unseen hands. "Damn it," she cried, but we could never catch the culprits. Stallkeepers ran out of food, and stayed open anyway. A blond girl made out with a Rasta man in the shadows, their bodies squirming with lust.

We set up the tent in a wooded back beach, and in the morning discovered we had camped in a graveyard. Tombstones leaned this way and that, buffeted by ancient storms, half buried in sand. Crabs crept from their holes then darted back in, like ball players trying to steal a base.

Along the beach toward town we passed traditional boats from Carriacou, Petit Martinique, Tobago, and Bequia, all in new paint. Crews and spectators intermingled. Class by class, the boats raced. The harbor teemed with clusters of white sails, each cluster of one species, like schools of fish.

The yacht race was next. Thomas, normally anything but serious, told Meg and me once more exactly how to pull the headsail over, and winch it tight. He had raced professionally for years. The starting gun went off, and we popped open the spinnaker. The other seven yachts fell quickly behind. We rounded the markers, Nabouya Island, then Jack-A-Dan Rock, Thomas snapping orders like a Marine Corps sergeant. Talk about overkill—we crossed the finish line a half hour before our nearest competitor!

"Everybody listen now, boat leavin' for Grenada eight o'clock, Monday morning," announced the captain of the inter-island ferry. What he meant, as everyone knew, was that people might start embarking at that hour, but the boat wouldn't leave until it was packed to the gunwales with carnivalers ready to go home. That didn't occur until Tuesday at eleven, giving Meg and me an extra day together. I was glad, because I loved her candor, and the way her brown eyes and wide mouth registered emotions, with the deliberateness of a good communicator, but ready for the shifts and ambiguities as well. Her legs were fantastic, too.

"I might be able to get some time off and visit you in Bequia this fall," she said.

"Let's work toward that."

Thomas and I sailed back to Bequia. The grind continued. Andy moved me into a vacant house he had bought across from the public market. I had the place all to myself, and fresh fruit and vegetables right across the street. I slept on an air mattress on the concrete floor, and worked around the lack of plumbing and electricity. I added greenheart caps to the leeboard rubstrakes, and laid on extra fiberglass where the ropes that hold the leeboards drape over the gunwales. I glassed this section then that, turned *Squeak* around, propped her at whatever angle allowed me to bear down with my tools. To keep some blood in my veins I burnt mosquito coils day and night. I learned how to spread insect repellent on my legs without getting it on my hands, by dripping it on and rubbing my legs together like a fly. I ate a cheap dish called *ital*—a mild stew of beans, rice, and vegetables—on those days when a Rasta man cooked it in a big cauldron on the beach. Otherwise I consumed avocados, bananas, carrots, whole-wheat bread, steamed grains or root crops. The diet was nutritious, cheap, and easy, but it was difficult to maintain appetite with such blandness.

I lived peacefully, if not intimately, among the blacks. The building I inhabited scarcely excluded them; its large windows were unglazed, its doors I left open to admit light. Four of their rum shops lay within a stone's throw. They socialized endlessly, pretending to transact business even if they had none. They clowned, conspired, greeted, shared the smallest details of their lives. They teased the village idiot, a whining, twisted wretch in torn trousers, calling him "Puss Man," from a suggestive song popular on the radio. They nicknamed me "Christopher Columbus." One Rasta brother even "had a vision" that I was the grandson of that controversial discoverer, whose name was on everyone's lips due to the 500th anniversary. Foul-mouthed boys teased me for walking with Charmaine. "You does like big-bottom girl, huh? It too big for you to con*trol,* mon," they laughed, jerking their arms and loins as if humping beach balls. Reggae boomed from passing vans, slow, with organ-chord offbeats, also *dub* and *soca,* other popular music styles. I imagined I heard Spanish being spoken outside, but it was always my mind converting incomprehensible West Indian into Spanish sound-alikes.

One day a heavyset gal came into the shop, looked me over.

"Where you wife?"

"I don't have a wife."

"Where you children?"

"Don't have any."

"Me want go wit a white man what him got a yacht. Me be your girlfriend, okay?"

This was rather sudden. "Well, perhaps we could go swimming together. Do you like to swim?"

"First you buy me a swimsuit."

"I don't think you and I are going to be very good friends," I said, nipping it in the bud.

A funeral parade filed past, rounded up, and came by again, a hundred people in somber, old-fashioned clothes, first elderly men in pairs, shouldering what appeared to be pool cues, then women and girls in their finest blacks and whites, no two dresses exactly alike. Revival meetings went on night after night. "Hallelujah! Praise the Lord!" over and over, with exaggerated feeling and overamplified singing. Meanwhile, up by Charmaine's there was barbecued chicken or corn on the cob, aunts and uncles and nephews and nieces sitting in the road, which never saw traffic. They were a shy people, their lives a carefully managed boredom. They had only their own cousins to marry, and hoped I would introduce some new, American blood.

When the fiberglassing was done I rebuilt the U-shaped seat that wraps around the footwell in *Squeak's* cockpit. I built a framework of fifty-four minutely fitted pieces of a blond mahogany the local boatbuilders called "silver valley" and covered it with a sheet of marine plywood. Twist-off deck plates provided access to storage compartments inside. It took a month to build, doing it right,

living for what will be
for the shape inside the wood, waiting to be free

for the curious, neck-arching geckos that
sculpt eye-blink paths over walls and window sills
for the scarlet blossoms of the poinciana tree
that burn holes in space, attract bees

curiosity and patience are my raw materials
a slight sharpening of the universe
a clarification, a careful stroke

I could tell Andy was getting tired of helping me out. Once again I depended on others. Now it was free shop space, other times it was living space, or access to word processors. This dependence rankled, because it ran counter to *Squeak's* purpose, which was freedom. Much of the boat work was design improvements—hopefully this would henceforth decline. *Squeak* has no engine or electronics to worry about. My use of alternative transportation, such as pickup trucks and ships, was resourcefulness, not dependence. I needed a word processor only because I had become allergic to writing by hand. Thus I rationalized the dependence, but it didn't make me feel better.

What did I lose by accepting free help? I offered payment if it was I who suggested the assistance, but people generally preferred the feeling of participation in what I was doing. That was good, because otherwise I'd have run out of money. Unfortunately, the benefactor sometimes tired of the arrangement before my need was satisfied. I was subject to his moods. Some may have thought association with me would change their lives, but it didn't. I wasn't a guru. I didn't want followers. The benefactor had every right to terminate the arrangement at will, but before doing so he usually went through a phase in which the good feeling he got from helping me conflicted with his fear of being taken advantage of. Feeling the vibes, I worked faster, and lowered my profile.

Andy and I were great buddies most of the time. He taught me how to drink rum, mixing it with lime juice, brown sugar, and water. He shared his perspectives of the island, which were useful because he had also lived in the States. He had no intention of using the building for some time, but it irritated him when the work took longer than I had estimated. Selfishly, I stayed on until the new cockpit was complete, and his generosity was exhausted.

I had still another project, so I took up another offer. At the invitation of owners Lars and Margit I sailed around to the Friendship Bay Hotel, on the south side of the island, and put *Squeak* in their warehouse. It was a large building, nearly empty, with a level floor and a leaky roof. Wasps and mosquitoes infested it, but the double doors, opened, admitted adequate light. The hotel catered to wealthy European vacationers. Its staff treated me kindly. I slept aboard *Squeak* in the warehouse, but I benefited as much as the paying guests from the beach and manicured grounds.

This final project was to reorganize my stowage. The original stuff-bag system had failed because everything tended to break, spill, and get wet. Also, it didn't lend itself to accessibility, or frequent loading and unloading, or to expansion as I accumulated equipment.

I needed boxes capable of thirty or forty pounds of gear apiece, with handles, lids, and hold-downs should *Squeak* roll over. The boxes must fit into the cabin like a hand into a glove, and also into the cockpit, at night, when it was time for my gear and me to trade places. I inventoried everything and decided upon one less-accessible box occupying the aft half of the "hold" (where my legs go when sleeping), continued use of the square buckets I had bought in Panama City in the forward half of the hold, and two longitudinal boxes, side by side, in the cabin.

To create the boxes' curved panels I covered the corresponding boat surfaces with plastic, then laid down fiberglass. I cut the plane surfaces from pre-glassed plywood. Box by box, I devised temporary clamps, glued all six sides together, cut off the top inch to serve as a lid, reinforced the seams, and added an interior coaming for the lid to fit over. I built non-protruding handles by cutting grip holes in the boxes' sides and covering these holes on the inside with enclosures large enough to accommodate my fingers. Wooden bars and straps held the boxes to the cabin sole.

Each of the three boxes took a week. I worried that Lars and Margit would get tired of the weirdo living in their warehouse, but they didn't. I felt my life ticking away, like I was trapped inside my perfectionism. None of the island women attracted me, but I visited Charmaine for companionship. I went to Port Elizabeth for food and building materials. As I crossed over the divide separating Friendship and Admiralty bays, a cruise ship was often in port. On those days the boutiques buzzed with tourists in bright, clean summer outfits, speaking in broad, North American accents.

I ate my meals on the lawn outside the warehouse, in the shade of palms. One day I saw I had spilled a grain of rice, and that it was being manhandled through the short, coarse grass by nine almost microscopic ants. Their combined mass was far less than that of the grain of rice, yet each ant gripped the rice with its mandibles and waved its legs in the air until it touched something to grab onto. Then that ant lifted rice and fellow workers all together, wheeling them around until his legs were dangling and another ant was lifting. By this method they worked their way through that seemingly impossible obstacle course. Could I ever match those ants in their fierce perfection? I yearned to be free again in a nature which demanded that perfection of me. My consciousness was like a beam of light, narrowing and expanding in accordance with ever-changing imperatives. I was tired. Overhead, the palms' long branches swayed and worked,

> like windmills in the engine of the trade wind sky
> in the tabernacle of the empty heavens

I caught a skinny mouse that had been gnawing my bread and bananas, and threw him into the sea. A wave washed him up onto the beach. I flicked him out again with my foot. He was so small relative to the surf that he was underwater most of the time, but he kept his orientation to land, and swam with all his might. Suddenly it was important to me that he not die, but where was he? Then I saw him crawling weakly up the sand, holding on as the waves slipped back into the sea. His skeleton showed through his wet fur. He could barely move. He kept wiping his big, black eyes—they stung from the saltwater. He dragged himself into the shelter of an empty coconut husk and stared into space, shaking like a leaf. I saw myself in him.

I was on a schedule. Meg was flying up on October 17 to cruise the coast of St. Vincent with me, then she would fly back to Grenada while I carried on. I completed the big boxes with time left over to build a tool box. Now only my writing was in arrears. That would have to wait. I had a boat whose new qualities I longed to try, and a chain of tropical islands to follow on my odyssey back home.

Meg arrived. We took a lovely room at the hotel for my final two nights on Bequia. The soft bed, lights, toilet, and shower delighted me. Everything was so clean and convenient. I would leave this place in style, like a regular guest!

I intercepted Charmaine on her way home from work, by the cemetery. I had told her I was leaving, but she hadn't seemed to accept it as fact.

"Charmaine! Hey, you know I'm leaving tomorrow. Come on, give me your address."

I hadn't told her about Meg; why hurt her feelings? But she must have heard. Her eyes were red, her voice indignant. "What, so you can put it in your little black book, with all your other girls? No thanks!" She turned and stomped away. I knew better than to try to stop her.

CHAPTER 24

ST. VINCENT TO ST. LUCIA

Considering the fuss that had been made over me during my three months in Bequia, there was little fanfare when, on October 19, 1992, I hoisted sail, got out my whistle, and tooted "Rio," the traditional shanty for weighing anchor for new lands. I cleared Friendship Bay, then coasted past the scenes of my various walks and dives: Ravine Bay, Hope Bay, Bequia Head.

The ten-mile crossing to St. Vincent was a close reach changing to a broad reach as a new front veered the wind in my favor. The southern tip of St. Vincent slowly took shape. I saw the tops of masts, then the anchored yachts beneath them, then entered a small bay south of Kingstown. At the Umbrella Beach Hotel I met Meg, who had taken the ferry over.

The next day we proceeded north together, past rocky drop-offs and forest enclaves. A pinnacle rising from the sea caught our attention. Leaving *Squeak* at its deserted landing, we climbed a spiral path carved from its vertical face. At the top we found the ruins of Fort Duvernette, built by the French in the early 1700s to defend the anchorage. The heavy masonry was cracked and overgrown, but eight cannons and one mortar still faced the harbor. The fort, and dozens more like it throughout the West Indies, were souvenirs of two centuries of mayhem perpetrated by the French and English against each other's settlements, corresponding to the many wars they fought in Europe during that period. How hardhearted, I thought, to have extended such musty belligerence to a clean new world!

We passed Kingstown Bay and continued along a sawtooth pattern of coves. At the first wilderness beach we stopped. It was Big Byahaut, an indentation a hundred yards wide, flanked by rocky, drowning ridges. A narrow green valley ran from the cove up into the island's mountainous center. Meg pitched the tent while I cooked a sweet potato stew.

Meg came down with something—hopefully not from my stew—so we stayed there two days. I hacked a path to a latrine, put the cuttings under the tent as bedding, and busied myself with packing arrangements and sewing. We had the place to ourselves except for the fishermen who rowed by each morning, setting nets.

The diving was superb: clear and calm with shattered rock, white sand, and vertical cliffs descending to unknown depths. I swam hard, with lots of down time. Two hundred and fifty yards north, in a final indentation before the coastal cliff jutted out into a point, I saw a cave opening.

It was a partly flooded arch, twenty feet tall, of sharply spalled, gray rock. The archway framed a black hole. Bat squeaks reverberated from it as I cautiously approached. The bottom became shallow with sharp rock. The sea surged gently in and out. Ten feet inside, the entrance ended at a narrow corridor running left and right. It was ten to twenty feet tall, and flooded to half its height. Small bats carpeted the walls and roof. They hung upside down, some asleep, some awake. They rustled, groomed, and fidgeted in short flights. Thousands of munchkin faces stared down at me with beady little eyes. There were so many bats, and the light was so dim, it was impossible to focus on any one. Their squeaks made a riotous, eery din. Hairless wings filled the air. It was a bat cave above, but a sea cave below, with the typical small reef fish. To my right the corridor was pitch black, uninviting, but to my left was a long, straight tunnel with a tiny light at the end.

I swam toward it. The tube narrowed. I lifted and dipped my eyes rapidly across the air/water boundary, coping with two separate environments: above, black cave walls that glistened with bats and slimy crabs; below, a shaft of blue light. A surge carried me forward. I flew with arms extended, like Superman. I thought about what those who have come back from death say it's like to die: a long darkness and a beautiful, spreading light. The bottom dropped away into a gorge with a floor of white sand, while the roof persisted low overhead. I dove down, hugging the gorge's floor, deeper, deeper, to the bottom of the gorge, while daylight spread over me, like an underwater dawn so beautiful I nearly forgot my need for air. Then I shot straight up, lungs aching, up, up, faster than the bubbles, toward the sun's glinting disk, until I emerged, dazzled and gasping, far from shore, in the wide-open bay north of Byahaut.

On the twenty-third Meg and I proceeded north. Being in the lee of tall mountains, the wind was light and fickle. We constantly changed places, lowered and raised sails, shipped and unshipped the oars. Meg trimmed the boat with her body weight while I drove her.

We stopped for provisions at a listless town named Barrouallie. Until some years before it had been a center for the hunting of pilot whales. Their skulls littered the sand like bleached boulders. In the shade of an almond tree four youths leaned against a broken longboat with a rusty gun mount in its bow. A dirt soccer field occupied the town's center. Barefoot beer-drinkers loitered against a tavern wall. A radio dribbled out sugary-voiced obituaries with organ-dirge accompaniment, while somewhere nearby an electric band practiced reggae hits. As we left, skinny black boys swarmed us, wanting rides. They spilled over *Squeak* and hung on to her extremities, screeching and splashing like a troupe of monkeys while I pulled away from the beach. One by one they fell away and swam ashore, laughing and waving their thanks to us.

We passed the northernmost town of Chateaubelair and hovered alongside a beach which we hoped to use as our base for an ascent of Soufriere ("that which emits sulfur"), St. Vincent's principal volcano. A work-worn longboat lay at anchor, neatly folded nets heaped high on its stern. A light surf washed over black sand. We dragged *Squeak* up into a coconut grove behind the beach, and pitched the tent.

"I'm up for the climb," said Meg, when the sun rose.

"Okay, baby, if you're sure!"

We hiked north along the beach, across a stream where two men were butchering a pair of *manicou* (opossums), and up a dry streambed. A mountain-farming couple showed us where the trail exited the stream bed and mounted one of the many ridges radiating from the crater. The man was heavyset, with short, spiky dreadlocks. He carried a *cutlass* (machete) in one hand, a satchel in the other. The woman, somewhat older, wore a plain red dress and a blue head-wrap. The landscape was a matrix of light forest and narrow patches of cultivation, oriented with the fall-line. The man paused to shift the tether of a bellowing cow while Meg and I examined a "coal pit:" a crib of sticks and vines in which alternating layers of green bows and oxygen-depriving earth produced charcoal for cooking.

We left our companions at their yam patch, which lay on a gullied slope a thousand feet above sea level, and continued up the ridge. The neighboring peaks began to show. Trees became heavier because older, being out of man's reach. Cultivation ceased. Wispy air roots bearing pepper-like fruits hung down over the trail—we parted them with our hands as if passing through a screen of beads. The canopy thinned. We transited a zone of tall grass, emerging finally onto a barren slope. A misty wind now chilled us. At three thousand feet we reached the lip of the crater.

It was three quarters of a mile wide, 750 feet deep, with a donut-shaped plain on the bottom. From the center of the plain rose a black, hemispherical plug of splintered rock, its top 500 feet below us. Steam rose from a streaky patch on the plug's side. Veils of cloud shifted in the high wind, revealing this feature, then that.

A rope had been strung between iron stakes down into the crater. I descended hand-over-hand, looking down over my shoulder. My footfalls sent loose pumice skittering down the slope.

The air inside the crater was calm and warm. Parched grass grew from the plain's gritty soil. We examined the sulfurous vents from which Soufriere got its name, then circled the crater clockwise. The cliffs to our left were inaccessible, the broken rock of the plug to my right equally uninviting. Opposite the access rope the plug impinged on the crater wall, forcing us to climb up over its massive shards of rock. On the far side, the plain tilted into a dry lake bed with a moist, clay surface. Past climbers had scratched their names in giant characters.

We returned to camp without incident, and the next day backtracked to Barrouallie. It was time for Meg to catch a bus to the Kingstown airport. She checked out buses while I obtained customs clearance from a policewoman with mountainous breasts under a starched white blouse.

"A bus *might* leave for Kingstown sometime after four o'clock," said Meg, mildly irritated. "That's all I can find out for now." To kill time we rowed to a cove north of town and dove, while four young men tried to chase a *manicou* out of a tree projecting over the edge of the cliff above us. Two on top, thrashing in the dense foliage, two on the beach shouting up instructions, and a pair of dogs at a complete loss as to how to contribute, all ultimately failed to dislodge the varmint, if it ever existed.

At four we returned and waited on the road, leaning against a whitewashed stone wall with a sharp ridge along its top to preclude sitting. Beside us a woman sold peanuts while plaiting painfully tight cornrows in her little girl's hair. Mother and daughter were like a single being, with steady, laconic eyes, full of slow purpose.

Just before sunset, as the bus came into view, we hugged good-bye for a full minute. It was sad, but easier than our good-bye on Carriacou, which in turn had been easier than our parting in Grenada. Greater distance separated us all the time, but our relationship had demonstrated a will to survive.

I rowed, lonely and free, to Wallilabou Bay, a mile up-coast. As I tied to a mooring among French and German charter boats, tourist-hardened boys paddled out on dilapidated surfboards. "Buy my *paw paw* (papaya)," they said. "Wood carvings, good price. Come on, how much you pay?" Those fancy yachts could have been square-riggers off the Malabar Coast, the surfboards could have been dugout canoes full of warriors in bizarre headdress, so great was the separation between the two cultures. Mutual curiosity had long since evaporated, leaving only exploitation. The boys approached me coldly, unsmiling, but I greeted them as they greet each other. "All right, mon, no need for that. Already cooking here." A light went on in their faces. They asked me questions, and gave me a "Right on!" for the courage to do a crazy thing. I had little curiosity to give them in return, but it was enough. They left, and I fell asleep thinking about the serious traveling I was finally prepared to do, and my most dreaded crossing: from St. Vincent to St. Lucia.

The next day I sailed toward Baleine (Whale) Bay, the slight indentation in the island's tapered, northern tip which I intended to use as springboard for the crossing. I kept a mile offshore, out of Soufriere's wind shadow. As I approached the latitude of Baleine, headwinds curled around the volcano, building nervous seas. The forested mountain rose starkly from the sea. I reefed and sailed toward it, down the long, advancing troughs, like walking through the revolving tunnel at an amusement park.

Baleine Bay was the seaward extension of a narrow gorge containing a small stream. The only improvement was a mooring buoy. It was reassuring to have a safe moorage, but there was a better way. At the mouth of the gorge was a narrow beach over which the stream flowed, as if over a weir, into the sea. Fresh and salt water collided in a confusion of waves and sheet flows, but the scale was manageable. I landed, lightened my boat, and pulled her up into the stream, which was barely deep enough to float her. The stream centrifuged around a concavity in the smooth cliff that made up the north side of the gorge. The trickle cut too tight a corner to negotiate, so I dredged sand with my hands. When the channel was wide enough I pulled *Squeak* into a lagoon the size of a large bedroom, and parked her on its seaward side.

The lagoon was cooler than the sea. A rainstorm hit, and quickly passed. Wearing only swim trunks, I walked up the gorge to a mist-filled chamber, the upstream wall of which was a fifty-foot waterfall. Smooth, wet stone paneled the chamber's walls. Ferns glistened in the flats and clefts. The water fell into a cupped pool. I dove in, opened my eyes, and saw the falling water penetrate the pool like reverse geysers, white with captured air. I surfaced into the falling water, mouth open and downward-facing to scavenge air. Water pummeled my scalp and shoulders, yanked my eyelids, stung my skin. A thunder filled my ears.

I replaced a deformed oarlock socket, then went to bed. St. Lucia lay twenty-five miles to the northeast, my widest windward crossing. Two days before I had seen its Pitons, the twin, needle-like peaks on its southwest coast.

October 27 dawned too hazy to see the Pitons. I launched at 6:30 A.M., and was soon in the full force of the maelstrom. Even with the main reefed and ten gallons of water ballast beside me, I had trouble keeping *Squeak* on her feet. She plowed into waves and belly-flopped off their crests, yet stubbornly held her course. Spray stung my face. My neck stiffened from twisting to the right to see the oncoming waves. I steered for the fleeting paths of smoothness between the rising and dropping surfaces, but new waves cropped up all the time. They sometimes broke over me, dumping a few gallons into the cockpit. But for every gallon that came over the windward gunwale, four came over the leeward gunwale. *Squeak* half-capsized several times, filling her cockpit. The weight of the water stopped her in her tracks. I just bailed and kept on sailing, frantically working the sheets and tiller.

The Pitons came into view as St. Vincent disappeared behind me. Other sailboats passed, their skippers eyeing me through binoculars. St. Lucia's various visible parts slowly coalesced. Having pinched into the direction of the wind, I was now able to bear off a little, increasing speed. At noon I started to enjoy the protection of the new island's lee. At 1:30 I reached its southwest point, for an average speed of four knots. The crossing had taken seven hours, three less than expected. *Squeak* had performed magnificently.

Rosy with success, I rowed into Anse des Pitons, the bay between the twin Matterhorn-like peaks. The view was that of a vast emerald amphitheater—breathtaking—but a hoity-toity hotel had claimed the entire beach. "Guests Only," said the signs. At the dock a sleek helicopter touched down beside a glitzy mega-yacht. Its rotors chopped the air. The thunder of its turbines ricocheted from slope to slope.

The map showed a customs station in the town of Soufriere, on the next bay up. En route, youths in outboard-powered boats with tomahawk prows swerved within a hair's breadth of me. Another bumped alongside, grabbed onto my gunwale, and callously looked *Squeak* and me over, probably wondering how to make money off me, then zoomed away. As I cruised along a seaside slum on the town's outskirts, loafers in ragged clothes yelled and waved at me to come over. Soufriere itself loomed, a lackluster French colonial town, full of streaky gray stonework. Loose cobbles covered a short, steep beach. A fleet of skiffs lay side-by-side beyond reach of waves. Already a mob was swarming. I got my passport and papers out before landing, so no one would see their hiding place, and covered up my compass with a little tent-shaped sign that said "Look, don't touch" on both sides.

I beached, and ten men brusquely yanked *Squeak* up into a gap between two boats. "Thanks!" I said. Men and boys pressed all around. They jockeyed for control, and flooded me with questions. I answered them while locking my hatches. Then I left *Squeak* to fend for herself, and found my way to the police station, three blocks away.

Behind the counter was a young duty officer in a stiff, blue uniform. A man and woman stood submissively before him.

"And at what time did you come home to find your door locked, sir?"

I couldn't make out his response.

"And you broke your door open and you hit her, is that it? What, with your fists?" He jotted notes in a ledger.

While the policeman took their statements, slapping sounds emanated from a room behind him, and muffled human cries. The wails seemed to express not so much pain as mindless, animal woe.

After the man and wife left I presented myself. "Hello. I'm on a boat, coming from St. Vincent, and I need to clear in."

The policeman frowned. He thumbed through a couple of manuals, made some phone calls. It was two hours later, and nearly dusk, before he had an answer.

"Sir? Customs says you must pay $25 E.C. for a 'Permit to Moor in Waters Other Than Port.' The permit is good for only twenty-four hours. Tomorrow you can enter officially in Marigot Harbour."

This disappointed me; why pay $10 US for one night? So I got out a snapshot of *Squeak* and put on my most forlorn and penniless expression.

"Please, you don't understand. It's just a little rowboat, not a yacht. Can you pretend I never walked in here? I'll just go back out to sea and enter Marigot tomorrow." I presented my case with utmost respect, anxious to avoid joining whoever was being beaten in the back room.

"Go on then," he said finally.

Eager to make myself as inconspicuous as possible, I rowed *Squeak* to a dark corner of Soufriere Bay and anchored a few yards off shore. Now a muscular black wearing nothing but athletic shorts started yelling from the beach, "Cap! Hey Cap!" He waved at me to come to him. To get my attention he experimented with various words, moods, tones, interjections, jumps, and claps, although I was obviously aware if his presence and ignoring him. He tried to get me to come ashore the same way he would try to catch a fish: patiently, to the utmost of his cunning, until he either caught the fish or something more promising came along. He was no more embarrassed that I ignored him than he would be embarrassed at not catching a fish. Finally some buddies came along and he forgot all about me, screwing around with them in high humor: snatches of song, lewd little dances, gymnastic feats. His mouth never stopped. Then some men in a skiff came along and set a net that arced from one point on shore to another, and he got involved in that too, adding his lusty voice to the welter of commands and recriminations that made up their decision-making process.

A rainstorm conveniently washed the saltwater off me as night deepened. I hung the foul weather gear over the boom to dry and tuned in to the biomechanics of moving heavy boxes around in a small, tippy boat. It was awkward, but there was a best way, a certain series of small moves from one balance point to the next. My new stowage system had made life much easier. Despite the crossing, the rainstorm, and a water container that had leaked several quarts, my stuff had stayed dry. Wonderful!

The airs were light the next day as I worked north in the island's lee. I stayed within a few yards of shore to get shade from the morning sun, and for diversion. The water was full of submerged rocks, fallen long ago from the eroding bluff. It delighted me to see the bottom through the crystalline water, and *Squeak's* shadow moving across it.

Fishermen buzzed by, five young males per boat. One stood in the bow with a sheaf of dry stalks in his hand. Occasionally he broke off a piece and dropped it in the water as a marker. When they had decided on a spot the first swimmer put on his mask and jumped in with the end of the net, while the motorman steered the boat the other way, in a circle, throwing net out with his free hand. Two more swimmers jumped in at intervals. They kept the circle in shape, watched the fish, and pounded the water with their fists. Meanwhile, the bow spotter threw stones ahead and outside of the boat's path to herd fish in the desired direction. The swimmers, mere boys, were especially beautiful. The sight of their bodies brought back memories of my freshman year of high school, when I turned out for wrestling, and watched muscles poke up all over my body, like painful flowers.

I tacked into Marigot Harbour at midday. It was a deep inlet, a pistol-shot wide, with steep flanks and a mangrove swamp at its head. It had remained undeveloped until a few years before when Moorings, the charter boat company, built a complex there. At the main landing, inside his little post, a customs official handed me a form without taking his eyes off the TV soap opera he was watching. Formalities concluded, I ignored posh restaurants on either side of the bay, and patronized instead a woman in a plywood booth. Hotel employees and souvenir salesmen sat around her on the beach sand, eating her stew of dasheen, plantain, and salt fish. I joined them. Next to me, a weaver of palm-frond hats, unable to afford even her prices, fried sardines on a stove fashioned from a steel wheel rim, set over burning charcoal. My fellow diners spoke some sort of French Creole, but switched to English when I addressed them.

At sunset, while refreshing myself with a row around the harbor, I noticed an old cutter-rigged yacht nestled stern-first into a leafy bank. Its American owners noticed me too. "We sailed in here in 1972 and haven't left since," said the man, after I'd told him my story. His plump face was covered with white whiskers.

"Yeah, we got barnacles on top of our barnacles," his wife added from under a straw hat. "Not like Tom there." She indicated a man running a circular saw on the dock next door to them. "He's a Johnny-come-lately. If you need a place to tie up tonight, you should talk to him. He can show you a better time than we could."

"Thanks. I'll do that."

Tom looked up from his work as I pulled alongside the dock. Switching off the saw, he brushed his hands on his jeans and walked over. The chest that showed though his partly unbuttoned, long-sleeve shirt was pockmarked and sunken, but his gait was purposeful.

"Yes, can I help you?" His lips moved economically under a gray mustache.

"Hi, I'm just passing through, and your neighbors said you might let me tie up to your dock."

"Sure," he said, with a nod. The voice was Texan, deep and affable, but I sensed an inner reserve. "Where you coming from, anyhow?"

I talked a while, then he said, "Me, I'm overseeing construction of a guest house further up this bank. Been here six months now. Pleased to have the company. Well hey, it's happy hour, isn't it? Come on in, have a drink with me."

We entered a small dockhouse. It had the feel of a cabin in the plains: tight little kitchen, bathroom, and bedroom with two single beds separated by a bed stand with a lamp on it. We pulled up chairs at the kitchen table. He poured himself a scotch and water and treated me to a can of cold beer.

"I built this place first," he said. "I'm staying here while the main house goes up."

"What'll you do when it's all done?"

"Oh, I may stick around and manage the place. The owner's a little up in the air about a few things. Not going back to the States, though, that's for sure. Gawd, I'm fed up with it up there. Politicians! I'm a Ross Perot man myself. Not that he stands a snowball's chance in hell of getting elected. He's too honest."

Tom looked away when he spoke bitterly, and back at me when his pendulum tipped toward hospitality and contact. He fixed us some hamburgers, and washed the dishes with a lemon-scented dish soap. The sky through the kitchen window was starry now.

"You keep a neat house," I said. "I like that."

"Phew," he puffed, and sat back down. "I had enough of wildness in my day. I'm just seeing if I can't resurrect something of the man in me. A man's a tidy animal, if he ain't poked at too much." He pulled on his drink, set it down, and swirled it on the table. "You ever own a motorcycle, Steve?"

"As a matter of fact, I've got a BMW 650 waiting for me at home. Far as I know she's being faithful to me."

"Haw! Yeah. Well, when I was seventeen I bought this Harley. Chopped it. Rebuilt it nine times. Painted it a different color every couple years. I ran with the bad boys. Went to some party once, got plastered, and caught this guy trying to steal my bike. People were always trying to steal my bike. It was the fastest around, and everybody knew it. So I shot him."

"You shot him?"

"Yeah. Hell, I shot two other guys trying to steal it before that. I just got in a whole lot more trouble the third time. Hurt him worse. He died eventually."

"So were you really bad, or did you just hang out with the wrong crowd?"

"Wrong crowd, for sure. I didn't exactly redeem myself either, but I usually worked for a living. I was an honest husband, a couple of times. Two divorces, I mean. Anyway, they put me in prison for killing a nobody we're all better off without." He chuckled wryly. "A nobody killing a nobody. This time the system was really pissed. Gawd. They hauled me in front of this board every year and played games with me, dangled their freedom in front of my nose. I told 'em to fuck off. Then they paroled me, and I went through the same thing with the parole board. They were determined to break me. I guess they finally did, in a way. Anyway, I saw I wasn't going anywhere, so six months ago"—his voice paused, his cheek muscles worked—"I sold the Harley. I'd had her thirty years. Took this job."

I felt his pain, and told him so.

"And here I am, like I lost my religion and I'm making up a new one. And here you are, a friggin' world traveler in a twelve-foot boat, asking if you can tie up to my dock for the night."

"Yeah."

"You can sleep in the spare bed, is what you can do. If you can handle the light being on. I read a lot."

We went to Castries together the next day, he for building materials, I for a pair of sunglasses and to mail letters. As we walked to the highway he talked with St. Lucians he had dealings with. He was good with them: personable, patient, not naive. On the highway we caught a van going the wrong way. "They're full on the way back," explained Tom. The van meandered through banana orchards, climbed a rural hillside, and turned around. On the way back it filled up with people who greeted each other familiarly. The road became congested with new Japanese compacts. A few miles north of Marigot we dropped down a steep ridge into a town. "Castries, population about fifty thousand," said Tom.

I had heard bad things about Castries, the capital of St. Lucia, but it seemed tame enough. We had lunch in a restaurant such as might cater to office workers in an American city, and bought dinner makings from an old lady seated behind a hunk of plywood covered with produce. The city was more modern than old, but the old parts interested me more, especially the cast-iron, turn-of-the-century public market and its surrounding district of sidewalk vendors and hole-in-the-wall shops. The red, yellow, and green symbolizing Haile Salassie and Rastafarianism showed up on baseball caps, plastic shoes, car decals. Young bloods greeted each other with the knuckles-to-knuckles, thumb-to-thumb press, like a clinking of glasses. The sudden gust blew that always meant rain would hit in about one minute. I stood under the shelter of a marquee by the taxi stand and waited for Tom to get back from the paint store.

Tom's hospitality was to my taste. "I'm not waiting on you," he said. "You just make yourself at home." I did, for a second night. Then there wasn't any reason to stay longer.

I shook his hand. The grip was rock solid. "Thanks, Tom."

"Any time," he said. Then he pulled his tool belt on and trudged up the hill.

I made it to Rodney Bay that day, stopping first at the ruins of Admiral Rodney's Naval Station, on a promontory at the bay's entrance. It had been an extensive military complex for its day, and the focal point of the drawn-out conflict between the French and the British. St. Lucia exchanged hands fourteen times before Britain finally prevailed. But France kept Martinique. From those lofty battlements the latter island looked close, due north across a twenty-four-mile passage.

I tacked up the narrow channel into the marina, keeping both leeboards down for lack of time to shift them, and tied to the dinghy dock at the center of a large complex. It was the international yachting scene at its zenith: hundreds of boats, flags from all over, yachters in crisp whites. I chatted with a quirky Brit named Marcus, who sailed a centerboard ketch. I flirted with a buxom German girl but she and her traveling companion had already fixed themselves up with local studs. In the end I spent the evening with a hyperactive Majorcan named Juanito. He saw my *El Viaje de Squeak* map on the aft hatch cover, and launched eagerly into Spanish. Before the night was over he wore me out with his emotional long-windedness. A year before, his dear father, a taciturn old fisherman, had shattered Juanito's life by throwing himself down a well. "Worse yet," he said, "he chose *my* well to do it in. Now why would a man who spent his life on the sea choose that particular means of suicide? And why my well and not my brother's?" I felt like I had come upon the scene of a bizarre accident with no knowledge of first aid. Not only was I unable to ease the suffering, I wasn't sure if the drama was a tragedy or a grotesque comedy.

The following morning, Saturday, October 31, the Rodney Bay customs office was crowded. A fleet of boats had sailed down from Martinique to race in a regatta, and their captains were plunking down stacks of passports and filling up all available space on their crew list forms. I laid down one passport and used a lot less ink. Where the clearance form asked for tonnage I wrote, with unnecessary accuracy, ".125."

An official frowned. "Scratch that out and just write 1," he said.

CHAPTER 25

MARTINIQUE AND DOMINICA

It was eleven A.M., a little late to start a wide crossing, but I quickly rounded the old fort and set a course for Cul-de-Sac Du Marin. The wind was south of east, so for the first time my sheets didn't have to be all the way in. Right in the middle a black squall passed. The ocean seemed to become a plain of ashes from which the downpour raised wisps of smoke that blew off before the wind. I reefed, fearful, but the squall only twisted the wind more in my favor, and by nightfall I had anchored in the calm water off Le Marin.

It was an affluent town of red tile roofs. Nobody mobbed me when I docked at the waterfront park. The natives were mulattos of all shades, the architecture French provincial. Renaults, Peugeots, and Citroens made squeaky sounds as their tires negotiated the narrow, well-paved streets. Sunday Mass was being given in the cathedral on top of the hill—I peeked through the massive doorway into a twilight full of solemn worshippers, and a smell of sweat and incense. In the corner grocery store a single banana cost five francs. I sat on a park bench and brushed up on my high-school French with a young couple from mainland France who were living on a small sailboat. They were like birds: lovely little people with clear, intelligent faces, full of nervous energy.

I proceeded west along the island's south coast, ecstatic to be sailing downwind in calm water. I scanned the successive beaches for pretty girls, my binoculars finally coming in handy. I saw some teenagers playing frisbee, landed, and joined the game. I answered their questions about my voyage, and watched the revelation flash on their faces. "Can life really be so free?" they seemed to ask.

The hills were low and green, the coast shoal and encrusted with coral. Fish traps littered the sea floor, each marked by a Clorox bottle on a string. I stood to keep better lookout, and dipped into each cove. I saw family picnics, and fishing villages, their colorful boats all home to roost. Then came that delicious time of day when I could take off my sunglasses and cap, and the light and temperature were perfect.

I stopped at the first west-facing bay. Nine other yachts were already there, their owners either well-to-do *Martiniquais* or transplants from mainland France. They asked me if I had heard of D'Abboville, the famous French solo ocean-rower, just as the Swedes at the Friendship Bay Hotel had asked if I knew Sven Lundin, *their* eccentric small boat hero. I cooked and slept at anchor, in long pants and sweatshirt. The nights were getting cool. I had lost my sleeping bag in Grenada, and discarded my leaky air mattress in Cali. A folded blanket under my torso sufficed, because *Squeak* held me like cupped hands.

Anse Mitan, across the roadstead from Fort-de-France, looked like the Riviera, with its beach hotels and pampered palm trees. I tacked up through the crowded anchorage and cruised the beach line, seeing and being seen. Then I tied to the *Mara*, the centerboarder I had noticed in Rodney Bay.

"Oh yes, the little boat. Good show! Come on aboard, have a rum and coke with me," said her owner, Marcus. He was a stringy, stooped fellow with spectacles and unruly hair, like a nerdy schoolboy suddenly pushing forty. His voice reminded me of that of Rex Harrison in *My Fair Lady:* very British, very cultured.

"Thanks," I said. "You remember me from St. Lucia, right?"

"Yes, and St. Vincent, too. You had a woman with dark hair with you, and particularly attractive legs, as I recall."

"Meg."

"Yes yes. I didn't see how the two of you could fit into that thing. What in the dickens did you do at night?"

I filled Marcus in on my sleeping arrangements, with and without company, while running my eyes over *Mara.* "She reminds me of this cathedral I saw in Panama City," I said. "Lovely, but a little run-down, if you don't mind my saying so."

He flushed, either from annoyance or shame. "*Mara.* Yes, well I'm bringing her back, slowly but surely. Had a new deck put on her by those rascals in Carriacou. God what a hassle! Ended up replacing the mast step too—rot everywhere, simply everywhere. Now if I can just make it up to St. Martin I'll get to work on this bloody cabin top. *Mara* was specially built in Nova Scotia, as a yacht for the captain of a fishing schooner. In 1956. Something to knock around in after a hard week fishing in the Grand Banks, I suppose. There's more seaworthiness in her bowsprit than in a whole fleet of these plastic bathtubs." He grimaced at the sleek yachts that lay anchored all around us, facing into the wind, their halyards slapping against their aluminum masts.

I liked him. "Where you from, Marcus?"

"I'm Scottish, actually." He crossed his legs, puffed off his cigarette, and cackled softly. "Oh, I'm very patriotic. You would be too if your money came from what was originally the Johnny Walker fortune. Me mum's grandad made a fortune in Scotch, see, and the family's lived off it ever since. I almost feel like a traitor drinking rum, but, when in Rome do as the Romans. Anyway, I get just a pittance now, enough to keep me in cigarettes, but I'll come into quite a bundle if my auntie ever dies, poor thing. She's a German baroness, believe it or not. Ho ho! And a dyke to boot. She and her old 'companion,' sipping tea in a castle in the Rhineland. Quite amusing, really." Marcus laughed nervously and stared into space.

The restaurants were all far too expensive for me so I ate from my stores aboard *Squeak,* and slept tied to *Mara's* stern. In the semi-privacy of first light I performed my toilet using rainwater collected in the cockpit. When Marcus woke, at nine, he offered me a tow into Fort-de-France.

It was the only Eastern Caribbean capital I would unreservedly call a city. Its downtown, on a small river delta, was dwarfed by suburban hills. Marcus and I split up at the harbor. He reacquainted with an old buddy named Hans, whom he saw on an anchored boat, while I tied up in the only space left at the dinghy dock. Peculiar air bubbles were surfacing there, like those from a scuba diver. I didn't think much of it.

I got a map of Martinique and roamed a grid of crowded streets. The buildings were common-wall, of even façade, two or three stories high. Parked cars covered the sidewalks. Fashion shops dominated the retail mix. A huge tricolor flag waved over the massive ramparts of Fort St. Louis, still an active military base.

I returned to the dock and was remarking to some bystanders upon the air bubbles surfacing under *Squeak's* stern when they erupted into a cone-shaped geyser six feet tall! It lifted *Squeak* and slammed her around like a toy, filling her cockpit with water. As I released the docking lines to rescue her the geyser sank back down into the water, leaving not even the telltale bubbles as proof that anything unusual had occurred. "What the heck was that?" I asked. Nobody knew.

"I'll be continuing north with Hans as soon as our plans clarify," said Marcus when I stopped by the *Mara.* "He seems to think we can make some money buying a load of French wine here, where there's no duty, and selling it in Antigua."

"Okay, we'll probably see you down the road, then."

I continued to St. Pierre, in the north of the island. This was the old capital of the French West Indies, destroyed by an eruption of Mount Pelee in 1902. Only one man survived, a prisoner in an underground cell. In the twinkle of an eye he leaped from a life of petty crime to a distinguished career with Barnum and Bailey's Circus, showing his burn scars to audiences all over the world. The city had thirty thousand inhabitants at the time of the eruption, and was famous for its picturesque streetscapes. In the historical museum I found this passage, written by a nineteenth-century traveler:

> No street is absolutely level; nearly all climb hills, turn, and describe brusque angles. Some are very steep, and at their base can be seen the blue sea, as if from the top of a cliff.

The museum displayed what were once boxes of nails, melted into lumps of iron by the blast. The citizens died in a ball of fiery gases. The ships in the harbor all capsized and burned. The shock wave sliced heavy stone buildings off at the level of their ground floor window sills. With no one left to pick up the pieces, the city never recovered. Most of the ruins were left in place. Rubble was recycled into retaining walls and road ballast. A few buildings were rebuilt—the boundary between the old stonework, below the sills, and the new, above, was clearly discernible. Eventually a smaller town sprang up, with little tie to the old.

I improved my mooring at the town dock by throwing my anchor out sideways to hold *Squeak* off, and by running stretchy bow and stern lines to restrain her against the forward-and-backward surge. Mt. Pelee loomed ominously over the town. Every now and then, sudden as the slap of an angry bear, a blast of wind slammed *Squeak* to one side or the other. It was the trade winds, eddying over the green and rust-colored volcano. I mixed a rum punch and enjoyed the sunset, chatting with the locals on the dock.

In the morning I was ready to leave for Dominica when a French singlehander, whom I had met in Anse Mitan, rowed up in his dinghy.

"I'm going to climb Mount Pelee, want to come?" asked Jean-Philippe, a merry Frenchman with brown eyes and rosy cheeks that protruded over a black beard.

"Sure!"

"*Fantastique!* Come on!"

We caught a bus to the village of Morne Rouge (Red Hill), on a ridge extending south from the volcano. Soon we were climbing steeply through moss and ferns. Wind-driven mist chilled us. We discovered a tarantula crawling slowly over reddish scree. On a path to our right, a mongoose eyed us warily. Jean-Philippe climbed briskly, the muscles of his tanned calves bulging in front of me as we ascended.

Unlike Soufriere, the top of Mt. Pelee was a vast pattern of broken calderas, false summits, boulders and crevices—dark, wet rock in infinite shapes. We picked our way to a slab projecting over the mountain's western slope. The chaotic wind was visible in a light rain that swirled about in restless parabolas. The cloud cover broke. Suddenly we had an unobstructed view of the Caribbean from 4,800 feet. It looked like a dull blue wall, as tall as the mountain on which we stood.

"Too cold to stay long time, isn't it?" said Jean-Philippe, bouncing up and down on the balls of his feet. "This is my third time up, and always before I go down the way I came. This time I would like to go down the west side, by the village of Le Prêcheur. *Ça va* (Okay)?"

"*Ça va.* After you."

I struggled to keep up as we descended a slick trail through wet, hip-high brush. The cheap shoes I had bought in Port of Spain were falling apart. At the tree line the trail became a concrete road that boldly followed the fall line the rest of the way down, with horizontal grooves for traction. Jean-Philippe filled our rucksacks with windfallen guavas and avocados, and picked small oranges from a tree. "They would otherwise go to waste," he said. "In Strasbourg, where I was a chef, I would die for such fresh fruit. Here, where it hangs heavy from all the trees, the *Martiniquais* don't eat them. But I love this tropical fruit! That's why I am searching for land, to build a farm. It must be on one of the mountainous islands. The low ones don't have enough rainfall."

In Le Prêcheur, where a plaque commemorated the birthplace of Josephine, Napoleon's wife, we caught a bus back to St. Pierre. I dined with Jean-Philippe on his wooden ketch, devoting half my attention to his talk of buying land and half to his chart of Dominica. It was more detailed than mine, so I transferred notes. Tomorrow I would make the crossing.

It was my widest passage yet, but also my most off-the-wind. I steered ten degrees east of my target to counteract the west-setting current, and romped along on a beam-reach at five knots. There was still plenty of motion, but less bailing, and none of the decelerations and belly-flops associated with sailing into oncoming waves. Dominica's multi-peaked outline grew until I rounded a promontory at the southwest corner of the island.

It was Friday, and I wanted to clear customs in Roseau, the capital, before the weekend hit. After the roller-coaster crossing, rowing into a light headwind was tedious. The island was as steep underwater as above, resulting in a rocky shoreline with few beaches. A road hugged the coast, connecting a string of villages. I stopped for directions at the Anchorage Hotel, on Roseau's outskirts, then rounded the flat bulge on which the town sits. At 4:15 I docked at the main terminal, where a ship with "GEEST" painted hugely on its sides was loading bananas.

I found the officer in charge, a tall, stern policeman.

"How long do you intend to stay in Dominica?"

"Thirty days, please," I replied, knowing "I don't know" is unacceptable.

"What will be your address during your stay here?"

"I'll be staying on my boat."

He eyed me suspiciously "You live on a twelve-foot boat?"

"Yes."

"How long is your vacation for?"

"I left home two years ago."

His composure broke. "How is it you have two years of leave?" he snapped, as if shattered by the idea that everyone did not have a fixed place in society. Just as quickly, he recovered. Tearing his eyes from me, he grabbed a form and wrote out a permit. "This is good for the weekend. You will present yourself at the Customs office, downtown, Monday morning. They'll give you an extension."

"But I don't want to wait in Roseau…"

"That's Monday morning, the Customs office. Any questions?"

"No. Thanks."

The Anchorage Hotel was a better place to spend the weekend. I rowed back there and slept at their dock, which had the same surge as the dock in St. Pierre. *Squeak* surged with it, smoothly, regularly, forward and back, as if tethered fore and aft by rubber bands. The sensation was strangely pleasant.

Roseau had retained more of its character than the other West Indian capitals. Dominica was the final refuge of the Carib Indians, therefore the last island to be settled by whites. Roseau never became a center of power or sophistication. Its nineteenth-century architecture had been preserved, if somewhat shabbily, by the lack of any reason to replace it. I saw brick buildings, plank cottages on mortared-cobble foundations, and cheek-to-jowl shops. Locals thronged the streets, not tourists. I walked fast and purposefully, to be more safe, and out of habit. The public was not admitted inside the ancient post office; one got one's mail through a wire-mesh window. There was enough money around for Levi jeans and Almond Joy bars, but not enough for Calvin Kleins or French restaurants.

The Botanical Garden was a welcome retreat: a vast expanse of clean lawn where I could sit and eat a cucumber sandwich in the shade of ancient trees from Surinam, Sumatra, and Singapore. I then strolled through a corner of the garden and saw three large, green-blue-and-red birds. They sat quietly together on sticks simulating the branches of a forest, under the shade of a metal roof, behind a wire fence. They were the Dominican parrot, the national bird, almost extinct. Time seemed to stand still inside that cage. I had seen the process underway in the Orinoco Delta, and this was the end: captured or killed, until only a handful are left, and we put them in a cage and bestow honors on them.

"Give me a dollar. Give me a dollar." I wheeled around. It was a young beggar with an imbecilic smile.

"I don't give money."

"Give me a cigarette."

"No! Go away!"

He edged closer, reached around me, and touched my daypack. I bluffed a lunge at him and he cringed, still smiling pathetically. I walked away, but the same kid panhandled me again at the hotel, fawning, never taking no for an answer. He disgusted me, as did my pointless anger at him.

Sunday morning I made my diary entry sitting Indian style on the cabin floor, my back against the main bulkhead. The hotel started to come alive. Diving instructors prepped their boats. Guests opened sliding glass doors to sit in deck chairs facing the sun. Nearly three weeks had passed since leaving Bequia. My "early to bed, early to rise" regimen had leveled out my metabolism. Constant exercise had toned me up. I had been wearing my black swim briefs twenty-four hours a day, only occasionally slipping long pants over them. Spray, swims, and rain kept me clean. The sky had been cloudy enough to prevent sunburn, yet sunny enough to tan me and bleach my hair. I felt like yelling, "Hey women, I don't get any better than this! What are you waiting for?" But I didn't see anyone to yell it to. The end of the voyage was closer, but still far away. It was about the right distance away.

I had planned to hike up to the Boiling Lake that day, but my calves still ached from climbing Mount Pelee. Instead I rowed north of Roseau to explore the Layou River. By midday I was looking up a narrow valley between parallel ridges. Gospel singing boiled out of a stone church in a village near its mouth. I couldn't see over the top of the beach, but I suspected from the lack of trees behind that it concealed a large lagoon. The waves were intense at the foot of the natural spillway where the lagoon emptied into the sea. I dismounted when it was shallow enough to wade, and some boys who had been swimming there helped me pull *Squeak* up through the thigh-deep current. One stayed on to guide me through the lagoon and up into the slow-moving river. A mile up, I tied to a palm tree and made sandwiches while my friend rustled up some coconuts and opened them with my machete.

After we had lunched I continued alone past the coastal highway bridge, until blocked by overhanging trees and shallow water. Seventy-five yards upstream, a Rasta man with rippling muscles and a slim, bare-breasted girl were lathering and lovemaking in the river. He hugged her from behind, ready to do it right there, but she slipped away, gently restraining him. I watched them from the right bank, unseen, through a screen of vegetation.

Behind me stood the ruins of a large sugar mill. A crumbling power house held an iron wheel twenty feet in diameter, its bottom half in a diversion trough littered with the decayed wood that had once been the wheel's paddles. River stones had been mortared together and their exposed surfaces cut smooth to create a river wall, an aqueduct, and a vat house with arched windows. The investment paid for a century or two, then the roofs collapsed, trees grew up, and vines and roots crept over the walls. Will our modern mills and power plants fade as gracefully?

I rowed back out the river and a mile further up the coast, to a hotel on whose beach I could safely leave *Squeak*. Tomorrow would be Monday, time to get my visa extended. While in Roseau I also hoped to have my oarlocks reconditioned by a machinist.

In the morning, as I removed the bolts securing oars to oarlocks, a woman in a black one-piece suit emerged from an early swim. Stopping on the damp sand at the water's edge, she leaned left then right, toweling her shoulder-length blond hair, then straightened and smiled at me. I approached her, oars in hand.

"Excuse me. I don't have any way of securing these oars while I go into town today. Any chance you could keep them in your room?"

"Of course, I'd be glad to."

I took a bus into Roseau, resolved visa and oarlocks, and returned in the afternoon. She greeted me with the same smile and invited me in. The balcony door was open, allowing the sea air to blow through. Her bed was neatly made. Yellow and red flowers stood in a vase on the end table.

"I'm Angela, by the way, from Berlin."

"Hi. My name's Steve, from Seattle, Washington. Know where that is?"

"Of course. Where you make your Boeing airplanes, nay?"

"You got it. Hey, want me to put a punch together? I bought some fruit in town." I'd done so with this moment in mind.

"That sounds marvelous!"

"Okay, let me get my machete."

Soon we were opening coconuts, squeezing oranges, and pouring from a bottle of Trois Rivieres rum. Angela got some ice from the manager. Then we sat on her balcony, she in a chaise lounge, I in a deck chair facing her, and sipped. "Oh, now this is really delicious!" she said, her face animated, playful. I wore my olive walking shorts and white T-shirt. She had on a silk robe that revealed shapely legs. Her waist was narrow. She was about forty, with blue-green eyes, a fine nose, and prominent yet delicate cheekbones and chin.

I told her my story, then asked, "What brings *you* to Dominica?"

The smile wilted. "Well, you see my husband is Dominican. I raised two daughters before I met him, but we thought it might be good to have a child together. So three years ago we adopted a nine-year-old Dominican girl, the daughter of someone he grew up with. Camilla, that's the girl's name. We loved her very much. At first all went well. We sent her to a good school and gave her every opportunity. But she eventually become quite hostile, especially to me."

"Why?"

"Oh, she rejected our white culture and demanded we return her to her true family."

"Is she old enough to make a decision like that?"

"You don't understand. She was making our life a hell. 'Camilla,' we said, 'you must decide this very carefully. We can't allow you to go back and forth, changing your mind. If we take you back, that's it, no second chance.' Still she demanded. Then my relationship with my husband became also bad, and now we are separated. I fought for a long time to keep us three together, but there was nothing to do."

"You mean—"

"I yesterday gave my Camilla back to her first mother. This woman has ten other children and no husband! She runs a rum shop in a small village. Now Camilla is living back there again!" Tears streaked down her face. She brushed them away, then smiled stoically.

"When's your return flight?" I asked, wondering how to cheer her up.

"Thursday."

"Would you like to sail with me to Portsmouth, on the north end of the island? It won't be very comfortable, but I'll take you there safely. We can have some fun."

"That sounds good, Steve. Really good. Can I tell you in the morning what I decide?"

"Sure." I leaned over and stroked the back of her head. "Now, I'd better turn in."

In the morning she greeted me with a bright hug. "Yes, I go with you, Steve," she said. "Never in my life am I so sure of something." And off we sailed with an extraordinary pleasure in each other's company. The sea was warm and calm. While I sailed, Angela sat counterbalancing me.

"Comfortable?" I asked.

"Oh, I'm just loving this." She inhaled deeply, nostrils flaring in the breeze. "Although my memories of the sea are good and bad. My father was an officer on a U-boat, you see, before I was born. The war did something to him, made him cold and bitter." She told me how her mother had come from an aristocratic Prussian family, but the shortage of men after the war forced her to marry below her station. When Angela was little they'd had a sailboat on the Baltic Sea, but she hated their outings because her father made her repeat commands and shout, "Aye aye, captain," like in the navy. At sixteen she left home and joined the student-worker revolts then sweeping Europe. She served as a courier for the Bader-Meinhof terrorist group, and married the leader of a revolutionary party. Then her husband became a drug addict. She lost interest in politics. She raised two daughters while secretly working as a call girl, choosing her clients, making good money. She put herself through acting school, divorced her husband, and at thirty began a new career. She became a TV news reporter, then hosted a popular dating game show. When she could no longer stand the lack of privacy she switched to voice-dubbing, and progressed to her current job as sound director for cinema. "My life has never been easy," she said. "I've never chosen the conventional way. But in everything I do I am very professional and proud, even my call-girl business. Especially now, I love my work. Always I have survived. I sense this in you too, Steve."

We tacked into Prince Rupert Bay, where Angela took a room at the Coconut Beach Hotel. We allowed the management to think I would sleep aboard *Squeak*. Actually I spent the night in her room.

The next day we rowed up the Indian River, at the head of the bay. It was wilder and more intimate than the Layou, with a marsh at its delta, and heavy swamp cypress lining its banks. We worked our way in until the river became a winding brook in a bed recessed several feet below the forest floor. Among the bed's pebbles I found a smooth pink shell like a child's fingernail, and gave it to Angela—she cherished it. We enjoyed the closeness of the forest, and each other, until late afternoon, then allowed the current to drift us back out to the mouth. Out in the broad bay, the wind took over, drifting us slowly out to sea. The scenery changed like a long movie. We watched it lazily, comfortable together. The sun slid out of the sky, and where it went down a furnace of light built up, to the zenith, and past, yellow to orange to red to violet to blue. The furnace stopped, cooled. The flames receded. Each tint, in the same order, slowly drowned in the ocean, pressed there by an invading blackness, punctured by stars.

That night Angela woke up crying, got out of bed, and felt her way across the room. A moment later she returned and pressed back into me as she'd lain before, her backside to my front, cupped. She no longer seemed frightened.

I lay my arm around her. "What was it?" I asked, sleepily.

"The shell. I dreamt I lost it, but it's still here. See?" Taking my hand she pressed a dull round edge into my palm. It was the little shell I'd given her. Then clenched it between her hands, brought them up to her chin, and went back to sleep.

Neither of us were cheery in the morning—it was Thursday. I gathered my belongings and stowed them aboard *Squeak* while Angela packed, then we met at the restaurant for juice. What to say? Her taxi came, we held each other, she left.

I needed to move around, so I followed the taxi onto the two-lane road and walked the way it had gone, toward Portsmouth, at the head of the bay. The quickness of our romance had left me dizzy. I needed to think.

Angela had talked for hours, intensely, intellectualizing her problems. "Joy is a great responsibility," she had said. "We must take seriously the erotic, sense everything, or we will have wasted our gift." "With myself I am honest, not with society." "Question, question everything." She had talked of these things too much, like she was filling space, or mending a tear in her soul. Sharing in it had drained me. I was relieved she was gone, and felt guilt at that relief. The shell—what did it represent? Her daughter, and what else? She couldn't have fallen in love with me so soon. Was it something she was afraid of losing, or something already lost?

The road crossed a small valley. To my left was the sea. To my right the valley led up into the foothills of Mount Diablotins. The sky was limpid, full of cool moisture from drifting showers. The setting sun cast its most golden glow. A rainbow arched across the valley, both legs firmly planted. It neither moved nor faded, but shone bravely, like a realistic hope. It was the same spectrum Angela and I had seen in the sunset the evening before. Its courage was also hers. For the first time I noticed how the colors complete one cycle from the inside of the visible band to the outside, like an octave of pitch, so I wrote it down:

red
red orange
orange
orange yellow
yellow
yellow green
green
green blue
blue
blue red (violet)
blue red (purple)
red

The following morning I returned to that valley and hiked up it. A dirt road ran through open meadow. I helped a farmer move a light shack away from the road, prying with poles and lifting while he set skidders. Then I continued through orchards of banana, passion fruit, and papaya. The road ended at a ford in the river, and continued as a trail on the left bank. I passed through unharvested coconut groves, where sprouting coconuts covered the forest floor. Yellow land crabs put up their dukes and edged away. Tracks led off to animal snares and secret plots.

I needed soothing, and hoped to find it in a hike in the rain forest. A map showed my trail cutting up to the left and following a ridge to the summit of Mount Diablotins, at four thousand feet. Instead it had disappeared in the bouldery stream. I'd seen no sign of a diverging trail, so I climbed straight up toward the top of the ridge. Maybe I would find the trail there.

The slope was forty-five degrees. Jagged hunks of hard gray stone protruded here and there from a thin layer of detritus. Fallen trunks and branches lay everywhere. The soil supported bright vines, ferns, and hardwood saplings. Flowers were few. A filmy lichen colored all the trunks green-gray. There were few branches except high up, where the trunks divided. The canopy obliterated all but a few specks of sky. The air smelled green.

I advanced slowly, clearing with my machete, seeking good holds. The thrill of being alone in wilderness overcame me, causing me to concentrate on my movements. I slashed unhurriedly, left, right. I adjusted the angle, tipped the blade, found the weak point in a hard stalk. The large-leafed succulents fell easily. I felt only slightly sorry for the destruction; the plants would quickly regenerate. Unable to see the top of the ridge I studied the opposite side of the valley. Knowing it was of comparable height, I estimated my distance to the top. The sky uphill from me began to show through at a lower angle, indicating decreasing slope.

The ridgetop was sharp and heavily wooded. I climbed a tree, jamming my hands and feet in the crotches. Much of the horizon was still obscured, but I saw my ridge and those on either side converge toward where I knew the mountain was. Now that I was immobile, mosquitoes homed in on me, back and forth, in high-pitched figure-eights. There wasn't any trail. It was midafternoon anyway, time to head back. My thoughts regarding Angela had settled. Everything would be okay—she was a survivor, like me.

I followed my track back down into the valley, ready to move on. With what remained of the day I rowed into the small town of Portsmouth to buy provisions and get my clearance for Guadeloupe. The market was a roofed, concrete slab. All available space was filled with piles of fresh-out-of-the-ground produce: taro root, banana, callaloo. Half the town was there, sitting beside their respective piles, milling around, trading, laughing. No danger of being introspective here—people gathered around *Squeak* and me, drawing me out, making new again the question-and-answer process that for me was already two years old.

"How you sleep, man?"

"How you cook?"

As I walked down Main Street in search of the immigration office, a bundle of rags on the sidewalk suddenly rolled and lifted itself a few inches. A grinning, toothless face appeared, a stubby hand twisted imploringly in the air. It was the face of a child—no, an ancient midget woman.

"Pleeease," she lilted, beaming sweetly.

I nodded a friendly "No," not breaking pace.

"Ayeeeee, sir!" she affirmed, cocking her head.

At the police station/immigration office I waited behind two German women reporting a stolen camera. "You've got to go to Customs first," he said when it was my turn, pointing to a pier a mile away. I rowed there and tied to a dock full of people engrossed in the drama of trying to unload panicky cattle from a cargo boat onto a truck. At the base of the dock I played yo-yo between two Customs men a quarter mile apart, each of whom insisted the other should take care of me. By the time one of them agreed to process me it was after four o'clock. "Sorry, you'll have to pay an overtime fee," he said.

"Nice timing," I grumbled.

In my comings and goings I had noticed the *Mara* at anchor in Portsmouth harbor, so I rowed there and knocked. "Oh yes, the little boat," muttered Marcus. "Come in."

The salon's ceiling was varnished. A huge centerboard trunk ran down the middle, separating the salon, to a height of four feet, into equal halves. Clothes, tools, and dirty dishes lay everywhere. Seated at a fold-up table, to starboard, was a husky, bristly-bearded man, about fifty, with tattoos all over his arms and chest. He was giggling convulsively, presumably about a story I had interrupted.

"You never really met Hans in Fort-de-France, did you?" asked Marcus.

The man perked up, and stared hungrily at the bottle of Trois Rivieres in my hand. "Already I like your friend, Marcus! He drinks good rum!"

Marcus picked through a cupboard until he found three reasonably clean cups, then poured us rum-and-cokes.

"So, you two are old friends?" I asked.

"We met first time in Brazil, right Marcus?" said Hans. "He helped me escape there by sailing beside me to French Guyana. We both had boats, see? But I had to get out of there quick because the police wanted me. No time to get food or water! I mean I had nothing, not even a map or compass, so I had to follow Marcus across ocean for four days and four nights, otherwise I'm lost. When I get hungry I go beside, and he throws me something to eat!" Again, his chest heaved with giggles, and his cheeks reddened under his dark tan.

"Yes yes, quite amusing," chuckled Marcus. "In Cayenne Hans sold his boat for a thousand dollars. I daresay it wasn't worth it. Then we got up to St. Martin just in time for Hurricane Hugo. I swear I don't know how I bring this luck onto myself. Hans here valiantly helped me lose my boat—no, not this boat, the one before. Twenty-four hours we battled. 'Oh, The Lagoon's safe in a hurricane,' everybody'd said. Bloody hell! We were damned lucky to get out of that alive. Gawd what a disaster. Smashed boats everywhere, simply everywhere."

"After, Marcus and I both got other boats and didn't see each other a long time," Hans said. "I find a way smuggling people out of Haiti, some people wanting to be refugees, and they pay me. Then the police catch me and throw me in prison. *Sheist,* that fucking place! Ha! They are burning people with blowtorches there! Finally the German consul gets me out. I go to Fort-de-France."

"Yes, and when I found him he was in a bad way indeed," said Marcus. "Drinking rum-and-cokes straight out of bed, not functional until four in the afternoon. Then this idea of his to smuggle wine into Antigua, but we couldn't find anybody to spot us the money. Anyway, I needed to get up to St. Martin and work on this cabin top, and to get there I needed a mate, so I offered him the position. Isn't that so, Hans?"

"I am so honored, Marcus, *mein capitan! Sieg heil!*"

"Oh, please go to hell."

We cooked a lentil-coconut stew and mixed more drinks. Marcus went on and on about "the insipid chatter of those retired Americans in their floating Winnebagos. They clutter up the single-sideband air waves exactly while I'm trying to listen to the daily BBC radio drama. 'Er, uh, *Flying Cow* this is *Sun Goddess.* Happy hour at your place tonight, over?' 'Sylvia? Sylvia honey this is Evelyn. Yeah, I was trying to make that cherry cheesecake you gave me that *simply fabulous* recipe for, but I just don't seem to have any red food coloring. Uh, do you think blue will work?'" He imitated the American accent with a dull, whiny voice.

"Marcus," I said, "you have the blackest humor of anyone I've ever met."

"Human fallibility, my friend! I should die of boredom without it."

With the Ecole Communale, Les Saintes, 11/14/92

CHAPTER 26

GUADELOUPE AND MONTSERRAT

The next day, November 14, 1992, I crossed from Dominica to Bourg. It was the only town in Les Saintes, a cluster of low, dry islands off the south coast of Guadeloupe. I landed on a white beach across a narrow street from a two-story building with the words "Ecole Communale" above the door. I followed the street as it wound through neatly plastered buildings with steep metal roofs to a plaza at the foot of a ferry dock. After Portsmouth, Bourg des Saintes seemed a fairy-tale village of charm and elegance. Slim, fashionable women strode past. Vacationers boarded ferries to and from Guadeloupe. Some of the townspeople were white, from mainland France.

"They call us who come from the mainland *metros*, as if we are all from Paris," said Claude, the schoolmaster of the Ecole Communale, or grade school. It was evening. He had called to me from the terrace of his second-story apartment, next door to his school, inviting me up for a glass of wine.

"Most of us are in our thirties or forties," he said. "We came here for the better environment. For years now I've had this work. Without it I couldn't live—only the children give me life. But there was a time when I expected more freedoms, more artistic expression." A wedge of black bangs hung over his expansive forehead. His lower face seemed compressed in comparison—small, square chin, hollow cheeks. "You remind me of what I used to hope for. It's a sweet yet painful memory."

"It's not all good, Claude. I miss my family, and having a girlfriend. You can only do so much in one life."

His eyes searched mine. "I think my students should learn about your voyage. Would you object to being the subject of a class project?"

"Of course not."

In the morning, as I prepared to leave, Claude approached wearing pleated jeans and a short-sleeved shirt. He held a tape recorder under his arm.

Behind were thirty smartly dressed kids, about ten years old. Their skin was every lovely shade of mulatto.

"Bonjour," he greeted, then turned to his students. "Quiet now, come closer. Group around. Natalie, Paulette! Sh!" He turned the recorder on. "Children, this is Monsieur Ladd, from *les Etats Unis,* and his little boat, *le Squeak*. They have come a very great distance to visit us here. Monsieur Steve, will you tell us about your route and reasons for travel?"

I talked, Claude translating. The children asked questions. "Do you see whales?" "Is America very far?" Afterward, Claude arranged for a group photo, I aboard *Squeak* in black swimsuit and black fanny pack strapped over a white T-shirt, he and the kids behind me along the starboard side—a solid backdrop of whispering, giggling kid energy.

Claude shook my hand. *"Merci,* Steve. I'll have them each write a paper about it. Who knows what impression it will make in their lives. We drop a pebble into a well, and cannot see the ripples. You are leaving now?"

"Yes, I'd better."

"Children, will you help the monsieur to launch his boat?" Each of them grabbed onto some little part of *Squeak*. At my *"Allez!"* they slid her into the water. I jumped in, and *Squeak's* momentum carried her out into the harbor.

"*Bon voyage*!" shouted thirty small voices. Their faces remained turned toward me, watching me row, while Claude shepherded them toward school, palms forward, scooting them along.

In the town of Basse Terre, Guadeloupe, I noted the prices in the supermarket. Better to eat little and travel fast, I thought. Garbage disfigured the steep beach leading north from town. Behind the beach cement-block houses formed a nearly solid wall. Dissatisfied with this close-up view, I drew away from shore and looked back toward Les Saintes. There they were, and Dominica, even Martinique, a hundred miles away. The islands telescoped away and slightly to the right, like an object reproducing itself smaller and smaller between two mirrors. Ahead I made out Montserrat, for a total spread of 150 miles. At dusk I stopped at a wild creek, rearranged stones to enlarge the channel, and pulled *Squeak* into a back-beach pool—my favorite sort of anchorage. I opened green coconuts and drank their jellywater. After I'd settled into bed, egrets roosted in a tree on the other side of the pond, fifteen feet away. They groomed languidly, and slept standing.

The next day a sailboat slowly gained on me while I rowed. She was a classic of yesteryear, with rust-streaked topsides and white-tipped masts—the *Mara!* The sea parted and curled under her bowsprit. At first her mainmast showed to the right of her mizzenmast, indicating she would pass me to seaward. Then her masts lined up—they'd seen me. The figures of Marcus and Hans materialized, looking for all the world like a pair of pirates. Marcus stooped and leered through his spectacles, jaw jutting, face ruddy. Hans stood at the helm, brown, bare-chested, hairy as Blackbeard. "Ahoy *Squeak!*" shouted Marcus, and threw me a line. I tied it to *Squeak's* mast, and climbed aboard.

Junk littered the cockpit. Cockroaches grazed on the dirty dishes in the galley. Clothes were strewn all over the salon. Still, it was more fun to hang out with Marcus and Hans than by myself in *Squeak,* so I cruised the length of Guadeloupe with them. Marcus gave me the driest bunk; only two deck leaks dripped water on me compared to three or four apiece onto my mates. Hans, the chef, specialized in pasta-and-corned-beef stews. The booze was rum-and-whatevers, no ice.

Hans loved to tell stories. "In World War II," he said, "my father was head of intelligence for the German army on the eastern front. I was eleven when the war finished. My father made sure to surrender to the Americans, and they helped us to move to New York because they wanted his secrets to use against the Russians." Later they moved to Venezuela, where Hans grew up to become a smuggler, drug- and otherwise. He told a humorous tale about having a sailboat shot out from under him by the Brazilian Navy, and another about fighting as a mercenary in 1975.

"I was fighting for the Spanish Legion against the Polisarios and the Moroccans, to keep the Spanish Sahara for Spain," he said. "But Franco died, and King Juan Carlos washed his hands of us. Then King Hassan of Morocco led a hundred thousand civilians south in the Green March. You heard about that? My company was captured and put in political prison. For two months they tortured us! They tied our wrists and ankles together, our hands behind, then they put a steel bar through behind our knees and pulled us up in the air so our heads fall down." Hans was giggling so hard he could barely get it out. "Then they beat the bottoms of our feet and give us electric shocks! Other times they put a hose in our mouths and push it down, and fill our bellies up with water!" With his hands he simulated blowing up like a balloon, then puffed his cheeks out and crossed his eyes. Marcus collapsed laughing.

"Steve, you must really see Hans do his dead fly trick sometime," he gasped between breaths. "I swear, he drowns a fly in water, stone dead, then he brings it back to life by sprinkling salt on it! Funniest damned thing I ever saw."

On Thursday, November 19, we left Guadeloupe, *Mara* and *Squeak* sailing separately. Montserrat was thirty-five miles away—a small, bell-shaped curve of blue slightly darker than sea or sky.

For five hours there was no wind. Then a front hit, a frightening ash gray with blackness behind, that took up the entire eastern sky. I braced myself as it swept over me, but its effect was good: a renewal of the normal, ten-to-fifteen-knot-trade wind. My butt had chafed from rowing so long, so I sailed standing up, balanced on a tripod consisting of two legs and tiller arm, bending each as necessary to keep upright, with a balance assist from a leeboard control line held like a rein in my free hand.

The wind came on the starboard quarter; the wake showed good speed. Still, watching Montserrat get closer was like watching the grass grow. It never seemed to get bigger except in comparison to Guadeloupe, which steadily shrank. Finally the white of crashing shore waves became visible. I wasn't going to get there before dark. There would be no moon. Fortunately, the landfall was simple. There were no odd coastal shapes, no off-lying hazards. Montserrat was a sleek volcano poking four thousand feet above the sea. Its color was the light green of salt-spray heath near shore, dark green of tropical forest above.

Night fell as I reached the island. I paralleled the coast, circling slowly clockwise. The wind dropped. I raised the rudder blade and steered by push-rowing, from which position I could see ahead, if there was anything there to see. I judged my distance from shore by the sound of breakers, by whether I could see their whiteness, and by the feeling of the waves passing under me. Were they rising up yet, getting ready to break? I passed lighted houses, then saw Plymouth, the only town. It faced southwest. I rowed through a confusion of construction barges and massive steel pilings. It wasn't a harbor, just a lee. The water was too rough to sleep properly. Nonetheless, I was greatly relieved to anchor among assorted small craft off what appeared to be the center of town.

At dawn I saw what looked like an ancient stone village on a short piedmont that sloped into tall hills a mile away. There was no landing or dinghy dock, but a sunken barge lay near shore. Its top was partly awash, and with each swell a geyser erupted from a hole in its steel deck. The narrow strip of water behind it was calm. I tied up there with a breast line to the riprap bank.

A street ran along the shore. Across it were the post office, taxi stand, and a small park consisting of palm trees, war monument, and two cannons. An old man tilling a few square feet of leftover ground leaned on his hoe to answer my questions. "That construction work in the water? That's the new pier they buildin'. Ol' Hurricane Hugo took out the old one couple years ago, along with every roof on the island. That there's the port," he said, pointing right, to a fenced compound. "You best go Customs there."

Marcus appeared while I waited at the Customs office. "We didn't like the looks of this anchorage," he said, "so we kept going up to Old Road Bay. With the wind blowing from southeast it's better there. I must say I'm rather worried, though. I took a bus here, and I'm afraid Customs will hammer me for going ashore without stopping at the Customs dock first. But when there *is* no Customs dock surely they can't quibble." I was guilty of the same crime, but whereas Marcus had illegally traversed several miles of sovereign territory, I had only crossed fifty yards of it. He fidgeted with his papers while we waited at a wooden counter.

A uniformed official strode stiffly in. His clipboard held a sheaf of forms with the letterhead, "The British Dependent Territory of Montserrat." Marcus smiled submissively and presented his story in the most innocuous light. "You took *a bus* to get here?" exclaimed the official, and proceeded to verbally flay him for a good twenty minutes. He even raised the specter of boat confiscation before sending us both on our way like a pair of schoolboys released from the principal's office.

My sunken barge made a convenient marina. In the square, idle taxi drivers popped up to offer me their services. "Excuse me, where can I buy an envelope?" I asked, and three old gents in slacks and T-shirts fell over themselves to point out the exact spot, with endless assurances that I couldn't possibly get lost.

I stopped by a church and noticed a single gravestone close against its west wall. The inscription was in archaic hand:

HEARLEYETH
THEBODYOF
ANDREWPOIXIER
WHODEPARTED
THISLIFETHE16OF
JANVERY 1720
NY36YEAROFHIS
ADOE

A 6"x10" bronze plaque had been added above the inscription:

1720 RESTED IN PEACE
1841 DISTURBED IN HIS SLUMBER
1954 RESTORED TO HOLY GROUND

A history brochure told how Montserrat had been a child of the "mother colony," St. Kitts. But the Englishmen who acquired title in 1632 relied on Irish indentured servants to till the soil. Frenchmen and Caribs regularly came to massacre the colonists and destroy their farms, as did periodic hurricanes. The Andrew Poixier of the churchyard had died during this epoch. When Irish labor became insufficient to grow sugar cane, Negro slaves were imported, and the population slowly became black. Then the sugar industry collapsed. In the latter half of the twentieth century white faces reappeared, as British and Canadians came there to retire. An American medical school was established. Montserratians working in England and Canada returned with savings. Thus, while the island had no industry or agriculture, there was enough money to import food, clothing, building materials, even a few Japanese cars. Learning such things occupied me for two days. Then I got a clearance for Nevis, the next island, and moved to a beach a mile north of town, ready to leave in the morning.

My first clue that my departure would be delayed occurred at one A.M., when a wave bashed *Squeak* to one side, waking me. Poking my head out the hatch, I saw that the surf had built up and was reaching the level to which I had dragged *Squeak*. I unloaded, pulled her up further, and went back to sleep. Again waves reached the boat. This time, with difficulty, I pulled her up a final grade and across the upper beach to the edge of the woods.

By morning, Sunday, November 22, the scene was very different from that of the evening before. As I would later learn, a gale in the central Atlantic, at the latitude of Florida, had generated huge swells. When they reached Montserrat, they bent around behind it and hit this southwest-facing shore from the west. Thus, they broke first on the cliffs to my right and continued past, down the beach toward Plymouth. Close offshore the swells rose to a height of eight feet, curled, and crashed on the beach so violently I felt the vibration through the sand. The curling breakers were walls of water, dark with suspended sand, flecked with foam. They washed far up onto the beach, then slid violently back just in time to collide with the next wave as it reared up, bowling it over, as a rolling log might topple a man.

My first reaction was annoyance at not being able to launch as planned. Then I realized the wind was blowing hard out beyond the wind shadow. The ground swell had arrived first, but now the gale itself reached Montserrat. But for the whim that had caused me to move to the beach, the swells breaking over the sunken barge would have forced me out to sea in the middle of the night. At best, I'd have had to ride it out at anchor, an ugly prospect. My little beach camp, at the foot of a wild ravine, looked better and better all the time. I put up my tarp and got comfortable.

By afternoon it was raining and the sea was rough. A large yacht sailed around the point to my right, the one separating Plymouth from Old Road Bay. Only her jib was flying, yet she was heeling hard and laboring. I got out my binoculars. It was the *Mara*—I'd thought she had already left for Nevis. She sailed to the vicinity of the new dock, but twenty minutes later she was off my beach again, a half mile out. Her sails were down. Marcus and Hans appeared to be running around on deck like ants. Then the tugboat employed to build the new pier came and towed them back to Plymouth.

When it stopped raining I hiked to the bay on far side of where the new pier was being constructed and stood on the shoulder of the coastwise road. The *Mara* lay at anchor three hundred yards out, but I couldn't raise them on my hand-held VHF.

"Beep beep!"

I turned to see a Toyota pickup truck stopped on the road behind me. The driver was a stranger with curly blond hair. Beside him sat Hans, beckoning. I hopped onto the bed of the truck, and we took off.

"Okay, Hans, fill me in," I said through the open back window.

"Fucking big storm, Steve! On Old Road Bay, the swells grew and grew until *Mara* dragged her anchor. We thought she was going onto the beach for sure. That damned engine of his wouldn't start, so Marcus and I had to pull the anchor in by hand. Oh, my back is aching from that! Then we raised the jib and sailed around the point, but Marcus then went below and found water a foot deep in the cabin—the force on the mast had opened up the seams below the chain plates. We anchored there in Sugar Bay, but we soon dragged again. Then the tug came and towed us back, and loaned us a pump with a motor. I came ashore and found Tom at the Yacht Club. Tom, this is Steve."

The driver, seated on the right due to Montserrat being a drive-on-the-left country, reached around with his right hand for me to shake it. "Pleasure, Steve!" he said, with an English accent.

"Hi, Tom! So where we going?"

"Get some rum," said Hans. "Also Marcus's dinghy. We had to leave it in Old Road Bay. Marcus, he stayed aboard *Mara* to man the pumps. He's scared, I tell you!" Hans laughed excitedly.

"Hans helped rebuild houses here after Hurricane Hugo, that's how we met," said Tom, a middle-aged man with the face of an overgrown child and a dimpled chin.

"You live here then?"

"Born and raised. My old man used to be Governor. But me, I'm only a humble T-shirt painter. And president of the Montserrat Yacht Club! A peculiar institution to have on an island with no harbor, no marine services, and no yachts, I grant you. But we do have a Yacht Club, consisting of a bar and restaurant. It's right by where we picked you up, on Sugar Bay. What kind of anchor does Marcus have, anyway?"

"An eighty-pound fisherman," said Hans.

"Let's hope it holds."

Given the magnitude of the situation I assumed we would be in a hurry, but we went to Tom's house, where we had a bite to eat and a few drinks with his fiancée. Then we dropped in at a bar called The Nest, at the foot of the dock at Old Road Bay, and had a couple more. By the time we had loaded *Mister Joe* (Marcus's tippy wooden dinghy), stopped at the store, arrived at the beach in front of the yacht club, and unloaded the dinghy, it was dark, and judgments were mildly impaired. The surf was pretty bad.

"You've gotta wait until a series of little waves goes by, then a series of big waves, then go when the next set of little waves starts," said Tom, sensibly.

"Right," agreed Hans.

Sure enough, the waves were big, then became small. We waited. They stayed small. Impatience set in. "Okay, now, quick!" We pushed *Mister Joe* into the water. I got in front, rowing, Hans in back. Our timing was perfect, but in reverse. Out of the corner of my eye I saw the first big wave coming, black and sleek, already breaking.

"Hang on!" It spun us and half filled the boat, but we were still afloat.

"Go! Go, quick!" yelled Tom from the shore.

"Go! Go!" yelled Hans. Another big one was coming.

"We're not going to make it," I muttered, and rowed as fast as I could. It promptly rolled us, and then we were scrambling around in the water looking for oars and bags.

"The rum! Where's the rum?" cried Hans. It was safe in my day pack, which I'd kept on, but we lost an oarlock and some clothes and diving gear. Hans and I righted the dinghy while Tom grabbed some paddles from the yacht club. We launched again, and made it this time.

We found Marcus on deck, fiddling with a portable pump. "Hans, where the dickens have you been? Bloody pump broke down two hours ago. The boat's not leaking so fast anymore, or I might have already sunk. We'll have to take turns on the little hand pump. My God, what a horrid day! Simply horrid."

Marcus distributed dry clothes. Hans cooked a stew. I poured drinks, and we enjoyed the high spirits that follow a calamity narrowly avoided.

In the morning I went back to *Squeak* for my mask, snorkel, and fins while Marcus and Hans bought flashing, roofing tar, and tacks in town. Reunited aboard *Mara*, we cut three-inch-wide strips of flashing and bedded them on one side with tar. Then I jumped in the water with a hammer, a pouch full of tacks, and a pair of needle-nose pliers to hold them while pounding. There were three open seams, each about seven feet long, two to three feet underwater. Getting the first few nails in was the hard part; I needed four hands, and *Mara* was bouncing a lot in the waves.

It took three hours to nail the strips on, and by then I had tar all over me. The only thing we had to take it off was gasoline. Some of it spilled on the head of my penis, causing a nauseating pain. I jumped in the water and thrashed around. I got back out and washed with soap and water. Nothing helped.

"I'm in some pain," I confessed. "I got gasoline on the head of my penis."

"Need a light?" asked Hans.

This gale was a taste of things to come because the Caribbean, like the Llanos, gets its heaviest winds from December through March. Harbor-less Montserrat had become an unhealthy place for boats. The remainder of the week we listened to the twice-daily weather forecast on Radio Antilles, ready to leave as soon as the storm abated. Marcus got his engine running while I whittled a new boomkin and mizzen sprit boom. The former had broken in Guadeloupe, the latter had become too springy to sheet the mizzen tight in heavy wind. Then it occurred to me to scout around for a computer on which to do some writing. I soon made an arrangement with a medical student living on the north end of the island.

By Friday the storm had died down enough for Marcus and I to move our vessels to Old Road Bay. I moved to be closer to the house with the computer, Marcus because Old Road Bay was again a better place to wait. That evening we went ashore for drinks at The Nest, a U-shaped bar on a concrete slab under a thatched roof, unenclosed except for a bathroom and storage room. Bottles covered the wall behind the bar. Marcus, Hans, and I sat at stools. I began talking to a stately Trinidadian woman on my right of mixed Chinese and Indian blood. Marcus, to far left, got smashed and began talking madly. He made absurd faces, jutted his chin, posed theories in stark absolutes, built cases founded in counter-intuitions, and sped up to a blur at his punch lines to clear his mouth for the giggles that quaked his bony shoulders. It was all black humor, rot and decay, failure and frustration, how jolly! For once Hans couldn't keep up, so he just sat in stitches, his merry little cheeks bulging above his beard.

With no one on his left to talk to, Marcus bypassed Hans and me to address the beautiful Trinidadian. I was certain he would disgust her, but she steeled herself and tried to make out what he was saying. The serene smile froze on her lips. The muscles around her eyes began to wince and work, revealing confusion, curiosity, fear. She looked like a Hindu princess, staring into the face of a swaying cobra. The spell snapped, however, when Marcus interrupted his monologue to order a fresh Cuba Libre. Released from his grip, the princess swiveled away, sat still for a moment, then shifted to another stool.

On Saturday morning I walked up a narrow asphalt road to the village of Salem, a climb of five hundred feet. There I caught a van to the house of

Mary Lou, the woman with the computer. She was a brusque, folksy biochemistry professor from Texas, in the process of adding an M.D. to her long list of credentials. Her voice was sharp, her body trim, her hair short and silvery. She could have played the role of a woman Army general. The house was luxurious and neat as a pin, but Mary Lou called it "camping out." Bob also lived there. He was a tall, thin, forty-five-year-old triathlete from California, with a cold precision and the face of an undertaker.

I worked until dark on the computer, in the spare bedroom, then hitched a ride back to The Nest. Hans was there, lit up like a Christmas tree. He and Marcus had gone to Plymouth with all their papers, gotten a clearance to sail to Nevis the next day, gone bar-hopping, and lost the papers. Gone were Marcus's passport, traveler's checks, and ship's papers. Hans, who'd had only a forged passport, now had no ID whatsoever. Marcus had gone back to his boat with orders that Hans not return until he found the packet of documents. "Of course, when anything goes wrong it's my fault," grumbled Hans, too drunk to be really peeved.

On Sunday I again worked at Mary Lou's. When I returned to The Nest, Jill, the emaciated English barkeep, asked, "Steve, have you seen Hans?"

"Not since last night. He said they'd lost all their papers."

"He found the papers all right," said Jill, tucking a strand of long blond hair behind her ear. "They were in the back seat of a car they'd ridden in. Then at about ten P.M. Hans left the bar without a word. I figured he was going back to the *Mara*. But neither Hans nor the dinghy have been seen since. Steve, I'm worried. So's Marcus."

The following morning, Monday, I rowed to *Mara*. Marcus said, "When I woke yesterday morning and saw Hans and the dinghy weren't here, I assumed he'd spent the night at Tom's . I didn't go ashore until late afternoon. Jill says, 'Marcus, where's Hans?' 'At Tom's probably,' I said. But she'd already called him, and everybody else she could think of. In fact, nobody's seen Hans since he left the bar, except that New Zealander on the yacht next to me. He swears he saw Hans swimming ashore from the *Mara* at nine o'clock yesterday morning. Even identified him by the tattoos on his arms. But I was awake at that hour, and *I* never saw him. Besides, none of Hans's things were touched. I tell you, I'm totally baffled, totally."

As Marcus and I discussed the matter, he developed three scenarios. "Maybe Hans lost the dinghy, and perhaps the papers again as well, and was too ashamed to come back to face me. In that case he's hiding somewhere on the island. Or, he capsized in the surf and drowned. I can see him doing that, frankly. He can't swim properly, you know, and if he ever lost that forged passport of his in the surf he'd have gone into an absolute panic to get it back—he considered it irreplaceable. Or, maybe he made it through the surf all right, then got blown out to sea. It was blowing like stink that night, as you recall, straight offshore. Thanks to you two losing that oarlock in the surf, we were paddling *Mister Joe* with one oar, like a canoe. If he drifted past the boats, he'd never have been able to work his way back. My God, what a fate."

"I hate to say it, but isn't there a fourth possibility?" I asked. "Couldn't Hans have taken off with your passport and eight hundred dollars worth of traveler's checks?"

"Mmm, no, that's not Hans. Not after everything we've been through..."

Marcus reported Hans's disappearance to the police Monday afternoon. They demanded to know why Marcus had waited so long to report it, and soon established another possibility: that Marcus had murdered him. They barred him from leaving the island pending further investigation, and sent a scuba team out to look around under the *Mara.* Marcus kept his wicked humor at bay during this process except with me, whom he treated to bloodthirsty scowls in support of the detectives' suspicions. The case made headlines in the local newspaper ("WHITE MAN DISAPPEARS OFF YACHT!") with Marcus's mug shot below as captain of the jinxed vessel. He commenced the process of replacing his passport and traveler's checks. He was extremely vexed at having to stay in that rolly, unsafe anchorage, and at Hans for disappearing.

"Bloody annoying," he said. "I found him down there in Martinique on his last legs and got him dried out a little, and he was doing pretty well. Then the first time I leave him ashore by himself he bloody well gets himself killed. He was just a child really, totally irresponsible."

The fourth night after his disappearance, Marcus and I made wind and current assumptions and plotted Hans's day-by-day positions, should he be adrift. He would by then have been forty miles south of St. Croix, Virgin Islands. In another two weeks he would wash up in the Dominican Republic. "If his luck's really bad, he might even wash up in Haiti, where they'll throw him straight back in jail," said Marcus. "Wouldn't *that* be choice."

Others predicted Hans would drift more south, toward Venezuela. The various coast guards had been notified, but it was unclear whether anyone had actually searched for him. Hans's Montserratian friends pointed their fingers at Marcus for waiting so long to report it, but they themselves may have felt a tinge of guilt for not organizing a search, especially Tom as Yacht Club President. I felt the guilt too. Why did we all wait for somebody else to do something? We should have assumed he was adrift immediately, when there was a chance of finding him.

Hans's disappearance lingered like a minor chord with the sustain pedal down. "Any news on Hans?" everybody asked, but they asked it less and less often. Wild new theories circulated, and died out. Marcus became depressed.

Eventually, at the mere mention of "Hans," everyone at The Nest would shift uncomfortably on their stools and stare off at different angles into space.

Meanwhile I wrote. I put *Squeak* on a patch of grass on the Old Road Bay jetty, and woke to the sounds of elderly Montserratians taking their daily bath in the sea. I walked the several routes leading toward Mary Lou's house. I hitched rides with a fleshy, middle-aged policeman, a housecleaner of Irish and black descent, and a landscaper who flew the Stars and Stripes from the grill of his automobile, "because most of my clients are Americans," he said. It was easy to hitch rides, but the vans were good too. Far from the "dour-faced and insular" formula I'd thought was universal among bus passengers, everybody was amiable. Once, while I rode back from Plymouth, the bus filled up one by one with country ladies in long skirts and wide-brimmed hats or head-wraps. I imagined them tending goats or bent over, weeding little plots. All had very different faces and body shapes. They gossiped spiritedly about a contemporary who had lived away most of his life and had now returned to Montserrat, finding it all changed. They contended for speaking time the way basketball players fight over the ball, and broke frequently into laughter. They dwelt on emphatic statements, repeating the best ones whenever possible.

Mary Lou was in the middle of finals, and too grouchy to be around. "Hey, I feel like you're in my space here," growled her roommate, whom I'd come to think of as Iron Man Bob. I worked on the computer while they were at school, then hitched back to Old Road Bay, said hello without stopping to the "expats" (expatriates) at The Nest, cooked a grim pot of something-or-other, and went to bed. Jill kindly kept the door to the bathroom open for me, and a light bulb I could twist on for reading if I couldn't sleep.

It was getting toward Christmas. The police promised to release Marcus from his house detention by then if nothing new turned up. Marcus, having given up on Hans, longed to continue to St. Martin. For that he needed a new mate. Meanwhile, Meg had some vacation time coming, and my work was about done. Our schedules were compatible, so we agreed that Meg would fly to Montserrat then sail with Marcus to St. Kitts, Statia, and St. Martin. I would shadow them in *Squeak*. The three of us would share housekeeping aboard the *Mara*, which Marcus promised to clean up before Meg came.

She arrived on December 19. I had almost forgotten how dark and wavy her hair was, how wide her smile. A bit awkwardly, we held hands and walked up to an ancient pasture surrounded by low, hurricane-scarred trees. A band of goats spooked and fled some yards down the slope. We sat and looked out over eroded volcanoes, town, and sea. What did I want from this tall woman, so serious and substantial? She was sexy, intellectual, eager to please. Was it fair to have had her come so far?

It mortified me to show Meg her quarters aboard the *Mara.* Marcus, demoralized by guilt and fear of storms, had squandered the month of December on a barstool at The Nest. He'd sprayed some poison around, killing half the cockroaches and enraging the remaining hordes. Otherwise, *Mara* was squalid as ever. Meg and I cleaned the boat ourselves, and instituted a new domestic regime. Marcus, relieved to have an orderly crew, paid a large provisioning bill.

At the last minute he became nervous. "I don't think it would be at all advisable for us to leave for Nevis tomorrow, given the present state of the sea," he said. He'd been listening to the Radio Antilles weather forecasts like a cautious investor deciding if the timing was right for a major stock purchase.

"We can't tell what the sea's like here in the wind shadow," I said. "Tell you what, I'll run up to open water at the head of the island tomorrow in *Squeak,* and take a look." I did so, and returned with my report: "Ten-foot seas, some breaking. Nothing unusual. I say we leave." My point was that if I could handle it in the twelve-foot *Squeak*, surely Marcus could in his forty-foot *Mara.*

"Very well then. Barring unforeseen events," he said.

Christmas Eve, 1992, I slept with Meg in *Mara's* forepeak, with *Squeak* tied astern. The wind slackened during the night. The swell jostled the two boats together. Nobody heard anything, but at five A.M., when I boarded *Squeak* to get a head start on the crossing, I saw that the boomkin had broken loose from its mounts and was floating in the water, attached by the sheet. That wasn't so bad; I could sail with main alone. Then I noticed one of my beloved oars was missing, together with its universal-joint oarlock. A wave of disgust came over me. "Great Christmas present," I muttered. I had no choice but to do what Marcus had preferred all along: sail with them aboard *Mara*, with *Squeak* in tow.

CHAPTER 27

TO PUERTO RICO

We sailed from Montserrat in midmorning under jib and reefed main, with *Squeak* and Marcus's vinyl inflatable dingy under tow. Unfortunately, the "Christmas winds" picked the dinghy up, broke its line, and blew it away like a birthday balloon, airborne most of the time, until it disappeared to leeward. Now *Squeak* was our only auxiliary. Noticing that spray and slop had filled *Squeak's* cockpit, I had Marcus heave to so I could bail her out. I hopped aboard, and back again, but doing so was too risky in that sea. Thenceforth *Squeak* would have to fend for herself.

I tried to shake off my irritation at Marcus, my self-anger for allowing *Squeak* to become damaged, and my fears of further damage. For all her flaws, *Mara* was magnificent. She'd been designed by Commodore Munroe, whose *Presto* was one of *Squeak's* design inspirations. Meg sat on the windward cockpit coaming, abaft the wheel, where the spray didn't reach and the sun could warm her back. If the motion bothered her, she didn't show it. She proved a reliable hand, and a scenic one in her black swimsuit.

"Hey, lookin' good!" I said.

"Oh, I'm *feelin'* good."

We anchored off Nevis, and the next day continued to St. Kitts, the other half of this two-island nation. A spine of sharp peaks ran down its center, skirted by fields of sugar cane. Ruined plantation structures of stone and brick dotted the lush slopes.

On Bequia I had read a book about St. Kitts' early role as the "mother colony" to both British and French planters. About the time the Pilgrims were landing at Plymouth Rock, another band of Englishmen, defying Spanish claims to the New World, landed here to establish an agricultural colony. A party of Frenchmen soon arrived as well. Knowing that only through a united effort could they prevail against the Carib Indians, the English kept the center of the long, slender island and ceded both ends to the French. They cooperated long enough to defeat their common enemy and send spin-off groups to the other Antilles. Dutch planters, recently expelled from Brazil, moved into the Caribbean as managers and traders, passing on what they had learned about growing tobacco, cotton, indigo, and sugar cane.

Ultimately the British pried the French from their strongholds. Basseterre, the little capital, boasted a central roundabout resembling London's Piccadilly Circus. The public buildings were pompously Georgian, the streets disproportionately wide. There were shops of quarried limestone and shingled homes with steep roofs of corrugated steel and hurricane shutters riding on wrought-iron hinges.

The people on the street, however, were not British. Wars, hurricanes, and low sugar prices had long since caused the white masters to abandon St. Kitts to their former slaves. The cabbies who bombarded us with offers of their services were Africans of the West Indian culture. An old woman in a long, plain dress selling nuts looked like the produce mongers I had been seeing since Trinidad.

"Hmmm, what are these?" Meg asked.

"Bread nuts."

"How do you open them?"

She demonstrated. We expected her to give us the sample, but instead she popped it into own her mouth and said, "That's how you do it!"

Meg laughed. "Yes, you certainly do make them look delicious. Give me a dollar's worth, please."

The anchorage was exposed, as they all are in that stretch of the Indies. That night the wind howled in *Mara's* tangled rigging. The lantern that swung from the ceiling of the salon, divided nearly in two by the massive centerboard trunk, lit a scene of dampness and disorder. We had no privacy. Marcus had been drinking all day, and now his tired eyes gleamed behind their coke-bottle glasses. His face was sunburnt, his hair short, wiry, and damp. He laughed at his own jokes and Monty Python imitations. He kept us awake with his compulsive dithering. He was a happy drunk, but with a dark and lonely undercurrent. Rainwater dripped all along the seam joining the cabin structure to the deck. Two-inch-long cockroaches scrambled over our bare skin.

Marcus repeated his act the following night, scaring Meg with confessions of fear and predictions of calamity. "I don't mind telling you," he said, his voice even in that state sculpted and pensive, "I'm bloody frightened. The odds are quite against us, at this time of year, in an unsound vessel, with a green crew. I dare say, we'll be lucky to make it to St. Martin alive. Very lucky indeed!"

Meg and I discussed how to escape his ill-starred ship, but in the light of day, with a painfully sober captain, the situation appeared less dire. We told him what he had said and suggested he cut back on his drinking. Ashamed, he followed our advice.

An ominous squall followed as we cleared Basseterre harbor. Fearful of jibing, Marcus ordered the mainsail down. We proceeded at a snail's pace, under jib alone, to St. Eustasias (Statia), fifteen miles downwind. We arrived in a chilling downpour. It was a small island with hills at one end, a volcano shaped like a huge barnacle at the other, and a flat plain between. A narrow strip of waterfront contained the ruins of the original Oranjestad, destroyed long ago by hurricanes. We were eager to clear into the Dutch Antilles before customs closed, so Meg and Marcus got into *Squeak* while I put my fins on and jumped in the water. Pushing her while swimming was the only way to get *Squeak* through some rocks and onto a scrap of beach.

The inhabited portion of the settlement was on the plain, a hundred feet up. We climbed a flagstone ramp to a village dominated by massive ruins, including those of the first synagogue in the New World. They dated from the seventeenth and eighteenth centuries, when Statia was a commercial hub for the Eastern Caribbean. Here African slaves were sold, privateer plunder was auctioned, and rum was stockpiled for shipment to Europe and the American colonies. Statia won its place in American hearts in 1776 when, by saluting the colors of the USS Andrea Doria, it became the first foreign power to recognize the new United States.

Now it was a quaint relic, with no harbor for modern commerce, no beaches to attract tourists, and little arable land. Still, it was tidy. The runoff from the storm, which still raged, collected in stone trenches and gushed through a spout over the edge of the bluff, to cascade down an erosion-proofed ravine. The black inhabitants spoke a queerly accented English more often than Dutch.

Continued bad weather kept us there two days. The swells, at right angles to the wind, caused *Mara* to roll sickeningly. Our unwashed bodies rolled back and forth in our berths like logs in the surf. Sour-smelling bilge water gurgled under the floorboards. Parts of the stove were missing and the utensils were worn and rusty, but Meg and I managed a corned-beef-and-cabbage, and we played a few hands of gin rummy. Two French charter boats, two tankers, and a fishing boat shared the miserable anchorage with us.

On the final day of 1992, after much fretting over weather reports, we hanked on a tiny storm jib, double-reefed the main, and left for St. Martin, thirty-five miles to the north. We met with standard Christmas winds—fifteen to twenty-five knots from the east—and seas to match. I had removed *Squeak's* masts and strapped air bags in the cockpit. Breaking waves sometimes knocked her on her side, but she always righted. She wandered alarmingly at the end of her taut, forty-foot towrope. Intervening seas often obscured her, then she would leap at us over a tumbling wave, in Marcus's words, "like a mad, one-eyed fish" (the single eye being the porthole on her starboard bow).

We inched past Saba, a lonely rock off to our left, and sighted St. Barthelemy, to the northeast. Marcus went below and I spelled him at the wood-and-brass wheel. The purchase and tie-off gear for her sheets were dilapidated, and the helmsman's seat wasn't bolted down. Apropos of nothing, the top two feet of the mizzen mast fell off and landed between our feet in the cockpit, but we didn't use that mast anyway. For want of proper stowage, pans and cooking staples kept crashing to the cabin floor. A dozen other problems demanded immediate attention, but the *Mara* thrilled me nonetheless. Old-fashioned, functional purity expressed itself in her every line. This was the closest I would ever get to being a sea captain in the days of commercial sail.

At sunset we entered Philipsburg harbor on the south, Dutch side of St. Martin, and anchored among yachts from all over the world. The island was populous and wealthy enough to support fireworks displays in three different locations, yet small enough that, from our vantage, two could be seen directly, and the third as rosy reflections in the overcast sky. Marcus went ashore in search of new company while Meg and I celebrated New Year's Eve cozily together. Cruise ships large enough to be seen from other planets blazed in the night like chandeliers. Wild young men with lusty voices crisscrossed the harbor in fast inflatables.

"If this is civilization, I feel detached from it," I said.

"I know what you mean," she said, "but I'm more concerned that you seem to be feeling detached from me, too."

"Maybe I am, but it's not from any inadequacy on your part. No, you're fantastic. Maybe I've just traveled alone too long to bond very well. Tell you what, let's get to The Lagoon as soon as possible and spend some time alone before you fly back to Grenada."

"The sooner we get off this scow the better. It'll be nice to have some privacy," she said, and gave me a squeeze.

We hurried Marcus through the process of buying a new dinghy, then motored to the entrance to The Lagoon. Marcus had to wait for the 5:30 bridge opening, but we didn't. I simply loaded Meg and our gear aboard *Squeak*, put on my fins, and pushed us, swimming, to a beach inside.

Much as the traveler should live in the present, he inevitably builds images of his approaching destinations. The image becomes better informed as he gets closer, but upon arrival it sloughs off, overwhelmed by direct sensory data, just as dreams are rarely remembered upon waking. Thus, I could hardly remember how I had imagined the famous Lagoon to look, but saw a body of water about a square mile in area, shallow, with one entrance on the Dutch side and one on the French side. It was enclosed by a narrow fringe of land all around, except that its east side adjoined the island proper, which was hilly and dry. Every few minutes a jumbo jet screeched out of the airport at The Lagoon's southern fringe. Hundreds of boats lay anchored and at moorings. It was luxurious to be in flat water again after such long exposure to ocean swells.

We set the main and sailed *Squeak* to a little island in the middle. A corner of it had been cleared of its native manchineel and planted with palms. Someone had neatly raked the golden sand in anticipation of 10:00 A.M., when the daily double-decker tour boat would come, leave its passengers there for an hour, then whisk them off to their next "experience." It was a stage set for someone else, a cunning imitation of nature. Grateful nonetheless, we beached and set up Meg's tent.

Our parting the next day was made tedious by the usual complications of air travel. Meg checked in while I sat against a wall on the terminal's linoleum floor, people-watching, and wondering why we don't all just stay where we are, with those whom we've come to love. Meg shed tears in our last embrace. Perhaps she sensed it was our last meeting. Then she was in the passenger-only terminal and I was alone again. I felt empty, guilty, relieved to no longer have to wait for others, not yet lonely.

As always, I had the voyage, like a mantra, to focus myself. I needed technology to get *Squeak* seaworthy again, and for that I was well-placed. The Lagoon is an international waterway. On the north side lies the chic town of Marigot. Casinos, resorts, shopping districts, and marinas dominated the Dutch side. A Creole- and Spanish-speaking underclass loitered around the shacks where lottery tickets were sold. The jets overhead were full of North American and European tourists and business people, and duty-free shoppers from all over the Caribbean. But they also shuttled the army of unskilled workers, especially Haitians and Santo Domingans, who kept the machine going, because the native black population was relatively small.

Marcus anchored in his habitual corner of The Lagoon, near the airport. I gravitated to Cole Bay, at the east end, because that's where the marine industries were concentrated. I chose the Lagoon Marina as my base because it was a mom-and-pop outfit, and because they were willing to charge me next to nothing for a slip too shallow for anybody else to use.

In nature I'd have been self-sufficient, but here I needed security, and a way of bathing other than in The Lagoon, which was polluted. Everywhere, old cane fields were being transformed into warehouses, and mangrove swamps into parking lots. Public works lagged behind, resulting in quagmires and traffic jams. Many lamented these problems, but always pessimistically, with detachment. Those just passing through saw it as someone else's problem, while the poor and newly affluent had not yet developed an environmental awareness.

My fellows at the Lagoon Marina were just passing through. Most were English or South African, of working-class background. The young ones were there to make money so they could resume cruising, the middle-aged ones had invested in small businesses, and the older ones were living on pensions. A couple of the guys fished for deep-sea snapper. Every night they all sat around little tables in the marina office, which doubled as a lounge, and drank cheap Santo Domingo beer. There was a hurricane-tracking chart pinned to the wall, and a library of worn-out paperbacks in the corner. The TV was always on but you could never hear it for the conversation. They did their best to draw me in, but I had little to add beyond the recounting of my voyage, which had become mechanical. They, keener than me on talking about themselves, used me as a springboard to entertain the group with tales of their own exploits.

"Was off the island of Milos I saw my worst storm," said John, a greasy metalworker from Birmingham. "Come around the western point and this mistral blows up. Pretty soon the waves was twenty feet high and curlin' over on top of us. Like to of shit my pants."

"Isn't that the Med for ya?" someone agreed. "Always too much wind or not enough."

A hippie-ish Frenchman had a section of broken mast he was willing to part with. It was straight-grain Douglas fir, like the oar it had to match. I cut a deal with the owner of a cabinet shop to use his facilities, and within a couple of days had cloned the surviving oar. Meanwhile, John the metalworker, operating out of a converted shipping container, made a pair of aluminum holders for my sliding boomkin, to replace the plywood ones that had popped off on Christmas Eve. He did a good job, so I commissioned him to make me a set of stainless steel oarlocks. Accustomed to Third World craftsmanship, I was pleasantly surprised when he got everything right the first time.

I had worked my way far enough north that the months of December through March, though still associated with stronger winds, were no longer associated with lower precipitation, as in South America. A tropical depression brought rain squalls. The wind continued at night, and the sea built up until even the fishermen stayed in port.

I needed better weather because my next task was to cross the Anegada Passage to the Virgin Islands, eighty miles away. It would be the first time I'd sail through the night, the first time I'd be out of sight of land, and my first passage straight downwind. That was too many firsts all at once to take lightly, so I spent time with Glenn and Pete, my fisherman friends, considering options. To reduce the odds of being run over I bought a light powered by a single D cell and devised a way to jam it into the top of my mizzen mast. Pete saved me $18.95 by giving me an old chart. A Danish sailor saved me $24.95 by showing me how to make a 1991 nautical almanac work for 1993.

Pete Hudson, the fisherman, didn't hang out with the others, but each time he passed me on the pier he offered to help in some way.

"I'm going over to the marine store in a little bit, need a lift?" or

"I've got some light line I don't use anymore. Want it?"

He was a robust man. Vigor had shaped him, but he was no longer vigorous. He looked like his spirit was fading before his body. I spent time with him on his boat, where he pointed out various improvements he intended to make. "But I come down here every morning and I don't feel like doing anything, so I just listen to the weather forecast then go back home. I'm finding it hard to keep my momentum up these days." He spoke bravely, calmly, like a man not given to complaint, for whom shyness is unnatural.

One day Pete drove me around the island. With us rode a Santo Domingan woman friend of Pete's. She and he could only converse in French, she and I only in Spanish, and he and I only in English, so one of us was always out in the cold. With me in the back seat was Pete's black lab, Sixty. He had been paralyzed from the waist back some weeks before by a blow from a human assailant. Pete was pretty sure who did it. He cleaned up the poor thing's uncontrolled excrement, and tucked his penis back into its sheath when it fell out in the course of dragging himself around. "We don't forget, do we, Sixty? We'll see how *he* looks with a broken back."

We completed our errands on the Dutch side of the island and proceeded to the French side. Pete stopped at Cul-de-Sac beach, where he had been bringing Sixty every day to "run" him in the shallow water along the shore. While Pete splashed alongside, Sixty worked his strong front legs. His hind end streamed limply behind, but he loved the sensation of being able to run again. "His rear legs are beginning to move a little, see?" said Pete.

In Marigot Pete treated us to lunch at a restaurant he was half owner of, and told me of his previous jobs as crewman, charter skipper, and owner/operator of a small freighter. "You should have seen Key West and St. Thomas in the sixties and seventies, Steve. The yachting scene was more counterculture back then, and fewer paradises had been lost. God we partied." We swapped stories, I that of the Frenchman whose throat had been slit for an outboard motor in Buenaventura. "I knew him!" exclaimed Pete. "He was a nice guy. What more can you tell me?" Later Marcus happened by, and he and I told the tale of Hans to Pete and other old-timers at the bar, adding another skein to the web of Caribbean lore, which tends toward the absurd or unexpected.

We continued counterclockwise around the island to his bungalow. Its focal point was a patio lush with plants and shady fish ponds. Like many fishermen, he had the touch of a farmer as well. On the table was a 1962 National Geographic with a picture of Pete as a blond, bare-chested deckhand aboard the tender of an experimental research submarine. It was a dramatic nighttime shot of the bathyscope suspended alongside after an emergency retrieval, with Pete spread-eagled, one foot on either vessel, securing a line. The virile youth was still visible in the paunchy but powerful man who gave me coconuts and spoke with such masculine sensitivity. With his balding head and pewter hair curling on his temples he could have posed for a bust of Caesar. In his every gesture he seemed to be turning something over in his mind, looking back. I didn't see how he could find anything but beauty in his soul. Yet he was in the grip of something I never identified, perhaps because he didn't know either.

The Christmas winds finally stopped. I bought new docking lines, spring-loaded clips, and a rectangle of clear plastic with parallel lines and a compass rose, for converting straight lines on the chart into compass headings, or vice versa. It was flexible, so I could employ it on the cylindrical surface of the seat deck. Not knowing when I would leave, I said good-bye to my friends as I saw them.

On January 18 I got a favorable weather forecast, then hurried to catch the eleven o'clock bridge opening. As I hoisted sail in the outer bay a gust flipped *Squeak* over. It was my first full capsize under sail, yet of no great concern. She slowly righted once I had released the mainsheet. I bailed out the cockpit and set a course for Dog Island, a speck of land fifteen miles north-northwest, to get some shut-eye at the westernmost jumping-off point.

It was a remote place: a steep, curving slope of bronze sand swept clean by each new surge, topped by low, untrammeled greenery. I couldn't land, so I dropped hook and laid down while the sun set over there, where I wanted to be. I needed to leave at night so as to make landfall during the day. I ate some bread and a can of mixed vegetables. Damned Radio Antilles skipped their evening weather forecast again. Pretty windy. Water too rough to sleep. Oh well, don't think, just do it.

At 11:30 P.M. I raised my four-pound Danforth and drifted until the mid-bay rock ghosted past, a blackness a shade denser than the moonless night. I hoisted the mizzen and hung it to starboard. I left the main down, sheeted its boom out to port, and pointed straight downwind. Thus canvassed, *Squeak's* helm was balanced, and hair-trigger sensitive. With only fifteen square feet of sail set, but displacing only 580 pounds, she went fast enough. I clipped a water bag to the starboard gunwale to balance my weight, which was to port. I kept my hand on the tiller, and found a star to steer by.

I strapped on a headlamp my brother David had sent me and periodically twisted it on to correlate stars with the headings on my compass.

The dark waves slid by underneath, their crests often sharp enough to slop a few gallons into the cockpit. I was cold from wind and wettings, but not to the point of shivering. *Squeak* pitched and yawed sharply. Soon I was fighting sleep. Periodically I allowed myself a second of dream activity, then jerked my eyes back open. The night glow of St. Martin slowly dimmed. The Sombrero Island light, twenty miles north, reflected off the clouds with each sweep. It shifted ever so slowly to the rear of my field of vision, then disappeared. A ship or two passed in the distance. I longed for the sun to rise.

Suddenly a flapping—the line controlling the forward end of the mizzen sprit boom had come loose. I resecured it. Another mad flapping! This one stupefied me. It seemed a living thing, and indeed it was. A silvery, yard-long needlefish had strolled into the cockpit and was beating itself to death at my feet. "All right, do that," I said. "I'll gladly eat you tomorrow."

My lodestars disappeared behind invisible scraps of cloud, and dipped below the horizon as the earth turned. I selected others, keeping her to due west magnetic, until the sun rose behind me, revealing something I'd never seen before from *Squeak*: no land anywhere.

I unstepped the mizzen mast and removed the running light. I had rather hoped Virgin Gorda, westernmost of the British Virgins, would be visible by now. To hasten her appearance I raised the main. Speed increased to about five knots. As the waves overtook me, situating me teeter-totter fashion atop their sharp crests, the water around me crushed into foam. It appeared *Squeak* might surf down the wave fronts, but happily she didn't.

Having heard that the current sets northwest, putting hapless boats onto Anegada Reef, I compensated by steering fifteen degrees south of my target. I left in time, theoretically, to reach land at two P.M. But by midmorning there was still no land in sight. I contemplated taking a sun sight with my sextant, which I'd never used, but the motion was too sharp to get an accurate angle. Besides, I'd have to heave to and deal with all those disgusting tables, when what I needed to do was get to land before dark. I hailed a passing ship with my hand-held VHF, hoping to get a position, but no one answered. Then I was alone again.

Perhaps because the horizon was uninterrupted, the sea looked different. The overcast was thin and patchy. As far as I could glimpse, eight-foot waves, some white-capped, marched westward in slow motion. A grand topography slowly evolved and expressed itself. My particular piece of the globe seemed, not just water, but a *place*, different from others. I thought of snowscapes in my native Cascade Mountains. Because clouds, waves, and I were all going the same direction, it seemed a harmonious world.

At eleven o'clock I saw what appeared to be an island far to the north-northwest. No. Yes! It was visible only from wave tops, in moments of relative clarity, but an island it was. Which? Whichever, I wanted to be there.

With wind and waves now on the starboard quarter, I semi-planed while traversing the smoother wave fronts. My island was the size and shape of a penny lying on the floor at the other end of a room, as viewed with one's head pressed to the floor. This geometric abstraction slowly became real, with vegetation, and weather. A white rainstorm obscured it, and moved on. Another marched past to the south.

My Defense Mapping Agency chart of the Anegada Passage showed Virgin Gorda to have a height of 414, and my Imray-Iolaire chart of the Virgins showed the small islands streaming off Virgin Gorda's southwest tip to be even higher. "My" island stood alone, so it couldn't be Virgin Gorda.

A second large island appeared to its left, further away, equally hilly. I hypothesized I was sailing toward St. John, and that St. Thomas had appeared to its left. Hills and smaller islands, as they revealed themselves, more or less fit the pattern. I tried calling a passing sailboat, but again no answer. Daylight was running out. I had to reach land before dark.

By 4:30 I had in view a complex geography tantalizingly close to that which I would see from my hypothetical position, but where were the islands to the right of St. John? Frustrated, I rejected all assumptions and started over. St. Croix? Too many islands. Anegada? Too hilly. Gods or mapmakers playing cruel tricks on me? Not funny. Virgin Gorda? I compared the maps again and realized the first had heights in meters, whereas the second was in feet. I'd thought they were both in feet. Everything suddenly popped into place: "St. John" was Virgin Gorda, and "St. Thomas" was Tortola. I promptly steered west-southwest for what I now recognized as the gap between Round Rock and Ginger Island. The latter had a faint, flashing light. Due to a faulty assumption regarding current, and faulty map-reading, I would be entering an unfamiliar passage after dark. But, with land now too close alee to spend the night adrift (horrid thought!), valor seemed better than discretion. Go for it.

The sun set. Light slowly drained from the sky. The breakers on Round Rock became visible: angry white explosions in the murk to my right. Not too close! Then I was through the passage and entering Sir Francis Drake Channel.

The sea calmed. The lights of Tortola blazed across the channel. Spanish Town was the nearest harbor, three miles north. An hour later I glided in, past buoys and anchored yachts, to a beach with gently lapping waves, lit by lamp lights. I threw my anchor like a lasso onto the dry sand, and let the land-muffled breeze hold me off. The water was clear, knee-deep. I'd made it! I could sleep, and in the morning explore a new archipelago, a new series of stepping stones leading back home.

Morning found me luxuriating in sun and stillness. What was that tune going through my head? With a snort of self-contempt I realized it was "Mary Had a Little Lamb," boldly rearranged through countless brain cycles. The needlefish, now thirty hours dead, was attracting bottle flies. I gave it away. After clearing customs I roamed through an antiseptic world of manicured lawns and newly opened gift shops. President Clinton was giving his inaugural address on a large TV screen in a courtyard restaurant crowded with somber Americans. Uninspired, I sailed south along the shore I had passed in darkness.

Virgin Gorda was a hilly island of palm trees and giant boulders. These rounded and split lumps of stone grew and multiplied until I reached The Baths where, piling one atop the other, they created in the dark spaces between them a network of sandy-floored caves, interpenetrated by the sea to form surging, dimly lit pools.

I landed on a pocket beach adjacent to The Baths and pulled up into the shelter of an elephant-colored megalith erupting from the sand at the beach line. The low, kinky sea grape of the upper beach had been cleared back to make room for a T-shirt stand and open-air bar. The skyline toward The Baths was close and tall: stone obelisks set off by palm crowns on reed-like trunks, never straight, but flaring delicately. The area was crowded with beach towels and lily-skinned sunbathers. *Squeak* stood out like a sea lion in a pelican colony, but no one told me to leave. Then the shadows lengthened and everybody left but me and the feral cats hanging around the garbage can.

The cheerful black vendors returned in the morning to open shop. Camera-toting New Englanders and Argentines walked down into the clearing, paused, and struggled to make sense of the strange collection of objects confronting them in that small enclosure. The curious minds took longer, while the lazy minds were soon staking out spaces for their beach towels. From the former group I selected an old man from Connecticut to help me wrap a collar of epoxy-soaked twine onto the mizzen mast to keep it from sliding down through its supports. Groups came and went. Someone touched one of *Squeak's* leeboards and asked if it was the rudder. Another pointed at the rudder and asked if it was the anchor. Most questions reflected fears.

"What do you do when it gets rough?"

"Aren't you afraid of sharks?"

"Don't you get lonely?"

One of my interrogators was a paunchy English gentleman with a silky voice and melancholy eyes. "Good show young man. The name's Tony Snell. Please, when you leave here visit my restaurant, The Last Resort. It's just across the channel, on a little island off Tortola. No, the island's too small to have a name, but you can't miss it. It's just beyond that headland there, see?"

That afternoon I sailed as he had instructed and presented myself at his dock. Tony situated me at his well-appointed bar, where my needs were attended to, then at a dinner table with himself and assorted guests. Tony had a quick bite, then got onto the stage and delivered droll comedy. He feted a birthday girl, introduced an intrepid explorer (me), and played humorous ditties on an extraordinary range of instruments. Periodically he exhorted his charmed audience to buy "Pusser's, the official rum of the Royal Navy—it's been killing British sailors for generations. And, yes, for each sale I receive a small commission. All the more reason!"

The evening wound down. I slept at the dock, and rose in the stormy dawn to explore the deserted nightclub. The tables and chairs had not yet been repositioned. A damp wind blew through. Raindrops splattered on the windows and ran off in rivulets. Through the panes, misty islands and gray sea bled together, like a watercolor left out in the rain. The nightclub walls were spangled with curiosities and memorabilia. One was a World War II photograph of a cocky young man standing before a fighter plane on an English field. It was Tony with the Spitfire he piloted in the Battle of Britain. On another wall a London showbill from the year 1960 caught my eye. It depicted a showman resembling Soupy Sales with various instruments swirling around his head. I suddenly realized that this too was my host, thirty-three years younger.

Tony came out in silk robe and slippers to see me off. He was casual and pensive when not in his show mode. "Stephen, it's been a great honor to have had you with us. Sure you'll be alright in this weather? Quite nasty today. Here, I'll fend you off. Best of luck!"

I paused a few days in Road Town, Tortola's main settlement, then exited the British Virgin Islands. The customs and immigration officers, not satisfied with charging me to enter, charged me again to leave. Each new country brought some new hassle, like unexplained fees or unreasonably short time allowances. My entry at St. John, U.S. Virgin Islands, however, was an exception. For the first time in two years I was on U.S. soil, and could stay as long as I damn well pleased.

The Virgins are divided politically, but otherwise they're alike: small islands with a West Indian cultural base to which massive Anglo-Americanism has been grafted. Tourism is the only industry, but there's a lot of it, and welfare programs are generous. By some perverse linkage, the Virgins have both the highest standard of living, and the highest crime rate, in the English-speaking Caribbean.

My first night I went to a bar teeming with young whites who had come down from the States to work in tourist-related industries. Sexy chicks in jeans and white blouses sucked on long-neck Buds while a band played such all-time hits as "You're an Asshole Too" and "Why Don't We Get Drunk and Screw," with fiddle, mandolin, and spoons accompaniment.

I asked an inebriated woman I'd seen up on the stage if she was with the band, and she replied, "I show my tits. I'm the tits-shower."

"I missed that part. Can I see them?" She gladly lifted her shirt. They were big.

"Can I touch them, too?" She wandered away without responding, but another guy grabbed her boobs, and he didn't even ask. She laughed and clouted him back into his seat. My own culture shocked me, but I could get used to it.

I set myself up on the beach, borrowed a laptop from a local radio personality, and caught up on my writing. Curious visitors weren't long in arriving: hippie cooks, female diving instructors, elderly tourists in dazzling Bermuda shorts. One day I even ran into Josef and Miriam, the Israeli Humphrey Bogart and Sophia Loren I'd known in Trinidad.

"Whoa, Stephen, all this time I am thinking, is my friend alive? I am sure I never see you again," said Josef with his huge, boastful smile. "Look, Miriam, can you believe it? The crazy American, he is still alive!"

"OK, so I'm crazy. Hey, I thought you guys were sailing to the Pacific. What're you doing here?"

"Oh, the owner he changed his mind," said Miriam. "Now he wants us to take the *Lady Dorothy* to Miami." She leaned over and added, in a fierce whisper, "And I promise you that when we get there Josef and I are splitting up for good. We have decided."

"Where will you be docking in Miami?"

"At the Miami Beach Marina," said Josef.

"I'll look you up."

I left in the pre-dawn of January 30. The black sky started absorbing the sun's rosy light. Then the still sea absorbed it, going from glossy black to gray blue, then transparent, like air. The sun rose, warming the land. This heat rose into the sky, creating a sea breeze which I caught in my sails. This was a new pattern. Sometimes the world was regular like this, like a great clock. Other times and places were marked more by change and discontinuity. I saw order and disorder playing tug-of-war with me as the rope. Such cosmological imaginings were probably shallow, but you have to think about something when you spend three years in a twelve-foot boat.

I rode the awakened wind through what looked like the San Juan Islands of my home state. Fancy hotels lined the beaches of St. Thomas. Villas dotted its hillsides. By midday I was in Charlotte Amalie, the old Danish city. Its commercial core had been preserved as a grand bazaar for liquor, perfume, and loose diamonds. In the harbor were more magnificent yachts than I had ever seen assembled. The cruise ships lining the wharf each struggled to be taller, whiter, statelier, more futuristic than the others. They were floating nirvanas, jostling for market share. But I remembered a survey I had read in *Holiday Magazine*. They had asked their readers for the "best and worst of modern cruise-making" and every respondent had the same complaint: that the other people assigned to their dinner table were invariably boring. I imagined banquet halls full of tables at which everyone thought everyone else was boring, and felt better about my solitude.

I picked up a raft of Christmas mail at the post office and read through it at a Wendy's Restaurant. There were a lot of letters—family, Jim and Eileen, Mariela, Meg—so I selected the all-you-can-eat lunch and stretched it out. Frankly, for $4.69 I ate both lunch and dinner, and snacked continuously in between. The letters made me cry, and the sentimental tears that splashed over my salads and casseroles added a delightful touch of salt.

These were days of easy travel. The weather was lovely, coves were numerous, and provisions readily available. I stopped at Isla de Culebra, part of Puerto Rico. It was another U.S. possession with little incentive to cast off Yankee imperialism. Just as I had marveled at the marriage of West Indian and American cultures, I was now entering a Latin America in which *los Estados Unidos* is not a remote powerhouse, but a day-to-day presence. Many of the locals worked at a pharmaceutical plant which had located there to avoid paying corporate income tax. Here were no crowds waiting to get into a U.S. Consulate, because anybody with the money for a plane ticket could fly to New Jersey and stay with relatives while looking for work.

Having decided to follow the south coast of Puerto Rico, which is the more sheltered, I sailed west from Culebra to Marina Palmas del Mar, on the east end of the island. Surrounding it were luxury condominiums of neo-Spanish architecture. I anchored just inside the breakwater, in an area reserved for the plywood runabouts utilized by the local fishermen. Expensive cars stood with their engines idling in a dirt turnaround at the landing. Middle-aged Latin men sat inside, kissing painted women. The fishermen were all in port, visiting with each other in Spanish and attending to small chores. When I spoke to them in their own language they responded in English, as if to say, "It's not necessary for you to understand our language. We understand yours."

The next day I rounded the southeast corner of the island and continued west, cutting across the openings of a dozen half-moon bays. It was a benevolent coast. I trailed a feathered lure and caught a yellow reef fish. Blue-green hills tapered down into a flat, blue sea. Each new headland began as a flat line the color of the sea. It appeared on the horizon suddenly, just as a fingertip touching water causes it to suddenly dimple upward. First the headland hovered flat, like a mirage. Then it grew, darkened, solidified. New headlands cropped up behind and to its left, depriving it of its saliency, until it lost itself in the hills' evolving skyline.

I found an opening in the coral reefs and mangrove cays that parallel the shore, and continued, still downwind, in the elongated lagoons behind. Manatees flapped their fan-shaped tails and dove as I passed. *Squeak's* sails billowed. Her wake hissed. The soft, flat water hypnotized me. I reflected on the years of designing and building it took to be able to sit there and go where I wanted to go, see what I wanted to see, with no more effort than a flex of the fingers of my right hand. It was worth it.

On February 7, I reached the relatively modern city of Ponce. It sprawled across a coastal plain, its colonial center set back several miles from the shoreline. I bought a cheap, battery-powered word processor at the local Radio Shack and spent the next three weeks writing, first on a deserted island at the entrance to the harbor, then on a beach at the Ponce Yacht Club. I cooked and took my meals in *Squeak*, or under such shelter as presented itself. When the nights became dewy I bought a blanket and stitched it up like a sleeping bag. When the white gas that powers my stove ran low I bought another can at K-Mart. In two and a half years I had used two and a half gallons. Every few days I trekked to a distant supermarket where groceries were inexpensive. Wherever I went I jogged, pack on back, map in hand, mind busy with routes. My frustrations were the same as in previous layovers, but I was thankful for the health which allowed me to pursue the voyage. I was weary, but it was the managed weariness of a runner nearing the end of a marathon.

My beach could only be approached by passing through the Yacht Club gate, so only well-heeled Puerto Ricans visited me. One, an earnest young engineering student of Cuban descent named Ricardo, saw that to draw me out would require effort, so he visited daily. He drove me around on errands and when I left, on February 21, gave me a T-shirt that said, "*Yo Amo A Puerto Rico* (I Love Puerto Rico)." The words were true for me, thanks largely to Ricardo himself. I gave him a copy of the poem of thanks I had written for Karen and the others in Cali, and which I reserved for my dearest benefactors.

From Ponce I sailed west along a low shore of brittle stone, then through vast, mangrove-fringed shallows. Eel grass carpeted the bottom. A coral reef, detectable only as a white line on the horizon, sheltered the water. I worked my way around the island's southwest corner and into Boquerón Bay. The hills were greener on this side. Several dozen seasoned cruising boats lay at anchor, their owners attracted by the relaxed atmosphere of the village. It had a dinghy dock at the foot of its main street, and a little plaza where one could drink cold beer and eat mangrove oysters in the company of other over-the-hill gringos.

I got a clearance for the Dominican Republic, then joined those salty dogs for happy hour. "Wasting Away Again in Margaritaville" played on a jukebox. They all had single-sideband radios, so I pumped them for weather forecasts. An unattached Englishwoman joined us, and one of the cruisers, a former Los Angeles fireman on a generous disability retirement, unabashedly put the make on her. "You know, you're really my type. What can I say? I like your looks. How'd you like to throw that bag of yours on my ketch and be my lady?" He was tall, blond, good-looking, but the woman was noncommittal. She just sat there, fidgeting with a handful of quarters, blushing slightly. "Instead of quarters those could be hundred-dollar bills," he offered, in a lower tone. She glanced at him, a modest smile in the corners of her pretty mouth. Unfortunately, I left too soon to find out whether she took the bait. A cold front was supposed to strike in about forty-eight hours. That left me just enough time to sail the forty miles to Isla Mona, rest up, then sail the remaining forty miles to Hispaniola.

At 2:00 A.M., when my wristwatch alarm went off, I left on a gentle breeze. Being in the lee of a mountainous island, it took two hours to enter into the full motion of the sea. It got light, and I stripped as the sun warmed me, then covered again as it threatened to burn my skin. A gray-brown seabird with beady black eyes kept circling, attempting to land atop the mainmast, but couldn't quite settle down on that sharp, swaying perch. I shifted between the various positions suitable for steering downwind. None of them were comfortable for long because I had to keep my weight centered, eyes forward, yet work the tiller behind my back. I realized I'd made an error of 20° in plotting my course, and compensated accordingly. Isla Mona was only five miles in diameter. Would I find it?

At nine A.M. I hailed a freighter on my VHF. "Ship with red hull steaming south, this is small sailboat one mile to your port, over?"

A British voice responded. "This is the *Mersey Victor*. I see you, barely. Can I be of assistance? Over."

"What's your position, over?"

A pause, then "That's north seventeen degrees fifty-three minutes, west sixty-seven degrees forty-one minutes. Over."

"Thank you. That's all. Over."

"*Mersey Victor*, over and out."

I set the tiller in one of its notches to maintain course, plotted the ship's position on my chart, and estimated my own. Then I calculated Isla Mona's heading, stood, and looked in that direction. There it was.

It began as an intermittent white line and grew into a flat, cliff-fringed pancake of land. The island looked as if it had been stamped out with a giant cookie cutter and misplaced in the shuffling of continents. The limestone cliff was eighty feet tall, pockmarked with caves, blackened in the sockets. Surf pounded heavily on a coral reef encircling the island.

At one in the afternoon I located a landing on the east side. It consisted of a narrow, ill-defined passage into a belt of still water behind the reef. To one side of the opening lay the bones of a wrecked freighter. I waited until a lobster boat entered, then followed in its wake. From a short, steep beach grew palms and shrubs that partly screened the cliff.

Now that I was safe, I realized this landing didn't suit me. I would need daylight to row back out through the passage, whereas I had to leave at two in the morning in order to arrive at Hispaniola with the sun still high. The fishermen told me of another landing on the lee side of the island, so I went back out and continued around the south side, careful to distinguish between normal whitecaps and waves breaking over coral heads. The water was transparent blue and green. I sailed over forests of staghorn coral like an airplane flying just above the treetops.

At the west end was a cove where divers and hunters lived in tents among the lofty palms. Excited by my arrival, they pulled me up into their camp and plied me with manta ray steaks and cold Budweisers.

"Where have you come from, señor?" one asked in Spanish.

I pointed out the map painted on the aft locker cover.

"*In that?*"

"Yes, in this."

"And where are you going?"

"Dominican Republic."

"Caramba! I hope we don't see your boat back here in a few days filled with *Dominicanos.* They are sneaking into Puerto Rico by boat, and they stop here first. Don't let them hijack you!"

These humble men scratched a living from the sea, or had come to hunt wild goats and boars. I longed to explore the immense caverns they told me about, and see the species of iguana that exists nowhere else in the world, but the good weather was due to end. Besides, what did it matter what I missed along the way as long as each day brought new experiences?

I set my alarm and went to bed early. When it went off I slid *Squeak* silently out of the camp and down the steep bank. Her keel left a groove in the sand, like the trail a mother turtle leaves when she waddles from her egg burrow back out to sea. But for that groove, my friends might have wondered the next morning whether my arrival was real or imagined.

CHAPTER 28

DOMINICAN REPUBLIC

It was February 25, 1993. A ship passed, its heading discernible by the relative positions of its high stern lights and low bow lights. It still seemed vaguely foolhardy to sail at night, blind to unlit hazards, but sailors have always done so. Like them, I relied on my reckoning as to where land lay, and hoped no flotsam or surfacing whales lay directly in my path.

The breeze was just adequate to maintain three or four knots. At 9:30 A.M. I spotted Punta Espada, fifteen miles north. An hour later an atmospheric discoloration on the western horizon became Isla Saona, a limestone plain the color of molding corn stalks.

I'd read much about Hispaniola's preeminence in the initial phase of the Spanish Conquest, but knew nothing about the modern-day Dominican Republic. Because the less I know about a place, the more it intrigues me, I burbled with excitement as I approached the shallow, coral-studded bay separating Isla Saona from the southeast tip of Hispaniola.

A rowboat or two tended fish pots, but there was no sign of man on the lush lowlands to my left nor in the mangrove swamps to my right. I came into the lee of reefs and flew through the flat water of the bay. Flecks of foam streamed from *Squeak's* stern. I stood tall on the seat deck and looked through the pale water as if through glass. Brown manta rays darted away like giant moths at my approach.

I exited the bay's western opening and continued northwest along a pristine shore. A whale spouted and thrashed his tail. A sea turtle lifted his head to eye me. I expected a native village, and soon saw one, but it was actually a resort complex in disguise. Thatched, onion-shaped roofs blended into palm trees. Windsurfers flitted along the beach like brilliant butterflies. Finally, I entered a quiet cove and anchored among a fleet of sail-powered fishing smacks, to stretch out and enjoy a full night's sleep.

The next day I landed at a military dock in La Romana, at the mouth of a small river. Armed men in T-shirts and fatigues excitedly conducted me to a dim room in which a little old man sat at a desk. His fingers rattled a manual typewriter. I sat facing him on a wooden bench and didn't move for two hours, reverent before the god of paperwork. Perhaps my piety touched the old man, because while he typed my customs papers he occasionally glanced up over his bifocals and smiled at me, as if to say, "Ah, youth!"

When the ceremony came to a close I walked cautiously up to town. It brought home to me how sanitized Puerto Rico had become under U.S. administration. *This* was the Latin America I knew: dirty, noisy, high-spirited, glorious. The chaotic public market and the central park full of stuffy homages to "heroes of the revolution" seemed straight from Panama or Colombia. The same dust choked me, the same panoply of smells persuaded me to breathe through my mouth. Black, white, and Indian blood intermingled; few people were full-blooded anything. Two dollars bought me a heaping plate of rice and greasy chicken. I returned to the docks and rowed up the river a piece, admiring the shanties that scrambled up the steep, garbage-strewn slopes. I gave the gleeful slum kids rides for a while, then sailed out the mouth of the river to spend the night on a nearby islet.

The islet was a limestone slab, barely above sea level. Its edge was vertical, undercut by wave action. Freestanding remnants were mushroom-shaped, with gnarly caps. I arrived on its lee side just as a cruise ship was departing, and landed on a freshly evacuated beach. Minutes before hundreds of tourists had been paying big money to be there, but the only people I shared the island with were a quartet of ragtag soldiers, garrisoned there to make sure nobody stole the island. They questioned me suspiciously for a few minutes, then resumed knocking coconuts out of trees with rocks. Meanwhile, I stretched out on a cushy beach chair and opened a can of beans. "Ah, yes!" I exulted. Then the sun went down and a million mosquitoes attacked me. The tourists had left just in time.

Two days' sailing down a low, regular coast put me in Santo Domingo, the capital. I entered the mouth of the Rio Ozama and searched among battered naval vessels and rafts of garbage and hyacinth for an appropriate berth. I found it under the stern of a replica of the *Niña.* The river was laced with raw excrement and a greasy tar that coated everything. A nearby power plant spewed a gritty soot night and day. The concrete wharf was suitably low, however, and watchmen provided twenty-four-hour security. The wakes were tolerable. Might as well write here.

From my berth I looked across wharf and a four-lane arterial to the ancient city wall. Subsequent research in local museums told me that Columbus had anchored here in the original *Niña* after the *Santa Maria* sank off the island's north coast. He chose this site to be the capital of New Spain. The docks were here in ancient times as well. Where *Squeak* now berthed once berthed the caravels and galleons by which Spain spread its empire. From here set forth the expeditions that colonized Cuba, Jamaica, Panama, northern South America, Puerto Rico, Florida, and Mexico, all within thirty years of the city's founding.

I walked through the Puerta de las Atarazanas (Gate of the Dockyards). There, among charming plazas and stairways, were the first church, monastery, university, hospital, court, mint, and customs house in the western hemisphere. Some were restored, others in picturesque ruins. All were built during those first, explosive thirty years. Spain's finest architects designed the city. The peaceful Taino Indians, of the Arawak culture, were forced to cut the limestone, lay the bricks, and work the gold mines, until mistreatment and disease wiped them out. The Spanish then brought in Indians from other islands. They too died. Finally, they imported Africans. They survived.

Imperial focus soon shifted to the richer gold- and silver-bearing deposits of Mexico and Peru. The ports controlling the flotilla routes—Cartagena, Veracruz, Havana—boomed while Santo Domingo became a backwater. No longer wealthy or progressive, it nonetheless remained the metropolis of what would become the Dominican Republic. Within a century or two it had overflowed its walled confines. In recent times a rural-to-urban population shift had brought sprawl.

I stayed there a week, admiring the inventive way doors and windows were arranged in the façades of the well-policed colonial zone, and the tumult of the inner city beyond the walls. For there it was carnival time, and brightly colored bird-like creatures festooned with mirrors, chains, and bells ran through the streets swinging plastic clubs. At night, as I hurried through urine-stained neighborhoods, groups of seated men beckoned—"Psss! Psss!"—trying to weasel rum money out of me. The hubbub thrilled me. Sensing danger, I minded my "envelope" as a defensive driver does in a car. I didn't move like someone unfamiliar with the city. I looked too hard and busy to be mistaken for prey.

Among the many to come and stare down at me from the wharf's edge while I sat in *Squeak,* tapping on my word processor, was a dark brown, sparrow-like woman. Her eyes were the shape of almonds. "Are you an Indian?" she asked, musically.

It was a refreshingly novel question. "No my friend, I'm a white man."

She nodded slowly, her lips parted in a childlike smile. "And is your little boat the son of this one?" she asked, indicating the *Niña's* tall stern. It rose above *Squeak* much as a hen's tail might tower over her chick.

I laughed. "No." *Wait,* I thought, *is she serious?* "Why? Do you think boats give birth?"

"I don't know. All the world is strange."

"No, I sailed here." I told her the story.

"You live in this boat? That too is strange." She marveled some more, her expression never changing, then, "Tomorrow I will bring you a little *tinto.*"

She returned in the morning with a cup of strong coffee on a saucer. When I had drunk it she said, "Want to come to my house?"

"Sure." After I'd locked up we walked through a blighted district just outside the city wall to what apparently had been a two-story factory. *"Bienvenidos al Caserón,"* she said. The syllables were staccato, gaily inflected. "Come." Touching my arm, she led me through a narrow entrance, past chattering adults and restless children, to a corridor that snaked between lean-tos propped against the building's tall brick walls. The second floor and roof no longer existed. The lean-tos pressed together under the open sky, as if shoehorned in place. Residents moved from one to another in cycles of work, play, fraternity. Their clothing was flimsy and worn, yet many laughed and sang. Their hair was black, eyes brown, teeth white and flashing. I smelled people, fried food, kitchen scraps.

"Caserón, Caserón. I don't know that word." I pulled out my dictionary. It read, "Caserón, *masculino,* big, tumble-down house, barracks."

"Caserón, of course. How many families live here?"

"Thirty-five. One moment." While she asked a woman in a blue shift something about children and meals I looked around. They had tapped into power and water lines and had broken a hole in the floor to access a drain. Doors were left open. Spanish rap music trumpeted from an unseen tape player. A toddler danced to it in the soiled corridor.

"I live here." We entered her shelter and sat down. It was too small for its table, three chairs, and bed. "What's your name?"

"Estevan. What's yours?"

"Cherí."

"How old are you, Cherí?"

"Twenty-six."

"Children?"

"Yes, two. They're with my sister right now." She smiled as if even these facts held wonder for her.

A child of three or four came whining for food. "He has no parents," she said. She left, arranged something. Soon the boy was at her table eating a bowl of fried plantain. She sat back down on her bed, facing me.

"Estevan. What a pretty name. I'll visit you every day."

She did so, and always was refreshing as a wild strawberry along a stony path. Such diminutive fruit cannot satisfy hunger, however. That is, our friendship remained innocent, and her limited awareness of the factors ruling my life allowed her to cure only part of my loneliness.

From Trinidad to Puerto Rico I had had the company of other yachtsmen, but by following Hispaniola's south coast I had exited the yachting path. I welcomed this renewed separation from my own culture as a final reintensification of my experience. When once I saw two gringos talking at a sidewalk cafe on the great plaza, I checked my urge to approach them. *You're here to be here, not to be there,* I thought. Not having expressed myself intimately for weeks, my emotional batteries begged to be discharged, but ever so selectively, on the razor's edge between making it happen and waiting for it to happen. I could accept frequent, weaker discharges, or wait for a greater one. I chose to wait.

I wrote no worthy poetry—the rigor of voyaging had exhausted me of that. I wasn't desperately lonely like in Cali before meeting Mariela. My self-worth was good. But again, in my deepened introspection, I tasted that elusive sensation of whose incalculable components the most discernible is a rarefied joy. And it could be something more: not proximity to a superior being, but rather a resonance between my own value and an overall value.

I sensed a harsh joy as I hugged the shady side of streets to avoid the scorching sun. When a girl with hair of orange-brown frizz seemed to have fallen in pace beside me I experimentally touched the nape of her neck, and when she recoiled, so did I at my own audacity. I spent twenty-four hours with a cadre of young Spaniards living carefree lifestyles where they could speak their native tongue without the mechanical oppresiveness of Europe. I trudged the arrow-straight Calle Duarte, with its endless consumer-goods shops—it was crushed with people, harsh and dusty. I met a fellow Seattlite, my age, an explorer of African rivers, a researcher of historical novels. We were jarringly similar; I didn't know who to be with someone so like myself.

The chaos of my life sang to me, because my hands were around the neck of chaos, squeezing it to my will. The harder I squeezed, the more tasks I checked off my list of things to do before sailing to increasingly frightful coasts: the horn of southern Hispaniola, then Haiti, Cuba. They frightened me because no information was to be had about them—no charts, no consulates, no one familiar with the way.

I checked off tasks until I found myself again in my rowing seat, pulling out the mouth of the Rio Ozama. I felt cleaner as the slimy river dissipated into the sea, fetid brown to limpid blue. But poor Sea! How much more punishment can you take?

Again I sailed a low coast, but southeast swells now crashed into pockmarks in the land's abrupt edge, and over the coral reefs that lay off its points. The fore and aft halves of a giant freighter, sundered by some hideous bygone violence, lay like body parts on a narrow, gray beach. Then beach grew into dunes, and brown-green mountains advanced upon the coast from the island's cloud-capped interior. Empty Clorox bottles littered the waves, each connected by string to a fish pot on the shallow sea floor.

I rounded the conjunction of sandy crescents that made up Point Salinas and landed at a wilderness fishing camp. A dozen men and boys, without a word from me, helped careen *Squeak* and scrape off the tar she had picked up in the Rio Ozama. They were a slight people, their skin the color of coffee with cream, wearing any old western clothing. At dusk they began shuffling off to some nearby village. By the time I had cleaned up and eaten, moving hands and feet constantly to frustrate the hungry mosquitoes, I was alone with my thoughts of the next day's sail.

It was a thirty-mile shortcut, west across a concavity in the island's great belly. From horizon to zenith the sky was the same pale blue until, Point Salinas now receding behind me, a jagged line developed across the sky ahead and to my right. The portion below the line became a darker blue, until I realized it was a mountain range. Smokes of slash and burn punctuated its remote slopes. They were meager hills—soil, but not much, rainfall, but not much. Two thirds of the way across, a massive peninsula protruded from the north, nearly intercepting my course, but it was bluff-sided, lee-less. I ate leftover spaghetti, and scrubbed the burnt pot with the fingertips of one hand, dipping it in the sea to rinse, careful that it not be jerked from my grasp. I passed a snowy bird with a whip-like tail sitting on the water. The tail arched up and forward, its tip dangling over the bird's forehead like a goad. I thought, with neither dread nor longing, of being home again, harnessed into the labor force, in the bosom of my family. I sang nonsense songs, and the few shanties of which I remembered the words, all lost in the surf on Isla Galera nearly two years before.

Now mountains to north and south framed the valley that pierces Hispaniola from east to west, thereby nearly connecting Bahia de Neiba on the Dominican side with Baie de Port-au-Prince on the Haitian. Were sea level to rise a few feet, Hispaniola would become two islands, each still split into two countries. The town of Barahona lay at the south side of the bay's entrance. The stacks and tall bulk of a sugar refinery materialized, then a street pattern suggested itself on a drab green piedmont. I stood up and a protective reef popped into view only a hundred yards away. *Where's the entrance?* I found it, jibing once, twice, cautiously hauling in the sheet then letting it burn through my hand, fingers braking its impulse, as the wind backed and slammed the sail to the other side.

I landed at a hotel beach populated by lackluster Germans and neatly uniformed security personnel. Plainclothes policemen with gold chains around their necks arrived, searched *Squeak*, and coldly withdrew. I trekked into town for provisions, shaking off guides, prostitutes, and moto-taxi boys on Honda Trail 70s. I returned to find a sailor in dungarees standing by *Squeak*. He looked to be about seventeen years old.

"Sir, I have orders to accompany you to the naval post at the town dock," he said, nervously.

"Oh that's just great. Okay, if they need to hassle me too, then help me push off. Now step into the cabin there and sit. Face forward, that's it. Don't tip me over." The idea I might be commanding the eighth or ninth most powerful vessel in the Dominican Navy suddenly amused me, so I sang "What Do You Do With a Drunken Sailor?" as I rowed him to the dock.

There, a clutch of swabbies and daintily dressed officers scrutinized my papers with an air of bewilderment. As far as I could tell, they didn't even have a boat. They were excited by my mission, but anxious that they might process me incorrectly and thereby incur the wrath of their commander.

"I am very sorry, señor," said the post's second-in-command, "but foreign vessels must have permission before landing at any port. Your clearance does not mention Barahona, only Cabo Rojo, on the border with Haiti."

"In a boat as small as mine, with no motor, I can't possibly know in advance where I'll be at nightfall. That should be obvious. So I didn't even try to guess. I just got a single clearance."

"I sympathize, but please, *el Comandante* must first approve your release, and he has gone home for the day."

"The police have already searched *Squeak,* and they didn't find anything."

"Scoundrels! They have no right to interfere in Navy jurisdiction!"

I spent the evening telling my story and sharing their supper, for they were kindly men. But my irritation returned as I wasted much of the following morning waiting for the elusive commander to give me the Supreme OK to continue minding my own business.

Finally the second-in-command came out. "Your new clearance is ready, my brave friend. But I'm sorry, he says you must pay a ten-dollar fine."

"Ten dollars! I can't afford that kind of money! Please, as a fellow seaman…" Calling him that was a low blow, so strongly did he wish it were true. He worked his mustache back and forth, tapped the table.

"Aiee, you'll cost me my stripes. Go, and God bless you. I'll think of something."

"Ciao, amigo. Thanks."

The delay wouldn't have vexed me so much if my next hurdle weren't to round that mountainous horn whose tip is Cabo Beata, forty miles south of Barahona. Worried about reaching a landing place before dark, I rowed hastily out the harbor and down a bluff, exposed coast.

This day there was no wind, but the sea was choppy nonetheless. My tired torso arched and counterbalanced. *Squeak* bobbed so drunkenly my oartips often grabbed at water that wasn't there, or caught prematurely on waves. It was too rough to read during meal breaks. It was as if the swells, knowing they would soon die on the sharp rocks, aroused themselves in a final agitation. Farther out it might have been calmer, but I needed to monitor my chances of finding a haul-out. I didn't want to spend a sleepless night off an unlit lee shore. My charts didn't show landings, nor had sailors or fishermen been of much help. They seemed incapable of quantifying distance, even in terms of travel time. They had flustered when I questioned them, like schoolchildren caught without answers, and made up something if they didn't know.

At four o'clock I reached a village with a few yards of beach sufficiently sheltered to land the crude dories native to that coast. Privacy would have been nice, but I appreciated their helping me haul up. I helped them heave their boats too, enjoying, as always, the good cheer associated with that manly ritual, that smooth orchestration of sweaty muscles. Their catch was meager, because the soil erosion that robbed the land of its fertility also, as sediment, had choked the life-giving coral reefs. Still, donkeys bore a few avocados, tubers, and coffee beans down from the hill, and the fishermen brought in a few mackerels at the end of the day.

In early twilight a certain seabird traced the surf zone, and the men sprang to their feet with a shout, twirl-casting baited hooks into the curling breakers. They froze and jerked with cat-like acceleration, then pranced back, rewrapping their lines onto hollow tubes with blurred speed. The waning moon rose fifty-five minutes later than the day before, on the same lagging schedule as the tides. I climbed into bed. My hands hurt from rowing too hard for my current state of callus buildup. The stars pulsed.

I dreamed—people were screaming from some hideous calamity. I awoke, triggering that mental loop in which, upon waking, I always forced into consciousness a picture of my location—always in *Squeak* but always in a different place. It was driving rain, but the closed hatch had kept me dry. What in my dream had been screaming was the surf, scouring the shore with unquenchable fury. If I hadn't found that landing, I'd have spent the night fighting for my life.

I had to clear Cabo Beata. The next day an east wind built up until I feared being capsized by the large seas overtaking me on the port quarter. I steered facing backwards, studying the coming waves, looking forward only when I was on their crests, about every thirty seconds. Only a few fishing boats were out, and they could only be seen when both they and I were on crests at the same time. The mountains fell away again and were replaced by low wasteland. I saw the cape itself, a chopped-off headland a mite taller than the rest. Because I wanted to reach its lee so badly, it arrived with maddening slowness. Degree by degree I bore around, jibed, and began to savor the cape's protection.

In a tiny cove at land's end was a cluster of stick huts. I stopped to question the populace, most of whom were Haitian-born blacks. A score of ragged scarecrows knotted around me, gaping with disbelief. One was anxious to share his knowledge of geography. "In passing these narrows you are leaving the Caribbean Sea and entering another. Very *big* sea."

"What is the name of the sea I am entering?"

"The Pacific, perhaps…or the Atlantic. I am not sure."

"Are there other places to land a boat ahead?"

"Oh yes, places much better than this," he frowned, disdaining his own bleak hamlet.

I proceeded through midafternoon along a shallow, surf-less gulf that curved sublimely through a fifteen-mile arc, with a shoreline of soggy limestone sand backed by dry lagoons and buttes of scrub and torrid cactus. The land was desolate, roadless.

The next day I cut off the remainder of the gulf's arc, sailing downwind for Cabo Falso. Having camped in the lee of mountains I realized too late that a gale was blowing. Soon I was down to mizzen alone and tensing up with stress. Wave tops blew away as spindrift, and the sea became very rough with only a few miles of fetch. I made the cape, and with the wind now abeam had to raise the reefed main to make for Cabo Rojo, eight miles north. The waves were small again, but the wind was too strong to keep her upright. Nor was luffing the main an effective safety valve because the boom, flying out perpendicular, caught in the water whenever *Squeak* heeled, dragging the sail back into an oversheeted position. Inevitably, I was knocked down and thrown into the water. *Squeak* floated high on her side. Hull windage kept her pinned there, so I swam her bow up into the wind and righted her. By this time it was too late to look for the bailer bucket I had built in Port of Spain, or the two water ballast bags which had broken loose from the gunwale. Mercifully, the wind lessened after that.

Cabo Rojo (Red Cape) is so called for the red bauxite it consists of. There was no village, only a terminal for loading the mineral onto ships, and a dusty naval post. Rusty hulks littered the sandy shore. The terminal was rarely used anymore, and the sailors were bored. They gave *Squeak* the obligatory search and typed me a clearance for Jacmel, Haiti.

To get an exit stamp in my passport I hitched a ride on an ore truck to Pedernales, fifteen miles away across a baked plain. It was a sluggish border town, bristling with low-tech military installations. Its people were mostly Haitians—they spoke Spanish with a fumbling lilt. I found the immigration official, an illiterate buffoon who hadn't the faintest idea what to do with the rubber stamps he carried in a crumpled, brown paper bag. He nonetheless wasted an hour of my time with absurd reasons why he couldn't possibly employ them in the manner I suggested, until I resentfully bribed him four dollars.

In places like Boquerón and Santo Domingo, when I said I was going to Haiti, people invariably looked at me like I was mad. The news from there was always incomprehensible: a hundred people shot by soldiers for trying to vote, a thousand people drowned when a ferry tipped over. Here, so close, my travel plans were received more matter-of-factly. But I had run off the edge of my chart, and knew nothing about the coast ahead except that Jacmel, sixty miles away, would be my port of entry, and that from there a road led across the southern peninsula to the Gulf of Gonâve. I hoped to arrange portage there, thus positioning myself to cross the Windward Passage at its narrower, northern entrance.

CHAPTER 29

HAITI

On March 14 I rowed across the shallow, crystalline waters off Cabo Rojo. A light headwind had succeeded the storm. The sun burned my lower lip, and my wrist where my wristwatch used to be, the band having broken. Ashore, white, pink, and red rocks rose into lifeless hills—Haitian hills. The coastline to Jacmel described a vast, concave arc. To cut the distance I rowed in a more direct line, and rejoined the shore later in the day to seek shelter.

In doing so I found a jumble of huts at the foot of a sheer cliff on which goats scrambled for forage. A reef sheltered a lagoon just large enough to anchor in, which I preferred to landing given the uncertainty of my reception. About thirty ebony-skinned people were massing. They wore cut-off slacks, long, dusty skirts, and plastic shoes. Various emotions could be interpreted in their agitated movements. They readied a dugout. To maintain the initiative I didn't wait for them to come out, but rather stripped down and swam ashore, wading the last bit through ankle-deep seaweed, mindful of sea urchins. I stepped into their midst with feigned nonchalance. They closed in tightly around me, no smiles, no welcome, no leader. I told them briefly, through one who spoke Spanish, what I was doing, and extracted from them the names of the upcoming villages.

"Give me money," demanded one young male.

"Papers!" ordered another, but I silently turned and swam back. A wail of protests rose. They were bluffing, trying anything short of physical violence to detain me. One followed me, mocking my mincing step, the way I swam, and the village roared with unkind laughter. Several came out in a dugout and pestered me, but returned when I firmly commanded them to. I sat in my boat cooking, making my bed, and all the while the villagers watched me from shore and cliff top. They gestured vigorously whenever I looked up: circular belly rubs, agitations of uplifted forearm. They shouted unintelligible propositions, discussed me among themselves, and simply stared, arms crossed, fingers to chins.

The sun set. The lagoon smelled of briny weeds. A pelican dropped, kersplash. A mile offshore a boat drifted toward Pedernales under a ragged sail. He wouldn't make it anywhere before dark. Was he afraid, like me?

There followed another day of fickle winds, spent well offshore. I passed a man and two small boys with wicker fish traps piled high on the stern of their rowboat. My main halyard's outer braid wore through inside the masthead sheave, making it impossible to lower the sail, so I battened hatches, tipped *Squeak* on her side, and replaced the halyard in the water, swimming.

At five o'clock, when I linked back up with the coast, it was a thousand-foot cliff. This time, apparently, I'd sleep at sea. But suddenly the old trade wind kicked back in, rather violently, and I aimed *Squeak* like a big, wavering gun at a far-off point I hoped might provide shelter.

Behind the point was a village in a green, funnel-shaped vale. The cove opened directly onto the heavy swell. No good. Further down, behind a wooded delta at the foot of a valley, was another indentation, slightly less exposed. Just outside the roaring surf, the depth and bottom were suitable for anchoring. It was rough. If the anchor dragged, *Squeak* would soon drift into the breakers. But it was safer than heading back out to sea, because if worse came to worst I could swim to the beach. I dropped anchor and dove down to check its set, feeling my way through the murk and suspended sand.

I had potatoes and onions half chopped when five men in an outboard-powered boat came out through an obscure, diagonal gap in the breakers. Had I noticed the gap before I'd have landed, but the tension I sensed in these men persuaded me to pull my machete out. They stopped ten yards away. One spoke Spanish. "The village is afraid," he shouted. "You must come in with us."

"No. I sleep here tonight."

"Yes!"

They conferred in Creole, then motored upwind of me and fished my anchor line out of the water. They intended to tow me.

"Okay, let go. I'll come in." I up-anchored and followed them in.

The gravel beach was packed with yelling, milling people. My boat was roughly searched, my papers examined, my machete and passport confiscated. The sight of all my exotic belongings spread over the cockpit and surrounding beach excited the villagers. One of the men who'd been in the motorboat said something to me in Creole.

"He's the sergeant," said the Spanish-speaker. The "sergeant" wore no uniform and seemed less intelligent and sympathetic than my interpreter. "He wants you to go with him to the army post, for your own safety."

"Tell him I demand the right to stay with my vessel. He can post a guard over me if necessary." The sergeant gave in, unsure of himself. I was allowed to cook my dinner, but not to eat in peace. Everybody talked to me at the same time, laughed, argued, handled my gear, asked to borrow my flashlight.

For all their gaiety, they were also afraid. The sergeant was unable to find anyone willing to guard me until a strapping young man agreed on condition that his cousin keep him company. When everyone else had gone home, these two stretched out on the ground, a machete between them. They had no bedding, nothing to cover their bare chests, arms, and legs. They jabbered excitedly, like kids at their first camp-out.

Morning revealed a half dozen gaudily painted boats, a fringe of banana and sugar cane, and dirt streets on a narrow plain. The village was called Marigot. The ancient French must not have been very imaginative in their place-naming, this being the third Marigot ("Swamp") I had visited. The houses were small, and painted with whimsical, weakly geometric designs. Many Marigotians had sailed in overloaded boats for America. I was the first American to sail to Marigot. Their Creole was unintelligible, but limited communication was possible in French, English, or Spanish.

The subdistrict army commander arrived, a small, ugly man everybody kowtowed to. He had *Squeak* searched again, minutely, then ordered the villagers to haul all my stuff to the army post. They marched off like a file of ants with my gear balanced on top of their heads. Meanwhile I was shoehorned into a sedan packed with rifles and soldiers and driven to the subdistrict *fortaleza,* in the next village down the coast.

It was straight out of an old French Foreign Legion film: thick walls, tall ceiling, no windows, with one huge double door in front and another in back. Furnishings consisted of a desk and chair for the commander and a wooden bench for anyone else so lucky as to be invited to sit. I was. He had lunch brought to me.

The commander decided he wasn't competent to pass judgment on a matter of such weight as myself, so he ordered me taken under guard to district headquarters. A soldier conducted me to a street corner where we climbed into the back of a flatbed truck bound for Jacmel, Haiti's southern city.

Two hours later we entered a two-story army compound. Soldiers in olive-green uniforms and heavy black boots clumped in and out, rifles slung over their shoulders. We waited in an anteroom in which four lieutenants sat around a table covered with soiled papers, administering state with an air of bored incompetence. File drawers were open and flowing over onto the floor. The wooden cabinet cases were full of termite holes.

"Captain Souffraunt will see you now," said an adjutant.

He was a refreshingly calm, middle-aged black, in a tan uniform with gold insignia pins on the points of his collar. My passport lay before him on his desk. "Pleased to meet you. I am commander of Haiti's Southeast District. Yes, I speak English. I was educated in the States, you see."

"Thank you for your time. Do you understand my situation?"

He asked a couple of questions, then said, "I'm sorry. We get so few visitors, especially now, with the UN embargo. I'll ensure that you encounter no further difficulties." He wrote on a scrap of paper, in French, a note telling the subdistrict commander to release me provided he found no contraband.

"Thank you, sir."

"Good day."

I'd had to pay my own fare to Jacmel, and paid again for my return trip. I exercised what little I remembered of my high-school French with my escort along the way. When we had returned to the subdistrict *fortaleza* he poked his head in and asked something. "The commander's at home," he said. "We're to go there."

We walked up a dirt lane to a blue, cement-block bungalow. The Japanese sedan I had ridden in that morning was parked in front. Broad-leaf shrubs shaded a yard of trampled earth. The subdistrict commander, in boxer shorts and T-shirt, lay smiling in a hammock on the porch. He was small and round as a pygmy chieftain. Beside him stood a tall, gaunt woman in a black dress.

I handed him the note. He read it and gave it back to me. Then he said something to the woman, who addressed me in Spanish. "This morning the commander had to drive to Marigot in his own car. Now because of you he has to go again. He thinks you should give him money for gas."

I didn't like the pygmy's smile, or the woman's tone. "No. I don't want to."

"Permit me to remind you that you are not free. Now, is it fair that the commander should have to pay out of his own pocket? Don't you realize he's doing you a favor?"

"If he orders me to pay I will, but Captain Souffraunt said nothing about that." I held up the note and slid it into my pocket.

The pygmy stopped smiling. He grunted something. The woman glowered at me, then went into the house. She returned with the man's trousers and shirt.

We drove back to Marigot, where another ant-like procession conveyed my gear back to *Squeak*. My hundreds of paraphernalia were again unpacked and individually examined. "To verify that all is intact…" said the commander, but he was obviously enjoying himself. He toyed with my C-clamps, O-rings, and Q-Tips. He asked, through an interpreter, what my protractor, earplugs, and silicone sealant were for. I demonstrated the use of frisbee, dental floss, and signaling mirror. The villagers, though they'd already oohed and ah'ed over everything twice, crowded around in greater numbers than ever. They were awestruck. One of the last articles to be checked off was my tin whistle. Because it looked like I would soon be freed, I put it to my lips and piped "The Maid of Amsterdam," an especially merry shanty. Every eye and mouth shot open. They howled with glee, danced, slapped each other on the back. "Ain't he somethin'!" they seemed to say.

The next morning I sailed unmolested to Jacmel. From sea the town was a jumble of red tile roofs on a low hill, set off by the twin rococo towers of a cathedral. Except for a sea-going tug stranded on the coral reef, there were no ships in the harbor. Skirting heavy breakers, I landed at a beach composed of equal parts of gravel and garbage, at the foot of a pier heavily damaged by ship collisions. Nine idlers helped me pull up. Soldiers came.

"Wait until your chief comes before you search my boat," I said. "I don't want to have to go through this more than once."

They waited until a junior officer came, then stripped *Squeak* down. It being my fifth search in five days, I had learned how to maintain a degree of control by handing things out to them and explaining as I went along. The soldiers were irritable. The bystanders didn't venture close except for a bent little man who shuffled inconspicuously around the group, hands clasped behind his back. His suitcoat was tattered. Twine held his pants up, and the soles of his shoes flapped like tongues. When he passed behind me he whispered in English, "I can help you!" His face was impassive, but he shot grave, conspiratorial glances at me as he continued to circle.

I'd had the right idea about making them wait for their superior, but I hadn't gone far enough. When they were finished an obese police chief pulled up with three plainclothes goons. The crowd drew back even further. The policemen repeated the search, then shoved me into their car and hauled me in front of Captain Souffraunt again.

"Yes, Mr. Ladd, how can I help you?"

I shrugged my shoulders and gestured toward the police chief.

Souffraunt addressed him curtly in Creole, something to the effect of, "Yes, yes, he's okay. I already freed him once. Now take him down so he can get his port fees settled."

The policemen, whose spirits had been high so long as they were my captors, now looked bored. "Take him," said the chief to one of his goons.

He took me to a room in the port office, where five officials gathered to set my port fee. It took them an hour, with my assistance, to figure out that a metric ton equals a thousand kilos, therefore *Squeak*, at 113 kilos, weighs

.113 metric tons. The fee, being based on tonnage, was only two dollars. Captain Souffraunt himself, in charge of one ninth of the country, had to sign off on it.

One of those in attendance was the old man with the flapping soles. It seemed he was the port pilot. He didn't say much, but when the meeting had broken up he intercepted me, gripping my arm. "My name is Marcel!" he whispered, his eyes darting to ensure privacy. "Had I known you were coming this morning I'd have rowed out to meet you! It's my job to show vessels how to come in."

"What happened to that tugboat out on the reef, then? Doesn't look like it's been there very long."

He flinched. "That wasn't my fault! I can't talk about that."

We returned to *Squeak* so I could put her back in order. Now that the soldiers and policemen had left, would-be guides and confidence men swooped down on me. Two English-speaking youths greeted me with particular warmth. Marcel gave way to them, but hovered in my field of vision. I mentioned my need for transport and they tried to take me to "someone who can help." Marcel, catching my eye, discretely drew his finger across his throat. I shook them off.

That evening I took Marcel to a cafe for dinner. "Don't trust anyone, especially those who want to be your guide," he warned. "Since the embargo they're like drowning men, and you're the only lifeboat!" Three years before, the military had overthrown Aristide, the first democratically elected president. To pressure the government to restore legitimacy, the United Nations had stopped all trade and tourism.

"The embargo has ruined me, too. Since then the harbor's been empty. I've had nothing to do, and I get paid by commission. I barely eat."

"Well you're eating now, and it's on me. What vessels have come here lately, besides me and that tugboat?"

"A sportfishing boat came in a year ago. We found it had been stolen in Puerto Rico, so we impounded it. Sometimes Colombian drug boats break down on their way to Florida and land here. Every couple weeks a small ship smuggles goods in from Santo Domingo—tell no one I said so."

"Do you think I'll be able to find a truck to haul my boat to Port-au-Prince?"

"I can help you with that. I tell you, I used to live in the States. I'm sixty-seven years old. I know the world. I'm not like these ignorant people you see here."

He was, in fact, courteous in a way that seemed out of place there, and pitiable. But I also sensed stealth, and desperation. "I prefer to make my own arrangements. There is a way you can help me, though. Can you get me information on Jacmel's history? The architecture's so French. It must have been very charming once."

"Yes. I'll see what I can do."

The next day Marcel located a pamphlet entitled *Jacmel, the City of Coffee.* It had been a wealthy emporium, but it burned in 1896, at the peak of its glory. The coffee barons rebuilt it in brick and cast iron, importing the materials from France. Whitewashed mansions were erected, with hipped roofs and second-story verandahs. Each, I saw, had two sets of double doors, large enough for a giant, symmetrically placed in the façade, which adjoined the sidewalk. The doors opened outward and were hinged to lay flat against the façade, in which position they remained during the day, to admit light and air. Yard-long iron hooks hung at eye level from ringbolts on the doors' exposed inner surfaces, for securing them when shut. Semicircular grooves were worn in the thick wood where the hooks had swung for nearly a century.

But the rebuilding proved a bad investment. By the 1930s Jacmel was economically finished, not by fire, but by deforestation and erosion. Coffee could no longer be grown. Waterfront warehouses were abandoned, sewers caved in, parks went to seed. Hurricane Hazel ripped further wounds in 1954. The embargo had only deepened a long depression.

It was livelier away from the harbor. The ornate iron marketplace beneath the rococo cathedral was packed with spitting women. They sat on low stools, knees spread, skirts gathered at the crotch, wares stacked before them. Refreshment mongers served vendors who wooed buyers who stretched their few pennies as far as they could, trying to put enough food on the table. A fight broke out between two women, causing a panic of merriment. I paid the equivalent of sixteen cents for a bowl of rice, corn mush, beans, cabbage sauce, and boiled yam.

The money system unnerved me. There was a bank exchange rate and a black-market rate. Prices were quoted in an abstraction called the Haitian dollar, which had to be multiplied by five to arrive at the price in *gourdes*, the physical currency. The Haitian coins were based on hundredths of a *gourde,* but U.S. coins circulated as well, based on hundredths of a Haitian dollar, so the U.S. coins were worth five times their *gourde* equivalents. I finally paid a shopkeeper $60 U.S. for 750 *gourdes.* I was careful not to be seen, but soon noticed a disheveled young man following me. It took several twists and turns to shake him.

The next day, March 18, I rose too late to defecate privately, and had to borrow a one-legged man's latrine, which was screened by a wall of sticks. I walked to the outskirts of town, admiring the schoolchildren's neat uniforms, a different color for each school. The colors mingled as they walked into town, and separated again as they approached their respective destinations.

Barefoot women shuffled in with banana bunches balanced on their heads. It was nice not to hear the eternal crashing of waves. Above a house, six pie tins made up a homemade TV antenna. A sweaty crew tossed wet cement, bucket-brigade fashion, to the second story of a house under construction.

That night a plainclothes policeman with a gold front tooth stopped me on the street to practice his halting English. He seemed torn between befriending me and shaking me down. The gleam in his eye got uglier as he grew more confident. Finally he held up a palm. "Give me five dollars," he snarled.

It was perfect. "Give you five? I'll give ya' five," I said, and slapped his palm. "Alright! Now you give me five. That's it, slap my hand!" He complied, smiling weakly, and left me alone after that.

My wanderings were aimed at finding a truck to portage *Squeak* to Port-au-Prince. I had resolved to take the shortcut if it could be arranged for a hundred dollars or less, otherwise I'd keep sailing west. Twice I made deals, and twice the truck never showed up. While waiting with *Squeak* at the foot of the pier, I offered to share my grapefruit and bread with the men standing around. My offer startled them. One took my food with a laugh and words to the effect of, "Hell yeah I'll eat the dumbshit's bread!" Others refused, suspicious. One accepted graciously, with embarrassment at the others' behavior.

At eleven A.M. on the nineteenth three strangers pulled up in a Daihatsu flatbed. They must have heard about me. I wasn't in the mood to haggle anymore. "Two hundred Haitian dollars. Yes or no?" The driver agreed. Five minutes later we were loaded up and gone.

I stood in back, tightening ropes and monitoring *Squeak*, while we jolted over the withered red mountains. When the road passed through a teeming country market the driver laid on his horn. Pedestrians parted and closed again behind, like water parting around a vessel. We passed a truck draped with goats, bound and hanging by their hooves—they twisted their heads upright to bleat their terror. When we reached the Gulf of Gonâve coast I rejoiced at its lack of surf. I wrote "Hotel Oloffson" on a slip of paper and handed it to the driver. Marcel had told me I might find safe haven there during my sojourn in the notorious capital.

The streets became clogged with pedestrians. We climbed to the foot of the mountains forming the city's southern flank and entered a hotel compound. I had been rehearsing what to say, wondering what to do if they refused to let me park *Squeak* there. The hotel owner wasn't in, so I charmed the receptionist into neutrality, quickly unloaded *Squeak* onto the grass by the compound wall, and paid the driver. The truck left, making my residency a fait accompli. I was elated.

The hotel was a tall, gingerbread museum piece with leaning turrets and rickety balconies overlooking a wheel-shaped formal garden. Here Graham Greene wrote *The Comedians*—the Hotel Oloffson was the "Hotel Trianon" in that novel of intrigue set in even worse times, during "Papa Doc" Duvalier's reign of terror in the late sixties. Tourism resumed in the seventies, only to evaporate again when Aristide was ousted in 1990. The UN imposed its embargo, and now the hotel's only guests were foreign correspondents, *Medicins Sans Frontiers* (Doctors Without Borders), and Organization of American States (OAS) observers. Still, it was enough to provide innumerable maids, watchmen, musicians, and masseurs with a meager living. The management, when it became aware of me, did not object to my anchoring in their front yard. I was a conversation piece who asked only to camp there until my business in Port-au-Prince was concluded.

Like Jacmel, the city had once been more glorious. Its wide boulevards, open spaces, and monuments were appropriate to a national capital. But grime now coated the solid old commercial structures. Garbage had built up in the streets like snowdrifts. In some districts the reeking, smoky mounds were so large as to block traffic and dam drains. Dogs and chickens dug around in them. The stench was terrific. The air alone made my clothes dirty.

Vendors took up the sidewalks, so I walked in the street, jostling with handcarts, pressing back to the sides when a truck rammed through. One merchant carried only kerosene lamps made from tin cans. Another carried only long bars of soap from which the buyer cut off the desired length. Old women sat all day behind a few used bottles or scraps of paper. Walking soft-drink salesmen tinkled their bottles; shoeshine boys rang bells. Woodworkers in a tiny, shaving-filled shop hustled to get something done during the two hours each afternoon when the city's electrical grid was switched on.

Transactions were difficult. Besides the language barrier there were no marked prices, no menus, no scales. Vendors asked whatever they thought you might be stupid enough to pay, and I, being white, looked pretty stupid. The old gambit of watching what other people paid didn't work because the *gourde* notes were too dirty and ragged to identify at a distance. There were no friendly greetings, no courtesy.

The system pressured me to hire a guide to do my bargaining, but I refused, and paid the consequences in frustrated harangues, miles walked, and meals uneaten rather than be overcharged. Beggars hit hard. "Psst," "meester," and "*blanc* (white man)" flew thick all around me. Sometimes I thought a guy intercepting me might be sincerely friendly, but it always ended up being a hard luck story, a manipulation. The faces were of many shapes, uniform only in their blackness. Too many were sad, bitter, miserable.

I closed myself off, felt selfish. To avoid being conned was hard, but maintaining my moral balance was harder. I wanted to give, but of my self, not money. I wanted to give by being curious about them and satisfying their curiosity about me. I succeeded with one young beggar who, after the initial disappointment of not getting any money, told me, with what little English he spoke, how he had stowed away on a ship to America. "For two years I be at Immigration Prison, New York. I very sad they send me back. American prison better than Haiti."

Poor people are sad only to the extent they realize others are less poor. The Haitians were very aware of their poverty. Few could afford even booze, which sad people usually buy a lot of. The tiny elite was inconspicuous. There was no night life, no glitter, no lasciviousness. There wasn't even much armed robbery, that having been monopolized, so I heard, by the same squads that also performed political terrorism on behalf of the ruling elite. These shadowy *zen-glen-do* exercised such restraint as necessary to retain their crime franchise, while negotiations continued, the military for the lifting of the embargo, the OAS for the resumption of democratic rule. Neither side showed any sign of giving in.

I ranged freely through the city in buses sheathed in gaudy plastic, overflowing with grim riders. I finagled my way into the docks and bummed used charts from Indian, Nicaraguan, and Greek ship captains. I sought out the grubby shops capable of repairing my broken zippers, locks, and hatch clamps. And I stayed home, in the shady peace of the hotel compound, writing, repairing gashes in *Squeak's* bottom, rebuilding the rudder fork, patching a sail, replacing a halyard. I laughed at the little brown lizards that watched me work, puffing their necks out, and doing their rapid-fire push-ups, as if it were me they were trying to impress. By a small, sustained force of will I again avoided losing any of my four screwdriver bits (two slot and two Phillips) that fit into my ratchet driver, even though the driver no longer gripped them securely. Throughout the voyage they'd wanted to fall out into sand, brush, or sea. I insisted they not. All four were still there in the plastic vial I stored them in, together with my pushdrill bits.

Shopping, I bought from children because they hadn't learned how to overcharge yet. When this wasn't possible I offered a reasonable price. If they refused I offered more next time, and the next, until they accepted. If they accepted I offered less next time, and the next, until they refused. Only by such testing and careful record-keeping could I divine local prices. I did this to save money, and to engage them as they engaged me: with every ounce of wit.

Changing money was the worst. I did so as needed, in small quantities, from money-changers who stood on street corners with stacks of dirty bills in their hands. Seeing I meant business, they rushed me like jackals, shoved their *gourdes* in my face, yelled, and elbowed each other out. The first hurdle was to find one willing to give me the premium street rate: 255 *gourdes* per $20 US. The second hurdle was to get past his short-change tricks while keeping my wits amid a din designed to confuse me.

Beggars grabbed my arm. They were little kids, cripples and amputees, baby-toting women, toothless ancients chanting supplications. Some weren't needy, but tried me anyway. Young men followed me for blocks, trying to "make friends." I walked faster, crossed the street, changed course. A taxi driver refused to give change until I raised my clenched fist in his face. People stopped what they were doing to stare at me, with the look of a cat seeing a flicker of mouse, or a hunter-gatherer sensing motion in a bush. There was no racial hatred, no threat of violence, just an intense vying for advantage. No one guaranteed their survival.

The hotel guests were committed to their work and absorbed in Haiti, but their respective investigations were finely focused. I never saw them in the markets or on the streets. Only with a young Harvard English professor and part-time journalist named George was I able to share my impressions. Together we explored the cemetery, where the dead repose in decorative, rectangular, above-ground crypts. As we left the main trail the crypts crowded in, closer, closer. Beyond the cemetery walls were steamy slums, but here all was still. We began to see signs of grave robbery—breached crypts, scattered debris. Then George peered into an open chamber and froze. "Bones," he breathed. The skeleton was disheveled but complete, swathed in decomposed funerary clothing. Deeper yet, the remains had been strewn about, until ribs, femurs, skulls, and bits of coffin clogged the narrow passage. The air was dry and musty. We were ready to leave, but the tombs formed a dense maze. There was nowhere to step but on bones that crunched underfoot. Our voices turned to whispers, our awe to near-panic. We climbed a crypt to get our bearings, then scrambled over vault after vault toward the exit. When finally we emerged, it was into the midst of a funeral procession—people crying and laughing in equal numbers, and a drum-and-bugle corps with cheap, gaudy uniforms.

The straw-hatted taxi men who hung around the hotel gate nicknamed me "busy man" because I always walked fast, out of the compound and down the Rue Capois, downtown. Sickness slowed me down, first amoebic dysentery then a cold that turned into bronchitis, but the *Medicins sans Frontiers* cured me with antibiotics. Inside the hotel, combos interpreted traditional Haitian ballads, and dancers simulated voodoo ceremonies in orchestrated melees of color and movement.

Another night the in-house rock band put on a dance. A rapport ensued between myself and a public-health consultant from Washington, D.C. She was soon sighing, and shifting her gaze from my eyes to my mouth. I forgot I was sick, and danced, and courted.

"Your boat or mine?" I asked.

"My hotel room, silly." There we made awesome love until morning, when she had to leave for the airport. I had met her on her last night in Haiti.

Easter arrived during my third week in Port-au-Prince. That night a procession flowed slow and hot as viscous lava down the damply glistening street, a few feet below me, on the other side of the wall from where I lay trying to sleep. It was Mardi gras jazz, with trombones and a sea of makeshift rattles, whistles, and one-note tooters. The music was fast, major key, repeating in the same two-chord progression for hours as they roamed the steep avenues of the city's south flank. The revelers drank a clear hooch called *clairin*, and danced, their bodies bent double at the waist, arms outstretched, heads cocking from side to side, feet swerving intricately, ecstasy on their faces. They were happy as ghouls. I watched from behind the wall, drawn yet fearful, because there was lawlessness in their mirth.

At dawn, mosquitoes, shut out by nets during the night, sought the warm dens where people had slept, positioning themselves to suck blood the following evening. At a stall in the crowded market I haggled with a vendor who wanted to give me more vegetables rather than the change she had promised me, while a second woman, naked and curled up under the counter, tugged at my pant leg and grinned up at me, urging me to lie down with her. I yanked my bill out of the vendor's hand and walked away.

I checked in with the American consul, a conscientious man. On the wall behind his desk was a map of Port-au-Prince with marks indicating the residences of American citizens. My experiences in Jacmel interested him. "Let me tell you a story about your friend Marcel, the pilot," he said. "Did you see that tugboat on the reef there?"

"Yes."

"Well that was an American tug, and that slimy little Marcel put it there. They were fifteen miles offshore. They weren't even going to *stop* in Haiti, but those brutes in Jacmel went out in a boat and—well basically they hijacked them. They forced them into port and were so busy shaking 'em down they plowed right onto the reef. Far as I can tell, Marcel was the ringleader. I've been trying to nail him ever since."

"Wow," I said. "He was nice to me but—this is a weird country."

"Very weird indeed, my friend. You watch yourself sailing up the Gulf of Gonâve. There's a colonel in charge up in Gonaives who's like something from the feudal ages."

"Thanks. I don't plan to go ashore very much."

"And I've been trying to reach Guantanamo Bay to get information on the Windward Passage for you, but the line's been out of order."

"You tried."

On April 13 I got a clearance to sail to Baracoa, Cuba, with a stop in Môle St. Nicolas. I had no good-byes to make. Richard, owner of the hotel and leader of the rock group, gave *Squeak* and me a ride down to the waterfront in his pickup. We had to hire a guide to find a place to launch, so blighted was the shore with new slums. The shallow gulf was filling in with sediment, and squatters were building on the mud flats. The landing was a leftover scrap of waterfront scattered with rusting hulks, rimmed by dredge spoils and middens of trash.

We arrived after dark. I was tired, but the place wasn't safe. So I assembled *Squeak* and shoved off, feeling my way through dead and living vessels, the latter recognizable by the voices and lamplight that emanated from them. I quietly tied off to a warp securing a grounded barge, but a half moon revealed me. Men came out in a rowboat. "I sleep here! Go away!" I cried in French. They did. The air smelled of sewage and putrefaction on a colossal scale, like the very earth was sick and lying in its own vomit. I felt vulnerable.

It was a relief to sail out of Port-au-Prince harbor at daybreak, through silted reefs that extended well out into the Gulf of Gonâve. The sea was calm, tepid, murky at first, gradually clearer. Native sprit-riggers crisscrossed the bay under baggy sails of quilted rags.

I intended to sail to Môle, at Haiti's northwest tip, then cross over to Cuba and follow its north coast to within striking distance of Florida. But none of the countries I had recently visited had diplomatic relations with Cuba. I'd tried for hours to telephone the U.S. Interests Section in Havana, to no avail. No one I'd met had ever sailed there. Weather forecasts were unavailable. There was no way of anticipating sailing conditions in the Windward Passage, or Cuba's reaction to my arrival. Furthermore, if I made it from there back to the States, I might be charged with violating the economic embargo against Cuba. But it was the straightest route, with the fewest crossings, and it interested me more than the Bahamas.

The uncertainty surrounding my arrival in Cuba was compounded by that of my remaining days in Haiti, because my reception would be uncertain wherever I stopped. The first night I camped at a Club Med resort that had closed down four years before due to political chaos. The second day I hoped to reach the south shore of Haiti's northern prong, but westerlies slowed my crossing. Sunset found me ten miles off Gonaives. The empty gulf smelled oozy, Paleozoic, as if its tepid waters might harbor trilobites and brachiopods. The sky seemed sad and out-of-time.

Suddenly the headwind became a tailwind. My sails snapped full. I steered

Squeak downwind over waves that hadn't had time to change direction yet—the rapid collisions gave a sensation of fantastic speed. The wind crescendoed. In the final light of dusk, a violent thunderstorm manifested in the sky behind me. The waves stopped, reversed, rose, steepened. The night was blinding, black, cold. To slow down I doused the flogging mainsail, sheeted the mizzen tight, and lifted the rudder blade. *Squeak* swung bow-to-windward and sailed stably backwards at two knots while I scrunched up in the cockpit, wishing I had a wetsuit. I remained like that all night, uncomfortable but reasonably safe, because the hatches were shut. I'd learned my lesson that night off Nuquí.

The storm passed. Morning broke with rays of hot sun. A zephyr blew me slowly up to the massive cape at the point where the west-trending coastline begins to swing north. The land was high, of broken rock. The gray of the rocks' tops bled down over the tan of their underbellies. Between the rocks grew scorched grass and "cactus trees"—thorny trunks with wide canopies of "leaves" that hung down like big, spiny pods. Wherever a boat could land, a few crude huts huddled together, as if afraid to be alone. I passed close by one such hamlet and a woman wrapped in a towel ran out and performed an unlady-like little dance for me, urging me to land.

A beamy, motorless, gaff-rigged sloop worked past me the other way, becalmed most of the time. It was loaded to ten feet above deck level with sacks of charcoal. Its gaff was peaked nearly vertical, and twice the length of its mast, against which the gaff crotched at a point just above the boom. The boom extended ten feet aft of the wide, flat transom.

Wicker traps dotted the longshore coral beds. Each was the shape of a bloated S, with inward-tapering fish entries in each of the two crotches. The buoys marking them were sections of bamboo. Their tenders rowed from trap to trap in carvel-built dinghies, or paddled one-man rafts consisting of three short logs pegged together, the center one turned up to form a prow. Dinghies and rafts tried to converge on me. The fishermen gestured obscurely, and called out in their thick-lipped speech. Fortunately, I was able to pull away. They scared me.

There were no anchorages. Afternoon headwinds again dashed my hopes of reaching a port. I dreaded placing myself at the mercy of the locals, but I needed to sleep, so I landed alongside some rowboats on a gravel beach at the foot of a ravine.

A dozen young men amiably hemmed me in while I did chores. Some had the look of savages: scowling, uncomprehending, bits of straw jutting from their woolly hair. One had had some schooling and thus spoke French about as well as I did—not very. Conversation was laborious. As bedtime approached one fellow got out a Santa Claus cap, of all things, and pulled it on. It wasn't a joke—he just wanted to keep warm and that's all he had. I laughed, and teased him with a "Ho, ho, ho, Merry Christmas!" That kept everybody in stitches for a while. Still, the exchange was stressful. I longed to hike, swim, stretch my legs, but to leave my things unguarded would have tempted them unduly. Soon they were begging for food, money, English books, cigarettes, liquor, drinking water. Only the last did I give. They were pitiful, with no shelter or bedding, and nothing to eat but a few miserable little pogies charred over a bonfire. But I wasn't running a relief operation.

The following day I sailed into Môle St. Nicolas Bay, strategically located at Haiti's northwest tip. It was like a fjord, bordered to south and east by open slopes and terraced cliffs, and on the north by a low, barren peninsula. Columbus landed there in 1492, after stops in the Bahamas and Cuba. Napoleon had forts built here after formally acquiring Haiti, then known as St. Domingue, in the Treaty of Ryswick. The batteries had long since gone to ruin. Rusty cannons lay scattered about as if, over the ages, various people had thought to take them home as souvenirs, but lost interest after hauling them a short distance. Someone said the U.S. Navy had long coveted the inlet as a base to take the place of Guantanamo, for the two harbors are equally convenient to the Windward Passage, which handles shipping between the Eastern Seaboard and the Panama Canal. There were also long-standing plans to build a resort on the bay's south shore, where the sand is white. Some trial irrigation and landscaping had already demonstrated the Mediterranean-like Eden into which Môle could easily be transformed.

But sandwiched between glorious past and possibly glorious future was a humdrum present, for Môle had no port facilities or tourism. The only industry was charcoal transshipment—rowboats carrying dusty sacks out to sloops such as the one I had passed. It was a village of several hundred inhabitants with an army post, a school, and an ancient church. I was unable to spend my remaining three dollars worth of *gourdes* constructively, so meager were the wares at the open market.

There wasn't much for me to accomplish there, but I was a welcome diversion for the villagers. The soldiers enjoyed searching my boat, and as usual I was the Big Chance, the Last Hope of various youngsters who sought to attach themselves to me. They believed no hope existed in Haiti except in the aura of foreigners. And perhaps my aura was especially bright, because they could relate only too well to what I intended to do, namely sail to America. But when *I* got to Florida no one would say I couldn't come in. Females were pushed forward with the words, "This one wants to go with you,"—an occasion for laughter, because everyone realized *Squeak* was a ship for one. The girls struggled and blushed, but they loved the attention. Their community was putting them on display, and in their shy eyes, mesmerized by contact with mine, was awe at the very concept.

I was unsure as to my strategy for crossing to Cuba. The winds in the Gulf of Gonâve had been patternless—how would they be in the Passage? Did the absence of trade winds stem from being in the lee of a large landmass, or had they actually stopped? Was a cold front impending? No one in the village was capable of discussing such matters. In Môle, "Is this weather normal?" was, for some reason, an imponderable question.

CHAPTER 30

CUBA

The following morning, April 17, a breeze blew toward Cuba. Had the Northeast Trades resumed? Anxious to get it over with, I set sail. Out the bay I flew, past the coast-hugging Haitian boats, beyond the wave shadow of the great island, to where two swell patterns merged: Caribbean to port, Atlantic to starboard. Spurred by my approach, flying fish leaped left and right from the sea. To prolong their flight they banked away downwind:

Silver splashes, darts of light
materialize from wave crests
to soar, not high, but far
on wings of blurred speed
Do they "flap?" yes, but so fast!

Neon in their spines, they tremble
strain for the last ounce of flight
bank, arc, swim through air
tails beating like atomic metronomes

to repierce the sea
flaming arrows, extinguished
without ripple or sound

And their flight lasted but an instant
but that instant was eternal
implying, perhaps
that divinity is an event, not a state
a yearning, not an achievement

I steered 320° for the southeast tip of Cuba, fifty-five miles away. The wind grew faint—I added oarpower. At dusk, just before Hispaniola's bony mass dissolved into the china-blue sky, I took a bearing on it. The result, being greater than 320's reciprocal, informed me of a north-setting current. I altered course to 310°.

The sea grew glassy. The sun set. Gladly I removed cap and glasses. Shut-eye would have been nice, but my body said, "No, not yet." Deepening night revealed a faint, periodic illumination ahead, and specks of light that moved slowly both ways across my field of vision. It was the Cabo Maisí lighthouse, and the shipping lanes off the tip of Cuba. As I row-sailed smoothly through the moonless night these lights expanded into a grand spectacle. Southbound ships were cutting around Cuba as close as international law allowed, then veering southwest for the opening between Haiti and Jamaica. Northbound ships followed the opposite course. A separation zone two miles wide kept them from colliding. At their turning point, opposite the lighthouse, the lanes were ten miles offshore. My chart showed it.

It was like crossing a freeway on foot, at night, on a vast scale, in slow motion. Ships marched in close succession, a few one way, a few the other. Distance made them seem slow, yet they were going five times my speed. I myself shone no light. I wanted them to follow their paths as orderly as planets.

The stars disappeared behind clouds. Lightning flickered dully in the sky north of the lighthouse. Ship engines drummed monotonously, louder, louder. At midnight a freighter passed a hundred yards off. *All clear—go!* I crossed the northbound lane at a forty-five degree angle. Now I was in the separation zone, at its turning point. My next goal was to cross the southbound lane and keep the lighthouse to my left as I rounded Cabo Maisí.

Suddenly the lighthouse blacked out! The breeze died. Something vast and violent was approaching. I downed the sails and fumbled into raingear and life preserver, panic tugging at my sleeve. A headwind smacked me in the face. In the sky, which I'd thought was already black, an arch or rainbow of denser blackness approached and grew until it framed me, like an arch as tall as the sky! *It's swallowing me!* Then the rain hit, the same wall of water that had blacked out the lighthouse. I was blind, disoriented. To minimize lost ground I deployed my sea anchor, bow to weather, and rowed to relieve pressure on the line, facing forward to illuminate the compass with my headlamp. Within minutes the cockpit was awash with cold rainwater. I bailed, hopped to the oars again, bailed, to control my shivers as much as anything. My skin pruned with prolonged wetness. The ships' trajectories now baffled me—I was in their vortex.

The rain died. The wind tapered as the night wore on, but I stayed at the oars. At dawn I hoisted sail and tacked north through a steep chop. The eastern tip of Cuba was a green plain rising to a distant plateau. Close ashore were small boats. I kept landward of the shipping lanes. I'd drifted seven or eight miles south during the night—a current was working against me. The day was cool and damp. A cold front had arrived.

By noon I still hadn't regained the latitude of the lighthouse. I'd never round the cape before dark unless I went in close, where the current might be less. I'd intended to stay offshore until I had a straight run into Baracoa, fifteen miles west along the north coast. I didn't want to be arrested prematurely—everything in due course—but better to be thrown in Castro's worst dungeon than spend another sleepless night on that treacherous treadmill.

When I was close ashore a peculiar formation approached: a steel fishing boat towing three smaller boats, all abreast. The skipper held up his thumbs and forefingers to me, linked like a chain: he was coming to tow me, too. I took his line, and *Squeak* swung into place beside the others, like an errant duckling returned to the flock. Two were fishing skiffs whose motors had conked out. The third was a military launch that had come to pick me up and whose motor had likewise conked out. The men in each boat were busy steering and fending off. Most were white, one was black, a few mestizo. They spoke clear, vibrant Spanish. When I answered in the same tongue the ranking soldier, a corporal with graying temples, eyed me curiously. Creases bracketed his mouth. All had tight, weathered faces and trim physiques. Their manner was keen, competent, unhurried. The skipper of the fishing boat was nonchalant about being pressed into service as a tug, but the soldiers appeared embarrassed at having intercepted me in such an undignified manner.

Just north of the Maisí lighthouse a gap in a coral reef gave access to a small harbor containing a pier. Upland were a few empty warehouses. Horseback villagers watched us impassively. A railroad terminated at the pier. The rails were dull and grown over. Broken-down Haitian sloops scattered the upper beach. Among other things, Maisí was an internment camp for boat people. At the moment, I was the only guest.

They pulled *Squeak* up onto the beach. My captors were firm, yet anxious that my stay be as pleasant as possible. "We're not used to receiving Americans," said the corporal. "Everything to do with our powerful neighbor to the north is sensitive." He and the others wore olive green uniforms with "GUARDAFRONTERA" or "DEPARTAMENTO DEL INTERIOR" labels. On the pier a fisherman in oil-stained clothes worked on his motor. A couple of local families, shy people with reddish, sun-bleached hair, had a look at me. The blacks and mestizos were indistinguishable from the others in speech and mannerism. It seemed an egalitarian society.

They searched *Squeak* and scrutinized my documents, maps, and manuscripts, then took me up to their *Guardafrontera* post. "Now sir, if you could tell us your plans," said the post commander, a fatherly man of fifty. His uniform was like that of his men.

"I'm an adventurer and a writer. I've been sailing nearly three years, and am trying to get back home. With your permission, I'd like to navigate Cuban waters to La Isabela, then sail to Florida."

"Are you associated with your government or any sponsor?" asked a man in a suit, probably a political officer.

"No. I'm acting on my own behalf."

"And what do you think of the U. S. embargo against Cuba?" He was formal, guarded.

"It doesn't make much sense to me. But my mission has nothing to do with politics. All I want is to go home." That seemed to satisfy him.

The *Guardafrontera* commander took over. "What ports would you stop in? What is your strategy?"

"I sail from beach to beach. I can't know in advance where I'll spend the night. I realize that might be difficult for you to allow. If it's unacceptable, okay. I'll sail home by way of the Bahamas."

"In Cuba nothing is impossible," he said. "Our policy is to encourage tourism and normalize foreign relations. We will see if we can grant you the navigational freedom you need, yet meet our security requirements. In the meantime we will assign a guard to you, for your own security."

I needed to recover from the crossing anyway, so my house arrest didn't bother me. Two soldiers took turns sitting on a chair beside *Squeak,* their rifles across their laps. They talked my ears off. One planned to be a policeman after fulfilling his military obligation, the other a barber. The post's cook brought me hot food. "Did you like the black bean soup?" he asked. "I'm so glad." He bowed, hand to chest. I was free to walk around as long as I stayed in sight. Military and civilians alike addressed me politely. No one begged.

That night it rained. I could stay dry, but my guard couldn't. "Shall we go to that warehouse?" I offered. "There you can guard me without shivering."

"Thanks, friend," he said, as we dashed to the derelict building.

We sat on the dusty floor, backs to the wall. I lit a candle. He was a handsome young man, eager to talk about women. His eyes lit up explaining Cuba's permissive sexual mores. He asked my opinion of a green-eyed schoolteacher who had stopped by that evening to look at the sea and flirt with him. He talked of how proud he was to be Cuban, too, but stiffly, as if it was expected of him.

I was about to write off a third day there when the post commander came down. "Good news!" he said. "Cuba welcomes you! They are expecting you in Baracoa this evening." We did some paperwork, then a launch towed me out of the harbor.

It had rained off and on since my arrival. The country was richly forested, another contrast to Haiti. It rose in vigorous, ancient shapes. Gorges gaped like mouths. Green ridges rose to an anvil-shaped mountain of solid rock. I sailed around the cape and on to Baracoa, a colonial town with a snug harbor. At the wharf three soldiers gestured for me to dock at three different locations; I obeyed the one with the most stripes, tying up behind a naval patrol boat. The port captain, a stiff man with white, crew-cut hair, wrote out an *acta de entrada*, or entry document.

"Am I free to walk around?"

"Yes," he said, unsmiling. He studied me closely.

"How long is my visa good for?"

"No limit." Another pleasant surprise.

The streets were dark and curvilinear. Transport consisted of Soviet-block motorcycles with sidecars, a few Russian cars and trucks, and horse-drawn buggies. The houses fronted on the street. Some were plank-built with peeling paint, others were of cold cement. Socialist slogans adorned the walls, eulogizing Fidel and Ché, calling for ever more *"sacrificios en defensa de la revolución."* Only I read them. Atop a hill was El Castillo. A plaque in English said the Army Corps of Engineers had rebuilt the fort during the U.S. occupation at the turn of the century. Now it was an INTUR hotel, catering to foreign tourists. I could eat in their restaurant and buy from their tourist shop, paying in dollars.

Good thing. I had no ration cards, and the town's shops and cafes had little to offer in any case. If a store had anything good, people stood in a line that ran out the door and around the block. At the bakery they waited patiently, each with their standard-issue shopping bag, while clerks briskly counted out one bun per person per day. I looked on with envy until a young bystander took up my cause. He went to the counter, spoke to a clerk, and came back with five buns. "Here," he said. "No charge. Foreigners have priority."

"You're the first person to approach me," I said.

"We can be charged with soliciting or possessing dollars. But no one watches me. Want to sample the local chocolate?"

"Sure."

He took me to a nearby row house. Its only light was an odorous kerosene lamp. The furniture was sparse and threadbare. An old woman in a torn dress cooed and fussed over me. "Oh, such a handsome, brave young man. I'll just bring you a little cup of cocoa. At least I have that. My sweet

Jesus, this poor life we lead, in your name. I tell you, He will punish those who have scorned Him. Take this, I want you to have it." It was a small cross.

Her daughter entered, a keen woman of thirty-five, mother of the two children who sat beside me on the divan. "Good evening, friend! Yes, I speak English. I teach it, you see. I've just now returned from a night class. How exciting to have such an honored guest!"

Due to her occupation, Oneida could be seen with a foreigner without arousing suspicion. I returned several times during my three days in Baracoa. Her husband, a policeman, was never home. She fed me yams, and answered my questions about Cuban life, police controls, and food availability. Once she was at work, and her mother gave me Oneida's bed to nap on. When she returned she tickled my feet, waking me. "Who's this sleeping in my bed?" she laughed. "Goldilocks?"

As our acquaintance matured, Oneida revealed grievances. She dropped her voice. "Shh, the neighbors." She pulled me into the kitchen. Humor vanished. "You must remember what I tell you. We want the world to know." Her grievances were many. She wanted to go to church, but feared her husband would lose his job. They couldn't finish the upper floor of their house because all the cement went into building underground bomb shelters, which everyone must help dig. "They'll be our tombs one day," she said. "Don't laugh!" Her stove was broken, the part unavailable. There were no matches, no cooking fuel, no shoes, not enough food. People were going blind from malnutrition. The authorities read people's mail and checked their ballots. Those voting incorrectly were punished.

All this was probably true, yet the people seemed happy enough. They interacted in relaxed, orderly ways. I sat on a park bench, and a pretty, bronze-skinned girl in white blouse and culottes smiled at me until I went up and introduced myself. She had in mind a fling with a foreigner, and I obliged her that night, and again the next, in trysts among the ruins of an apartment building. "If only you can give me a little soap," she said. I got her some liquid hand soap at the INTUR shop. Her tenderness toward me seemed sincere, but the soap mattered too.

I bought fruit and vegetables from the hotel restaurant staff. Oneida gave me some plantains. This food would have to last me until the next INTUR facility. Oneida sold me twenty dollars worth of Cuban pesos. I was unable to buy anything with them but postage stamps and a vial of antifungal cream that burned my skin.

Once the port captain had given me my sailing papers he wouldn't let me go back into town. I couldn't meet my lover and tell her good-bye as we'd planned. I rowed out of the harbor while she waited for me on that street corner, or perhaps she climbed some vantage point and watched me go. We hadn't exchanged addresses. Incommunicado forever.

A wet north wind chilled me and hampered progress. At day's end I came in behind a coral reef and anchored in a foot of water. An uninhabited islet hid me from the mainland, but there were eyes about. I had just gotten snug when a sound prompted me to look through the porthole. Two wary soldiers were approaching me in a rowboat. When they were ten yards away the one not rowing clicked the safety off his automatic rifle. I opened the hatch and slowly sat up, facing him.

"Unsafe to sleep here," he said. "You must come with us to Yamanigüey."

We rowed there side by side. It was a village on the mainland, at the edge of the mangrove-lined bay. We stood stoically at the foot of a watch-tower in the pounding rain, waiting for their superior to come, dancing and slapping at the ravenous mosquitoes.

"How do they avoid getting washed out of the air?" I asked.

"Who knows."

The commander never showed up—I didn't blame him a bit. "Sleep well," said the soldiers, and climbed into the watchtower. I slept tied between two pilings.

In the morning I beat my way out through the lagoon's narrow opening, straight into a nasty blow, tacking just shy of where the waves broke over the sharp coral heads. I rounded Punta Guarico, and swung *Squeak's* stern to the wind and seas. I worried about broaching as I passed the mammoth nickel mills east of Moa. The coast was one vast reef, pierced here and there by jutting headlands. I coveted the calm water of the lagoon, which was two miles wide in places, and twenty miles long, but the waves crashing on the reef were an impenetrable barrier. I was relieved to finally enter the harbor opening.

Moa was a new industrial city with a socialist rawness and insensitivity to nature. Mineral wastes had tinted the lagoon red. Most of the people lived in sprawling apartment complexes. Officials from Immigration, Customs, the Port Captaincy, and the *Guardafrontera* all met to work out a grand paper-work scheme that hopefully would carry me to La Isabela, with local clearances along the way. The first mate of a Cuban freighter gave me an excellent set of charts, drawn by their own hydrologic institute, which would get me all the way to Florida. The military shared their beans and rice with me, but their rules required that I moor at their dock, which was too tall and exposed. That night, high winds kicked up a chop that made sleep impossible, while lightning split the sky, and torrential rain obliged me to bail the cockpit.

The morning was warm and fair. Hurray! The trade winds had returned! Now the sailing was intense. With stiff tailwinds and the long spring days, forty-, fifty-, even sixty-mile days were possible. The spray evaporated on my sunglasses, leaving residues of salt which I melted by sucking the lenses in my mouth. Speed was a constant four to five knots. I shifted between several *almost* comfortable positions for sailing downwind, and wished I had a third arm projecting straight backwards to work the tiller.

When it was especially rough I sailed no further than a mile offshore, so I could swim to the beach if worse came to worst. I monitored the waves approaching from behind. During its life span each slowly built up, until nearly vertical at the crest, then broke. Whether that wave then ceased to exist or merely repeated the process I could not discern. Normally *Squeak* simply rose and the wave passed underneath, but if the wave was breaking it pushed *Squeak* forward in a surfing motion. She accelerated instantly to perhaps double her normal speed, and wanted to yaw. Foam is less dense than water, so as the dying wave passed, *Squeak* settled into its frothy crest, like a hen into a downy nest. Then another wall of water took its place. The knuckles of my tiller hand whitened with stress. A breaking wave might roll me, so I deviated from my course as necessary to take them stern-on. *Squeak's* responsiveness was a blessing then.

Yet all this worry was perhaps unnecessary. On April 25 a wave turned *Squeak* sideways to the wind and rolled her ninety degrees, dumping me in the water. All I had to do was swim around to the windward side, climb in (righting her in the process), and sail on while bailing the cockpit. A half hour later the same thing happened again. The only casualty was my mop-up towel, which I hadn't secured, and therefore lost.

Cuba was never-endingly beautiful. Its smooth, green shapes dissolved gently, one into the other. It was a lush, low plain of variable depth, backed by velvety green mountains. The lowlands were a series of horizontal lines that diverged and converged, demarcating variations of distance and color—sand, green of brush, darker green trees. My eyes probed and judged distance. My mind imagined it in plan view, and identified features on the chart matching that image. Low-lying points and keys (or cays) didn't show themselves on the horizon until I was within five miles, seven miles if I stood up. Shallow bottleneck bays invaded the lowlands every five or ten miles, providing easy refuge. They were ringed with mangrove swamp, therefore full of wildlife, but that wildlife included mosquitoes and sand flies. Much of the shoreline was barrier reef, in which case I needed only to find an opening to land on the surf-less white sand inside.

Squeak and I sailed the indigo water offshore, and the aquamarine shallows. We flew over thousands of acres of sharp coral. Everything up to thirty feet deep was as clear as if air, not water, separated us. If the lagoon was long and continuous we might sail inside, over water that glowed with a pale blue light, more the white of sand than the blue of sky. Pillboxes and defensive tunnels had been built where the shore lent itself to amphibious invasion, but they were generally unmanned. Once while passing a watchtower I heard a gunshot—the damn soldiers wanted me to stop. I turned back, landed, flashed my sheaf of papers, and chewed them out royally. "I have every right to sail here! Why do you shoot?" Chagrined, they released me without a search. Boats were rare because only trusted fishermen were allowed to go out in them; anybody else might run off to Florida. Few of those endless beaches and longshore islands were inhabited.

Every two or three days I reached a tourist hotel. The guests were retired German couples, Canadian nurses, middle-aged Italians with sexy Cuban girlfriends. Bikini girls—the Cubans called them *jineteras*—hung around those places, seeking to attach themselves to a foreigner, happy to sleep with a man for a bar of soap or a pair of sunglasses from the dollar-only store. They were just girls dying for a little brightness in their lives, not hardened prostitutes.

I came down with amoebic dysentery again, so I holed up for a few days at the INTUR complex near Nuevitas. I was weak and low in appetite. But I enjoyed the beach, the enforced inactivity, and the Cubans who made such a fuss over me, all so eager to be my friends, to render any service.

In the open-air hotel lobbies I found comfortable chairs, near restrooms (vital), where I sat and read as long as I wanted. I joined a Canadian gentleman in orange trunks on the beach. He was partying with three plump Cuban women. Havana Club Rum, Coca-Cola, snacks, and sun tan lotion lay scattered on the sand. The Canadian, who was funding the party, tried to nod off, but his girlfriends cooed, "No, we love you too much, we want to party!" Conceding defeat, he opened a new bottle of rum with a humorous little fanfare—"Da da da da-da, da da da da da-da"—that was part of their repertoire of cherished diversions. The ladies wrapped their brown arms around him, tousled his hair, kissed his cheeks. "I love to see people happy," he said.

A fawning soldier boy guarded me each night on my patch of beach at the foot of the Nuevitas pier—they didn't want *Squeak* to sneak off with a Cuban aboard. A restaurant employee boiled my stove in vinegar to free a clogged jet. Two young guys working at the jet-ski rental befriended me. They were inseparable friends, one short, one tall. I hung out with them in their single room. "Go on, use the shower!" they said. Their girlfriends washed my clothes and fed me choice morsels of chicken while we all watched Rambo III on TV. The censors must have been sleeping to have let that one through—the communists were the bad guys!

My friends and their gals weren't concerned with political correctness. They didn't parrot the Communist Party propaganda, nor did they wish to leave Cuba. They knew socialism was flawed, but they defended their Revolution. The Soviet Union had dissolved the year before, withdrawing its support. The U.S. added another nail to the coffin by prohibiting ships that called at Cuba from calling at any U.S. port. The economy, already weak, was contracting ever further. As in Haiti, there was a feeling that deep political change might occur at any moment. "The common people are powerless," they said, "but we have fun whenever we can."

I stood alone looking seaward while waves sucked the sand from under my feet, undermining me. I was nearly within striking distance of southern Florida. One way or another, the voyage would soon end. Repairs and maintenance unrelated to seaworthiness could wait. Maybe I could afford to run my body ragged too, and recuperate at home. The voyage still absorbed me, but glimpses of a life after began to penetrate.

By May 5 my Metronidazol pills still hadn't cured me, but I felt strong enough to travel. I launched, and over the next few days skirted the vast Archipelago of Camagüey, off Cuba's north-central coast. It was the off season, yet the tourist facilities remained heavily staffed. They were all glad to have someone to fuss over, especially a *"gran aventurero,"* as they made me out to be. One guy even made a sign and stuck it in the sand in front of his restaurant, to commemorate my having slept there.

But most of these keys were untouched. That portion of the archipelago exposed to the sea was marked by barrier reefs and shorelines of sand or sponge-textured coral bedrock. The ground cover indicated moderate precipitation: grass, brush, a few juniper trees and midget palms. In contrast, the inland bays were labyrinths of mangrove and weedy shallows. It was faster to stay outside.

Twice dusk found me far from any Cuban security installation. Those nights I luxuriated in the privacy of nature. Other nights I stopped at *Guardafrontera* stations, knowing they'd seen me. If I tried to camp elsewhere they'd just come and get me. Each post called up the next one to inform them of my approach.

The air was chilly these days, and I wasn't well. Diarrhea and mosquitoes are a bad combination—every time you open the hatch to relieve yourself they swarm in. But what of that? I had great wind, favorable current, moderate seas, and easy access to sheltered water. Turtles and turkey vultures were numerous, and the seaweeds and coral growths exhibited great variety. Killdeer-like birds chirped up minor storms, running to and fro in water knee-deep to them. My environment and activity were health-inspiring, even if I carried in my gut a seed of discontent.

This was the Old Bahama Channel at its narrowest. On the other side, ten miles northeast, was the Great Bahama Bank, an area as big as the Florida Peninsula, but slightly below sea level instead of slightly above it. Freighters and sailboats navigated the Channel, hugging its centerline. Toward my fellow sailors I felt a connection, and also a disconnection, as if I were invisible to them. I was inside Cuba's hermetically sealed defense envelope. They were outside, in international waters.

The keys to my left were too numerous for names. Besides, how big, and how dry, and how separate from its neighbors at what stage of tide must a spot of soil be to qualify as an island? Whatever the cutoff, much of the archipelago was neither one nor the other but something in between: tidal thickets fragmented by filamentous sloughs, or barely inundated mud flats with mangrove saplings peeping hopefully up, like flowers through melting snow.

On May 9 I abandoned the deep blue water and sailed into the jade green. It was a crystalline jade where the lagoon was calm, milky jade where rough. Either way the sun, blazing in the turquoise sky, lit it up like neon. The waves still broke here, shocking white explosions, like black people smiling. The seascape boiled with a monotonous, pastel energy. More than beautiful, it was chic, *arte nouveau.* The waves, crossing a shallow threshold, broke into even surf. I sailed right through it, my confidence in such conditions much improved over my days on the Pacific coast.

Inside there was still plenty of water for *Squeak* to sail, kicking up her rudder blade as necessary. Eel grass carpeted the bottom. No real land was visible, just the pyramidal, weblike tangles of mangrove roots and the dense green of their small leaves. I entered a channel that slowly narrowed and shoaled until I dragged keel in the muck. Still I sailed, arriving finally in a marshy cul-de-sac. There, a tidal creek just wide enough to squeeze through gave access to the next bay. As I crossed it the sun went down through the bulk of a stranded freighter, illuminating her delicate, rusty ribs. On the far side lay La Isabela, at the mouth of the Sagua La Grande River. Straight into the setting sun I sailed, sorting out the shapes of a small port town. The river mouth was like a pair of lips, puckered out into a small delta. I found the opening, and gave my docking line to the soldiers who waited for me on a concrete pier surrounded by rowboats.

By the time various authorities had searched me and processed my paperwork, supper time had passed. The army officers retired to their post at the base of the pier. A private ignited a searchlight and began probing the river for anyone trying to enter or leave. "I'm sorry," he said. "There will be nothing to eat in town now until morning."

When the sun came up I looked for food. La Isabela ran three blocks wide down a strip of land between river and a saltwater boat basin. The clapboard row houses sagged like ancient breasts. None had seen a drop of paint in decades. Many lots were vacant, and the old customs house was a ruin. Tongues of ugly mud flat invaded the town's margins, as in Nuquí. But the people here were white, and not even particularly tanned. They looked more Appalachian than Latin.

"Hurricane Kate destroyed the houses that used to be here," said Abelardo, a shipping agent whom I met while asking directions to the bakery. "After the hurricane, Fidel and his brother, Raul, came here and promised us a glorious *new* Isabela, south of here, on higher ground. That's where my wife and I live. Do you want to see it?" The smile beneath Abelardo's graying mustache was sincere. His chest and legs were thin. He seemed to be the only man in town who wore a tie—a limp, navy blue tie with white polka dots.

"First some lunch," he said. We went to the workshop of the agency responsible for maintaining buoys and similar aids to navigation. "My wife cooks here," he explained. We entered an employee cafeteria and sat at a plywood table with six or seven workmen. Everyone got a scoop of rice, a thimbleful of pork, three slices of cucumber, an unripe banana, and a glass of fake orange juice. Their faces revealed disappointment, but nobody complained.

We got in Abelardo's car and drove south through flat farmland. Along the way he picked people up and dropped them off, like a free taxi service. "I've known them all my life," he said. "I'm a Party member, so I have a car, but really it belongs to all of us." Abelardo's generosity was repaid when he ran out of gas a couple miles short of home. The first person to come along, a young farmer on a motorcycle/sidecar, stopped and siphoned two beer bottles' worth of gas out of his tank. "We all carry siphoning hoses now, don't we, Paulino?" Abelardo laughed, and clasped his shoulder.

Nueva Isabela was a six-story apartment building, lost in sprawling fields of sugar cane. "The rest of the project was tabled when the Soviets pulled out," he said. Now, three years old, the building looked more like thirty. Abelardo's one-bedroom apartment was dim and shabby, like inner-city public housing in the States. "See, it's on the ground floor, and bigger than most. Refrigerator, too." His pride sounded hollow, as if he were trying to convince himself. "I want to show you my Beatles collection," he said, and pulled out a folio full of fan club stuff: photos, write-ups, some old 45s. "And here's my collection of imported beer cans." About twenty of them stood stacked on a low table, from breweries in Amsterdam, Copenhagen, St. Louis, Milwaukee. Next came a photo of his daughter, and his Communist Party card. "See," he said. "Fidel himself signed it." The signature had flair, but the card was faded. He rushed from one memento to another.

"They're nice, Abelardo. But I'm surprised you're interested in things like, oh, beer and rock music."

Abelardo sank down on the couch next to his beer can pyramid. "How old are you, Steve?"

"Thirty-nine."

"Same as me. Cuba's not on a different planet, you know. It hurts me that America is so hostile toward Cuba. Why? What threat are we? I love America, but I love Cuba too." He wrung his hands. "Working with foreign shipping companies, I know what free enterprise is. I know our socialism doesn't work, and that we'll have to change. There are eight people in my office, but three could easily do it all. We pretend to work, they pretend to pay us. A fisherman is twice as well off as me, because he can charge market prices. All I get is worthless pesos."

"Why did you join the Communist Party?"

He looked away. "It was the only sensible choice. My wife and I believed in the future. We worked like dogs, and took the perks that came our way—the car, the access to foreign newspapers. It's not what we had hoped."

His eyes were misty. "You're a good man, Abelardo. Come on. I need to get back to La Isabela. Immigration said they'd have my exit papers ready at two P.M."

"You're not still leaving today, are you? You're so skinny. Are you up to crossing the Straits of Florida? It's no joke out there."

"I am twenty pounds underweight," I confessed. "But there's no INTUR around here, nothing I can legally buy. And I'm sure as hell not going to gain weight eating lunch with you!"

Abelardo smiled weakly. "I suppose not."

"Better I leave now, while I've still got some food in my food buckets. The weather's good. The moon still shines during the morning hours, but it's rising an hour later every night. Soon it'll be no help at all."

"Okay. I'll see if I can get you something to eat on the way."

We drove back. Abelardo rounded up a sack of fresh rolls while I readied *Squeak* for sail. "Adios, amigo," he said. "Remember Cuba."

"I will. Thanks for everything."

I tacked out the river mouth and up to Cayo Hicacal, one of the outermost keys. I anchored in a knee-deep cove, in a bed of sand and coral-stone, rich with tiny life. The sun set, and the phosphorescence came on, a pale radiance in the water that the merest stir released. A fishing boat lay at anchor not far away, but nobody bothered me. Here it was calm, but the Atlantic beat heavily only yards away, across a spit of land. This, Cuba's true edge, was known to few Cubans. The archipelago added a physical shield to the political and economic barriers around the greatest of the Greater Antilles.

The wind whistled as it had at Dog Island, before my crossing of the Anegada Passage. I set my wristwatch alarm for four A.M. and lay down. My goal was Sal Cay, a speck of land forty-three miles out. I knew that it belonged to the Bahamas, and little else. Maybe there'd be people there. If I passed through their immigration maybe the U.S. authorities would think I'd been in the Bahamas all this time. I'd spent sixty-three dollars in Cuba; would the Treasury Department prosecute me for that? Would they confiscate *Squeak* and sell her to pay off the national debt? If I found Sal Cay I would rest up before crossing the Gulf Stream. If not, I'd do it all in one piece.

CHAPTER 31

HOME

No matter how many times I did this it would never feel sane: to get up in the cold night, make my tent a ship and myself a sailor, break out my puny anchor, drift away from a perfectly safe haven while I stow anchor, hoist sails, lower rudder, and steer around the point into that angry sea, knowing how long the hours will be, how cold the wind and spray, and how uncertain the outcome. Still it possesses for me a terrible beauty: falling away into a darkness so powerful it seems an aching void, a horizontal abyss. Worse, a vertical one: drop a penny in the ocean and imagine what happens to it, how long it falls, and what it looks like where it comes to rest, forever. I am only a tiny cork in that sea, but I am concentrated, a pinpoint of intelligence. I create coordinates in nothingness by being at their juncture. Painful discovery powers my movement through the chaos. Thus I followed the course I had laid for Sal Cay that night of May 11, one month shy of my fortieth birthday.

The moon glinted on the waves, suggesting their fast-changing shapes. I wore everything capable of cutting wind or insulating me while wet. Still, I was cold. I had stars to steer by, but only up high, where they're inexact guides. The hemispherical float inside my compass jiggled around inside its bowl too fast to read its numbers. Or was the bowl jiggling around outside the float, or were both jiggling relative to me, or me to them?

Daylight brought perspective. Already Cuba was gone. Breaking waves were slinging *Squeak* sideways. I tried putting the leeboard down to control side slippage, but it tended to trip her, inviting capsize. Better to compensate by heading up a tad. I met bad waves by rounding up or rounding off, whichever came fastest.

The sun came out. A ship passed in the distance. At 12:30 P.M. I took a reef out of the sail. Sitting back down, I saw an island about three miles away to northeast. Sal Cay! I'd almost missed it. Now hard on the wind, I closed the gap. The sea went from indigo to pale electric blue: Sal Cay Bank, a Rhode Island-sized shoal in the center of the triangle formed by Cuba, the Florida Keys, and the Great Bahama Bank. Sal Cay itself lay at the southwest corner of its bank. The island was low, about a half mile by a mile, lightly vegetated. On its lee side were a few buildings and a flagpole flying an aquamarine, black, and gold flag. There were no boats, no people on the beach. I landed in front of a sign that said, "SAL CAY, HER MAJESTY'S BAHAMIAN SHIPS."

Country western music drifted from an open door. I knocked, and a young black in T-shirt and shorts came out. "Hello?" he said, with a slight West Indian accent.

I explained myself and asked what sort of facility it was.

"We with the Bahamian Navy," he said. "They five of us. I'm the midshipman. Navy keep us here so's the Cubans don't come invade again, like they did couple years ago. Was them built this place, you know."

All five came to look at *Squeak*, smiling shyly, none in uniform. The midshipman processed my entry into their country. Otherwise they seemed at a loss for words.

"Am I free to explore the island?"

"Sure. You can use that extra house there," he said. They went back inside.

A day that had started so recklessly could not have ended more serenely. I showered and napped in a vacant bungalow with Spanish graffiti on its walls. In the heavy sunshine of late afternoon I walked around the island, admiring its brackish lagoon and gentle contours. Then the guys shared their dinner of macaroni and cheese and fried conch with me in their television room. "No need to pay," they said. We relaxed together in front of the tube. The programming came from Miami. The weather man predicted light southeast winds.

North American culture is an engine of such power that its rumble is heard even in distant lands. I'd been sneaking back up on the States by obscure paths. No one knew I was almost home. But I knew it, by the types of litter washed up on the beach, by the clothes my hosts wore, and by the U.S. Coast Guard helicopter that buzzed over the island the next morning.

I had left home saying I'd be gone a year, maybe eighteen months. Then the North American rivers took longer than I'd expected. Then Isla San Jose happened, and Bahia Piñas, and all the other stops, until I gave up predicting my rate of travel. It wasn't until Montserrat that I'd had enough experience in the Caribbean to consider how long it might take to finish the voyage. There I had examined my track record since Bequia and estimated I might be back in Seattle by August 9, the third anniversary of my departure. For once I was conservative. Though at such places as St. Martin and Ponce I had felt bogged down, the favorable winds and currents were bringing me home sooner.

Squeak and I were a serious traveling machine. I loved my life with her. I wasn't anxious to get back home, but neither did I contemplate any detours, to Africa, say. Like a good novel, the voyage had its own sense of rhythm, of beginning, middle, and end. Now it was ending.

Sal Cay was peaceful and warm. Hundreds of coconuts lay wasting, so I opened a few and drained their nutritious water into a container. At noon, when I felt ready to go, the entire garrison was off hunting conch on the other side of the island. I buried my Cuban papers in the sand at the foot of a palm tree and shoved off from Sal Cay twenty-four hours after my arrival.

The wind diminished as I sailed north over the bank. Its shallowness, ten meters on average, allowed local waves but barred ocean swells.

Double-Headed Shot Cays, at the northwest corner of the bank, weren't quite what I had expected. It was dusk, and I wanted to sleep again before the main crossing. But rather than sand and palm trees, these keys were sponge-textured extrusions of coral rock: an ancient reef, uplifted, eroding in weird, inhospitable shapes. There was no holding ground in their lee, just a slab of submerged stone. Beyond that the bottom dropped off evenly to a depth of a thousand meters. The cays were like a row of teeth, each fifty to a hundred meters long, five to ten meters high, with narrow gaps between. The entirety curved the way a mouth curves on a dental chart. The rock at sea level had been eaten back a meter or two by undercutting waves, creating an overhang below which a submerged wall ran down ten feet to the stone bottom.

I only needed a few hours of rest before crossing to Florida, so I found a low saddle in one of the keys where the wind was unobstructed. There I rowed up close, lodged my anchor in a bubble-shaped cavity at chest height, fed out line, and trusted the wind to hold me off. I converted *Squeak* to sleeping mode, feeling precarious, like I was lying in a hammock in a tree that might fall. I calculated my crossing as follows:

Wind	E to SE, 10 knots
Current	1.5 knots average
Direction of Current	45°
Course	315°
Distance	60 miles
Speed	4 knots?
Elapsed time	15 hours
Leave	midnight
Arrive	3 P.M.

Crossing the Gulf Stream would be like crossing a sixty-mile-wide river. The current is about three knots in the center, tapering to zero at the edges. My course made good, keeping the keel pointed at 315°, would be an S-shaped curve. I would aim for Big Pine Key, but land somewhere around Lower Matacombe, eighteen miles downstream. The current was beneficial in that it would take me toward Miami, but someone in St. Martin had told me how monstrous the Straits can get when the wind blows perpendicular or opposed to the flow of the Stream. Nobody in Cuba had known anything, because whoever made it to Florida never came back to talk about it. I didn't know what sort of surf to expect. The trade winds appeared to be winding down. Sleep eluded me.

At midnight I retrieved my anchor and fell off into the Straits. I stayed warm and dry, the wind being lighter and more aft, but it continued to die and swing clockwise. Was another cold front coming? Now I fought sleep. The moon rose, sad and lovely. Then the fierce sun.

At noon I began seeing white specks ahead. It turned out to be a big tournament to see who could catch the most "dolphin," or dorado as they call them in Mexico. Soon high-powered boats with flying bridges were zipping all around me. One gave me a position. We were in the axis of the Stream, eight miles downstream of my projected track.

The wind reached southwest and stayed there, never quite dying, just enough to ghost along. There, the top of a lighthouse! An hour later I began seeing an endless line of trees and structures. The Stream still carried me sideways, but less and less. I passed through a line of piling-supported lighthouses set about ten miles apart along the intermittent reefs at the edge of the peninsular shelf. Coral sand now shone through the water, but land was still four miles away. To pinpoint my approach I scrutinized the comings and goings of speedboats. The Keys formed a line broken by random gaps, like a message in Morse code. They were covered with…what? Resorts, condominiums, shops, restaurants, bars, bridges, power poles, warehouses, radio towers, water tanks, billboards, marinas, cars, people, money.

I rowed into a small boat basin. Around its margin, men and women were sipping cocktails and being photographed alongside dolphins that hung from a row of heavy hooks. Death had muted the fishes' once-luminous blue-greens. Somebody yelled at me in good humor, "Hey, watch your wake, buddy!"

"Okay, I'll go slower next time! Where am I, anyway?"

"Holiday Isle Resort, Windley Key."

Every square inch, to a height of two or three stories, was devoted to making money. The American Bartenders Association was holding their annual convention in the hotel next door. The Tiki Bar was cranking out "rumrunners" by the hundreds, at $4.75 each. Tourists crowded the dive shops, gift shops, art shops, and fast-food joints. The mood was upbeat, informal. Complete strangers shot good-natured barbs at each other. Women paid for their own drinks. Nonconformity was "in." I was back in the USA.

The place was too busy for the arrival of a pipsqueak boat and her skinny skipper to arouse much notice. No girls kissed me. But a couple of old geezers, realizing I'd come from at least the Bahamas, extended welcoming hands. The management let me tie up to a work float near the fuel dock, no charge. I checked in with Customs over the telephone. They didn't ask me anything about Cuba, so I didn't mention anything. "Entry logged, no inspection necessary," the woman said. I called home, and to Meg in Grenada. I was relieved, proud, tired. One phase of my life was ending, another was starting. Hard to fathom. Too much emotion, no one to share it with. Sleep.

I rested a day, then rode the Gulf Stream like a slow train up to Miami. The air stilled, leaving only the oppressive sun. I longed to nap while drifting, but it was too hot. For once, I was ready for the voyage to end.

A south breeze sprang up in the afternoon. It carried me on into the night, toward a galaxy of lights. Half-lit skyscrapers reared up, singly and in clumps. The glow of the metropolis, reflecting on the water ahead of me, silhouetted jetties and buoys. Four islands make up Miami's shoreline. Where was the shipping channel? Tools close at hand—map, pencil, hand compass, dividers, course plotter, headlamp—I watched the lights of running speedboats where they passed shore lights, and noted which blocked the other when they met. A barely submerged pipeline temporarily blocked my path, then a riprap breakwater—I was cutting against the grain. At 2:30 A.M. I entered the Miami Beach Marina, found the *Lady Dorothy,* and tied up alongside, so *Squeak* would look like her dinghy.

Thump! Thump! The sound of someone beating on my cabin top woke me. I opened the hatch, wincing at the sunlight. Josef was leaning over the *Lady Dorothy's* rail, his prizefighter face hovering over me, full lips parted in astonishment, swarthy cheeks stubbly with a two-day beard. "Stephen! I don't believe!" he said, then threw back his head and laughed. "Come here, you crazy! You tell me! Tell me everything!"

Wiping my eyes, I took the hand that pulled me up over the rail and into a bear hug.

"Okay, Josef, okay!" I laughed. "Good to see you too!" He loosened his grip and drew me down into the dark, teak-trimmed salon of the yacht he still skippered. I recounted my travails since our last encounter in St. John, Virgin Islands, while Josef rifled through the cluttered refrigerator. He pulled out Camembert cheese, cinnamon rolls, cranberry juice. As usual, the owner wasn't aboard. Nor was Miriam.

"Miriam, aw, she go back to Israel, long time ago. All over." Josef frowned, then shifted to a happier topic. "Oh, my friend, you won't believe this English woman I meet yesterday." He started waving his arms about. "I'm riding down the street, see, on my motorcycle. I pull up to a stoplight, and this *beau*tiful woman is next to me in a convertible, looking at me. I bring her here last night, and, Stephen! she *fuck* me, I tell you, over and over, all night long! Never enough. Such hot woman! She's coming here again tonight..."

She was a rich, fashionable girl with family homes in Miami and London. Still flush with the newness of their romance, anxious that it work, each asked me in private what I thought of the other. I kept my skepticism to myself. Josef hosted me well during my two days in Miami, but I felt myself disengaging. Yes, the danger and discomfort were past. I had time. Since leaving home nearly three years before I had spent only $12,000. I still had a little money. But my discipline couldn't stop just like that. It propelled me on. I had to get *Squeak* home.

In the center of a campus of palm trees and flapping flags stood the marina office, a concrete-and-glass building full of potted ferns and impressionist paintings in the nautical theme. On May 17 the ladies at its front counter exchanged my dollar bills for quarters and loaned me their *Miami & Dade County Yellow Pages.* I opened to "Automobile Transporters & Drive-Away Companies," jotted down a list of phone numbers, thanked them, and walked to a pay phone.

Eight dollars worth of quarters later, a voice on the other end of the line said, "Yeah, it belongs to Paul Marriott. Ya know? Of Marriott Hotels. 1989 Cadillac limousine, white. Needs to go to Portland, Oregon. Can you come by this afternoon?"

"Okay, I'll be there at, um, two o'clock. Right."

Next I looked up "Trailers—Boat." A dealer in West Miami had one for $225.

By the following morning, May 18, 1993, limousine, trailer, and *Squeak* were hooked up and ready to roll. My contract with AAMCO Nationwide Transport said "No towing," but they would never know.

Miami Beach was fun, with its Cuban-American families, potbellied old New Yorkers, and dark young men with rakish new hair styles, all making the beach scene. Colombian gangsters sat on the sand, shiny black pistols protruding from the waistbands of their flowered shorts. A pair of pretty girls in bikinis played frisbee, breasts bouncing, then stared coldly when I asked if I could play too. I sensed an East Coast decadence, or callousness. With determination, and my new wheels, I could have cut a wide swath. But not for long—the limo was due in Portland in ten days.

Night found me driving north on I-95:

in Georgia I bought pecans
the cruise control came in real handy in Kansas
I inhaled the high plains of Colorado and Wyoming
still laced with old snow
the soil soggy and raw
with the newness of spring

On May 23, 1993, I parked *Squeak* on the fresh-mown grass of my parents' back yard, in Bremerton, Washington. Mom laughed when she saw me pull up in a limousine, and cried when she saw how skinny I was. My Haitian intestinal parasites soon died off, however, perhaps due to homesickness, while Mom's chicken casseroles and Mexican salads started putting flesh back on my bones. My tan seemed to wash away with the first hot shower. My chronic jock itch cleared up from not being wet all the time.

My wanderlust didn't itch anymore either. I had scratched that craving so hard and long it wasn't likely to pester me again soon. It was pleasant to sleep in my old bed. But material comforts don't matter. People do.

Mom and Dad fussed over me. "When's the book going to be done?"

KOMO TV sent a news crew over.

Squeak left to spend a month on display at the local library.

Jim and Eileen hosted a fortieth birthday/welcome home party.

When the commotion had died down, Mike and Cathi invited me to their place near Renton. I pulled up in their driveway on my motorcycle, dismounted, and was taking my helmet off when a three-year-old Brian bolted out of the front door. "Uncle Deve! Uncle Deve!" he shouted, and climbed up on me like a squirrel into a tree. Leaving him there to explore my upper reaches, I walked inside, sat on their nubby brown sofa, then peeled him off and held him squirming in my lap.

The microscopic rivers didn't show in his face anymore. Now his skin was tan, his hair glossy, blue eyes wide open. Teeth like little pearls flashed through a curvy mouth. "My voyage began the day you were born, Brian-buddy. Now I'm back, but you're just getting started. Aren't you?"

"Yes!" he said, with a tone of friendly challenge, and yanked at my mustache. I worked his hand loose with little loss of hair.

"Brian, be nice to your Uncle Steve!" said Cathi. She pulled two Budweisers from the refrigerator, settled into the chair to my right, and handed me one. "Mike should be home from work any minute now."

We both sipped.

"So, have you changed?" she asked.

I was tired of my commonplace answers to that question. "You know, I don't remember how I felt before, but now I feel rich, like I've got the

Hope Diamond in my pocket." I pretended to fish a gem out of my pocket and turn it in the light. "Look at those dreamy shapes, glinting in there…"

That reminded me. After riding back home, late that night, I took a little wicker basket down from the top shelf of my bookcase. Mom and Dad were in bed. The house was dark but for my desk lamp. I flipped through envelopes full of photos to the one that said, "Me, historical," and pulled out the snapshot taken in Kabul, Afghanistan in 1971.

There I was, in the crisis of my youth. Weary perhaps. Overawed, like I could start crying at any moment. Our lives are so big—how can we not get lost in them? My own drama was my clearest window onto the greater drama, in which everyone takes part. Both my 1971–72 and 1990–93 journeys had tapped into something universal. I'd felt it on the *Tramarco Trader's* heaving deck, at Isla San Jose when the *Alefa* sailed away, and on the Orinoco River the time I woke in the furnace-like heat and plunged myself into the river: pathos, reverence, thrill.

Yes, the youth in the photo was me. Now to remember it.

In Kabul, Afghanistan, 1971

THE END

ABOUT *SQUEAK*

. . . a self-righting, beachable, row/sail boat that sleeps one

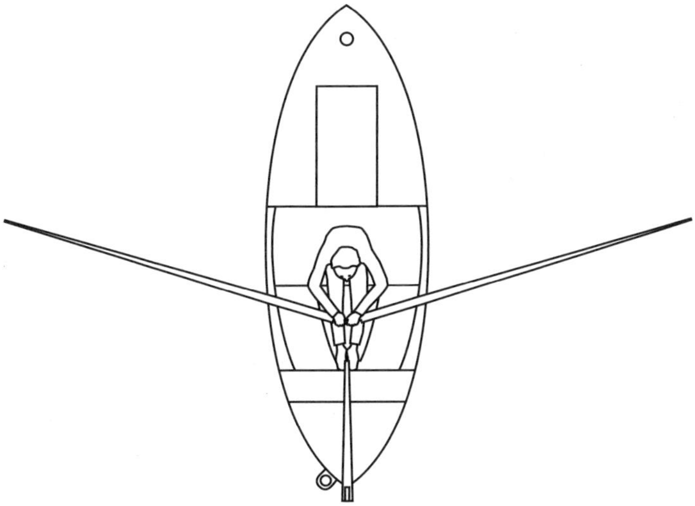

Length overall:	12 feet	Weight, empty:	250 lbs.
Length on waterline:	11 feet	Weight, full:	50 lbs.
Beam (width):	4 feet	Draft:	8 inches
Freeboard:	17 inches	Sail area:	68 sq. ft.

Purpose:	long-distance coastal, river, and island cruising
Construction:	2 layers of 1/8-inch fir, epoxy-bonded diagonally, sheathed in fiberglass
Accommodations:	cabin with full-length sea berth & four watertight stowage compartments
Sailing rig:	sprit-boom cat yawl, modified windsurfer masts, leeboards, kick-up rudder
Materials cost:	$2000 in 1990
Time to build:	1200 hours

ABOUT THE AUTHOR

Steve Ladd was born in Bremerton, Washington in 1953. As a child he was happy to sit in a corner reading books, often of history or geography. After high school he traveled for a year in Europe, Asia, and Africa, inadvertently witnessing the Indo-Pakistani War of 1971 and spending a month in a Moroccan prison due to involvement in a motorcycle accident.

Upon return Steve studied urban planning, obtaining degrees from Western Washington and Harvard universities. From 1976 to 1990 he worked for various Puget Sound counties and cities, helping to manage their growth and development. His outdoor interests included backcountry skiing, mountain climbing, and canoeing.

After the events related in this book Steve continued his city planning work until 2007, when he and his now-wife, Ginny, began preparations leading to a five-year voyage in a 21-foot boat, including an exploration of the Orinoco, Amazon, Paraguay, and Paraná river systems. That journey will become the subject of another book.